UNDERSTANDING
AND MANAGING
PUBLIC
ORGANIZATIONS

Hal G. Rainey

UNDERSTANDING AND MANAGING PUBLIC ORGANIZATIONS

Jossey-Bass Publishers · San Francisco

UNDERSTANDING AND MANAGING PUBLIC ORGANIZATIONS
by Hal G. Rainey

Copyright © 1991 by: Jossey-Bass Inc., Publishers
350 Sansome Street
San Francisco, California 94104

Library of Congress Cataloging-in-Publication Data

Rainey, Hal G. (Hal Griffin), date
    Understanding and managing public organizations / Hal G. Rainey. —
1st ed.
        p.   cm. — (A joint publication in the Jossey-Bass public
    administration series and the Jossey-Bass management series)
    Includes bibliographical references and index.
    ISBN 1-55542-344-2
    1. Public administration.   I. Title.   II. Series.
JF1351.R27   1991
350—dc20   90-28985
                                                                 CIP

Manufactured in the United States of America

The paper used in this book is acid-free and meets the
State of California requirements for recycled paper
(50 percent recycled waste, including 10 percent
postconsumer waste), which are the strictest guidelines
for recycled paper currently in use in the United States.

The ink in this book is either soy- or vegetable-based and during
the printing process emits fewer than half the volatile organic
compounds (VOCs) emitted by petroleum-based ink.

JACKET DESIGN BY WILLI BAUM

FIRST EDITION

HB Printing   10 9 8 7 6 5 4

Code 9147

A joint publication in

**The Jossey-Bass
Public Administration Series**

and

**The Jossey-Bass
Management Series**

Contents

Preface

Public organizations perform crucial functions, and they need effective management. The elaborate body of writing and research on organizations and their management that developed over the last century has valuable applications to the management of public organizations. *Understanding and Managing Public Organizations* reviews major topics in that literature, including organizational environments, strategy, decision making, structure and design, effectiveness, change, communication, conflict, leadership, and motivation. The book includes suggestions from the literature about managing the political environments of public organizations; attaining power and influence; developing managerial strategy and organizational mission; alternative structure and design; motivating employees; effective leadership, including transformational leadership; managing group decisions and conflict; and managing organizational change and development. To consider all these topics in public management settings, the book also draws on a comprehensive review of the evidence, including very recent contributions, on the distinctive characteristics of public managers and organizations.

The material on organizations and management usually takes a generic approach. Its developers have worked to produce insights that apply to all types of organizations, and for very good reasons. We need general knowledge because management and organization involve similar challenges in all settings. About fifteen years ago, however, a number of writers began to argue that this literature pays too little attention to public organizations. Some of these writers reported on their experiences as executives in public and private organizations. Academics pointed out that the generic management field did not take into account what political scientists and economists had written about public organizations as a distinct category. Researchers also have reported more and more evidence on the similarities and differences among public, private, and nonprofit organizations.

Understanding and Managing Public Organizations brings together the generic management literature with the research on public organizations. Many authors and officials who have called for a better analysis of public management complain that the writing on public bureaucracies from political scientists and economists consists of descriptive anecdotes and untested theories (for example, Perry and Kraemer, 1983). They say that it pays too little attention to organizational and managerial issues which the management literature has developed extensively. Other experts and official reports complain that public management suffers from a number of deficiencies—too many constraints on the managers, too little incentive to manage effectively, too much ineffective management in general. For all these reasons, various authors have called for a closer integration between the management literature and what we know about managing and organizing in the public sector. This book provides such an integration (although debate continues over whether public organizations actually differ from other types, such as private firms, so no book can yet provide a conclusive integration).

Although public management is often cast in a very bad light, this book repeatedly argues that public organizations and managers often perform much more effectively than is generally supposed. It provides many examples of successful management in the public sector and also considers the evidence on whether public and private organizations actually differ. Many management experts contend that assertions about these differences usually amount to crude stereotypes; business organizations, after all, face many of the same problems and shortcomings as do governmental bureaucracies. The evidence shows that it is hard to prove that private organizations show great superiority over public ones—and whether they do or not, public managers and organizations play indispensable roles in all societies. We have no alternative but to seek ways to enhance their effectiveness.

Audience for the Book

Understanding and Managing Public Organizations is addressed to practicing managers, people in policy-making positions (such as legislative staffers or elected officials), and academics and graduate students in the fields of public administration, business administration, and public policy. Some of my colleagues suggest that writing for such a diverse audience invites disaster. However, all these groups contribute to the discussion of public management, and they all must play a part in improving it and in developing the body of knowledge to support such improvements.

Public Managers and Officials

Public managers should find useful the summary review of major topics in contemporary management and organization theory, which includes suggestions about how to manage the various dimensions of organizations. For example, managers should know what the literature says about conditions for successful change in large organizations and the examples it provides of successful and unsuccessful change efforts in public organizations. They should find interesting the evidence on motivation and work satisfaction among government managers and employees, how it relates to motivation theory and practice, and the leadership and motivational techniques used in many government agencies. Managers should be aware of what we know about the structure of government agencies as compared to that of private organizations. They should know about the controversies over whether governmental organizations resist change and abolishment more than do private firms, and whether public organizations are subject to more red tape than are private firms.

Public managers and elected officials provide some of the most important contributions to this discussion. The book's evidence includes testimonies of former executives and government reports and surveys prepared for and by policy makers and managers. Many public managers and policy makers remain keenly interested in the question of what government can borrow from the private sector (President's Council on Management Improvement, 1987), and they should find useful the comprehensive summary of comparisons of the public and private sectors.

In addition to suggestions about managing public organizations, the book covers much academic research and theory. While there is a widespread belief that active managers find that kind of material too dry and abstract, many governmental policies and administrative actions have a basis in some form of theory—often an inadequate one. Better analysis of the public administration theory and related theories, such as of motivation, could improve such policies and actions.

Public managers sometimes complain that too many people enter administrative positions in government on the basis of their knowledge of a profession or policy area or because of political connections. Their preparation for managerial roles and their awareness of the body of knowledge on organizations and management are often weak. Similarly, experts and managers (Warwick, 1975; Lynn, 1981; Mintzberg, 1989) frequently complain that elected and appointed officials, and even news reporters and citizen groups, impose outmoded conceptions of management on public organizations. Some of these people operate as if effective management consisted of a strict hierarchy of authority and tight administrative rules and controls. This orientation not only involves an outmoded view of management, it aggravates tendencies toward unnecessary bureaucracy. In sum, those who have recently entered managerial positions within public organizations, or who oversee them from official elective positions or from the media, need to consider the issues and evidence in this book.

Business and Nonprofit Managers

Relations between business and government have become so elaborate that many business executives spend more time handling governmental relations and issues than anything else. They and managers in nonprofit organizations often serve as integral components of governmental policies and service delivery. Their roles can become analogous to those of public managers in that they must pursue social or public service goals under governmental regulatory oversight or funding. The book's discussion of the nature of public organizations can aid business and nonprofit managers' thinking about characteristics of their own roles, and it can aid their understanding of the governmental agencies and managers with whom they deal.

Academic Audiences

Understanding and Managing Public Organizations can serve as a companion to an organization theory book in courses on public management or organization theory in public administration. It can also serve as a primary text in such courses, with supplements on classical and contemporary contributions to the organization and management theory literature.

Theorists and researchers should find plenty of grist for their mills in the book as well. The debate over the distinctive nature of public organizations involves questions as profound and significant as any in the social sciences. The distinction between societal control through markets on the one hand and through government on the other represents one of the major theoretical and practical policy issues facing nations of the world. This book in large part concerns the implications of that distinction for organizations and management. The review of ongoing controversies and evidence from recent studies underscores many issues for continuing research and theoretical development. At many points, the book offers evidence that is relatively strong, by the standards of the social sciences, of distinctive aspects of public organizations and managers. At other points, it overturns oversimplifications about such distinctions. Generally, the analysis of the distinctive features of public organizations and management has received insufficient attention from researchers. Its further development raises challenges and exciting prospects for management, organization theory, and public administration.

Overview of the Contents

The Introduction describes the importance of the topic of analyzing and understanding public organizations, offers examples of its significance for theory and practice, and elaborates the theme of and the points made in this preface. The chapters in Part One consider the operating context of public organizations. Executives and researchers regularly cite the governmental environments of public organizations as the most important reason to consider such organizations distinctive; the absence of economic markets and the presence of intensive oversight from other governmental authorities exert major influences on their operations and characteristics. Chapter One discusses how public organizations are defined and the problems involved in analyzing whether they have distinctive characteristics. It also introduces many of the assertions, which will be further examined in later chapters, about how they supposedly differ from other organizations.

Chapter One details many of the assertions about the influence of political and nonmarket environments on public organizations. Organizational researchers have been attributing increasing significance to the environments in which organizations operate. Chapter Two summarizes this generic literature and its implications for understanding public organizations. The chapter points out that the generic conceptions of environment attend only vaguely to the elements of the political environment that political scientists and economists emphasize in their discussions of the public bureaucracy. Chapter Two begins the discussion of those elements by setting them forth and describing the complex of values that the governmental environment imposes on public organizations in the United States. Chapter Three elaborates on these influence processes by showing how other authorities and political actors impose values and directives on public organizations. The chapter discusses power within the political system and the power and authority relations among the elements of the governmental environment, public managers, and organizations.

Part Two reviews the evidence on the influences of environmental factors on public sector organizing and managing. Each chapter reviews the literature on one or more major dimensions of organization and management and that dimension's implications for public organizations. Each chapter also examines evidence concerning distinctive aspects of public organizations that the general management literature does not adequately cover. Chapter Four reviews managerial strategy, decision processes, and power relations inside organizations. These purposeful orientations both determine and are influenced by organizational structures and designs. Chapter Five discusses structure and design, including the controversy about whether public organizations have particularly bureaucratic structures. Chapters Six through Eight concern organizational behavior, which organizational purposes and structures heavily influence. Chapter Six reviews research and theory on motivation and related concepts, such as work satisfaction, and reports the available evidence on comparative motivation and satisfaction in government and business organizations. Chapter Seven covers leadership and organizational culture, and Chapter Eight discusses groups, communication, and conflict in organizations.

Part Three concentrates more directly on effective management and improvement of public organizations. Chapter Nine discusses organizational effectiveness. Chapter Ten turns to the challenge of bringing about organizational change and improvement, and it emphasizes what we know about changing and improving public organizations, including pressures against change and examples of organizations that have very successfully instituted changes and improvements. Chapter Eleven reviews studies of excellent business firms and public organizations and offers concluding suggestions and exhortations for improving public management.

The book assumes on the part of the reader no great knowledge of organization and management theory. The Appendix, however, offers a historical overview of major developments, themes, and contributions in the study of organizations and management over the course of the past century. Readers who have not done any extensive reading or course work on those developments—who do not, for example, know who Frederick Taylor and Max Weber were or what the Hawthorne Experiments did—should find that discussion useful.

Athens, Georgia   Hal G. Rainey
March 1991

Acknowledgments

I wish to thank Steven Cohen, Barton Wechsler, and Jay White for very valuable reviews and critiques of the manuscript. Glenn W. Rainey, Jr., and Dorothy Olshfski provided useful, constructive comments on parts of the manuscript. Jeffrey Brudney, in one of the most generous contributions that any colleague has ever made to my work, provided extensive comments on the manuscript, including many demanding and constructive suggestions. Michelle Wulfhorst provided excellent research assistance for the development of many parts of the book. Julia Tillman, who helped with the later phases of the book, also provided valuable assistance.

At many points in the book, the references reflect my indebtedness to coauthors from whom I have learned a great deal about public organizations over the last decade, including Bob Backoff, Barry Bozeman, Brint Milward, Jim Perry, Frank Sherwood, Bart Wechsler, and the friend we now miss so badly, Charles Levine. I also appreciate what I have learned from more recent coauthors, such as Barry Blunt, David Coursey, Ed Kellough, Pam Reed, and Carol Traut. So many colleagues and friends at Florida State University and the University of Georgia enriched my experiences at those institutions that I cannot name them all here. Many students in my classes have taught me far more than I have taught them. I owe particular thanks, however, to those with whom I worked most closely and discussed matters related to this book, including David Ammons, Paul Beck, Richard Chackerian, Del Dunn, Bob Durant, Bob Golembiewski, Tom Lauth, Jerry Legge, Joe Whorton, and others already mentioned. I also appreciate my association with many more colleagues than I can name, who are members of the Public Sector Division of the Academy of Management, the Public Administration Section of the American Political Science Association, and the American Society for Public Administration.

The many references cited throughout this book in part reflect my gratitude to numerous scholars, journalists, and practitioners for their research and experienced accounts. I have a list of useful references not included in this book, left out more because of the limits of page length, time, and my own cognitive capacity than because they do not deserve mention. Later editions, if any, and later books and articles will make up for these omissions.

Lynn D. W. Luckow and Alan Shrader of Jossey-Bass have been insightful, helpful, firmly persistent but understanding, and, best of all, highly competent. Many others at Jossey-Bass, among them Vivian Koenig, have been very helpful as well.

My parents, Professor Glenn W. Rainey (deceased) and Dorothy Q. Rainey, have provided years of intellectual stimulation and encouragement, a generosity that I aspire to match in my own behavior as a parent, and examples of moral courage. My wife, Lucy, has been supportive and patient, as always, and courageously so. She has faced, without complaint or self-pity, an extremely serious illness and a husband writing a book, probably unable to decide which was more difficult to endure. Even though my children, Willis and Nancy, devoted their boundless energy, ingenuity, and charm to delaying its completion, I owe this book to them more than to anyone else.

Finally, in keeping with a theme of the book, I wish to express my gratitude to those people in public service, in and out of government, who have the courage to care and who serve with effectiveness and integrity.

HGR

The Author

Hal G. Rainey is professor of political science at the University of Georgia. He has published numerous articles on the comparison of public, private, and hybrid organizations and managers; on incentive systems and work-related attitudes in public organizations; on the nature of public organizations and management; and on citizens' perceptions of government. He received his B.A. degree (1968) from the University of North Carolina at Chapel Hill in English and psychology and his M.A. degree (1972) in psychology and Ph.D. degree (1978) in public administration from the Ohio State University. He has served as chair of the Public Sector Division of the Academy of Management and has held various offices with divisions of the American Society for Public Administration and the Public Administration Section of the American Political Science Association. He has served on the editorial boards of the *Academy of Management Review, Administration and Society,* and seven other journals in the management and public administration fields. He served as an officer in the U.S. Navy and as a VISTA volunteer.

UNDERSTANDING
AND MANAGING
PUBLIC
ORGANIZATIONS

The Challenge of Excellence in Public Management: Using Theory and Research to Improve Practice

All nations struggle with decisions about the roles of government and private institutions in their societies. An antigovernmental trend around the world during the last decade spawned a movement in many countries to curtail governmental authority and to foster more private activity. Although the United States joined in this trend, it did so with ambivalence. Even as efforts to curtail government went forward during the 1980s, we continued to bestow massive funding and authority on government officials.

While the skepticism about government implies sharp differences between government and privately managed organizations, numerous writers argue that we have too little sound analysis of such differences. They contend that we have an elaborate body of knowledge on management and organizations but that it pays too little attention to the public sector. At the same time, a large body of scholarship in political science and economics about governmental bureaucracy has too little to say about management of that bureaucracy. This critique has elicited a growing interest in public management and public organization theory, an interest also fueled by recurrent complaints about ineffective public management. Ironically, however, prominent initiatives to improve management of public agencies have often failed, frequently because they violated principles espoused by contemporary management experts. These attempts underscore the need for more careful analysis of organizational and managerial issues in government.

This chapter elaborates on these points, developing the theme of the book: We face the dilemma that we couple legitimate skepticism about public organizations with recognition that they play indispensable roles. We have no choice but to seek ways to maintain and improve their effectiveness. We can profit from bringing together major topics from general management and organization theory with the rapidly increasing evidence of their application in the public sector. That evidence indicates that the governmental context strongly influences organization and management, often sharply constraining performance. Just as often, however, government organizations and managers perform much better than is commonly acknowledged. Examples of effective public management abound. They usually reflect a combination of managerial skill and effective knowledge of the public-sector context. Experts continue to research and debate the nature of this combination, however, as more evidence appears rapidly and in diverse places. This book seeks to base its analysis of public management and organizations on the most careful and current review of this evidence to date.

Recent Hostility and Ambivalence Toward Government

During the 1980s, European, African, and Asian nations pursued privatization policies, seeking to sell their state-owned enterprises to private operators. The spreading conviction that excessive governmental controls had wrought economic disaster added momentum to dramatic changes in the Soviet Union and Eastern European countries. These countries began to allow more private enterprise, sometimes trying to sell state-owned enterprises to private operators.

A wave of antigovernmental sentiment also swept the United States during the 1970s and 1980s. Opinion surveys found seething resentment of taxes and the widespread conviction that governmental activities operate in wasteful and ineffective ways. Tax reduction referenda appeared on the ballots in many states, with California adopting a particularly drastic one. Angry criticisms focused on the governmental bureaucracy with such intensity that the term *bureaucrat bashing* came into use. Jimmy Carter and Ronald Reagan attacked the federal government and its bureaucracy in their election campaigns. President Carter pressed for deregulation of industry, reduction of federal red tape, and major civil service reforms to combat alleged sloth and inefficiency among federal employees. President Reagan more aggressively impugned government and sought reductions in funding and authority for federal programs and agencies (Raines, 1981).

Various writers and officials touted an American version of the privatization movement. Some proposed that all levels of government employ more contracts with the private sector for provision of services, employ more user fees, and adopt voucher systems whereby clients could choose among providers. Others called for privatizing the U.S. Postal Service and the Social Security system. Privatization of state and local government functions increased dramatically (Ehrenhalt, 1990; National Academy of Public Administration, 1989; Wise, 1990).

Such developments around the world reflect two central premises: first, that governmental activities differ from those controlled by private actors and organizations; and, second, that governmental activities are performed less effectively and efficiently. In the United States, these beliefs serve as fundamental principles of the political economy. Many political ideologues and economic theorists treat them as truisms. Surveys find that the majority of citizens accept them (Lipset and Schneider, 1987; Katz, Gutek, Kahn, and Barton, 1975).

Americans regard government with more ambivalence than hostility, however. Government in the United States, at all levels, stands as one of the great achievements of the nation and one of the most significant institutions in human history. No major nation operates without a large, influential public sector. Government in the United States accounts for a smaller proportion of the gross national product than do governments in most of the other major nations of the world, including economically successful ones.

Americans show implicit recognition of these facts. The same surveys that find waning faith in government also find fundamental support for a strong governmental role. Lipset and Schneider (1987) found declining confidence in both governmental and other institutions, such as private business corporations. Their respondents saw government as wasteful and inefficient but strongly supported an active role for government as a countervailing power against business and labor unions. Katz, Gutek, Kahn, and Barton (1975) found that many of their respondents expressed unfavorable attitudes about federal agencies and employees in general. When asked about the treatment that they had received in actual encounters with government workers, however, the respondents gave much more favorable evaluations. Even during the antigovernment trend of the 1980s, typical surveys found that most respondents opposed cuts in public services. Many wanted government to do more in a variety of areas. Almost daily, some commission, group, or expert called for a stronger governmental effort to pursue some policy or combat some problem.

Sentiments for and against governmental activity wax and wane cyclically in the United States and other countries (Hirschman, 1982). By the beginning of the 1980s, the antigovernment sentiments of the preceding decade had softened. Californians, for example, voted to increase taxes for use in maintaining transportation facilities, and some surveys showed declining opposition to taxes. President Bush moderated the antigovernment rhetoric of preceding administrations and by 1990 reversed a campaign pledge by agreeing to tax increases to reduce the federal budget deficit. Commentators increasingly belittled the overblown claims for privatization and governmental cutbacks of the 1980s (Donahue, 1990). Public policy issues such as environmental protection received more and more attention. Americans continued to play out a time-honored paradox by conferring massive funding and responsibility on government officials even as they castigated and ridiculed them (Whorton and Worthley, 1981; Sharkansky, 1989).

To the basic beliefs mentioned above, this ambivalence adds another.

While Americans tend to regard government as different from and less efficient and effective than business, most of them also regard government as crucial. Thus, the United States struggles with a complex version of the dilemma faced by all nations. We know that both government and private activities have strengths and weaknesses. The challenge lies in designing the proper mix and balance of the two and doing what we can to attain effective management of both (Lindblom, 1977).

General Management and Public Management

Given the worldwide significance of the topic of how governmental management differs from business management and how public organizations can be managed effectively, it has received far too little attention. Because this contention is open to controversy, it needs clarification.

Organization Theory, Organizational Behavior, and Management

First, we need to clarify the areas of academic research on which this book draws. Scholars in sociology, psychology, business administration, and related fields have developed an elaborate body of knowledge on the fields of organizational behavior and organization theory. The study of organizational behavior had its primary origins in industrial and social psychology. Researchers of organizational behavior typically concentrate on individual and group behaviors in organizations, analyzing motivation, work satisfaction, leadership, work-group dynamics, and other attitudes and behaviors among members of organizations. Organization theory, on the other hand, has been based more in sociology. It focuses on topics that concern the organization as a whole or sets of organizations, such as organizational environments, goals and effectiveness, strategy and decision making, change and innovation, structure and design, and birth and death. Organizational behavior is often considered to be a subfield of organization theory; the distinction is primarily a matter of specialization among researchers, reflected in the relative emphasis in textbooks (Daft, 1989; Gordon, 1990) and in the organization of professional associations.

The term *management* is used in widely diverse ways, and the study of this field includes the use of sources outside typical academic research, such as government reports, books on applied management, and observations of practicing managers about their work. While there are many elements crucial to effective management—financial management and control, management of information systems, inventory, purchasing, production processes, and others—this book concentrates on the topics treated in the fields of organizational behavior and theory.

A strong tradition that pervades organization theory, organizational behavior, and general management rejects the belief that public organizations differ fundamentally from private ones. As discussed in Chapter Two, most of the major figures in this field, both classical and contemporary, claim that their theories and insights apply to most or all types of organizations. They have worked to build a general body of knowledge about organizations and management, with important theoretical and practical justifications for doing so. Some pointedly reject any distinctions between public and private organizations as crude stereotypes. Current texts on organization theory and management contain applications to public, private, and nonprofit organizations (Daft, 1989).

In addition, management researchers and consultants work frequently with public organizations, using the same concepts and techniques that they use with private businesses. They argue that their theories and frameworks apply to public organizations and managers, since management and organization in governmental, nonprofit, and private business settings face similar challenges and follow generally similar patterns.

Public Administration, Economics, and Political Science

In a sense, we already have a body of knowledge on public management. We have a huge government, which represents a massive beehive of managerial activity. City managers have become highly professionalized. We have a huge body of writing on public administration. Economists have developed theories of public bureaucracy (Downs, 1967). Political scientists have written extensively about governmental bureaucracy (Seidman and Gilmour, 1986; Meier, 1987; Rourke, 1984). Many political scientists and economists, however, treat the public bureaucracy as quite different from private business. Political scientists concentrate on the political role of public organizations and their relations with legislators, courts, chief executives, and interest groups. Economists analyzing the public bureaucracy emphasize the absence of economic markets for its outputs. They usually conclude that absence of markets makes public organizations more bureaucratic, inefficient, change-resistant, and exposed to political influence than private firms (Barton, 1980; Breton and Wintrobe, 1982; Dahl and Lindblom, 1953; Downs, 1967; Niskanen, 1971; Tullock, 1965). They codify into theory the general public belief in the inferiority of public organizations, a belief that the management literature tends to reject as a crude stereotype.

In the late 1970s, authors began to point out this divergence between the management and the public bureaucracy literatures and to call for better integration of these topics (Allison, 1983; Bozeman, 1987; Hood and Dunsire, 1981; Lynn, 1981; Meyer, 1979; Perry and Kraemer, 1983; Pitt and Smith, 1981; Rainey, Backoff, and Levine, 1976; Wamsley and Zald, 1973; Warwick, 1975). These authors note that organization theory and behavior offer elaborate models and concepts for analyzing structure, change, decisions, strategy, environments, motivation, leadership, and other important topics. In addition, researchers tested these frameworks in empirical research. Because of their generic approaches, however, they paid too little attention to the issues raised by political scientists and economists. They virtually ignored the internationally significant issue of whether governmental auspices and economic market exposure make a difference for management and organization.

The critics also faulted the writings in political science and public administration for too much anecdotal description rather than systematic theory and research (Perry and Kraemer, 1983; Pitt and Smith, 1981). Scholars in public administration generally disparaged as inadequate the research and theory in that field (Houston and Delevan, 1990; McCurdy and Cleary, 1984; Kraemer and Perry, 1989; White, 1986). In a national survey of research projects on public management, Garson and Overman (1981, 1982) found relatively little funded research on general public management and concluded that the research that did exist was highly fragmented and diverse.

Although economists offered impressive intellectual exercises in developing abstract theory, they relied on simple, very general assumptions. They assumed, for example, that since public administrators cannot gain from profits in the economic market, they do not strive for efficiency and innovativeness, and that since they have no clear performance indicators from sales and profits, they administer through a profusion of rules. In addition, economists seldom directly tested the validity of their theories through empirical research. Neither the political science nor the economics literature on public bureaucracy paid as much attention to internal management — designing the structure of the organization, motivating and leading employees, developing internal communications and teamwork — as did the organization theory and general management literature. From the perspective of organization theory, many of the general observations of political scientists and economists about motivation, structure, and other aspects of the public bureaucracy appeared oversimplified.

Issues in Education and Practice

The debate involved more than a squabble among academics over the adequacy of their theories. It mirrored practical concerns about the practice of public management and the education necessary for it. In the wake of the upsurge in government activity during the 1960s, educational programs in public administration spread among universities around the country. The National Association of Schools of Public Affairs and Administration began a process of accrediting such programs. Among other criteria, this process required M.P.A. programs to emphasize management skills and technical knowledge rather than providing modified master's degree programs in political science. This implied the importance of identifying how the M.P.A. program resembles the M.B.A. program in preparing people for management positions. At the same time, it raised the question of how public management differs from business management.

These developments coincided with expressions of concern about the adequacy of our knowledge of public management. In 1979, the U.S. Office of Personnel Management organized a prestigious conference at the Brookings Institution. The conference featured statements about research needs for public management by prominent academics and government officials. It sought to address a widespread concern among both practitioners and researchers about "the lack of depth of knowledge in this field" (U.S. Office of Personnel Management, 1980, p. 7). At around the same time, various authors produced a stream of articles and books arguing that public-sector management involves relatively distinct issues and approaches. They also complained, however, that too little research and theory and too few case exercises directly address the practice of active, effective public management (Allison, 1983; Bower, 1983; Bower and Christenson, 1978; Brock, 1984; Chase and Reveal, 1983; Lynn, 1981, 1987).

The term *public management* has been used for decades. Educational courses and case exercises in public management have been available for years. Yet a sense of insufficiency drove the critique of its knowledge base and a growing attraction to the public management concept. Critics have argued that we have too little knowledge of this topic, especially as compared to the development of business management and general management (U.S. Office of Personnel Management, 1980). *Public management* connotes active, effective management of government organizations, as opposed to preoccupation with politics or acceptance of a caretaker administrative role.

Ineffective Public Management?

Recurrent complaints about inadequacies in the practice of public management have also fueled interest in the field. Generally, we recognize that large bureaucracies, and especially governmental ones, have a pervasive influence on our lives (Chackerian and Abcarian, 1984). They often blunder, and can harm and oppress people inside and outside of them (Denhardt, 1984; Hummel, 1982), and we face severe difficulties in assuring both their effective operation and their control through democratic processes. Some analysts contend that our provisions for pursuing this balance of effective operation and democratic control often create disincentives and constraints which prevent many public administrators from assuming the managerial roles that managers in industry typically play (Warwick, 1975; Lynn, 1981). Too many public managers, they say, do not seriously engage the challenges of motivating their subordinates, effectively designing their organizations and work processes, and otherwise actively managing their responsibilities. Politically elected and politically appointed officials face short terms in office, complex laws and rules that constrain the changes they can make, intense external political pressures, and sometimes their own amateurishness. Many concentrate on pressing public policy issues, at worst exhibiting political showmanship and paying little attention to the internal management of agencies and programs under their authority. Middle managers and career civil servants, constrained by central rules, have little authority and incentive to manage. A National Academy of Public Administration (1986) report pointed out that federal government administrators responsible for programs involving hundreds of millions of dollars often had to go through elaborate processes of obtaining approval to send one of their staff members to a brief training program or to obtain minor facilities or equipment. (The cover of the report contained a picture of Gulliver lashed down by the innumerable tiny threads of the Lilliputians.) The report called for revitalization of federal management by relieving federal administrators of picayune entanglements and constraints.

Experts also complain that too many of the elected officials charged with oversight of public organizations know and care very little about their management. Elected officials have little political incentive to attend to "good government" issues, such as effective management of agencies. They often have little managerial background, and they tend to interpret managerial issues in ways that would be considered outmoded by management experts. Warwick (1975) argues that many legislators and politically elected or appointed executives adhere to an "administrative orthodoxy." They believe that sound management requires a strict hierarchy of accountability in government agencies, strict accounting and control, elaborate reporting requirements, and tightly specified procedures. This orientation conflicts sharply with contemporary management thought and the practices of many of the most successful business firms.

The Dilemmas of Improving Public Management

Examples of the dilemmas of trying to control the federal bureacracy, coupled with the prevailing public hostility toward it, illustrate the need for better analysis of how external political processes influence organization and management in government. They reveal the constant struggle for political control of the bureaucracy and show how that effort often leads to negative, control-oriented approaches that backfire.

Having attacked the federal bureaucracy in their election campaigns, Presidents Carter and Reagan moved to control and curtail it. Carter administration officials developed the Civil Services Reform Act of 1978 as a management improvement initiative. Its provisions included steps to make it easier to discipline federal employees, to base pay more directly on performance, and to make it easier for politically appointed agency heads to select and transfer the career civil service managers who work under them. It created a Senior Executive Service to include higher-level executives in federal agencies. Yet administration officials also saw too little political support for a "good government" initiative. They found that they could mobilize support most effectively by stressing the difficulty of firing lazy, incompetent civil servants. Newspapers seized on this angle enthusiastically (Kettl, 1989). Later, surveys of federal managers found high levels of insecurity and discouragement resulting from the effects of the reform act.

President Reagan even more aggressively attacked federal agencies and worked for cuts in their authority, funding, and staffing. Reagan administration officials sought to increase the president's authority over the agencies and to squelch resistance to his initiatives from career civil servants. These officials used Senior Executive Service appointments to aggressively expand the number of political appointees to the higher levels of federal agencies. This action demoted career civil servants by placing administration loyalists in positions above them (Volcker Commission, 1989). Aggressive cutbacks disrupted many agencies (Rubin, 1985). Some agencies floundered when politically appointed executives were indicted for illegal actions.

Similar effects of the hostile climate were felt at state and local levels. Political candidates accused those governments of wasting money and promised cutbacks and reforms. Many states adopted poorly designed pay-for-performance schemes for their government employees (Sherwood and Wechsler, 1986). A highly respected long-term official in one of the largest cities in Florida stated in an interview that he was discouraged by the climate of criticism and disrespect for government employees. Moreover, he found it more and more difficult to attract and motivate high-quality government employees.

By the mid 1980s, experts were warning of a crisis in the public service (Volcker Commission, 1989). Many career executives left federal government service, some for higher-paying positions in the private sector. Surveys found serious morale problems, with large percentages of career managers reporting that they intended to leave government and that they would advise their own children against a career in federal service. Other surveys found that students showed little interest in public-service careers. Paul Volcker, who had chaired the Federal Reserve Board during the Carter and Reagan administrations, served as chair of the National Commission on the Public Service (later known as the Volcker Commission), which brought together a panel of distinguished public servants to direct an analysis of the crisis and recommend remedies. The commission's report (1989) recommends steps to improve public support for the public service, to improve pay, performance, recruiting, and training, and to improve relations between political appointees and career civil servants.

Numerous incidents suggested that the crisis seriously affected the performance of public agencies. For example, when the space shuttle *Challenger* exploded, the greatest disaster to befall the American space program, analysts blamed the catastrophe in large part on political orientations overriding the judgments of professional personnel within the National Aeronautics and Space Administration (Romzek and Dubnick, 1987). Late in the Reagan administration, a scandal broke regarding illegal activities in the contracting processes of the Department of the Navy. Officials and journalists attributed the problem to the weakening of the professional civil service in the Defense Department. Senators and representatives discussing the scandal on "The MacNeil/Lehrer News Hour" gave such interpretations, and Kelman (1988) cited the emasculation of the career service as a major cause of the problem. Another scandal erupted over illegal contracts by the Department of Housing and Urban Development (HUD), which wasted billions of dollars meant for the poor. Analysts attributed these problems to incompetent and unethical political appointees, who often overrode objections from career HUD staff members to improperly award contracts to political allies (Waldman, Cohn, and Thomas, 1989). Others also attributed the problems to lack of a public and congressional constituency for sound internal management of agencies such as HUD (Sperry, 1990). Cutbacks in regulatory staff at the Federal Home Loan Bank Board aggravated the massive savings and loan scandal during the Reagan and Bush administrations by weakening the board's oversight capacity. Reagan administration officials had denied requests for staff increases, emphasizing their policy of deregulation and the need to let the free market correct the situation (Rosenbaum, 1990b; Gerth, 1990).

These and other examples illustrate the irony that demeaning career governmental managers and diminishing their authority, while touted as a way of controlling the bungling federal bureaucracy, actually demonstrated the essential role that those career bureaucrats play. The problems cited above stem from many causes besides the Carter, Reagan, and Bush administrations and reflect ongoing dilemmas in controlling and managing public organizations. Later chapters describe a variety of management reforms in government that have come and gone with dubious results. They raise the question of whether government organizations inherently resist effective management.

Excellence in Public Management

Hostility toward government has evoked a counterattack from authors who argue that public bureaucracies perform better than is commonly acknowledged (Doig and Hargrove, 1987; Downs and Larkey, 1986; Goodsell, 1985; Milward and Rainey, 1983; Tierney, 1988). Others describe successful governmental innovations and policies (Osborne, 1990; Poister, 1988b; Schwartz, 1983). Wamsley and others (1990) call for increasing recognition that the administrative branches of governments in the United States play as essential and legitimate a role as the other branches of government. Many of these authors point to evidence of excellent performance by many government organizations and officials and the difficulty of proving that the private sector performs better. Claims for the superiority of private businesses typically overlook innumerable failings on their part. The attacks on government agencies often misplace the blame, targeting the public bureaucracy for problems originating in legislative and interest-group pressures. In addition, government bureaucracy serves as an easy target because of public stereotypes and misunderstanding. A Roper poll asked a representative sample of Americans how much of every $100 spent on the Social Security program goes to administrative costs. The median estimate was about $50 out of every $100. The actual figure is about $1.30 out of every $100 (Milward and Rainey, 1983).

The Perennial Amateur Hour

The controversies noted above show the inadequacy of blithe observations about the public-private distinctions, which have become the most hackneyed statements in the administrative literature: There is really no difference between the public and private sectors. The classic distinctions no longer apply. Yet diametrically opposite conclusions about the inferiority of government organizations pass for wisdom among many intellectuals and officials. Neither pattern of oversimplification resolves the complex issues.

The Challenge: Sustained, Serious Attention and Analysis

The controversies reflect fundamental complexities of the American political and economic system. That system has always subjected the administrative branch of government to conflicting pressures over who should control and how, whose interests should be served, and what values should predominate (Waldo, 1984). Management involves paradoxes that require organizations and managers to balance conflicting objectives and priorities. Public management often involves even more complex paradoxes.

Those on both sides of the debate over performance of the public bureaucracy and whether it represents a unique or generic management context are correct in a sense. General management and organizational concepts can have valuable applications to government. Unique aspects of the governmental context, however, must often be taken into account. In fact, examples of effective public management in later chapters of this text show that there is often a necessity for both. Managers in agencies apply effective management procedures, but they also skillfully negotiate the external political pressures and administrative constraints to create a context in which they can manage effectively. The real challenge involves identifying how much we know about this process and when, where, how, and why it applies. As the Volcker Commission and many of the authors cited in this book have said, we need researchers, practitioners, officials, and citizens to devote sustained, serious attention to developing our knowledge of and support for effective public management.

This book contributes to that process a review and analysis of some of the important topics: what we know about distinguishing public organizations from other types, what we can draw from the major topics in research and theory on management and organizations, and what we know about the public-sector context and its implications for those topics. This effort raises challenges of its own. Research and writing on public management have been appearing rapidly in many different places, and this analysis covers as much of the evidence being presented as possible. The body of potentially relevant material overwhelms any single volume. Scholars have turned more attention to political economy, societal institutions, and the economics of organization, adding to an already vast literature in economics, political science, and organization. The public and private sectors that this analysis covers involve myriad variations in organizational level, type, and setting, about which we have not yet developed systematic frameworks. For each of the topics or variables covered in the analysis — power, political processes, motivation, leadership, organizational structure, and others — there exists an extensive, diverse body of research, filled with controversies and inconclusive in some ways. Yet these challenges represent realities we must confront, just as we must confront the inescapable paradoxes and conflicts inherent in public management.

PART 1

꒦꒦꒦꒦꒦꒦꒦꒦꒦꒦꒦꒦꒦꒦꒦꒦꒦꒦꒦꒦꒦꒦꒦꒦꒦꒦꒦

THE DYNAMIC CONTEXT
OF PUBLIC ORGANIZATIONS

Chapter 1

What Makes
Public Organizations
Distinctive:
Reexamining Common Views

We face a fascinating and important controversy. Leading experts on management and organizations spurn the distinction between public and private organizations as a crude oversimplification or a relatively unimportant issue. Other very knowledgeable people call for development of a field recognizing the distinctiveness of public organizations and public management. Meanwhile, policy makers around the world struggle with decisions involving billions of dollars and concerning privatization of state activities and the roles of their public and private sectors.

This chapter discusses important theoretical and practical issues that fuel this controversy and begins to develop some answers. First, it examines in more depth the problems with the public-private distinction. It shows that research and leading figures in organization theory have downplayed this distinction. In addition, the chapter describes the overlapping of public, private, and nonprofit sectors in the United States, which erodes simple distinctions among them. The discussion then turns to the other side of the debate: the importance and meaning of the distinction. If they are not distinct in any important way, why do public organizations exist? Answers to this question point to the inevitability and the distinctive attributes of public organizations. Still, given all the complexities, how can we define public organizations and managers? The chapter discusses some of the confusion over the meaning of the public category and then describes some of the best-developed ways of conducting research to clarify it. After analyzing some of the problems in conducting such research, the chapter concludes with a description of the most frequent observations about the nature of public

15

organizations and managers. The remainder of the book examines research and debate on the accuracy of these observations.

Public Versus Private: A Dangerous Distinction?

Many authors caution against oversimplified distinctions between public and private management (Baldwin, 1987; Bozeman, 1987; Golembiewski, 1985; Murray, 1975; Weinberg, 1983). Objections to such distinctions require careful examination, because they provide valuable counterpoints against invidious stereotypes. The objections also point out realities of the contemporary political economy and raise challenges that we must face when clarifying the distinction.

The Generic Tradition in Organization Theory

A distinguished intellectual tradition bolsters the generic perspective on organizations; that is, the position that organization and management theorists should emphasize commonalities among organizations in order to develop knowledge applicable across most or all organizations, avoiding such popular distinctions as public versus private and profit versus nonprofit. As serious analysis of organizations and management burgeoned early in this century, leading figures argued that their insights applied across the commonly differentiated types of organizations. Many of them pointedly referred to the distinction between public and private organizations as the sort of crude oversimplification that theorists must overcome. From this point of view, such a distinction poses intellectual dangers: It oversimplifies, confuses, misleads, and impedes sound theory and research.

Typical historical reviews of organization theory describe it as beginning with an emphasis on uniform, highly structured organizational designs and work processes for all organizations. (For a more detailed discussion of these developments, see the Appendix.) Then, over the course of the past century, those in the field came increasingly to recognize that organizations can and should adopt a more diverse variety of forms, including more flexible and adaptive structures. As some people put it, the field evolved from the search for one best way to organize toward a view that proper organization depends on the particular contingencies that an organization faces. Throughout this evolution, however, the distinction between public and private organizations received short shrift.

Early in the twentieth century, Max Weber founded the field of organization theory with his analysis of bureaucratic organizations, which he argued applied to both government agencies and business firms. Later, Frederick Taylor led the scientific management movement, whose proponents used time-motion studies and other procedures to design the most efficient ways for workers to perform tasks. Taylor applied his scientific management procedures in government arsenals and other public organizations, and such techniques are widely applied in public and private organizations today. Similarly, members of the administrative management school sought to develop standard principles to govern the administrative structures of all organizations. Luther Gulick and other leaders of this group espoused such principles as strong executive authority, clear chains of command, narrow spans of control, and clear job descriptions. These guidelines purportedly applied to all types of organizations.

Later in the century, the Hawthorne Experiments and other research underscored the importance of social and psychological factors in the workplace. More and more writers began to attack the earlier perspectives as dehumanizing because they overlooked the importance of worker participation, self-esteem, autonomy, and interest in work. Douglas McGregor called on managers in industry to abandon Theory X, the theory that workers have weak motivation and little capacity for self-direction, and to accept Theory Y, the theory that workers can motivate and direct themselves. Industrial organizations that adhere to Theory Y adopt such approaches as decentralization, job enrichment, and participative management. This orientation pervades organizational development procedures that consultants apply frequently in government agencies today (Golembiewski, 1985).

In the meantime, researchers on topics in organizational behavior, such as motivation and leadership, constructed theories and churned out mountains of research. Often, they tested their theories in government agencies and military units just as they did in business firms. Again, however, they expressed their theories and concepts generally, to apply across all such settings.

Around the middle of the century, Herbert Simon (1946) attacked the administrative management school from a different angle. He rejected that group's principles of administration as "proverbs," too vague and too contradictory to guide managers in real decisions. More importantly, his interest in managerial decision making led him to the insight that won for him the Nobel Prize in economics. He noted that much of administrative theory and economic theory relied heavily on assumptions that managers make decisions in very systematic, highly rational patterns. The administrative management school depicted executives as rationally applying objective principles in designing the optimal organization, and economic theory depicted managers as rationally calculating the means to maximize profits. In reality, Simon said, managers face too many uncertainties, too much information, too many possible alternatives, too many constraints on their own mental capacities to "maximize" by performing elaborate rational calculations to find the optimum alternative. Rather, they must "satisfice" by selecting the best alternative available after the most reasonable search that they can perform within their limited time and resources.

Interestingly, Simon implicitly framed this argument as applicable to all organizational settings, both public and private. Beginning as a political scientist, he coauthored one of the leading texts in public administration (Simon, Smithburg, and Thompson, 1950). It contains a sophisticated discussion of the political contexts of public organizations. It also argues, however, that there are more similarities than differences between public and private organizations. Accordingly, in his other work, he concentrated on general analyses of organizations (Simon, 1948; March and Simon, 1958). He thus implied that his insights about satisficing and other organizational processes apply across all types of organizations. Thus, the leading intellectual figure of organization theory clearly assigned relative unimportance to the distinctiveness of public organizations. In so doing, he never addressed key questions about political economy — whether, for example, satisficing responses in organizations exposed to economic markets are different from those in organizations under governmental oversight and funding.

Still, Simon's work had sufficient importance for the field of economics to earn him the Nobel Prize. His focus on decisions under constrained rationality and uncertainty became a central theme in the field of organization theory. As researchers performed more studies of organizations, they found the "principles of administration" not only theoretically inadequate but inaccurate as depictions of reality. They found that organizations follow not one standard set of organizing principles but rather a variety of approaches, depending on the conditions that they face. Research indicated that complex, unstable operating environments and complex, highly variable tasks impose great uncertainty on organizations and managers. Under such conditions, classical principles dictating clear chains of command, tight job descriptions, clear rules, and authoritative superiors break down. Organizations often move to more decentralized, informal, flexible structures, which purposely violate the classical principles of administration.

These observations developed into the *contingency theory* perspective on organizational structure and design. According to this theory, organizations adapt their structures to key contingencies that confront them. The primary contingencies include environmental uncertainty and complexity, the variability and complexity of tasks and technologies (the work that the organization does), organizational size, and strategic decisions of managers. Thus, even though this perspective emphasizes variations among organizations, it downplays any particular distinctiveness of public organizations. James Thompson (1962), a leading figure among the contingency theorists, echoed the generic refrain — public and private organizations have more similarities than differences.

During the 1980s, the contingency perspective evolved in many different directions, some involving more attention to governmental and economic influences (Scott, 1987; Nord, 1983; Barney and Ouchi, 1986). Still, the titles and topic coverage in management and organization theory journals and excellent overviews of that field (Daft, 1989; Hall, 1987; Pfeffer, 1982) reflect the generic tradition. Public organizations as a distinctive category receive sporadic, speculative attention, but with the clear implication that this distinctiveness plays a minor role relative to other influences.

Findings from Research

Objections to distinguishing between public and private organizations draw on more than theorists' claims. Studies of variables such as size, task, and technology in government agencies show that those variables may influence government organizations more than anything related to their governmental auspices. These findings agree with the commonsense observation that an organization becomes bureaucratic not because it is in government or business but because of its large size.

Major studies analyzing many different organizations to develop taxonomies and typologies have produced little evidence of a strict division between public and private organizations. Some of the prominent efforts to develop a taxonomy of organizations based on empirical measures of organizational characteristics have failed to show any value in a public-private distinction (Haas, Hall, and Johnson, 1966). Others have produced inconclusive results (Pugh, Hickson, and Hinings, 1969). Haas, Hall, and Johnson (1966) measured characteristics of a large sample of organizations and used statistical techniques to categorize them according to shared characteristics. A number of the resulting categories included both public and private organizations. Organizations' tasks and functions can have much more influence on their characteristics than public or private auspices. A government-owned hospital obviously resembles a private hospital more than it does a government-owned utility. Consultants and researchers frequently find in both the public and the private sectors organizations with highly motivated employees as well as severely troubled organizations. They often find that more proximal factors, such as leadership practices, influence work motivation and satisfaction more than whether the employing organization is public, private, or nonprofit.

Pugh, Hickson, and Hinings (1969), classifying a sample of some fifty-eight organizations into categories based on measures of their structural characteristics, had predicted that the government organizations would show more bureaucratic features, such as more rules and procedures, but they found no such differences. They did find, however, that the government organizations showed higher degrees of control by external government authorities, especially over personnel procedures. This study included only eight government organizations, all operating as local government units with functions similar to those of business organizations (for example, governmental vehicle repair unit and a water utility). Consequently, the researchers interpreted their findings as inconclusive as to whether government agencies differ from private organizations in terms of structural characteristics. Studies such as these have consistently found the public-private distinction inadequate for a general typology or taxonomy of organizations (McKelvey, 1982).

The Blurring of the Sectors

In addition to the research findings, those who object to the claim that public organizations make up a distinct category also point out that the public and private sectors overlap and interrelate in a number of ways.

Mixed, Intermediate, and Hybrid Forms. An important population of government organizations are designed to resemble business firms. A diverse array of state-owned enterprises, government corporations, government-sponsored corporations, and public authorities perform crucial functions in the United States and other countries (Seidman, 1983; Musolf and Seidman, 1980; Walsh, 1978). Usually owned and operated by government, they typically perform business-type functions and generate their own revenues through sales of their products or other means. Such enterprises usually receive a special charter to operate more independently than government agencies. Examples include the U.S. Postal Service, the Resolution Trust Corporation, the National Parks Service, port authorities in many coastal cities, and a multitude of other organizations at all levels of government. Such organizations are sometimes the subjects of controversy as to whether they operate in sufficiently businesslike fashion, on the one hand, and whether they show sufficient public accountability, on the other. On the other side of the coin are the many nonprofit and third-sector organizations that perform functions similar to those of government organizations. Like many government agencies, many nonprofits obviously have no profit indicators and incentives and often pursue social or public-service missions. Finally, many private, for-profit organizations work with government in ways that blur the distinction between them. Some corporations, such as defense contractors, receive so much funding and influence from government that some economists equate them with government bureaus (Weidenbaum, 1969).

Functional Analogies—Doing the Same Things. Obviously, many people and organizations in the public and private sectors perform virtually the same functions. General managers, secretaries, computer programmers, auditors, personnel officers, maintenance workers, and many other specialists perform similar tasks in public, private, and hybrid organizations. Organizations located in the different sectors—for example, hospitals, schools, and electric utilities—also perform the same general functions.

Complex Interrelations. Government, business, and nonprofit organizations interrelate in a number of ways (Kettl, 1988). Governments buy many products and services from nongovernmental organizations. Increasingly, nongovernmental organizations deliver government services. Through contracts, grants, vouchers, subsidies, and franchises, governments arrange for the delivery of health care, sanitation services, research services, and numerous other services by private organizations. These entangled relations muddle the question of where government and the private sector begin and end. Banks process loans provided by the Veterans Administration and receive Social Security deposits by wire for Social Security recipients. Private corporations handle portions of the administration of Medicare by means of government contracts, and private physicians render most Medicare services. Private nonprofit corporations and religious organizations operate facilities for the elderly or for delinquent youth using funds provided through government contracts and operating under extensive governmental regulations. In thousands of examples of this sort, private businesses and nonprofit organizations become part of the service-delivery process for government programs and further blur the public-private distinction.

Analogies in Social Role and Context. Government uses laws, regulations, and fiscal policies to influence private organizations. Environmental protection regulations, tax laws, monetary policies, and equal employment opportunity regulations either impose direct requirements on private organizations or establish inducements and incentives. Here, again, nongovernmental organizations share in the implemention of public policies. They become part of government and an extension of it. Even working independently of government, business organizations affect the quality of life in the nation and the public interest (Hall and Quinn, 1983). Members of the most profit-oriented firms argue that their organizations serve their communities and the well-being of the nation. Government agencies, on the other hand, sometimes behave too much like private organizations. One of the foremost contemporary criticisms of government concerns the influence that interest groups wield over public agencies and programs. According to the critics, these groups use the agencies to serve their own interests rather than the public interest.

Conclusion: *The Importance of Avoiding Oversimplifications*

Theory, research, and the realities of the contemporary political economy show the inadequacy of simple notions about differences between public and private organizations. For management theory and research, this poses the challenge of determining what role a public-private distinction can play, and how. For practical management and public policy, it means that we must avoid oversimplifying the issue and jumping to conclusions about sharp distinctions between public and private.

That advice may sound obvious enough, but violations of it abound. Some public managers too quickly assume a sharp distinction between their context and the context of those in private organizations. Experienced consultants find that their management ideas are as applicable in many public organizations as in business firms, yet public administrators often resist those ideas, claiming that one simply cannot do such things in government. Robert Golembiewski (1984), a prolific researcher with extensive consulting experience in government and industry, calls this tendency the "Dr. No" syndrome and says that he runs into it in many public agencies. Surveys show that public managers often have stereotypes about business managers and business organizations and vice versa (Stevens, Wartick, and Bagby, 1988; Weiss, 1983).

In matters of public policy, some calls for privatization oversimplify the distinction between public and private (Donahue, 1990; Wise, 1990). They often call for government contracts with private or nonprofit service providers that may impose elaborate constraints, eliminate competition, and otherwise restrain free-market conditions. Similarly, proposals for voucher systems and other quasi-market arrangements often assume that making things a little more like a market and a little less like government produces great improvements.

For all the reasons discussed above, clear demarcations between the public and private sectors are impossible, and oversimplified distinctions between public and private organizations are misleading. We still face a paradox, however, because scholars and officials use a public-private distinction repeatedly in relation to important issues, and public and private organizations differ in some obvious ways.

Public Organizations: An Essential Distinction

If there is no real difference between public and private organizations, can we nationalize all industrial firms — or privatize all government agencies? Private executives earn significantly higher pay than their government counterparts, and the financial press regularly lambasts the absurdity of corporate executive compensation practices. Can we simply put these executives on the federal executive compensation schedule? Such questions make it clear that there are some important differences between public and private administration. Scholars have provided useful insights into the distinction in recent years, and researchers and managers have reported more evidence of distinctive features of public organizations.

The Purpose of Public Organizations

Why do public organizations exist? The answers to this question lie in both political and economic theory — even some economists who strongly favor free markets regard government agencies as inevitable components of free-market economies (Downs, 1967).

Politics and Markets. Decades ago, Robert Dahl and Charles Lindblom (1953) provided a useful analysis of the raison d'être for public organizations. They analyzed the alternatives available to nations for controlling their political economies. Two of the fundamental alternatives are political hierarchies and economic markets. In advanced industrial democracies, the political process involves a complex array of contending groups and institutions that produces a complex, hydra-headed hierarchy, which Dahl and Lindblom call a *polyarchy*. Such a politically established hierarchy can direct economic activities. Alternatively, the price system in free economic markets can control economic production and allocation decisions. Most nations use some mixture of markets and polyarchies.

Political hierarchy, or polyarchy, draws on political authority, which can serve as a very useful, inexpensive means of social control. It is cheaper to have people relatively willingly stop at red lights than to work out a system of compensating them for doing so. However, political authority can be "all thumbs" (Lindblom, 1977). Central plans and directives often prove confining, clumsy, ineffective, poorly adapted to many local circumstances, and cumbersome to change.

Markets have the advantage of operating through voluntary exchange as a form of social control. Producers must induce consumers to willingly engage in exchanges with them. They have the incentive to produce what consumers want, as efficiently as possible. This allows much freedom and flexibility, provides incentives for efficient use of resources, controls production in the direction of consumer demands, and avoids the problems of central planning and rule making inherent in polyarchy. Markets, however, have a limited capacity to handle certain types of problems, for which government action is required (Lindblom, 1977; Downs, 1967). Such problems include the following:

- *Public goods and free riders.* Certain goods, once provided, benefit everyone. Individuals have the incentive to act as free riders and let others pay, so government imposes taxes to pay for such goods. National defense is the most frequently cited example; education and police protection are others. Even though private organizations could provide these services, government provides most of them because they entail general benefits for the society.

- *Individual incompetence.* People often lack sufficient education or information to make wise individual choices in some areas, so government regulation is required. For example, most people would not be able to determine the safety of particular medicines, so the Food and Drug Administration regulates the distribution of pharmaceuticals.

- *Externalities or spillovers.* Some costs may spill over onto people who are not parties to a market exchange. A manufacturer polluting the air imposes costs on others that the price of the product does not cover. The Environmental Protection Agency regulates environmental externalities of this sort.

Government acts to correct problems that markets themselves create or are unable to address — problems of monopoly, need for income redistribution, and instability due to market fluctuations—and to provide crucial activities too risky or expensive for private competitors to undertake. Critics also complain that market systems produce too many frivolous and trivial products, foster crassness and greed, confer too much power on corporations and their executives, and allow extensive bungling and corruption. For example, 80 percent of all newly introduced food and grocery products fail to sell and must be withdrawn from store shelves (Shapiro, 1990). Public concern over such matters bolsters support for a strong and active government (Lipset and Schneider, 1987).

Conservative economists argue that markets eventually resolve many of these problems and that government interventions simply make matters worse. Advocates of privatization claim that government does not have to perform many of the functions supposedly justified by market failures and that government provides many services that private organizations can provide more efficiently. Nevertheless, American citizens broadly support government action in relation to many of these problems.

Political Rationales for Government. A purely economic rationale for government does not effectively address many political and social justifications for government. In theory, government in the United States exists to maintain systems of law, justice, and social organization, to maintain individual rights and freedoms, to provide national security and stability, to promote general prosperity, and to provide direction for the nation and its communities. In reality, government often simply does what influential political groups demand. In spite of the blurring of the distinction between the public and private sectors, government organizations in the United States remain restricted to certain functions. For the most part, they provide services that are not exchanged on economic markets, but are justified on the basis of general social values, the public interest, and politically imposed demands of groups.

The Meaning and Nature of Public Organizations and Management

While the idea of a public domain within society is an ancient one, beliefs about what is appropriately public and what private, in both personal affairs and social organization, have varied among societies and over time. The word *public* comes from the Latin for "people," and dictionaries define it as a reference to matters pertaining to the people of a community, nation, or state (Guralnick, 1980). The word *private* comes from the Latin word that means to be deprived of public office or set apart from government as a personal matter. In contemporary definitions, the distinction between public and private involves three major factors (Benn and Gaus, 1983): *interests* affected—whether benefits or losses are communal or restricted to individuals; *access* to facilities, resources, or information, and *agency*—whether a person or organization acts as an individual or for the community as a whole. These dimensions can be independent of each other and even contradictory.

For example, a military base may operate in the public interest, acting as an agent for the nation, but deny public access.

Approaches to Defining Public Organizations and Managers. The multiple dimensions along which the concepts of public and private vary make for many ways to define public organizations, most of which prove inadequate. For example, one time-honored approach defines public organizations as those that have a great impact on the public interest (Dewey, 1927). Decisions about whether government should regulate have turned on judgments about the public interest (Mitnick, 1980). In their prominent typology of organizations, Blau and Scott (1962) distinguish between *commonweal* organizations, which benefit the public in general, and *business* organizations, which benefit their owners. The *public interest,* however, has proved notoriously hard to define and measure (Mitnick, 1980). Some definitions directly conflict with each other; for example, definitions of the public interest as what a philosopher king or benevolent dictator decides and as what the majority of people prefer. Most organizations affect the public interest in some sense, especially large business firms. Manufacturers of computers, pharmaceuticals, automobiles, and many other products clearly have tremendous influence on the well-being of the nation.

Alternatively, researchers and managers often refer to auspices or ownership, an implicit use of the agency factor mentioned above. Public organizations are government organizations, and private organizations are nongovernmental, usually business firms. This simple dichotomy has kept the debate going by producing impressive research results (Mascarenhas, 1989). The blurring of the boundaries between the sectors, however, shows that we need further analysis of what this dichotomy means.

Agencies and Enterprises as Points on a Continuum. In their analysis of markets and polyarchies, Dahl and Lindblom (1953) treated the public-private distinction as a complex continuum of types of organizations, ranging between *enterprises* (organizations controlled primarily by markets) and *agencies* (public or government-owned organizations). For enterprises, they argued, the price system automatically links revenues to products and services sold. This creates stronger incentives for cost reduction in enterprises than in agencies. Agencies have more trouble integrating cost reduction into their goals and coordinating spending and revenue decisions, since legislatures assign their tasks and funds separately. Their funding allocations usually depend on past levels, and if they achieve improvements in efficiency, their appropriations are likely to be cut. Agencies also pursue more intangible, diverse objectives, making efficiency harder to measure. The difficulty in specifying and measuring objectives causes officials to try to control agencies through enforcement of rigid procedures rather than evaluations of products and services. Agencies also have more problems of hierarchical control, such as red tape, buck passing, rigidity, and timidity, than do enterprises.

More important than Dahl and Lindblom's oversimplified comparison of agencies and enterprises is their depiction of these organizations as lying on points along a continuum. They conceptualize various forms of agencies and enterprises ranging from most public to most private as illustrated in Figure 1.1. Dahl and Lindblom did not explain how their assertions about the different characteristics of agencies and enterprises apply to organizations on different points of the continuum. Implicitly, however, they suggested that agency characteristics apply less and less as one moves away from that extreme, and the characteristics of enterprises become more and more applicable.

Ownership and Funding. Wamsley and Zald (1973) pointed out that the government-private continuum involves at least two major dimensions, ownership and funding. Organizations can be owned by government or privately owned. They can receive most of their funding from governmental sources, such as budget allocations from legislative bodies, or they can receive most of it from private sources, such as donations or sales on economic markets. Putting these two dichotomies together results in the four categories illustrated in Figure 1.2: public organizations, such as typical government agencies; publicly owned but privately funded organizations, such as the U.S. Postal Service and government-owned utilities; privately owned but governmentally funded organizations, such as certain defense firms funded primarily through government contracts; and privately owned and funded organizations, such as supermarket chains and IBM.

This scheme does have limitations; it makes no mention of regulation, for example. And many corporations, such as IBM, receive funding from government contracts but operate so autonomously that they clearly belong in the private category. Nevertheless, the approach provides a fairly clear way of identifying core categories of public and private organizations.

Economic Authority, Public Authority, and "Publicness." Bozeman (1987) draws on a number of the preceding points to try to conceive the complex variations across the public-private dimension. All organizations have some degree of political influence and are subject to some level of external governmental control. Hence, they all have some level of "publicness," although that level varies widely. Like Wamsley and Zald, Bozeman uses two subdimensions — political authority and economic authority — but treats them as continua rather than dichotomies. Economic authority increases as owners and managers have more authority over the use of income and financial assets of the organization and decreases as external government authorities have more control over their finances.

Political authority is granted by other elements of the political system, such as the citizenry or governmental institutions. It authorizes the organization to act on behalf of these other elements of the political system and to make binding decisions for them. Private firms have relatively little

Figure 1.1. Agencies, Enterprises, and Hybrid Organizations.

The continuum of choices ranging between government ownership and private enterprise. Below the line: arrangements colloquially referred to as public, government-owned, or nationalized. Above the line: arrangements popularly considered neither public nor private. On the line: organizational forms usually referred to as private enterprise or free enterprise.

	Government Agency →					→ Private Enterprise
Above the line		Private nonprofit organization totally reliant on government contracts and grants (Atomic Energy Commission, Manpower Development Research Corporation).	Private corporations reliant on government contracts for most of revenues (some defense contractors, such as General Dynamics, Grumman).	Heavily regulated private firms (heavily regulated privately owned utilities).	Private corporation with significant funding from government contracts but majority of revenues from other private sources.	Private corporation subject to general governmental regulation (affirmative action, Occupational Health and Safety regulations)	Private Enterprise
On the line				Government ownership of part of a private corporation			
Below the line	Government Agency	State-owned enterprise or public corporation (Postal Service, TVA, Port Authority of NY).	Government-sponsored enterprise, established by government, but with shares traded on stock market (Federal National Mortgage Association).		Government program or agency operated largely through purchases from private vendors or producers (Medicare, public housing).		

Source: Adapted and revised from Dahl and Lindblom (1953).

Figure 1.2. Public and Private Ownership and Funding.

	Public Ownership	Private Ownership
Public funding (taxes government contracts)	Department of Defense Social Security Administration Police department	Defense contractors Rand Corporation Manpower Development Research Corporation Oak Ridge National Laboratories
Private funding (sales, private donations)	U.S. Postal Service Government-owned utilities Federal Home Loan Bank Board	General Motors[a] IBM General Electric Grocery store chains YMCA

[a]These large corporations have large government contracts and sales but attain most of their revenues from private sales and have relative autonomy to withdraw from dealing with government.

Source: Adapted and revised from Wamsley and Zald (1973).

of this authority. They operate on their own behalf and only insofar as they support themselves through voluntary exchanges with citizens. Government agencies have high levels of authority to act for the community or country, and citizens are compelled to support their activities through taxes and other ways.

The publicness of an organization depends on the joint level of these two dimensions. Figure 1.3 illustrates Bozeman's depiction of possible combinations. As in previous approaches, the owner-managed private firm occupies one extreme (high on economic authority, low on political authority) and the traditional government bureau the other (low on economic authority, high on political authority). A more complex array of organizations represents various combinations of the two dimensions. Bozeman and colleagues have used this approach to design research on public, private, and intermediate forms of research and development (R & D) laboratories, and other organizations. Later chapters describe how they found important differences between the public and private categories, with the intermediate forms falling in between (Bozeman and Loveless, 1987; Crow and Bozeman, 1987; Emmert and Crow, 1988; Coursey and Rainey, 1990).

All these efforts to clarify the public-private dimension cannot capture its full complexity. Government and political processes influence organizations in many ways, through laws, regulations, grants, contracts, charters, franchises, direct ownership (with many variations in oversight), and numerous other ways (McGregor, 1981; Hood, 1983; Salamon, 1989). Private market influences also involve many variations. Perry and Rainey (1988) suggest that future research can compare organizations in different categories, such as those in Table 1.1. Analyses of the external controls on organizations could determine whether they are influenced primarily by polyarchies or by markets. Waste (1987) has developed measures of polyarchy for classifying cities, and such measures could be developed for organizations. One could also classify organizations by ownership and funding to develop a set

Figure 1.3. Publicness: Political and Economic Authority.

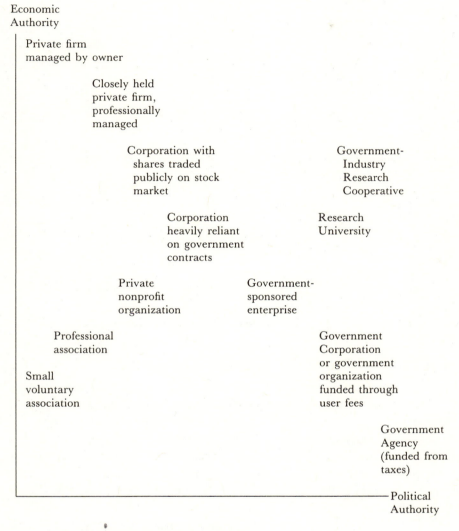

Source: Adapted from Bozeman (1987).

of types that could be compared in research. No standard nomenclature exists for the hybrid organizations listed in Table 1.1. Such terms for hybrids as *government corporation* and *state-owned enterprise* are often used interchangeably (Seidman, 1983). Yet one could more carefully designate such categories and, within various industries and policy areas, compare organizations representing these different categories along the public-private continuum. Later chapters describe many useful studies comparing more limited sets of categories, such as state-owned enterprises versus private enterprises. Further refining such comparisons should help to clarify the effects of governmental and market influences on organizations.

While this topic needs further refinement, these analyses of the public-private dimension clarify important points. Simply stating that the public

Table 1.1. Typology of Organizations Created by
Cross-Classifying Ownership, Funding, and Mode of Social Control.

	Ownership	Funding	Mode of Social Control	Representative Studies
Bureau (for example, Bureau of Labor Statistics)	public	public	polyarchy	Meier (1987)
Government corporation (for example, Pension Benefit Guaranty Corporation)	public	private	polyarchy	Walsh (1978)
Government-sponsored enterprise (for example, Corporation for Public Broadcasting)	private	public	polyarchy	Musolf & Seidman (1980)
Regulated enterprise (for example, private electric utilities)	private	private	polyarchy	Mitnick (1980)
Governmental enterprise	public	public	market	
State-owned enterprise (for example, Airbus)	public	private	market	Aharoni (1986)
Government contractor (for example, Grumann)	private	public	market	Bozeman (1987)
Private enterprise (for example, IBM)	private	private	market	Williamson (1975)

Source: Adapted and revised from Perry and Rainey (1988).

and private sectors are not distinct does little good. The challenge involves conceiving and analyzing the possible differences, variations, and similarities. In starting to do so, we can think with reasonable clarity about a distinction between public and private organizations, although we must always realize the complications. We can think of assertions about public organizations applying primarily to organizations owned and funded by government, such as typical government agencies. At least by definition, they differ from privately owned firms, which get most of their resources from private sources and are not subject to extensive government regulations. We can then seek evidence comparing these two groups, and in fact such research often shows differences—although we need much more. The population of hybrid and third-sector organizations raises complications about whether differences between these core public and private categories apply to them. Yet we have increasing evidence that organizations in this intermediate group—even within the same function or industry—differ in important ways on the basis of how public or private they are. Designing and evaluating this evidence, however, involve some further complications.

Problems and Approaches in Public-Private Comparisons

Defining a distinction between public and private organizations does not prove that important differences between them actually exist. We need to consider those supposed differences and the evidence for or against them. First, however, some intriguing challenges in research on public management and public-private comparisons need consideration, because they figure importantly in sizing up the evidence.

The discussion of the generic approach and contingency theory introduced some of these challenges. Many factors, such as size, task or function, and industry characteristics, can influence an organization more than government auspices. Research needs to show that these alternative factors do not confuse analysis of differences between public organizations and other types. Obviously, for example, if you compare large public agencies to small private firms and find the agencies more bureaucratic, size may be the real explanation. Also obviously, one would not compare a set of public hospitals to private utilities as a way of assessing the nature of public organizations. Ideally, an analysis of the public-private dimension requires a convincing sample, with a good model that accounts for other variables besides the public-private dimension. Ideally, also, studies would have huge, well-designed samples of organizations and employees, representing many functions and controlling for many variables. No one has had the resources or inclination to conduct such studies. Researchers and practitioners have adopted a variety of less comprehensive approaches.

Some theorize on the basis of assumptions, past literature, and their own experiences (Dahl and Lindblom, 1953; Downs, 1967). Similarly, but less systematically, some books about public bureaucracy simply provide a list of the differences, based on the authors' knowledge and experience (Gawthorp, 1969; Mainzer, 1973; Woll, 1977). Other researchers conduct research projects measuring or observing public bureaucracies and draw conclusions about their differences from private organizations. Some concentrate on one agency (Warwick, 1975), some on many agencies (Meyer, 1979). Although valuable, these studies leave doubts because they examine no private organizations directly.

Many executives and managers who have served in both public agencies and private business firms make emphatic statements about the sharp differences in the two settings (Blumenthal, 1983; Cervantes, 1983; Rumsfeld, 1983; Weiss, 1983). Quite convincing as testimonials, they apply to the executive and managerial levels. Differences might fade at lower levels. Other researchers compare sets of public and private organizations or managers. Some compare the managers in small sets of government and business organizations (Buchanan, 1974, 1975; Rainey, 1979, 1983; Porter and Lawler, 1968). Questions remain about how well the small samples represent the full populations and how well they account for important factors such as task. More recent studies with larger samples of organizations still leave questions about representation of the full populations. They add more convincing evidence of distinctive aspects of public management, however (Coursey and Bozeman, 1990; Coursey and Rainey, 1990; Hickson and others, 1986).

To analyze public versus private delivery of a particular service, many researchers compare public and private organizations within functional categories. They compare hospitals (Savas, 1987, p. 190), utilities (Atkinson and Halvorsen, 1986), schools (Chubb and Moe, 1988) and others. Somewhat similarly, other studies compare a function, such as management of computers, in government and business organizations (Bretschneider, 1990). Still others compare state-owned enterprises to privae firms (Hickson and others, 1986; Mascarenhas, 1989; MacAvoy and McIssac, 1989). They find differences and show that the public-private distinction appears meaningful even where the same general types of organization operate under both auspices. Studies of one functional type, however, may not apply to other functional types. The public-private distinction apparently has some different implications in one industry or market environment (hospitals, for example) as compared to another (refuse collection). Still another complication is that public and private organizations within a functional category may not actually do the same thing or operate in the same way (Kelman, 1985). For example, private and public hospitals may serve different patients, and public and private electric utilities may have different funding patterns.

In some cases, organizational researchers studying other topics have used a public-private distinction in the process and have found that it makes a difference (Hickson and others, 1986; Chubb and Moe, 1988; Tolbert, 1985; Mintzberg, 1972; Kurke and Aldrich, 1983). These researchers have no particular concern with the success or failure of the distinction per se; they simply find it meaningful.

A few studies compare public and private samples from census data or large-scale social surveys or national studies (Smith and Nock, 1980; U.S. Office of Personnel Management, 1979; U.S. General Accounting Office, 1990). These have great value, but often such aggregated findings prove difficult to relate to characteristics of specific organizations and the people in them. In the absence of huge, conclusive studies, we have to piece together evidence from more limited analyses such as these. Many issues remain debatable, but we can learn a great deal from doing so.

Common Assertions About Public Organizations and Management

In spite of the difficulties, the stream of assertions and research findings continues. During the 1970s and 1980s, various reviews compiled the most frequent arguments and evidence about the distinction (Fottler, 1981; Baldwin, 1987; Meyer, 1982; Rainey, Backoff, and Levine, 1976). There has been a good deal of progress in research, but the basic points of contention have not substantially changed. Table 1.2 shows a recent summary and introduces many of the issues that later chapters examine. The table and the following discussion of it pull together theoretical statements, expert observations, and research findings. Except for those mentioned, it omits many controversies about the accuracy of the statements, which later chapters consider. Still, it presents a reasonable depiction of prevailing views and issues about the

Table 1.2. Distinctive Characteristics of Public Management and Public Organizations: A Summary of Common Assertions and Research Findings.

I. Environmental Factors

I.1.   Absence of economic markets for outputs; reliance on governmental appropriations for financial resources.

     I.1.a.   Less incentive to cost reduction, operating efficiency, and effective performance.

     I.1.b.   Lower allocational efficiency (weaker reflection of consumer preferences, less proportioning of supply to demand).

     I.1.c.   Less availability of relatively clear market indicators and information (prices, profits, market share) for use in managerial decisions.

I.2.   Presence of particularly elaborate and intensive formal legal constraints as a result of oversight by legislative branch, executive branch hierarchy and oversight agencies, and courts.

     I.2.a.   More constraints on domains of operation and on procedures (less autonomy of managers in making such choices).

     I.2.b.   Greater tendency to proliferation of formal administrative controls.

     I.2.c.   Larger number of external sources of formal authority and influence, with greater fragmentation among them.

I.3.   Presence of more intensive external political influences.

     I.3.a.   Greater diversity and intensity of external informal political influences on decisions (political bargaining and lobbying, public opinion, interest-group, and client and constituent pressures).

     I.3.b.   Greater need for political support from client groups, constituencies, formal authorities, in order to attain appropriations and authorization for actions.

II. Organization-Environment Transactions

II.1.   Public organizations and managers are often involved in production of public goods or handling of significant externalities. Outputs are not readily transferable on economic markets at a market price.

II.2.   Government activities are often coercive, monopolistic, or unavoidable. Government has unique sanctions and coercive powers and is often sole provider. Participation in consumption and financing of activities is often mandatory.

II.3.   Government activities often have a broader impact and greater symbolic significance. There is a broader scope of concern, such as for general public interest criteria.

II.4.   There is greater public scrutiny of public managers.

II.5.   There are unique public expectations for fairness, responsiveness, honesty, openness, and accountability.

III. Organization Roles, Structures, and Processes

(The following distinctive characteristics of organizational roles, structures, and processes have been frequently asserted to result from the distinctions cited in I and II above. More recently, distinctions of this nature have been analyzed in research with varying results.

III.1.   Greater goal ambiguity, multiplicity, and conflict.

     III.1.a.   Greater vagueness, intangibility, or difficulty in measuring goals and performance criteria; the goals are more debatable and value-laden (for example, defense readiness, public safety, a clean environment, better living standards for the poor and unemployed).

     III.1.b.   Greater multiplicity of the goals and criteria (efficiency, public accountability and openness, political responsiveness, fairness and due process, social equity and distributional criteria, moral correctness of behavior).

     III.1.c.   Greater tendency of the goals to be conflicting, to involve more trade-offs (efficiency versus openness to public scrutiny, efficiency versus due process and social equity, conflicting demands of diverse constituencies and political authorities).

III.2.   Distinctive features of general managerial roles.

     III.2.a.   Recent studies have been finding that public managers' general roles involve many of the same functions and role categories as those of managers in other settings, but with some distinctive features: a more political, expository role involving more meetings with and interventions by external interest groups and political authorities, more crisis management and "fire drills," more of a challenge to balance external political relations with internal management functions.

Table 1.2. Distinctive Characteristics of Public Management and Public Organizations: A Summary of Common Assertions and Research Findings, Con't.

III.3. Administrative authority and leadership practices.

 III.3.a. Public managers have less decision-making autonomy and flexibility because of elaborate institutional constraints and external political influences. More external interventions, interruptions, constraints.

 III.3.b. Public managers have weaker authority over subordinates and lower levels as a result of institutional constraints (for example, civil service personnel systems, purchasing and procurement systems) and external political alliances of subunits and subordinates (with interest groups, legislators).

 III.3.c. Higher-level public managers show greater reluctance to delegate authority and a tendency to establish more levels of review and approval and to make greater use of formal regulations to control lower levels.

 III.3.d. More frequent turnover of top leaders due to elections and political appointments causes more difficulty in implementing plans and innovations.

 III.3.e. Recent counterpoint studies describe entrepreneurial behaviors and managerial excellence by public managers.

III.4. Organizational structure.

 III.4.a. Numerous assertions that public organizations are subject to more red tape, more elaborate bureaucratic structures.

 III.4.b. Empirical studies report mixed results, some supporting the assertions about red tape, some not supporting them. Numerous studies find some structural distinctions for public forms of organizations, although not necessarily more bureaucratic structuring.

III.5. Strategic decision processes.

 III.5.a. Recent studies show that strategic decision processes in public organizations can be generally similar to those in other settings but are more likely to be subject to interventions, interruptions, and greater involvement of external authorities and interest groups.

III.6. Incentives and incentive structures.

 III.6.a. Numerous studies show that public managers and employees perceive greater administrative constraints on administration of extrinsic incentives such as pay, promotion, and disciplinary action than do their counterparts in private organizations.

 III.6.b. Recent studies indicate that public managers and employees perceive weaker relations between performance and extrinsic rewards such as pay, promotion, and job security. The studies indicate that there may be some compensating effect of service and other intrinsic incentives for public employees and show no clear relation to performance of the differences in perceived reward-performance relations.

III.7. Individual characteristics, work-related attitudes and behaviors.

 III.7.a. A number of studies have found different work-related values on the part of public managers and employees, such as lower valuation of monetary incentives and higher levels of public service motivation.

 III.7.b. Numerous highly diverse studies have found lower levels of work satisfaction and organizational commitment among public than among private managers and employees. The level of satisfaction among public-sector samples is generally high but tends consistently to be somewhat lower than that among private comparison groups.

III.8. Organizational and individual performance.

 III.8.a. There are numerous assertions that public organizations and employees are cautious and non-innovative. The evidence for this is mixed.

 III.8.b. Numerous studies indicate that public forms of various types of organizations tend to be less efficient in providing services than private counterparts, although results tend to be mixed for hospitals and utilities. (Public utilities have somewhat more often been found to be more efficient.) Yet other authors strongly defend the efficiency and general performance of public organizations, citing various forms of evidence.

Source: Adapted from Rainey, Backoff, and Levine (1976) and Rainey (1989).

nature of public organizations and management, which amounts to something of a theory.

Unlike private organizations, most public organizations do not sell their outputs on economic markets. Hence, the information and incentives of economic markets are weaker or absent in them. Some scholars theorize (as many citizens believe) that this reduces incentives for cost reduction, operating efficiency, and effective performance. In the absence of markets, other governmental institutions (courts, legislatures, the executive branch hierarchy) use legal and formal constraints to impose greater external governmental control of procedures, spheres of operations, and strategic objectives. Interest groups, the media, public opinion, and informal bargaining and pressure by formal authorities also exert an array of less formal, more political influences. These differences also arise from the distinct nature of transactions with the external environment. Government is more monopolistic, coercive, and unavoidable than private organizations, with a greater breadth of impact, and therefore requires more constraint. Government organizations operate under greater public scrutiny, subject to unique public expectations for fairness, openness, accountability, and honesty.

Internal structures and processes reflect these influences, according to the typical analysis. These factors also complicate the goals and evaluation criteria of public organizations: the absence of the market; the production of goods and services not readily valued at a market price; value-laden expectations for accountability, fairness, openness, and honesty, as well as performance. Goals and performance criteria are more diverse, conflicting (with more difficult trade-offs), and intangible and hard to measure. The external controls, combined with the vague and multiple objectives, generate more elaborate internal rules and reporting requirements. They cause more rigid hierarchical arrangements, including highly structured and centralized rules for personnel procedures, budgeting, and procurement.

The constraints and diffuse objectives allow managers less decision-making autonomy and flexibility than their private counterparts have. Subordinates and subunits may have external political alliances and merit system protections that give them relative autonomy from higher levels. Striving for control because of political pressures on them but lacking clear performance measures, executives avoid delegation of authority and impose more levels of review and more formal regulations.

Critics complain that these conditions, aggravated by rapid turnover of political executives, push top executives toward a more external political role, with less attention to internal management. Middle managers and rank-and-file employees respond to the constraints and pressures with caution and rigidity. Critics and managers alike complain about weak incentive structures in government and lament the absence of flexibility in financial rewards and other problems with governmental personnel systems. Complaints about difficulty in firing, disciplining, and financially rewarding employees generated major civil service reforms in the late 1970s, at the federal level and in states around the country.

In turn, expert observers assert and some research indicates that public employees' personality traits, values, needs, and work-related attitudes differ from those of private employees. Some research finds that public employees place lower value on financial incentives, show somewhat lower levels of satisfaction with their work, and differ in some other work attitudes from their private counterparts.

Intriguingly, the relative performance of public and nonpublic organizations and employees figures as the most significant issue of all and the most difficult to resolve. It also generates the most controversy. As noted earlier, the general view has been that government organizations operate less efficiently and effectively than do private organizations. Many studies have compared public and private delivery of the same service, mostly finding the private form more efficient. Efficiency studies beg many questions, however, and a number of authors defend government strongly. They cite client satisfaction surveys, evidence of poor performance by private organizations, and many other forms of evidence to argue that government performs much better than generally supposed.

This is a fair characterization of the prevailing view of public organizations that one would attain from an overview of the literature and research. The picture is fairly unfavorable. Yet, for all the reasons given earlier, it is best to regard this as an oversimplified and unconfirmed set of assertions. The challenge now is to bring together literature and research evidence to work toward a better assessment of these assertions and a better understanding of their real meaning.

Chapter 2

The Environment
of Public Organizations

Management consultants exhort managers to analyze their environments, but that is no simple matter. The relevant environment can differ for different issues and at different organizational levels (Starbuck, 1983). Public organizations are often embedded in larger government structures (Meyer, 1979). The Food and Drug Administration, for example, operates as a subunit of the U.S. Department of Health and Human Services and, in turn, of the U.S. government. The larger units of government impose system-wide rules (Warwick, 1975) on all agencies. In many agencies, different subunits operate in very different policy areas and often have stronger alliances with legislators and interest groups than with the agency director (Seidman and Gilmour, 1986; Kaufman, 1979). All this can make it hard to say where the environment begins and ends.

In addition, members of the organization often *enact* the environment (Weick, 1979). They choose the matters to pay attention to and to try to change. Their actions determine the nature of the environment. For example, leaders of the Ohio Bureau of Mental Retardation adopted a "deinstitutionalization" policy. They moved patients out of large treatment facilities operated by the agency and into smaller private-sector facilities. This changed the boundaries of the agency and the set of organizations with which the agency worked. Organizations create or shape their environments as much as they simply discover them. That complicates the analysis of environments but makes it all the more important.

General Dimensions of Organizational Environments

One typical approach to working through some of the complexity of environmental analysis simply lays out general dimensions or conditions, such as in Table 2.1.

Table 2.1. General Environmental Conditions.

- *Technological conditions:* the general level of knowledge and capability in science, engineering, medicine, and other substantive areas; general capacities for communication, transportation, information processing, medical services, military weaponry, environmental analysis, production and manufacturing processes, and agricultural production.
- *Legal conditions:* laws, regulations, legal procedures, court decisions; characteristics of legal institutions and values, such as provisions for individual rights and jury trials, as well as the general institutionalization and stability of legal processes.
- *Political conditions:* characteristics of the political processes and institutions in a society, such as the general form of government (socialism, communism, capitalism, and so on; degree of centralization, fragmentation, and federalism) and the degree of political stability (Carroll, Delacroix, and Goodstein, 1988). More direct and specific conditions include electoral outcomes, political party alignment and success, and policy initiatives within regimes.
- *Economic conditions:* levels of prosperity, inflation, interest rates, and tax rates, as well as characteristics of labor, capital, and economic markets within and between nations.
- *Demographic conditions:* characteristics of the population such as age, gender, race, religion, and ethnic category.
- *Ecological conditions:* characteristics of the physical environment, including climate, geographical characteristics, pollution, natural resources; nature and density of organizational populations.
- *Cultural conditions:* predominant values, attitudes, beliefs, social customs, and socialization processes concerning such things as sex role, family structure, work orientations, and religious and political practices.

Anyone can provide examples of ways in which such conditions influence organizations. Technological and scientific developments gave birth to many government agencies, such as the Environmental Protection Agency and the Nuclear Regulatory Commission. Technological developments continually influence the operation of government agencies as they struggle to keep up with developments in computerization and other areas. Demographic trends currently receive much attention, as analysts project increasing percentages of women and minorities in government employment. This raises the challenge of *managing diversity* in the workplace, as it is called. Public administrators attend carefully to legal developments, such as changes in public officials' legal liability for their decisions. Much of the rest of this book concerns political influences on organizations. The discussion of public organizations often becomes preoccupied with politics, but organization theorists remind us that many other determinants shape organizations. As Chapter Four describes, strategy-making teams often use frameworks such as the list above for *environmental scanning,* to consider trends that they may have overlooked and to raise new possibilities. Consultants urge public managers to do this to break out of their sense of confinement under governmental constraints.

Another common approach lists more specific elements of the task environment, such as important organizations and groups. A typical depiction includes competitors, customers, suppliers, regulators, unions, and associates (Griffin, 1987). Similarly, Porter (1985) analyzes the major influences on competition within an industry: industry competitors, buyers, suppliers, new entrants, and substitutes. Consultants working with organizations on strategy formulation sometimes use such frameworks in *stakeholder analysis*, to identify key stakeholders of the organization and their particular claims and roles (Bryson, 1988, p. 52).

Research on Environmental Variations

Organizational researchers have also produced more specific evidence about the effects of environments. As Chapter One described, early theorists paid little attention to external environments, but research increasingly demonstrated their importance. Selznick (1966) helped lead this trend with a study of a government corporation, the Tennessee Valley Authority (TVA). He found that environmental influences play a crucial role in *institutionalization* processes in organizations. Values, goals, and procedures become strongly established, not necessarily because managers choose them as the most efficient means of production, but in large part as a result of environmental influences and exchanges. The TVA, for example, engaged in *co-optation* processes, through which organizations absorb new elements into their leadership to avert threats to their viability. The U.S. government established the TVA during the New Deal years to develop electric power and foster economic development along the Tennessee River. It operated in decentralized fashion, involving local organizations and groups in decisions. This gained support for the TVA but also brought in these groups as strong influences on values and priorities. In some cases, they shut out rival groups, putting the TVA in conflict with other New Deal programs with which it should have allied. Thus, an organization's needs for external support and consequent exchanges with outside entities can heavily influence its primary values and goals. (The above discussion is based in part on Hall's discussion [1987]).

Later research made the importance of the external environment increasingly clear. Prominent studies that led to the emergence of contingency theory (described in the Introduction and the Appendix) found more and more evidence of the importance of environmental uncertainty and complexity. Burns and Stalker (1961), for example, studied a set of English firms and classified them into two rough categories. *Mechanistic* firms emphasized clear hierarchy of authority, with direction and communication through the chain of command, and specialized, formally defined individual tasks. Other firms were more *organic,* with less emphasis on hierarchy and more lateral and network communication. Tasks were less clearly defined and more frequently changing. Managers in these firms sometimes spurned organization charts as too confining or even dangerous. The mechanistic firms succeeded in stable environments—those with relative stability in new products, technology, competitors, and demand for the firm's products. In such a setting, they could take advantage of the efficiencies of their more traditional structures. Other firms, such as electronics manufacturers, faced less stable environmental conditions, with rapid fluctuations in technology, products, competitors, and demand. The more organic firms, more flexible and adaptive, succeeded in this setting.

Lawrence and Lorsch (1967) studied firms in three industries with different degrees of uncertainty in their environments as a result of rapid changes and complexity. The most successful firms had structures with a degree of complexity matching that of the environment. Firms in more stable environments could manage with relatively traditional hierarchical structures. Firms in more unstable, uncertain environments could not. Different subunits of the firms faced different environments. As these different environments imposed more uncertainty on the managers, the successful firms became more *differentiated*. The subunits differed more and more from each other in their goals, the time frames for their work, and the formality of their structures. This increased the potential for conflict and disorganization, however. Successful firms in more uncertain environments responded with higher levels of *integration*. They had more methods for coordinating the highly differentiated units, such as liaison positions, coordinating teams, and conflict-resolution processes. This combination of differentiation and integration made the successful firms in more complex, uncertain environments more internally complex. The authors' general conclusion advanced one of the prominent statements of the contingency idea: There is no one best way to organize; organizations must adopt structures as complex as the environments that they confront.

As many studies of this sort accumulated, James Thompson (1967) synthesized the growing body of research in a way that provided additional insights. Organizations must contend with the demands of their tasks and their environments. Organizations try to isolate the technical core, their primary work processes, so that the work can proceed smoothly. They use buffering methods to try to provide stable conditions for the technical core. For example, they use boundary-spanning units, such as inventory, personnel recruitment, and research and development units, to try to create smooth flows of information and resources. Yet environmental conditions can strain this process. In more complex environments, with more geographical areas, product markets, competitors, and other factors, organizations must become more internally complex. They establish different subunits to match the environmental segments. More unstable environments create a need for greater decentralization of authority to these subunits and less formal structure. The shifting environment requires rapid decisions and changes, and it takes too long for information and decisions to travel up and down a strict hierarchy.

Researchers have debated the adequacy of contingency theory, and many have moved off in other directions. Yet recent texts commonly treat the contingency-theory message about organizational environments as standard and central in organization theory (Daft, 1989; Griffin, 1987): There is no one single best way to organize. An organization's structure must be adapted to environmental contingencies, as well as other contingencies. In more simple, homogeneous, stable environments, organizations can success-fully adopt more mechanistic and centralized structures. In more complex and unstable environments, successful organizations must be more organic, decentralized, and differentiated into many departments with correspond-ingly elaborate integrating processes.

Scholars have also further developed the contingency-theory concepts into more carefully conceived environmental dimensions. Table 2.2 illus-trates prominent examples. Clearly these dimensions apply to public orga-nizations. Tax revolts and pressures to cut government spending in recent

Table 2.2. Descriptive and Analytical Dimensions of Organizational Environments.

Aldrich (1979)

Capacity: the extent to which the environment affords a rich or lean supply of necessary resources

Homogeneity-heterogeneity: the degree to which important components of the environment are similar or dissimilar

Stability-instability: the degree and rapidity of change in the important components or processes in the environment

Concentration-dispersion: the degree to which important components of the environment are separated or close together, geographically or in terms of communication or logistics

Domain consensus–dissensus: the degree to which the organization's domain (its operating loca-tions, major functions and activities, and clients and customers served) is generally accepted or disputed and contested

Turbulence: the degree to which changes in one part or aspect of the environment in turn create changes in another; the tendency of changes to reverberate and spread

Dess and Beard (1984)

Munificence: the availability of needed resources

Complexity: the homogeneity and concentration of the environment

Dynamism: the stability and turbulence of the environment

Miles (1980)

Static dimensions

Complexity: the number of different external components and characteristics with which an orga-nization must deal

Routineness: the degree to which relations with the environment are routine and standardized

Interconnectedness: the degree to which environmental components and processes are intertwined such that changes at one point reverberate and spread

Remoteness: the immediacy and directness of an organization's relations with particular environ-mental components

Dynamic dimensions

Change rate: the rate of change in important elements and conditions

Unpredictability of change: the degree to which changes are patterned or predictable, as opposed to being sudden and difficult to anticipate

Receptivity dimensions

Resource scarcity: availability of needed resources

Output receptivity: demand for products and by-products and external constraints and opposi-tion to outputs

Domain-choice flexibility: the extent to which an organization is free or constrained in choices of domain (that is, populations to be served, geographical areas in which to operate, technol-ogies or procedures to apply, and goods, services, and functions to provide — what the organi-zation does, where it does it, how it does it, and for whom it does it) years show the importance of environmental *capacity, munificence,* or *resource scarcity* for public organizations. The federal government operates through a regional structure, reflecting the influence of environmental *heterogeneity* and *dispersion.* The Florida Department of Health and Rehabilitative Services, one of the largest state agencies in the country, adopted a regional structure in the 1970s, partially in response to the heterogeneity and dispersion of its environment. The state created regional districts, in part to make the department more responsive to the different service needs in various parts of the state.

Even organization theorists who attach little significance to the public-private distinction agree that public organizations face particular complications in *domain consensus and choice* (Miles, 1980; Hall, 1987; Van de Ven and Ferry, 1980; Meyer, 1979). Jurisdictional boundaries and numerous authorities, laws, and political interests complicate decisions about where, when, and how a public organization operates. Research strongly supports this observation that public status influences strategic domain choices (Mascarenhas, 1989), although later chapters show how public managers often gain considerable leeway to maneuver.

Turbulence and *interconnectedness* characterize the environments of most public organizations. Studies of public policy implementation provide numerous accounts of policy initiatives that had many unanticipated consequences and implications for other groups. Public managers commonly encounter situations where a decision touches off a furor, arousing opposition from groups that one would never have anticipated reacting (Chase and Reveal, 1983; Cohen, 1988). Similarly, environmental *stability, dynamism,* and *change rate* have major implications in public organizations. Rapid turnover of political appointees at the top of the agencies and rapid external shifts in political issues have major influences on public organizations and the people in them. As one example, researchers find evidence that turbulence and instability in the environments of public agencies damage the morale of managers in the agencies, and impede their acceptance of reforms (Ban, 1987; Rubin, 1985).

These environmental concepts developed by organizational researchers are useful for enhancing our understanding of public organizations. As the discussion shows, however, no conclusive, coherent theory of organizations explains how these dimensions are related to each other and to organizations. In addition, organization theorists have defined the environmental concepts at a very high level of generality. Certainly they apply to public organizations, but for understanding public organizations we need to add more specific content to the environmental dimensions. For doing that, there is a body of useful research and writing on public bureaucracies, to which this discussion turns after a review of very recent work on organizational environments.

Current Research on Organizational Environments

Some of the most prominent current research in organization theory concentrates on organizational environments and moves beyond contingency theory. *Population ecology* theorists, for example, analyze the origin, development, and decline of populations of organizations, using biological concepts (Hannan and Freeman, 1989). As biologists analyze how certain populations of organisms develop to inhabit a particular ecological niche, population ecologists analyze the development of organizational populations within certain niches, or available combinations of resources and constraints. They have produced interesting findings about change rates in populations of organizations, but mostly, so far, with rapidly changing populations of small organizations such as semiconductor firms.

Some ecology theorists reject the contingency-theory depiction of organizations as rational, speedy adapters to environmental change. They see the environment as selecting the organizational populations in a Darwinian fashion (Hannan and Freeman, 1989). This brings some criticism from other scholars, who complain that they overlook the importance of management strategies (Van de Ven, 1979). It also raises a profound question about management that is relevant to the public-versus-private debate. These prominent researchers imply that what managers do does not ultimately matter very much because environmental conditions determine outcomes. Consider this in relation to the claims that public managers face more constraints than do private ones. These theories in effect argue that all managers operate under sharp constraints, and public managers do not appear unique. In addition, they look at political influences on populations of organizations, such as laws and regulations that influence entry and exit in industries. They see many organizations influenced by governmental constraints, and this again reduces the distinctiveness of public organizations.

On the other hand, this general view of organizations raises some fascinating questions about public organizations that more research may enlighten. For example, why do some populations of organizations, such as schools, mostly inhabit the public sector? (About 80 percent of the schools in the United States are public schools.) This puts us back into the hunt for the meaning of public organization.

Resource-dependence theories analyze how organizational managers try to obtain crucial resources from their environments—materials, money, people, needed support services, technological knowledge. Organizations can adapt their structures in response to the environment, or change niches. They can try to change the environment by creating demand or seeking government actions that can help them. They can try to manipulate the way the environment is perceived by people in the organization and outside it. In these and other ways, they can pursue essential resources. These theorists stress the importance of internal and external political processes in the quest for resources. Chapter Four discusses how their analysis of resources in internal power relations applies to public organizations. They express their theories very generally, however, to apply to resource-dependency issues in most or all organizations. They, too, thus imply that public organizations do not represent a particularly distinct group (Pfeffer and Salancik, 1978, pp. 277–278).

Transaction-costs theories analyze managerial decisions to purchase a needed good or service from outside, as opposed to producing it within the organization (Williamson, 1975, 1981). Transactions with other firms and people become more costly as contracts become harder to write and supervise. The firm may need a service very particular to itself, or it may have problems supervising contractors. Managers may try to hold down such costs under certain conditions by merging with another organization or permanently hiring a person with whom they had been contracting. These theories, much more elaborate than summarized here, have received much attention in business management research and have implications for government contracting and other governmental issues (Bryson, 1988). Yet they usually assume that managers in firms strive to hold down costs to maximize profits. Governmental contracting involves more political criteria and accountability and different or nonexistent profit motives, so leading theorists in this group express uncertainty about applications to government (Williamson, 1981).

Recent studies of *institutionalization* processes hark back to the work of Selznick. They analyze how certain values, structures, and procedures become institutionalized in and among organizations—widely accepted as the proper way of doing things. Tolbert and Zucker (1983) show that many local governments reformed their civil service systems by adopting merit systems, because merit systems had become widely accepted as the proper form of personnel system for such governments. In addition, the federal government applied pressures for the adoption of merit systems. Meyer and Rowan (1983) argue that organizations such as schools often adopt structures on the basis of "myth and ceremony." They do things according to prevailing beliefs and not because the practices have been clearly proved as means to efficiency or effectiveness. DiMaggio and Powell (1983) show that organizations in the same field come to look like each other as a result of shared ideas about how that type of organization should look. Dobbin and others (1988) found that public organizations have more provisions for due process, such as affirmative action programs, than do more private ones. These studies have obvious relevance for public organizations. Pfeffer (1982) suggests that this approach proves particularly applicable to the public sector, where performance criteria are often less clear. There, beliefs about proper procedures may substitute more readily for firmly validated procedures. Public and nonprofit managers encounter many instances where new procedures or schemes, such as a new budgeting technique, become widely implemented as the latest, best approach—whether or not anyone can prove that it is. In addition, some of the research mentioned above shows how external institutions such as government impose structures and procedures on organizations. Some of these theorists disagree among themselves over these different views of institutionalization—whether it results from the spread of beliefs and myths or from influences from external institutions such as government (Scott, 1987).

These developments show how elaborate and diverse the work on organizational environments has become, and each one provides insights. In fact, scholars are currently arguing more and more frequently that there is a need to bring these models together, rather than argue about which is the best of them (Hall, 1987, p. 314; Tolbert, 1985). Obviously, they deal with processes that influence organizations in some combination, and all are true to some degree.

The Environments of Public Organizations

The work on organizational environments provides a number of insights, many of them applicable to public organizations. The preceding review of the literature on organizational environments also shows, however, why people interested in public organizations call for more complete attention to public-sector environments. The contingency-theory researchers expressed environmental dimensions very generally. They paid little attention to whether government ownership makes a difference or whether it matters if an organization sells its outputs on economic markets. They depicted organizations, usually firms, as autonomously adapting to environmental contingencies. Political scientists, however, see it as obvious that external political authorities often directly mandate the structures of public agencies regardless of something called "environmental uncertainty" (Warwick, 1975; Pitt and Smith, 1981). The more current perspectives on organizational environments bring government into the picture, but they also express their concepts very generally, subsuming governmental influences under broader concepts. Sometimes they concentrate on business firms.

Major Components and Dimensions

Public executives commenting on public management and political scientists and economists writing about public organizations (Downs, 1967; Meier, 1987; Hood and Dunsire, 1981; Pitt and Smith, 1981; Wamsley and Zald, 1973; Warwick, 1975; Wilson, 1989) typically depict environments as illustrated in Table 2.3.

General Institutions and Values of the Political Economy

As Chapter One elaborates, public agencies, owned and funded by government, operate under political authority. The political system of the nation and its traditions, institutions, and values heavily influence the exercise of that authority. The U.S. Constitution formally states some of these values and establishes some of the primary institutions and rules of governance. Other values and rules receive less formal codification but still have great influence. For example, Americans have historically demanded that government operate with businesslike standards of efficiency, although the Consti-

Table 2.3. Major Environmental Components for Public Organizations.

General Values and Institutions of the Political Economy

Political and economic traditions
Constitutional provisions and their legislative and judicial development
      Due process
      Equal protection of the laws
      Democratic elections and representation (republican form)
      Federal system
      Separation of powers
Free-enterprise system (economic markets relatively free of government controls)

Values and performance criteria for government organizations

      Competence
         Efficiency
         Effectiveness
         Timeliness
         Reliability
         Reasonableness
      Responsiveness
         Accountability, legality, responsiveness to rule of law and governmental authorities, responsiveness to public demands
         Adherence to ethical standards
         Fairness, equal treatment, impartiality
         Openness to external scrutiny and criticism

Institutions, Entities, and Actors with Political Authority and Influence

Chief executives
      Executive staff and staff offices
Legislatures
      Legislative committees
      Individual legislators
      Legislative staff
Courts
Other government agencies
      Oversight and management agencies (GAO, OMB, OPM, GSA)
      Competitors
      Allies
      Agencies or governmental units with joint programs
Other levels of government
      "Higher" and "lower" levels
      Intergovernmental agreements and districts
Interest groups
      Client groups
      Constituency groups
      Professional associations
Policy subsystems
      Issue networks
      Interorganizational policy networks
      Implementation structure
News media
General public opinion
Individual citizens with requests for services, complaints, and other contacts

tution nowhere expresses this criterion (Waldo, [1947] 1984). These general values and institutional arrangements heavily influence the values, constraints, and performance criteria imposed on public organizations. They translate into direct, practical influences on public organizations and managers, to an extent not adequately recognized in much of organization theory.

The assertion mentioned in Chapter One that public organizations pursue multiple, intangible, conflicting goals appears as the most frequent observation in all the relevant literature. It refers in part to the nonprofit, nonmarket nature of most public agencies. Since they produce services not sold on markets, they lack profit and sales indicators. In addition, however, the assertion about goals refers to the multiple, conflicting values imposed through political direction. This point is related to some of the most controversial issues about public management. As Chapter Nine points out, organization theorists find that *all* organizations have multiple, hard-to-measure, conflicting goals. The distinctiveness of public organizations becomes surprisingly hard to prove through empirical evidence (Rainey, 1983), so we need to examine the arguments about how external authorities impose these values. Later chapters consider evidence of their influences on structure and behavior in public organizations, which augments the examples given here.

Separation of Powers, Federalism, and Limited Government

The U.S. Constitution establishes a separation of powers among the judicial, executive, and legislative branches of government. State and local governments follow similar patterns of dispersed authority. The system of federalism reserves certain powers for lower levels of government. Also, at present, much federal spending is actually granted to or channeled through states and localities. Guarantees of freedom of the press and of association and expression have further empowered other elements of the political system, such as the press, political parties, and interest groups. Government also operates under principles protecting individual rights, such as rights to due process of law and equal protection of the laws.

While protecting individual rights, the government is also supposed to do what the majority of the people want it to do, as indicated by elections and other processes of representative democracy. By implication, government should do so effectively and efficiently. The system was not designed, however, for high levels of efficiency but places more emphasis on constraining the power of governmental authorities (Wilson, 1989; Huntington, 1981). The American political system thus embodies a dynamic tension among conflicting values, principles, and authorities.

Controversy over whether this system works as intended never ends. Nevertheless, the political authorities and actors representing these broader values and principles impose on public organizations performance criteria such as those listed in Table 2.3. Authors use various terms to express the diversity of these criteria. Fried (1976), for example, refers to democracy, efficiency, and legality as the major performance criteria for public bureaucracy in the United States. Rosenbloom (1989) considers law, management, and politics as three dominant sources of administrative criteria. The table uses Meier's (1987) distinction between *competence* and *responsiveness* criteria.

Competence Values

Public organizations operate under pressure to perform competently. Demands for *efficiency* come from all corners. Newspapers and television news departments pursue indications of wasteful uses of public funds at all levels of government. Political candidates and elected officials attack instances of waste, such as apparently excessive costs for components of military weaponry. The U.S. General Accounting Office (GAO), auditors general at the state and local levels, and other oversight agencies conduct audits of government programs with an emphasis on efficiency. In 1979, the GAO set up a nationwide telephone hot line to receive reports of waste and fraud in federal programs. Legislative committees and city councils conduct hearings and reviews of agencies with a similar concern. Special commissions, such as the Grace Commission organized under the Reagan administration, investigate wasteful or inefficient practices in government.

Public managers remain sensitive to these pressures because they know that evidence of inefficiency can damage public agencies and programs. They know of examples such as the severe pressures on the Department of Defense in 1987 arising from allegations of excessive costs in defense contracts. At one point, a defense official temporarily suspended all contracts with the corporations involved. Surely this involved troublesome steps that defense officials did not want to take.

External authorities, the media, interest groups, and citizens also demand *effectiveness, timeliness, reliability,* and *reasonableness,* even though these criteria may conflict with efficiency. Efficiency means producing a good or service at the lowest cost in resources, assuming a constant level of quality. These additional criteria concern whether a function is performed well, on time, dependably, and in a logical, sensible way. Government often performs services crucial to individuals or to an entire jurisdiction. People *want the job done,* often with efficiency as a secondary concern. The connection between the service and the cost of providing it is often difficult to see and to analyze. Evidence that police, fire fighters, emergency medical personnel, and the military lack effectiveness and reliability draws sharp responses that may push efficiency to lesser status. Casper Weinberger said in a television interview that the rapid military buildup he led as secretary of defense cost more than it would have if conducted more slowly. He argued that the imperative to upgrade the military made the faster, more expensive changes necessary.

Sometimes one element of the political system imposes some of the criteria more strongly than others (Pitt and Smith, 1981). This can increase conflicts for public managers, since different authorities emphasize different criteria. For example, the judiciary often appears to emphasize effectiveness over administrative efficiency because of its responsibility for upholding legal standards and constitutional rights. Judges rule that certain criteria must be met in a timely, effective way, virtually regardless of cost and efficiency. The courts have ordered that prisons and jails and affirmative action programs must meet certain standards by certain dates. They protect the rights of clients of public programs to due process in decisions about whether they can be denied benefits under the programs. This increases the burdens on the agencies to conduct costly hearings and reviews and maintain extensive documentation. The courts in effect leave the efficiency and cost considerations as problems for the agencies to worry about. The press and legislators, meanwhile, might criticize the agency for slow procedures and expensive operations.

Casework by members of Congress, state legislators, and city council members can also exert pressure for results other than efficiency. (Casework means action by an elected official to plead the case of an individual citizen or group who makes a demand of an agency). A congressional representative or staff member may call about a constituent's late Social Security check, A city council member may call a city agency about a complaint from a citizen about garbage collection services. While these requests can promote effective, reasonable responses by an agency, responding to sporadic, unpredictable demands of this sort can tax both its efficiency and its effectiveness. Some of the worst abuses in the savings and loan scandal allegedly occurred when senators and representatives intervened with regulatory officials on behalf of one of the major savings and loan executives.

Responsiveness Values

The responsiveness criteria in Table 2.3 often conflict sharply with competence criteria and also with each other. Public managers and organizations remain accountable to various authorities and interests and to the rule of law in general. They must comply with laws, rules, and directives issued by governmental authorities and provide accounts of their compliance as required. (Chapter Three describes some of the means by which external authorities hold them accountable.)

Public organizations and their managers are often expected to remain open and responsive in various ways. These pressures sometimes coincide with accountability, in the sense of responding to directives and requests for information from governmental authorities. Yet public agencies also receive requests for helpful, reasonable, and flexible responses to the needs of clients, interest groups, and the general public. As they are public organizations, their activities are public business, and citizens and the media demand relative openness to scrutiny (Wamsley and Zald, 1973). For some programs, the enabling legislation requires citizen advisory panels or commissions to represent community groups, interest groups, and citizens. Administrative procedures at different levels of government require public notice of proposed changes in government agencies' rules and policies, often with provisions for public hearings at which citizens can attempt to influence the changes. The courts, legislatures, and legal precedent also require that agencies treat citizens fairly and impartially by adhering to principles of due process through appeals and hearings.

A related criterion, *representativeness*, pertains to various ways in which officials should represent the people. One of the most important recent representativeness issues has been equal employment opportunity. Representativeness also means that identifiable ethnic and demographic groups should be represented in government roughly in proportion to their presence in the population. The advisory groups mentioned above reflect criteria of representativeness in another sense. These criteria add to the complex set of objectives and values that public managers and organizations pursue and seek to balance.

Later chapters describe examples and evidence of how these multiple conflicting values and criteria influence public organizations. They pose very practical challenges for public managers. External authorities and political actors intervene in management decisions in pursuit of responsiveness and accountability and impose structures and constraints in pursuit of equity, efficiency, and accountability. Sharp conflicts over which values should predominate — professional effectiveness or political accountability, for example — lead to major transformations of organizational operations and culture (Maynard-Moody, Stull, and Mitchell, 1986; Romzek and Dubnick, 1987). Before examining these effects on major dimensions of organization and management, however, Chapter Three considers the external authorities and interests that seek to impose these values and criteria and their exchanges of influence with public organizations.

Chapter 3

⌐⌐⌐⌐⌐⌐⌐⌐⌐⌐⌐⌐⌐⌐⌐⌐⌐⌐⌐⌐⌐⌐⌐⌐⌐⌐⌐⌐⌐⌐⌐⌐

The Impact of
Political Power
and Public Policy

One of the most deceptive oversimplifications of public bureaucracies depicts them as existing for no reason and against everyone's better judgment. A public organization that no one wants is the easiest target in all the organizational world. Recent U.S. presidents have had trouble reducing federal spending largely because one cannot find a government service or program that does not have staunch backing from some fairly hard-to-fight political coalition. This staying power provides one of the reasons that the public bureaucracy seems very influential in the political system. For decades, presidents have struggled to control the federal bureaucracy and wrest from it powers that they considered excessive. Yet experts disagree about bureaucratic power. Some authors describe the bureaucracy as immensely powerful, while others emphasize its subservience (Kingdon, 1984).

Both views have some truth to them. Public organizations engage in a dynamic exchange of influences with the elements in their environments described in Chapter Two. Their activities and financial resources require authorization from governmental authorities. They must have political support to survive and prosper. In a classic essay, Norton Long (1949) declared that "the lifeblood of administration is power" (p. 257).

Public Organizations and the Public

Public organizations need support from what political scientists call *mass publics,* or broad, diffuse populations, and especially from *attentive publics* — more organized groups, more interested in the agency.

51

Public Opinion and Mass Publics

General public opinion influences the management of public organizations more than much of the management literature acknowledges. Two types of mass opinion figure importantly: attitudes toward government in general and attitudes toward particular policies and agencies. The Introduction described the antigovernment strain of the last two decades and how elected officials responded with efforts to reform governmental bureaucracies. When President Carter reformed the civil service system, changing pay and disciplinary procedures and provisions for senior executives, he promoted the reform as a means of motivating federal workers and making it easier to fire lazy ones. President Reagan more aggressively attacked the federal bureaucracy, cut agency budgets and staffing, and sought to diminish the authority of career federal administrators (Rubin, 1985). Morale in the federal service plummeted. Surveys found many career civil servants expressing an intention to leave the service and saying that they would discourage their children from pursuing a career in federal service (Volcker Commission, 1989). The general climate of unfavorable public opinion about the public bureaucracy thus had very significant effects on the morale and work behaviors of government employees, the structure of the federal government, and the functioning of major federal agencies.

The sharp public outcry in 1989 against a proposed pay raise for members of Congress, federal judges, and federal executives provides another good example of the effects of general public opinion on government employees and organizations. In opinion polls, more than 80 percent of the public opposed the increase. Ralph Nader and the National Taxpayers' Union fought the raise aggressively, exhorting voters to write and call their representatives to object to it. Congress overwhelmingly voted the raise down. After the defeat of the raise, stories in the *New York Times* and elsewhere reported bitter reactions by federal managers, including many who would not even have been in positions to receive the raise. They expressed sharp disappointment over the symbolic rejection of their value to the society.

In state and local governments around the country, similar reactions to bad public feelings about government led to reforms of government pay systems aimed at tying a government employee's pay more closely to his or her performance to remedy allegedly weak motivation and performance. The efforts have apparently caused a lot of confusion and discouragement (Gabris, 1987; Sherwood and Wechsler, 1986).

Ambivalence and Paradox in Public Opinion

The ambivalence of public attitudes about government also influences public managers and their agencies (Lipset and Schneider, 1987; Whorton and Worthley, 1981). Surveys consistently find that respondents say that they would like lower taxes but do not want public spending reduced for most types of services (Ladd, 1983; Beck, Rainey, and Traut, 1990). Surveys have also found that when respondents are asked how they feel about federal agencies in general, they give unfavorable responses. When asked for specific evaluations of how they were treated by a particular agency in a specific instance, they give much more favorable responses (Katz, Gutek, Kahn, and Barton, 1975).

These ambivalent public attitudes contribute to the challenges of public management. In the absence of economic markets as mechanisms for measuring need and performance, public officials and public organizations often struggle with difficult questions about what the public wants. In recent decades, elected officials have often responded with reforms and decisions that directly influence structure, behavior, and management in public organizations. Nations cycle in and out of periods of anti-government sentiment (Hirschman, 1982), and the climate in the United States may change. Nevertheless, these examples illustrate the influences on public management of general public sentiments.

Public Opinion and Agencies, Policies, and Officials

The general level of public support for a particular agency's programs affects its ability to maintain political support. Certain agencies hold a more central place in the values of the country (Wamsley and Zald, 1973) than others, and the public regards their work as more crucial. The Department of Defense, police departments, and fire departments typically retain strong general public support because of the importance that people attach to national defense and personal security. Some social programs, such as those perceived to involve "welfare" payments to the poor, receive weaker support in public opinion polls.

Media Power: Obvious and Mysterious

The importance of public opinion bolsters the power of the news media. Congressional committees or state legislative committees summon agency executives before them to explain the events surrounding an embarrassing news story about an agency. Whistle blowers who go public with news about agency misconduct or incompetence have often received such harsh treatment that the federal government has made special provisions to protect them (Rosen, 1989). Bad press can sledgehammer an agency or an official, damaging budgets, programs, and careers. Chapter Ten describes a case in which bad press caused the removal of the head of a mental health services bureau and major changes in the bureau's operations.

Close media scrutiny of government plays an indispensable role in governance. The news media also report aggressively on scandals in private business (Dominick, 1981), yet they appear to emphasize scrutiny of government even more. Government is often more accessible and more appropriately watched, since government spends the taxpayers' money. In Columbus, Ohio, local newspaper photographers regularly checked the parking lots of bars and restaurants during normal working hours to try to take pictures of the license tags of any government vehicles parked there. An Atlanta, Georgia, television station carried a series of stories about the high costs of the furniture in the office of one of the county commissioners.

News reporters usually take a strong adversarial stance. They want to avoid seeming naive or co-opted. They need to focus on the serious problems and to generate an audience by reporting on controversial issues. The Volcker Commission (1989) report describes how Carter administration officials had trouble attracting interest in their proposals for civil service reforms until they developed a twenty-six-foot chart illustrating the tortuous steps it took to fire a bad federal employee. The news media immediately focused on this and provided more coverage. This apparently led the president to emphasize this more negative, punitive aspect of the reforms in trying to build support for them. This emphasis almost certainly contributed to the disgruntlement of federal managers. Thus, media coverage influenced the tenor of reforms that shaped the personnel practices of the federal government and influenced the morale of employees throughout it.

Instances such as this make concern about media coverage part of the lore of government (Linsky, 1986). Officials and experts from Washington speak of management in the "goldfish bowl" (Allison, 1983; Cohen, 1988), where media attention plays a stronger role than it does in business management (Blumenthal, 1983). Some federal executives apparently devote more time to creating a splash in the media than to performing well as managers (Lynn, 1981). Many public employees appear to feel that they will not get into much trouble for poor performance but will get into a *lot* of trouble for creating bad publicity (Lynn, 1981; Warwick, 1975; Downs, 1967). City and county officials will pack an auditorium to listen to consultants speak on how to handle media relations, and they regularly complain about unfair media coverage.

This apparent power of the media has mysterious qualities. The potential damage from bad coverage is often unclear. Ronald Reagan earned a reputation as the "Teflon president" by maintaining popularity in spite of sharp criticism in the media. For a long time, many experts argued that the media exercise little influence over public voting choices and attitudes about specific issues. Lichter and others (Lichter, Rothman, and Lichter, 1986) now argue that the media exert powerful influence on public attitudes, but in a diffuse way. Media coverage develops a climate that pervades the informational environment, which in turn influences public opinion.

Media attention also varies. Some agencies regularly get more media attention than others. Hood and Dunsire (1981) found that the Foreign Office and the Treasury get particularly high levels of press coverage in Britain, while other central government departments get relatively little. As the example about the Carter civil service reforms shows, the media often seriously neglect administrative issues. For years before the savings and loan scandal erupted as a major crisis, the media scarcely noticed the growing problem. Yet public officials also know that media attention can shift unpredictably. In one large state, where the Department of Administration ordinarily received little public attention, the director decided to change the set of alternative health insurance plans by private insurance companies from which the state's employees chose their coverage. Many employees disliked the new set of alternative plans. An outburst of complaints from state employees caused a sudden wave of coverage in the newspapers and television news around the state. A legislative committee soon called the director before special hearings about the changes.

Officials at higher levels and in political centers (capitals, large cities) often pay a great deal of attention to media strategies. Many city governments issue newsletters, televise city council meetings, and use other methods of public communication. Some federal and state agencies invest so heavily in issuing public information that it becomes controversial (Yarwood and Enis, 1987). Even so, many public managers resist suggestions that they should devote time to media relations, regarding themselves as professionals rather than "politicians." More active approaches usually prove most effective (Linsky, 1986), however, so experts (Cohen, 1988; Chase and Reveal, 1983) discuss ways of carrying out suggestions such as these: Understand the perspective of the media—their skepticism, their need for information and interesting stories, their time pressures. Organize media relations carefully—spend time and resources on them and link them with agency operations. Get out readable press releases providing good news about the agency; be patient if the media respond slowly. Respond to bad news and embarrassing incidents rapidly, with clear statements of the agency's side of the story. Seek corrections of inaccurate reporting. Use the media to help boost the agency's image, to implement programs, and to communicate with employees. To carry all this off effectively, make sure that the agency performs well, and be honest.

Interest Groups, Clients, and Constituencies

The support of organized groups also determines the political well-being of public agencies. The role of organized interests in American politics generates continuing controversy. Special-interest politics poses the danger that the system has become too fragmented into self-interested groups, making it resistant to central coordination and hence unmanageable (Lowi, 1979). Critics say that the system favors richer, more powerful groups over the disadvantaged (Miliband, 1969) and allows private interests to control major domains of public policy. Influence peddling abounds in this system and creates ethical dilemmas for many public managers. Some face temptations, for example, to go easy on industries that they regulate so as to enhance their chances for lucrative jobs in them.

Yet public managers also face the reality that interest-group activities are not all bad. They play important roles in the current system and provide important information. As pointed out in Chapter Two, legislation requires that public managers consult with interested groups and their representatives. Often, the groups voice reasonable-sounding demands — help my industry so we do not have to lay people off, help us with the economic development of your jurisdiction, help defend the country with this new weapons system, support education, aid the disadvantaged. Sometimes the demands from different groups are reasonable but sharply conflicting.

Given the importance of groups, many public managers have to cultivate the support of interest groups and constituencies (Doig and Hargrove, 1987; Meier, 1987; Rourke, 1984; Wildavsky, 1988; Chase and Reveal, 1983). Strong support from constituencies helps an agency defend itself against budget cuts and achieve more success in getting budget increases from legislative bodies (Meier, 1987; Wildavsky, 1988). It can also help agencies defend themselves against unwanted directives from legislators and chief executives. Constituent groups can also promote the agency in ways in which it cannot properly promote itself (Rourke, 1984). Interest groups can also block an agency's actions, sometimes popping up unexpectedly as a manager tries to act (Chase and Reveal, 1983).

What kind of group support bolsters an agency? Apparently, the most effective support comes from well-organized, cohesive groups, strongly committed to the agency and its programs. On the other hand, *capture* of the agency by a constituency can damage an agency and bias it toward the self-interested priorities of that group (Rourke, 1984; Wilson, 1980). Critics accuse some regulatory agencies of being captives of the industries or professions that they supposedly regulate and complain that other agencies are captured by the clientele who receive their services (allegedly, the Forestry Service by the timber interests, the Bureau of Mines by the mining interests). Agencies appear to have the most flexibility when they have the support of multiple groups. They can satisfy some, if not others, and even have them confront each other about their conflicting demands (Chase and Reveal, 1983; Meier, 1987; Rourke, 1984).

Viteritti (1983) points out that an important distinction sometimes exists between *clients* of a program, who should receive its services, and *constituents,* who have demands. He notes that research shows that bureaucratic rules in urban agencies actually defend equitable distribution of services. In some cases, however, broader constituencies may pressure public managers *not* to apply rules on behalf of certain clients. For example, community groups may press against having minority or handicapped clients put in school classes with their children or against location of homes for the mentally retarded in their neighborhoods. The public manager faces challenges in sorting out the demands of clients and constituencies.

Several studies report that managers in state and local government agencies often see interest-group involvement with their agencies as beneficial and appropriate. State and local agency managers regard interest groups as having less influence on the operations of their agency than the chief executive (governor or mayor) or the legislature. When groups do exert influence, they often provide useful information about policy issues and group positions (Abney and Lauth, 1986; Brudney and Hebert, 1987; Elling, 1983). Abney and Lauth found additional evidence that agency managers at the urban level see interest-group involvement as appropriate when it focuses directly on the agency and inappropriate when channeled through the city council or the mayor. The managers may be too forgiving of interest-group influences, but the findings also suggest a more positive or at least necessary side of relations with interest groups. Experienced public managers see these involvements as a necessary part of their work, often frustrating but also challenging and helpful. Public managers have to be accessible to such groups, seriously attentive to what they have to say, patient and self-controlled when the groups are harshly critical, and honest (Chase and Reveal, 1983; Cohen, 1988).

Legislative Bodies

Congress, state legislatures, city councils, and county commissions exercise as much formal, legal authority over public organizations as do any other entity. Formal authority always operates in a political context, which may weaken it or bolster it in practical terms. Even so, the legislative bodies have formidable powers.

Formal Authority

Power of the Purse. Legislative bodies provide the money. They exercise the final power of approval over budget allocations to the agencies. They can fund new initiatives or cut and curtail aggressively.

Legislation. Governmental agencies are often born through legislation, especially at the federal and state levels. (At local levels, the agencies of a city government are often required under state guidelines.) Such legislation states the basic missions and duties of the agencies and provides authorization for their activities. Additional legislation can give an agency new duties. Its policies and programs can be extended, given to some other agency, reformed, or abolished.

Much of this legislation transmits vague, idealized directives to the agencies. For example, authorizing legislation for various regulatory agencies instructs them to promote "just" and "reasonable" practices in the public interest and for the common welfare (Woll, 1977). These broad grants of authority give the agencies considerable discretion (Lowi, 1979). Yet legislatures sometimes also do the opposite. They delve into precise details of agency management and procedure and engage in "micromanagement"

(Harris, 1964). They sometimes reform the general structure of the executive branch, combining certain departments and splitting others apart. They sometimes dictate the subunit structure of major agencies, including the bureaus to be established. They produce legislation governing the details of personnel procedures for the agencies within their jurisdictions or dictating other administrative procedures very precisely. For example, the state legislatures sometimes include in legislation detailed specifications about the types of computer records that a state regulatory agency must maintain.

Oversight. Legislative bodies regularly conduct hearings, audits, and investigations into agency activities (Rosen, 1989). Hearings are a normal part of the appropriations process and of the process of developing legislation. Investigatory and oversight agencies are established under the authority of the legislative branch to carry out inquiries into agency activities and performance. The General Accounting Office at the federal level and auditors general or similar offices in the states conduct audits to support legislative oversight.

Formal Authority of Committees. Particular legislative committees oversee particular agencies, conduct hearings and oversight, and develop legislation pertaining to them. Names of some committees correspond almost exactly to names of major federal and state agencies. City councils often have a committee structure as well, with committees corresponding to the major departments and functions of the city government. Some observers of the federal government conclude that its committee structure casts the administrative agencies as "creatures of the Congress," relatively independent of control by the president and the courts (Woll, 1977). Harold Seidman, one of the leading experts on federal administrative reforms, argues that if one wants to reform the federal bureaucracy, one must first reform the Congress. The congressional committees jealously guard their authority over the corresponding agencies (Seidman and Gilmour, 1986). An appropriations committee chair once objected to extending the president's power to veto legislation, saying "we don't want the agencies taking orders from the President. We want them to take orders from us" (Miller, 1990).

Less Formally Authorized Legislative Influences

Legislative influences can be relatively informal, rather than codified into law. For example, legislators call administrators on the phone to press them for information or ask for certain actions. State and federal administrators trying to relocate their agencies' offices or facilities to save money or to reorganize operations frequently hear from outraged legislators whose districts will lose the facilities and jobs. During the 1960s, the U.S. Labor Department sought to better organize the diverse work-training programs run by various bureaus by bringing them under the authority of a newly created

Manpower Administration. In committee hearings, powerful members of Congress told the head of this new agency that he should leave the Bureau of Apprenticeship and Trades (BAT) alone; it should not be brought into the new structure (Ruttenberg and Gutchess, 1970). Labor unions wanted to maintain a strong influence on BAT and had lobbied the members of Congress to oppose moving BAT under the new structure. Similarly, legislators press for the hiring or against the firing of political friends and allies in the agencies (Warwick, 1975). None of these actions is necessarily formally authorized, and some are quite improper. They illustrate an additional dimension of legislative influence on the bureaucracy and show why legislators strive to defend their alliances and influences with the bureaucracy.

Limits on Legislative Power

Some experts insist that, even armed with all these powers, legislative bodies exert little real control over administrative agencies (Woll, 1977). The agencies are specialized and staffed with experts, who know much more about the functions of the agency than legislators and their staffs can know. Legislators often have little incentive to be aggressive in supervising agency performance (Meier, 1987; Ripley and Franklin, 1984). Such "good-government" activities offer little political profit, since constituents often cannot see the results. In addition, tough oversight of the agencies could jeopardize relationships with them as potential sources of favors for constituents, which translate into political support. The agencies also have independent sources of support from interest groups and from parts of the legislative bodies and executive branches that they can play off against other parts.

Legislative authority also varies across jurisdictions. Certain states, such as Florida, have relatively powerful legislatures, based on legal and institutional arrangements in the state (Abney and Lauth, 1986). The authority and power of city councils and county commissions vary from place to place, depending, for example, on whether there is a "strong-mayor" or a "weak-mayor" government in a city.

The Chief Executive

Presidents, governors, and mayors rival the legislative branches for the role of strongest political influence on the agencies. Presumably, these chief executives have the greatest formal powers over the public bureaucracies in their jurisdictions. Yet, as with legislative bodies, the influence patterns are complex and dynamic, and chief executives face similar challenges in taming the unwieldy bureaucracy.

Appointments

Chief executives appoint heads of executive agencies and usually an additional array of patronage positions in the agencies. The chief executive's ability to influence agencies through these appointments varies by agency, jurisdiction, and political climate. President Reagan mounted an aggressive effort to influence federal agencies through appointments. He filled top positions of some major agencies with executives committed to reducing the regulatory role, size, and influence of the federal bureaucracy. Certain agencies sharply curtailed staffing and activity (Rubin, 1985). Administration officials also added new levels of political appointees at the tops of agencies. This added layers between the top executives and the highest career civil servants, demoting career service managers. These steps had so much impact that the Volcker Commission (1989) called for reductions in the number of appointments that the president makes. This example illustrates the potential power that the appointment authority gives a chief executive with a strong electoral backing. In certain states and localities, many major or cabinet-level agency executives are independently elected and thus not beholden to the chief executive through appointments. Jurisdictions also vary in the degree to which they have patronage appointments within agencies.

Executive Staff Offices

The executive offices of the U.S. president and of governors and mayors around the country give the executive staff resources that can bolster his or her influence. Units within an executive office can represent special constituencies and functions. A governor might have an office of minority affairs or veterans' affairs as a way of demonstrating concern for that constituency. Other subunits might concentrate on press relations and relations with the legislative branch. Some governors and local executives have inspector generals located in the executive offices to conduct investigations into allegations of improprieties in agencies.

Budget Authority

The most significant of the staff offices are those that wrestle with budgets — the Office of Management and Budget (OMB) in the Executive Office of the President and similar offices on the staffs of mayors and governors. The legislative branch ultimately approves the budget, but the chief executive assembles the agency budget requests and submits them to the legislature for approval. The chief executive tries to hammer his or her priorities into the budget by proposing extensions or cuts in funding for programs. The executive's influence over the budget depends on many factors — anticipated tax revenues, programs needing attention, developments in the political climate (such as strong midterm election results for the chief executive's party or strong popularity ratings). The legislative body may fight back, of course, putting money back into programs that the chief executive tries to cut, and vice versa. Agency officials engage in various ploys to maintain their funding and avoid cuts (Wildavsky, 1988). Their ability to do so depends on factors already described, such as group support. Yet through this process the chief executives have significant potential influence on public policy and the agencies.

Policy Initiatives and Executive Orders

Chief executives have certain formal powers to tell agencies what to do through directives and executive orders. For example, some of the original equal employment opportunity (EEO) initiatives were implemented through executive orders from President Eisenhower and later presidents. They directed federal agencies to establish EEO programs and instructed private companies holding federal contracts to develop such programs. Chief executives can also prompt agencies to develop programs and policies that the executive will support through the budgeting process.

The Courts

As with the other institutions surrounding public organizations, some experts say that the courts exert powerful controls on the public bureaucracy, while others see them as ineffectual. Various experts point to the courts as the strongest ultimate check on the power of the public bureaucracy, while others see bureaucratic power overwhelming the courts.

The federal and state courts operate under fairly conservative principles (Woll, 1977). Courts overrule the actions of agencies for two main reasons. They can stop an agency from going beyond the intent of the legislature in authorizing legislation. They can also prevent an agency from violating correct procedures, such as those required under the due process of law provisions of the Constitution and related legal precedents. These standards actually focus the courts on preventing agency actions, rather than proactively directing policies and programs. In addition, a number of relatively conservative legal principles support the position of an agency in any dispute with a citizen or group. Examples of these include principles that hold public officials immune to many types of liability and that require citizens with complaints against agencies to exhaust all possible remedies that they can seek through the agency before the court will hear their complaint. Also, someone has to initiate a lawsuit for the courts to act. This is expensive and can take a long time. The agencies win a lot of suits because they have high levels of specialization and legal expertise and an obvious interest in doing things as they see fit (Meier, 1987).

In a sweeping critique of the contemporary governmental process in the United States, Lowi (1979) cites vague legislation as a major problem in weakening judicial oversight of the bureaucracy. To achieve compromise among diverse interests in the legislative process, Congress and other legislative units give diffuse grants of authority to agencies by passing legislation with very general objectives and standards. Courts then have difficulty enforcing adherence to the intent of Congress. The sheer size, complexity, and specialization of the administrative branch and the technical complexity of many of the policy issues that may come before the courts make it extremely difficult for them to exercise strong control over bureaucratic actions (Stewart, 1975).

Yet under the right circumstances, the courts wield immense authority. Through injunctions, they can force or block an agency's actions. They can award damages against agencies, thus making administrators very careful about assessing the legal implications of their rules and procedures. The principles limiting the courts' interventions concerning, for example, citizens' abilities to sue government officials and exhaustion of administrative remedies have relaxed over time (Meier, 1987). A ruling making it easier for citizens to sue social welfare caseworkers when children under their supervision suffer child abuse changes the procedures and expenses of agencies across the country. In surveys, administrators report that court decisions influence the allocation of funds at state and local levels for education, prisons, hospitals, and other services (Meier, 1987).

Congress has moved toward more specific standards in some legislation (Wilson, 1989), and court rulings sometimes focus powerfully on one particular aspect of an agency's operations. Courts sometimes intervene in particular agency activities, often on behalf of some constitutional principle such as due process of law or equal protection of the law. On occasion, courts have in effect taken over schools and prisons in certain jurisdictions. Lawsuits to force agencies to comply with legislation requiring environmental impact statements prior to any major building projects have delayed many projects in many agencies. The courts wait in the background in a sense, directly intervening in day-to-day operations of a public organization only on occasion. Yet they pose an ominous background presence. Administrators frequently take actions and establish procedures expressly because of what a court has done or very mindful of what a court *might* do.

Other Agencies and Levels of Government

Public organizations both work together and fight with each other. The participants in this contest represent all the different levels of government, the various agencies, and certain oversight agencies concerned with personnel administration, budgeting, and central purchasing. Later chapters describe many examples of ways in which this affects management within the organizations.

Higher levels of government try to direct and regulate the lower levels in various ways in the course of intergovernmental relations in the federal system. Some programs, such as Social Security, are actually carried out by state personnel following federal guidelines. Behind this general cooperative structure, however, patterns of mutual influence operate.

Grants from higher levels carry some of this influence. Merit systems of personnel administration have been disseminated throughout state and local governments in the United States in part because federal grants were made available to localities to set up such systems. Federal laws can mandate that federal money for programs be matched in certain ways by states and localities. Under federal law, for example, states must contribute to Medicare payments for individuals, in addition to the amounts paid by the federal government. With these funding arrangements come influences on structure and procedure. In Florida, the Department of Health and Rehabilitative Services adopted a new structure that brought together many service outlets (for indigent medical care, family and youth counseling, and others) in the same government offices and established a regional district structure. Yet federal vocational rehabilitation officials forced the department to exclude vocational rehabilitation activities from this arrangement and to organize those services separately. The rules for their programs require that they have a separate, independent organization.

Laws and regulations, whether or not attached to grants and funding, also transmit such influences. Environmental protection regulations from the state and federal levels and growth and economic development mandates directly impose decisions from higher levels about how lower levels must be managed. Federal legislation sometimes directs a federal agency to do certain things in every state unless a state does those things in such a way as to meet certain minimum standards established by the federal government. An example of this is the federal government's policy regarding mine safety regulations, under which the federal government would run mine safety regulation within a state unless the state could finance and manage the program itself at least at the level of federal standards.

The relationships may be very smooth in many instances, but the so-called lower levels do not necessarily take this higher-level influence lying down. During the Reagan administration, many state governments refused to carry out directives from the Social Security Administration requiring that they review the cases of many disability payment recipients and deny payments to some under more stringent rules. Early in the Bush administration, many states were very slow to comply with federal laws requiring that they increase their share of Medicare payments (Tolchin, 1989). Localities also work hard to influence state and federal legislation that may bear significantly on their activities. They have associations such as the League of Cities that lobby at state and federal levels for legislation that they feel they need.

Organizations at a given level of government also cooperate and compete in many ways. The delivery of many local services in the United States often involves a complex network of joint agreements and contracts among localities. State and federal agencies typically have overlapping responsibilities and engage in joint planning and activity. The Equal Employment Opportunity Coordinating Commission was established to coordinate the various agencies at the federal level that had responsibilities in carrying out affirmative action and equal employment opportunity policies. Early in the

Bush administration, a coordinating council was proposed as a means of facilitating the relationships between the various units of government with some responsibility for programs that address homelessness. Agencies also compete with each other for the time and attention of higher-level executives (Chase and Reveal, 1983) and compete over turf, seeking to block other agencies and authorities from gaining control over their programs (Wilson, 1989).

Public Managers' Perceptions of the Political Environment

Later chapters describe a variety of studies that pertain to how public managers respond to these components of their political environments and how those environments influence public organizations. Some studies mentioned above, however, provide evidence of how public managers perceive various aspects of the political context, such as the relative influence of the chief executives, legislatures, and interest groups (Abney and Lauth, 1986; Brudney and Hebert, 1987; Elling, 1983). These studies indicate that state agency managers see the legislature as most influential, with the governor coming second, although there are variations among the states in relative power of the governor and legislature. Local managers see the chief executive — the mayor — as most influential. State and local agency managers rate interest groups as much less influential on their agencies than the legislative bodies and chief executives but often see them as valuable contributors to decision making.

Aberbach, Putnam, and Rockman (1981) provide a similar indication of the strong influence of the legislative branch, at the federal level. They analyzed contacts between administrative officials and other actors in the federal systems of the United States and five other industrial democracies. In the United States they found much higher levels of contact between civil service administrators in agencies and congressional committee members than either of these two groups had with the executive heads of the agencies. The civil service managers had even more contacts with constituent groups than with Congress, however. Aberbach, Putnam, and Rockman referred to this pattern in the United States as the "end run" model because it involves civil servants and legislators going around the executive agency heads more than in any of the other countries they studied.

Studies seeking generalizations about how public managers perceive the nature of their own political activities are rare, but Olshfski (1989, 1990) identifies three conceptions of politics that emerge in state agency executives' descriptions of their political activities: *political astuteness,* the understanding of the political system and the processes of government and their own departments; *issue politics,* the political activities, such as bargaining and coalition building, necessary to advance an issue or achieve an objective; and *electoral politics,* the knowledge and activity related to gaining general political support for themselves, an elected official, or their departments.

The Public Policy Process

The analysis of public policy has burgeoned over the last several decades, as has the recognition that public organizations play essential roles in the formation and implementation of public policies. The research on this policy process helps to explain many of the characteristics of public organizations and their management. It adds insights about the dynamic interplay of the political institutions and groups discussed above.

Many Arenas and Programs

Government activity at all levels encompasses a diverse array of functions and policy domains. Without any standard nomenclature, scholars and government officials refer to policy categories such as defense, health, science and technology, social welfare and poverty, environmental protection, energy, economic and fiscal policy (including tax policy), agricultural policy, industrial development policy, educational policy, and regulatory policy. Government activities at state and local levels, sometimes referred to as *service-delivery categories* rather than public policy, include a similarly diverse list: industrial development, zoning and land use, police and fire-fighting services, transportation (including streets and roads), garbage collection, prisons and jails, parks and recreation, and many others. As mentioned earlier, state and local governments are also part of the policy process for major federal policies. Within these policy areas and spanning them, many specific programs operate at various levels of scope, size, and complexity.

Many Actors and Levels

All the institutions, levels, authorities, and groups discussed above play parts in shaping policy and carrying it out. Adding to the complexities already described, governmental policies draw many private organizations into the policy process. Many government programs operate largely through purchases and contracts with nongovernmental organizations, such as weapons manufacturers, or private nonprofit organizations that seek, for example, to help troubled youths. Many people know about the massive contracting in the federal construction and procurement process but not about the similar linkages between government and the so-called private sector in most other areas of public policy and service delivery.

Government actually creates private or quasi-governmental organizations in some cases (Ripley and Franklin, 1982). Under human resource training or "manpower" programs, nonprofit organizations were established to conduct research on labor policies. This increasing reliance on private contractors creates complications for public managers. They are responsible for the performance of contractors but often have trouble holding them accountable (Rosen, 1989). In addition, the arrangements become so complicated that even public officials have trouble keeping up with them. In 1986, a new governor took over in the state of Florida, having campaigned on the promise to cut waste in government through businesslike administration of public programs. The governor's aides conducted discussions with the director of the Department of Health and Rehabilitative Services (DHRS), a huge state agency that administers social welfare programs. The aides felt that more contracts with private organizations for the delivery of services would make the agency's operations cheaper and questioned the director about working harder on contracting out. The director had to explain politely that about half of the agency's budget of around three billion dollars was already administered through contracts with other organizations — a fact of which the governor's aides had been unaware.

Policy Subsystems

As discussed above, the policy process is fragmented into a number of policy areas. For a long time, political scientists described these domains as dominated by "iron triangles," which are tight alliances of congressional committees, administrative agencies, and interest groups that control the major policy areas, such as defense or environmental policy. Key people in the agencies, groups, and committees exchange political favors and support. Other authorities outside this triangle, even the president, can wield little influence over it. This situation has long been lamented as one of the fundamental problems of government in the United States. Ronald Reagan complained about iron triangles in one of his last public statements as president.

Although it refers to a very significant problem, political scientists now point out that the iron-triangle analogy oversimplifies the true complexity and dynamism of these coalitions. Competitions and conflict among groups and agencies may flare within the so-called triangles, making them much less solid than the analogy implies. Lawyers may fight doctors over a change in legislation on malpractice suits. One group of large corporations may line up on the other side of an issue from another group of equally large corporations. In addition, as problems change, different groups, organizations, and individuals move in and out of the policy arena. The iron-triangle analogy fails to depict the instability and flux in the process. It also suggests grim power politics as the driving force in influence patterns (Kingdon, 1984, p. 131).

Recently proposed terms better characterize the situation. Heclo (1978) refers to "issue networks" of experts, officials, and interests that form around particular issues and that can shift rapidly. Milward and Wamsley (1982) describe the characteristics of policy networks, or complex and shifting aggregations of groups, experts, public and private organizations, governmental authorities, and others whose interplay shapes formation and implementation of policy. Others refer to subgovernments' implementation structures (Hjern and Porter, 1981), public-service industries, policy subsystems (Rainey and Milward, 1983), and policy communities (Kingdon, 1984).

The public policy process in which public organizations and managers participate is balkanized into domains akin to those suggested by the iron-triangle idea. These subsystems or networks prove unwieldy and resistant to external control or coordination with other networks. Yet the depiction of the problem as one of staunch control by self-serving bureaucrats, politicians, and private interests oversimplifies the problem. Often, the difficulties in coordination and control result largely from the flux and complexity of the issues, the interests, and the participants in the process of trying to solve very difficult problems.

The Agenda-Setting Process and the Agenda Garbage Can

Public policy researchers also help to characterize the complex context of public managers by analyzing how certain matters gain prominence on the public agenda while others languish outside of public notice. John Kingdon (1984) describes this process as resembling the "garbage can model" of decision making developed by James March and his colleagues. As described in more detail in Chapter Four the garbage can model depicts decision making in organizations as much less systematic and rational than commonly supposed. People are not very sure about their preferences and how the organization works. Streams of problems, solutions, participants, and choice opportunities flow along through time, sometimes coming together in combinations that shape decisions. (An example of a choice opportunity is a salient problem that has to be addressed by a newly formed committee with sufficient authority to have a chance to get something done.) The process is more topsy-turvy than the organization chart might suggest. Sometimes solutions actually chase problems, as when someone has a pet idea that he or she wants to find a chance to apply. Sometimes administrators simply look for work to do. Choice opportunities are like garbage cans in which problems, solutions, and participants come together in a jumbled fashion.

Kingdon revises this view when he applies it to public policy, referring to streams of problems, policies, and politics flowing along and sometimes coming together at key points to shape the policy agenda. Problems come to the attention of policy makers in various ways: through indicators (unemployment figures, figures on the budget deficits); through focusing events such as crises; through feedback such as citizen complaints and reports on the operation of programs. Policies develop within the "policy community" as various ideas and alternatives emerge from the "policy primeval soup." Like microorganisms in a biological primeval soup, they originate, compete, evolve, and prosper or perish. They are evaluated in think tanks, conferences, staff work in legislative bodies and government agencies, and interest-group activities. They may be tried out in partial versions in programs or unsuccessful legislation, and a long period of "softening up" often follows the original proposal, in which the alternative becomes more and more acceptable. Some alternatives have a long history of implementation, shelving, alteration, and retrial. For example, various versions of public works and job-training camps have appeared at different levels of government since the days of the Civilian Conservation Corps during the New Deal and the Job Corps during the Johnson administration's War on Poverty. At times, events in these streams converge to open "windows of opportunity" in which the political climate and forces align in support of a policy alternative for a particular problem, moving this combination to a central place on the public agenda.

In Kingdon's portrayal, the agenda-setting process appears difficult to predict and understand clearly but not wildly out of control. Processes of gestation and evaluation focus considerable scrutiny on ideas and alternatives and their workability. Still, this analysis illustrates the dynamism of the policy process in which public managers must operate. In later chapters, the idea of identifying "windows of opportunity" figures usefully in the discussion of managing change in public organizations. Many of the challenges facing a public manager turn on effective assessment of the political feasibility of particular actions and alternatives and of the array of political forces shaping or curtailing opportunity.

Policy Implementation: The "Too Many Cooks" Problem

The study of implementation of public policy once it has been formulated has also grown tremendously in the last two decades. Such studies describe the complications of implementing public policies involving many levels, authorities, and interests that the policies affect. Government has to use directives and inducements to try to influence far-flung individuals and organizations. The system thus involves many "veto points," which can hinder implementation.

More recently, researchers offer better conceptions of implementation to replace the older case studies. They analyze such factors as the tractability of the problem that the policy addresses, the types of inducements used by higher levels of government, and the capacities of lower levels—including their organizational structures and personnel (Goggin, Bowman, Lester, O'Toole, 1990; Mazmanian and Sabatier, 1981). These analyses have not yet been integrated with many of the managerial issues that the remaining chapters take up. Analyzing these relations remains a challenge for the field (Lynn, 1987). Nevertheless, the work on policy implementation adds meaning to the assertions about complex objectives and constraints in public management. It also supports some suggestions in later chapters about how this implementation process may affect such topics as structure and motivation in public organizations.

Public managers, especially at higher levels, have to manage skillfully their relations with these external authorities, actors, and policy processes. They also have to operate effectively within the pattern of interventions and constraints that these actors impose. As the discussion now turns to key dimensions of organizing and managing, the importance of these relations in the handling of those dimensions comes up again and again. It also becomes clear that, while many rank-and-file managers and employees have little direct involvement with this external political and administrative milieu, it shapes the context of their work. Evidence and examples will show how it effects organizational characteristics and individual attitudes and behaviors throughout public organizations.

PART 2

KEY DIMENSIONS
OF ORGANIZING AND MANAGING

Chapter 4

Formulating and Achieving Purpose: Power, Strategy, and Decision Making

Faced with the diffuse and complex purposes of public organizations and with many constraints on their authority, effective public managers nevertheless work intensively to determine and achieve those purposes. This chapter examines processes that pertain to purpose—power and influence over decisions, decision processes themselves, and strategic decision making.

Power and Politics Inside the Organization

External power and politics influence internal power and politics. Political scientists have long recognized the role of external politics in determining the power of public organizations and that units within the government bureaucracy engage in power struggles and turf warfare (Wilson, 1989). Yet, aside from case descriptions, political scientists have paid little attention to developing frameworks for studying power relations *within* public bureaucracies. Writers on management have started looking at power within organizations only recently, but they have done more to analyze it than have political scientists. Early management theories depicted managers as basing decisions on rational choices of the optimal alternatives. Researchers increasingly realized, however, that politics and power relations figure importantly in all organizations (Pfeffer, 1981). Some make a point of claiming that the politics in business firms and government agencies are very similar (Yates, 1985). Management writers now warn managers of the dangers of overlooking power and politics within their organizations and exhort managers to assess these dimensions of their setting (Yates, 1985). They also discuss power in a positive sense, as necessary to performing effectively and, when shared, as a means of motivating people (Kanter, 1987; Block, 1987).

The many rules and controls imposed by external authorities and political actors on public organizations weaken the authority of managers. Political alliances between people in an agency and interest groups and legislators further weaken the authority of higher-level executives. This suggests that, in spite of the claims of management writers that business firms resemble public agencies in such matters, issues of power and influence become more complex for government managers (Allison, 1983). At the same time, rather paradoxically, observers typically depict the bureaucracy as quite powerful. Although constrained in many ways, then, public managers clearly can attain considerable power and authority within their organizations.

They also vary in power, just as agencies do. Agency power can be enhanced by a number of factors: strong, well-organized constituencies, skillful leadership, organizational esprit or cohesion (a relatively strong commitment to the agency and its role, as with the Forestry Service or the Peace Corps), and expertise — specialized technical knowledge required for the delivery of a service that the public values highly (Rourke, 1984; Meier, 1987). By implication, these factors also determine the power of people and units within public organizations. This chapter considers how concepts from the management literature can help us further to sort out some of the determinants of power. A recent example of a power play in the federal bureaucracy provides a useful beginning. Newspaper accounts dramatized it as a perfect example of how power works in Washington. Yet it also makes important points about how power does not work and illustrates the importance of analyzing the dimensions of power.

Shortly after Ronald Reagan left office, major newspapers carried reports on a controversial aide to the secretary of the Department of Housing and Urban Development (HUD) who had gained considerable power in the department. The reports claimed that the aide had little background related to housing and had gained her appointment because she came from a prominent family. According to the reports, the secretary had inattentively allowed her to make heavy use of his autopen — an apparatus that automatically signs the secretary's name — to influence major decisions on funding and agency policies. She garnered support from members of Congress by channeling projects and grants to their constituencies. She also allegedly used the authority of the secretary to move trusted associates into key positions in the agency where they could give her early information about the unit heads' plans so that she could devise ways to overrule them and channel their projects toward her supporters. In spite of her maneuvering, however, when she was nominated for the position of assistant secretary of HUD, Congress would not confirm her appointment because of her lack of credentials and qualifications. Ultimately, her influence on spending decisions in a housing rehabilitation program received intense scrutiny from federal auditors and news reporters and brought a deluge of bad publicity and the threat of legal action (Maitland, 1989; Waldman, Cohn, and Thomas, 1989).

Bases of Social Power

The HUD official's inability to attain sustained, successful power raises the question of how one does so. Social scientists usually refer to French and

Raven's (1968) typology of the bases for power in groups: *Reward* power is the power to confer or withhold rewards that others want, such as pay. *Coercive* power comes from the ability to take forceful action against another. A person has *referent* power over others if they see him or her as someone they wish to be like, as a standard for them. *Expert* power derives from the control of knowledge, information, and skills that others need. A person holds *legitimate* power if others accept his or her authority to tell them what to do.

These types of power have important implications for managers. One might think of coercive power as the ultimate mode of influence. The capacity to tax, arrest, imprison, and execute individuals is a fundamental attribute of government. These powers justify strong controls on public organizations, which often have a coercive character themselves. As for their own leadership behaviors, however, public managers need to recognize that management theorists have long emphasized the relative clumsiness and costliness of coercive power (Etzioni, 1975). Forcing and threatening people requires costly vigilance and oversight and can make enemies.

Managers may have authority to coerce, but their real challenge is in finding ways to reward (Barnard, 1938); as Chapter Six describes, public managers face particular constraints on their power over certain rewards. Managers may have some legitimate authority because of their rank and position, but they have to maintain the less formal legitimacy that exists in the eyes of their subordinates and external authorities. To do so, good managers invest heavily in setting a good example and performing well in order to attain referent power and expert power. For all the politics that surrounds public managers, experienced officials and observers still report that the skill, integrity, experience, and expert knowledge of a public administrator can give that administrator a positive form of power with members of the organization and with external authorities.

The HUD official described above rewarded certain supporters, illustrating the importance of political alliances. Yet her relatively coercive treatment of some agency officials probably contributed to her ultimate troubles. Also, she allegedly abused legitimate power (the secretary's autopen) and lacked sufficient legitimate, expert, and referent power to sustain her position. Later chapters provide examples of more effective approaches. They also involve development of constituencies, but with more effective visions of a contribution to society, sustained by reputations for expertise and integrity (Cohen, 1988; Doig and Hargrove, 1987; Chase and Reveal, 1983).

Dependency and Strategic Contingencies

In analyzing power, organization theorists also draw on the concept of dependency—how much others must depend on a person or group for resources. Groups and units that have the most to do with attaining key resources for the organization gain power. Studies of business firms find that their members rate the sales and production divisions of their firms as the most powerful units (Kenny and others, 1987; Perrow, 1970a). The firms depend on these units to produce and sell the products essential to bringing in money. Others can also depend on a person or unit for information, completed tasks, and services.

Similarly, power accrues to units that manage *strategic contingencies,* or the factors and events that figure crucially in the operations of the organization and its ability to achieve goals (Hickson and others, 1971). Units that handle the biggest problems facing the organization gain power. Earlier chapters discussed the central role of *environmental uncertainty* in analysis of organizations in recent decades; strategic contingencies include circumstances that impose major uncertainties on the organization, and those who handle these uncertainties become important. During the 1970s, many city governments faced the prospect of affirmative action suits, and many mayors and city managers began spending more time with their city attorneys and personnel officers to determine what kind of affirmative action plan would be legally defensible. The requests for support and resources from these officers and their units—for more funding and new personnel—and their capacity to tell other units what to do increased noticeably in some cities.

The study by Kenny and others (1987) further suggests that these concepts apply to public organizations, but with important distinctions. They analyzed major decisions in thirty public and private organizations in Britain. The private organizations included manufacturing and service firms. The public group included local governments, health districts, and government enterprises, such as a chemical manufacturer and an airline. The researchers asked managers of both types of organizations which internal and external units became involved in major decision making and how much influence they had. The two groups had similar patterns of unit involvement. For example, accounting, auditing, and production units were most frequently involved. In the public organizations, however, external government agencies became involved much more often. Sales, marketing, and production units had a great deal of influence in both groups. Yet in the public organizations, adjudication units—committees or commissions that decide on resources and policies, such as a health services district commission—had the strongest influence rating. This type of unit approached the lowest rating in the private organizations. Surprisingly, also, external government agencies were rated as having little influence in the public organizations, in spite of their frequent involvement, but as very influential in the private organizations. The authors suggest that this might mean that public-sector managers take for granted the influence of external agencies, while business managers react more sharply to government interventions.

Overall, the study indicates that units that produce and distribute primary goods and services wield strong influence in both types of organizations. Even in this group of public organizations with high market or client orientations—including government manufacturers, a health district, and so on—the institutional authority of government affects internal influence patterns; external agencies often become involved. The strong role of adjudication units reflects the authority conferred on them by the institutions of government. Those units also handled key strategic dependencies by representing external constituencies and making policy decisions. Later we will see that the same researchers also found that the strategic decision processes of the public organizations also reflected the effects of government auspices.

Power at Different Organizational Levels

Management experts also consider how people at different levels and in different units attain power. Daft (1989) points out that top managers have a variety of sources of power. They have considerable authority by virtue of their formal position, such as authority to control key decisions. They can influence allocation of *resources*. In government agencies, in spite of external constraints and politics, the agency heads usually exert considerable influence over funding for subunits and allocation of other key resources, such as personnel. Top managers can control *decision premises* — fundamental values or principles that guide decisions — and *information* (Simon, 1948). Robert Dempsey, director of the Florida Department of Law Enforcement, became interested in Peters and Waterman's (1982) *In Search of Excellence,* which emphasizes approaches such as concern for employees and open communication. Dempsey made it clear to his managers that the agency would adopt these orientations through open-door policies, improved communications, and other steps. This position became a guide for decisions by the other managers. When an employee asks to speak to a manager, the director has provided clear guidelines on how to respond to such a question — you listen! The basic decision premise guides subsequent, more specific decisions. (Chapters Seven, Ten, and Eleven provide further examples of managers' efforts to communicate major values and premises to others.)

Top managers can also take advantage of *network centrality*. They occupy the center of networks of information, personal loyalty, and resource flows. The HUD official placed loyal associates in key positions to develop a network of information. This worked effectively until deficits in other dimensions of power eroded her position (Maitland, 1989).

Lower-level members can have substantial power as well. They may serve as experts on key tasks. They can attain influence through effort, interest, informal coalitions, such as patterns of friendship, or formal organizations, such as unions. They can use rules and other organizational norms to their advantage. In his analysis of "street-level" government service providers, Lipsky (1980) points out that they have considerable autonomy. Civil service rules, vague performance measures, and extensive rules governing service delivery constrain higher officials' authority over them.

Middle managers fall between executives and employees and have some of the influence potential of both groups. Management experts interested in "empowerment" as a means of making managers more effective have lately focused increasing attention on these managers (Kanter, 1987; Block, 1987). These authors often focus on business firms, but empowerment also has intriguing implications for public agencies. Middle managers occupy positions below corporate vice-presidents or major division and department heads. In government, this would include those below assistant secretaries or major bureau heads, such as managers in GS 13–15 positions in the federal government.

Kanter (1987) argues that middle managers in business firms have so little power that they cannot perform effectively. Many rules and routines govern their work, with few rewards for innovation. They rarely participate in important conferences and task forces. They lack resources and support to do useful things, such as rewarding excellent subordinates or pursuing a promising initiative. Higher-level managers must bestow a positive form of power on these middle managers. They must relax rules, increase participation, assign important tasks, and reward innovation (Kanter, 1987). This sharing of power *expands* power, giving more people in the organization the capacity and incentive to do good work. Excellent corporations and effective leaders employ such policies (see Chapter Seven).

Interestingly, Kanter's analysis of problems in industry sounds like the complaints about heavy constraints on managers in government. The proposed solution, however, contrasts sharply with common approaches in government. Elected officials and top agency executives often impose *more* rules to try to improve performance and maintain control (Wilson, 1989; Lynn, 1981; Warwick, 1975); President Reagan aggressively sought to *dis*empower career federal civil servants. The accountability pressures in government complicate empowerment approaches. Yet government officials face a serious challenge of finding ways to allow civil servants sufficient authority and participation to maintain a competent and motivated public service (Volcker Commission, 1989; National Academy of Public Administration, 1986).

Power Among Subunits

Pfeffer and Salancik (1978) apply similar thinking to the analysis of power distributions among subunits. A department or bureau has more power when there is more dependency on it, when it has more control over financial resources and more centrality to the important activities of the organization, when there is less *substitutability* of services (when others have few or no alternatives to dealing with the unit for important needs), and when it has a larger role in coping with important uncertainties facing the organization.

Getting and Using Power

When they draw practical suggestions from this literature, management writers offer advice such as this (Daft, 1989):

- Move into areas of great uncertainty or strategic contingencies facing the organization and play an important role in managing those areas.
- Increase other departments' dependence on your own by making them depend on you for key resources and information. Incur obligations by doing additional work for others.
- Provide resources for the organization by bringing in money and other resources from external sources.
- Build coalitions and networks with others by building trust and respect through helpfulness and high motivation. Involve many people, including those who disagree with you.
- Influence decision premises by such means as influencing the flow of information about one's department and shaping the agendas of important meetings.
- Enhance the legitimacy and prestige of your position and department.
- Be reasonably aggressive and assertive, but be quiet and subtle about power issues — do not make loud claims or demands about power.

Suggestions as general as these certainly apply in most management settings. For public management, they need to be interpreted in light of the points made here about legitimate authority and external political authority.

Decisions in Organizations

Decision making is closely related to power issues, since power determines who gets to decide. As with power issues, the literature often suggests that public organizations should have distinct decision processes because of factors different from those faced by private organizations, such as political interventions and constraints and more diverse, diffuse objectives. The most recent evidence supports such assertions. Although it shows that the general decision processes of public organizations often resemble those of private organizations, it also indicates that major decisions in public organizations involve more complexity, dynamism, intervention, and interruption than those in their private counterparts. These conditions help to explain why, when demands for accountability and efficiency have led to schemes for rationalizing government decision processes, they have often failed. At the same time, however, public employees engage in much routine decision making that can be highly standardized. This raises another key challenge for public managers — deciding when to try to standardize and rationalize decision processes. Concepts from general organization theory help in the analysis of this issue.

Many contemporary management scholars (for example, Daft, 1989) analyze decision processes according to a contingency-theory perspective of the sort described in the Introduction. In some situations, managers can successfully adopt highly rationalized decision processes. Others involve too much uncertainty for such structured approaches and require more complex, intuitive decision making.

Rational Decision Models

Rationality has various meanings and dimensions, but in the social sciences, a *strictly* rational decision process would involve the following components:

1.   Decision makers know all the relevant goals clearly.
2.   Decision makers clearly know the values for assessing those goals and levels of attainment of them, so they also know their preferences among the goals and can rank-order them.
3.   They examine all alternative means for achieving the goals.
4.   They choose the most efficient of the alternative means for maximizing the goals.

These strict conditions seldom are met except in the most simplified situations, but we know that simplified situations that require decisions come up all the time. A bureau chief receives a careful committee report demonstrating that three alternative vendors can sell the bureau identical copying machines. The bureau chief chooses the least expensive machine. To do otherwise would invite others to question the chief's competence, ethics, or sanity.

Rational Decision Techniques in Public Organizations. Public agencies apply techniques akin to those of scientific management when they have consultants or in-house experts analyze work processes to design more efficient, effective work procedures. In one case, a client services agency conducted such an analysis when purchasing new computer terminals for use in recording intake interviews with new clients. The original plan called for the client to sit to the right of the interviewer while the interviewer keyed the client's responses into the computer. However, a consultant hired to conduct a time-motion study discovered that the terminals should be placed where the interviewer could face the client. The interviewers wanted to face the clients to make the interview more personable. In addition, if the client sat to the side of the interviewer, the interviewer would keep turning to face the client, wasting time and energy. A rational technique not only aided efficiency but supported the objectives of human relations with clients as well.

Similarly, management science techniques have wide applications in government (Downs and Larkey, 1986). These techniques involve mathematical models or other highly structured procedures for decision making. Linear programming, for example, uses mathematical formulas to determine how many units of output can be produced with given levels of inputs and thus to determine the best mix of inputs for a production process. Other mathematical techniques support design of work flows and queuing processes. Many discussions of such techniques emphasize the greater difficulty of successful applications in government because of such factors as vague performance criteria and political interventions (Drake, 1972; Morse and Bacon, 1967). For many technical areas of governmental work, however, these techniques have applications in government just as in industry.

Many of the proposals for improving government operations over the past several decades advocated approaches that involve elements of rational decision making (Downs and Larkey, 1986; Lynn, 1981). Lyndon Johnson issued a presidential directive ordering that the planning and program budgeting system (PPBS) be implemented in the budgeting processes of the federal agencies. PPBS involves a systematic process of organizing budget requests according to major programs, with plans and objectives for those programs specified and justified. Advocates proposed PPBS as a reform of previous budgeting techniques that concentrated on the items or activities to be funded, with little attention to objectives for programs. The Department of Defense had used the system with some success prior to President Johnson's order. Problems in implementing PPBS more widely, however, led to the order's cancellation a few years later.

When Jimmy Carter campaigned for president, he proposed the use of zero-based budgeting (ZBB) techniques as a way of exerting greater control over federal spending. This technique involves looking at the requests for funding of various activities as if their funding levels were zero. The idea is to force a very systematic, rational review of major commitments and possible reallocations, rather than simply taking existing programs for granted. The procedure never came into use in any significant way.

Others have proposed that the public sector can use management by objectives (MBO) techniques as well as the private sector does (Morrisey, 1976). These techniques, discussed in more detail in Chapter Six, involve careful negotiation and specification of the primary objectives for individuals and units, with performance evaluations to concentrate on whether those objectives have been achieved (Swiss, 1991). As with the previously discussed techniques, debate goes on over prospects for such a systematic and explicit technique in public organizations (Sherwood and Page, 1983; Bowsher, 1990).

Some public organizations use elements of these techniques, but their general implementation has foundered. Apparently, the public-sector conditions of diffuse goals, political complications, and highly complex programs often overwhelm such highly rationalized procedures.

Rationality Assumptions and the Behaviors of Public Managers and Officials.
Another role that the concept of rationality has played in analyzing public organizations revolves around the use of such assumptions to interpret the behavior of public managers and other governmental officials. "Public choice" economists have developed a body of theory using approaches typical in economics to analyze how citizens and officials make political decisions. They argue, for example, that in political just as in economic contexts, individuals rationally maximize utility. Voters vote in their own self-interest, and political officials in essence try to buy their votes by providing them with government programs and services that they want. Since no economic market process ensures that one has to pay directly for the goods and services that one receives, groups of voters use the political system to benefit themselves at the expense of others. They demand that their elected officials give

them services and subsidies that *they* need, sometimes shifting much of the burden of paying for them to other voters. When these theorists turn to the public bureaucracy, they suggest similar problems. In some of the most prominent, widely cited academic works on the public bureaucracy, they suggest that government bureaucracies strive for ever greater budgets (Niskanen, 1971) and tend toward rigidity (Downs, 1967) and information distortion (Tullock, 1965). Public organizations have no economic market for their outputs, so their administrators seek higher and higher budget allocations (Niskanen, 1971). Part Three discusses evidence and controversy about these assertions. It argues that some evidence supports them, but that they are at least oversimplified (Bendor and Moe, 1985), if not largely inaccurate.

Political scientists also have interesting perspectives on rationality and public organizations. Warwick (1975) proposes that an administrative orthodoxy governs many decisions about the structure and control of government agencies. Many officials feel that government should have a highly rationalized structure, with clear chains of command and strict lines of accountability, just as prescribed in some of the earlier, highly rational views of management described above. In turn, Warwick argues, many appointed executives at the heads of agencies strive for tight controls over the agencies, issuing rules and approval requirements and maintaining narrow spans of control. Lynn (1981) describes a similar tendency, which he calls "inevitable bureaucracy." These tendencies run counter to the most current prescriptions for profit-oriented firms that appear in the management literature (Peters, 1988).

The Limits of Rationality. These countertrends toward less emphasis on highly rational decision processes help to explain why rational techniques do not apply well in complex decision settings. The countertrends began around the middle of the century when Herbert Simon (1948) advanced his observations about the constraints on managers' ability to follow such procedures (see Chapter One and the Appendix). Simon argued that, for large-scale decisions, the deluge of relevant information and uncertainties overloads the cognitive capacity of managers to process all the information. Managers strive for rationality — they are *intendedly rational.* But cognitive limits, uncertainties, and time limits cause them to decide under conditions of *bounded rationality.* They do not maximize in accordance with rationality assumptions; they "satisfice." They undertake a limited search among alternatives and choose the most satisfactory of the alternatives after as much consideration as they can manage within the constraints. Interestingly, one of the prominent tests of Simon's ideas concentrated on business firms. Cyert and March (1963) studied business firms and found that they approached major decisions largely as Simon had suggested. Rather than making decisions in highly rational modes, managers in the firms followed satisficing approaches. They engaged in "problemistic search." They started searching for alternatives and solutions in relation to problems that came up, rather than in a systematic, explicitly goal-oriented pattern. They engaged in "sequential attention to alternatives," turning from possibility to possibility and looking at an alternative until they saw some problem with it and then turning to another. They tended to use benchmarks and rules of thumb rather than a careful explication of goals and how to maximize them. For example, without conclusive evidence to justify doing so, they might set a target of a 5 percent profit increase per year for the next five years because they had been achieving almost that in the past.

Contingency Perspectives on Decision Making

Current views of management typically follow this pattern of regarding strictly rational approaches to decision making as applicable within relatively limited domains of managerial activity. Where tasks and the operating context afford relatively stable, clear, simple conditions, managers find such approaches feasible. As conditions become more complex and dynamic, however, the deluge of information and uncertain conditions overwhelms procedures that require highly explicit statements of goals and painstaking analysis of numerous alternatives. More intuitive and experience-based judgment comes into play, supplementing or supplanting highly rationalized procedures.

James Thompson (1967) suggested a contingency framework to express these variations. Decision contexts vary along two major dimensions: the degree to which the decision makers agree on goals and the degree to which they understand means-ends or cause-effect relationships—that is, the degree to which they have well-developed technical knowledge about how to solve the problems and accomplish the tasks. Where both goal agreement and technical knowledge are high, very rational procedures apply. The example above concerning the design of procedures for computerized claims intake interviews illustrates a situation where everyone agreed on the goals. Everyone wanted more efficient, effective interview procedures. In addition, the consultants had well-developed ways of analyzing the efficiency and effectiveness of the interviews in the trial runs. A rational procedure served very well.

The Internal Revenue Service deals each year with problems in receiving the flood of tax returns and extracting and sorting them correctly. State departments of motor vehicles and the U.S. Social Security Administration process many routine applications and claims. In decisions about activities such as these, management science techniques and other forms of highly rationalized analysis have valuable applications (as long as they are properly implemented, in humane and communicative fashion). For example, the U.S. Navy once effectively implemented a planned maintenance system with elaborate scheduling charts that directed when the various pieces of machinery and equipment on a ship should receive maintenance. Instruction cards detailed the maintenance tasks to be performed, with a system of recording the completion of those tasks. In effect, the ships followed a strict recipe for maintenance.

At the other end of the scale, where decision makers have no clear consensus on goals and little clarity as to the technical means of achieving them, one can hardly follow a simple blueprint. Measurement, mathematical models and analysis, and strict guidelines for decisions become more tenuous. Under these conditions, managers engage in more bargaining and political maneuvering and more intuitive, judgmental decision making.

Incremental Decision Processes

Much more in political science than in management, scholars have debated whether governmental decision processes follow an *incremental* pattern. This perspective on public-sector decisions has features similar to those of the bounded rationality perspective and related intellectual origins. Incrementalism in decision making means concentrating on increments to existing circumstances, or relatively limited changes from existing conditions. Those who regard the policy process as having this character argue that major, wrenching changes to federal budget categories seldom receive much consideration. The officials formulating the budget instead concentrate on the limited increments, up and down, proposed in any given year. Policy makers restrict the size of the changes that they propose. The bigger the change, the more opposition one stirs up, and the more analytical the complexities.

Political scientists have debated intensively over whether incrementalism accurately characterizes the policy process and the budgeting process. In addition, they debate its desirability. Some argue that incremental processes reflect useful bargaining among active political groups and officials and guard against ill-considered radical changes. Others complain that they make the policy and budgeting processes too conservative and shortsighted and too supportive of existing coalitions and policies.

The debate became mired in difficulties about what is meant by an increment — how large a change has to be to be large. It has led to the conclusion, however, that policy and budgetary changes tend to be incremental but are not always. Fairly drastic cuts in some portions of the federal budget during the Reagan administration, along with fairly sharp increases in military spending, illustrate that however one identifies an increment, cuts or increases can greatly affect public managers and their agencies (Rubin, 1985). More generally, however, the decision processes of public organizations play out within these larger incremental policy processes. Policy changes that agencies initiate or that influence them involve a complex interplay of political actors tugging and hauling over any significant change.

In fact, these aspects of the governmental context lead to prescriptions for using incremental approaches as the most feasible alternative. Charles Lindblom's (1959) article "The Science of Muddling Through" represents the classic statement of this perspective. He notes that the requirement for political consensus and compromise results in vague goals for public policies and programs. In addition, public administrators carrying out these policies must maintain political support through public participation and consensus building. They have to remain accountable to elected officials who usually have less experience than they themselves. As a result, stated goals and ends for policies provide little clarity, and means become inseparable from ends. Administrators find it difficult or politically unacceptable to state a precise societal impact at which a program aims. They must identify a package of means and ends that can achieve political consensus and support. Far-reaching, original procedures and goals evoke particularly strong opposition and usually must be modified if support is to be maintained. In addition, the need for political support often outweighs such criteria as efficiency and substantive impact. Thus, in formulating their packages of means and ends, administrators must strive for satisfactory decisions — that is, they must satisfice — after examining a relatively limited set of alternatives. Often they rely heavily on past practice. A good deal of intelligence may enter the decision process through involvement of many groups, experts, and officials. Generally, however, the approach involves avoiding major departures and concentrating on relatively limited, politically feasible steps.

One can see why critics worry about the implications of such an approach (Rosenbloom, 1989). It can lead to unduly conservative decisions. It can favor politically influential groups over disadvantaged and less organized groups. Some critics end up calling for some version of greater central control by Congress or the president. The feasibility of these proposals, in turn, comes into question (Lindblom, 1977; Lowi, 1979).

Mixed Scanning. Etzioni (1967, 1986) proposes an approach aimed at reaching a compromise between the extreme versions of rational decision making and incrementalism. He argues that administrators and other officials make both decisions with large-scale, long-term implications and decisions of more limited scope. The latter often follow major directions already selected in the former. Etzioni suggests that decision makers strive through mixed scanning to recognize the points at which they concentrate on broader, longer-range alternatives and those at which they focus on more specific, incremental decisions within major directions. Decision makers need to mix both perspectives, taking the time to conduct broad considerations of many major issues and alternatives to prevent the shortsightedness of incrementalism. Yet these broad scans would not involve all the comprehensive analysis required by highly rational models. More intensive analysis would focus on decisions within areas of pressing need.

Logical Incrementalism. Quinn (1980) suggests a pattern of logical incrementalism in which long-range strategic decisions set a framework for incremental steps aimed at carrying out the broader objectives. Focused mainly on business corporations, the approach involves careful consideration of long-range, general priorities for the firm. Implementing these priorities, however, involves limited, experimental steps. Decision makers must recognize that the priorities need adaptation and that compromise remains important. These suggestions are consistent with some prescriptions for successful large-scale change in organizations discussed in Chapter Ten.

An Incremental Model of Decision Processes Within Organizations. Political scientists usually apply the concept of incrementalism to broad public policy and consider decisions within government organizations only by implication. Mintzberg, Raisinghani, and Theoret (1976) studied twenty-five major decisions in organizations and formulated an incremental decision process model. The model depicts decisions, even major ones, as involving numerous small, incremental steps, moving through certain general phases. During this process, "decision interrupts" can occur at any of the incremental steps, causing the process to cycle back to an earlier point. The identification phase involves recognition of the problem and diagnosis of it through information gathering. Then, in the development phase, a search process that identifies alternatives is followed by design of a particular solution. Finally, in the selection phase, the solution is evaluated, and through an authorization step the organization makes a formal commitment to the decision.

This process seldom flows smoothly. "Decision interrupts" at any of the steps make the decision process choppy and cyclical, rather than smooth and carefully directed. An internal interruption may block diagnosis of a problem. Even when a solution has been designed, a new option may pop up and throw the process back. For example, a new executive may come in and refuse to authorize a decision otherwise ready for implementation, or an external interruption such as a governmental mandate may cause higher executives to push a proposal back for further development.

The Garbage Can Model

The tendency to regard major organizational decisions as complex and dynamic rather than smoothly rational now dominates the management literature. It reaches its apex in the garbage can model. The garbage can metaphor comes from the observation that decisions in organizations are made when particular decision opportunities or requirements arise. Like garbage cans, these instances have a diverse array of material cast into them in disorderly fashion. As noted above, James March participated in research validating Simon's observations about constrained rationality in organizational decisions (Cyert and March, 1963). In addition, March and his colleagues also observed that organizational decisions involve much more internal political activity than generally supposed, with extensive bargaining and conflict among coalitions (March, 1962; Pfeffer, 1982).

These observations evolved into the garbage can model. It holds that in organizational decision processes, participation, preferences, and technology (know-how, techniques, equipment) are ambiguous, uncertain, and rapidly changing. Organizations tend to be "loosely coupled" (Weick, 1979; March and Olsen, 1986): The members and units have loose control and communication with each other. It is often unclear who has authority to decide what and for whom. In addition, people may loosely engage even with very important issues, because other matters preoccupy them. People come and go in the organization and in decision settings such as committee assignments. Problems and potential solutions also come and go, as conditions change. Choice opportunities also come up—a committee may look for decisions to make, or a manager may look for work to do. A solution may go looking for a problem: A promising alternative may become available that virtually begs for some type of application, or a person or group may have a pet technique that they want to find a way to use. Thus, problems, decision participants, solutions, and choice opportunities flow along in time relatively independent of each other.

Decision making occurs when these elements coincide in a way that is conducive to a decision—the right problem arises when the right decision participants are receptive to an available solution, all coming together in a choice opportunity. The model emphasizes that the linkages between these elements are more temporal than consequential; that is, they result as much from coincidence as from rational calculation (March and Olsen, 1986).

The model has considerable intuitive appeal, since anyone who has worked in a complex organization knows of chaotic or accidental decisions. In addition, a number of studies have found that the model accurately depicts decision processes in a variety of organizations. March and Olsen (1986) stress that they intend the model not as a replacement for other perspectives on decision making but as a supplement to them, thus implying that they do not claim that it perfectly accounts for all decision processes and contexts. They do not rule out relatively rational approaches in certain instances. In addition, they point out that the model does not imply that all decisions involve unavoidable bedlam and chaos. Dominant values and norms, historical contexts, and other factors can guide or bias decisions in systematic ways. They also suggest guidelines for relatively purposeful action by managers in garbage can settings, to which we return in Chapter Seven.

The proponents of the model do not state very clearly just where and when it applies. Early on in their theoretical work, they suggested, without explaining, that the model applies mainly to public and educational organization (March and Olsen, 1976; Cohen, March and Olsen, 1972). Most of the applications apparently have concentrated on educational and military organizations and courts. Yet at times they also suggest that it applies to business firms and generally to all organizations (March and Olsen, 1986, p. 12). Still, the model has important implications for public management. As discussed below, Hickson and others (1986) found that this type of decision process occurs more frequently in public organizations than in private firms.

Managerial Strategy

Although most experts on managerial decision making emphasize the rather chaotic nature of the process, by no means do they deny that managers do and should engage in purposeful, goal-oriented actions. In fact, the topic of strategic management has advanced prominently in recent decades. Strategy *is* purposeful behavior. The term comes from the idea of military strategy, of using the resources and strengths of a military force to achieve goals — military victory, usually — by forming plans and objectives and executing them. The concept is more attractive than similar rubrics, such as planning and business policy, because of this emphasis on assessment of one's own general goals, one's strengths and weaknesses, and the external threats and opportunities that one faces in order to formulate long-term plans and actions for deploying one's forces to best advantage in pursuit of the goals.

Prescriptive Frameworks for Strategic Management

Management consultants and experts propose a variety of approaches for developing strategy. Bryson (1988) concludes that managers can apply all of them in the public sector, although with provisos discussed below. Some of the models, such as that of the Boston Consulting Group, focus on high-level corporate decisions about the relative priority of the corporation's business activities. The Boston Consulting Group's "portfolio model" exhorts executives to treat the mix of business units in a large corporation as if they represented stocks in an individual's portfolio of assets. Executives assess the business units in the corporation on two dimensions — market growth and size of market share. The businesses high on both of these dimensions are "stars." They should receive priority attention and reinvestment of profits. Units with small shares of slow-growing markets — low on both key dimensions — are "dogs" and candidates for divestiture. Mixed situations provide opportunities for strategic shifting of resources. A unit with a high market share in a slowly growing market brings in a lot of money but does not have strong growth prospects. These activities should be treated as "cash cows" and used to provide resources for units that provide growth opportunities. Units in rapidly growing markets but not yet in command of a large share of the market should be considered for infusions of resources from other units, especially the cash cows. The approach sounds cutthroat, but it actually emphasizes *synergy* — the effective meshing of all the activities to produce overall gains beyond what the activities would gain as the sum of their independent operations.

Ring (1988) applies a modified portfolio model to public-sector strategy making. He uses "tractability of the problem" and "public support" as the key dimensions. Where problems are manageable and public support is high, public managers can seek to gain resources that they can then use to deal with more difficult policy problems in settings where public support is high but the problem is very difficult to solve. Where public support and tractability are both low, public managers simply seek to shift priority away from those problems. Similarly, Rubin (1988) suggests that strategic patterns will differ according to whether the time horizon for the policy issue is long or short and whether the policy plays out within a disruptive or an anticipated environment.

Other approaches emphasize different levels and issues (Bryson, 1988). *Strategic planning systems* propose methods for formulating and implementing strategic decisions and allocating resources to back them up across units and levels of an organization. *Stakeholder management* approaches analyze how key stakeholders evaluate the organization and form strategies to deal with each stakeholder. (Stakeholders include individuals or groups who have a major interest in the organization, such as unions, customers, suppliers, and regulators.) *Competitive analysis* approaches analyze major forces acting on an industry, such as the power of buyers and suppliers, the prospects for substitute products, and competition in the markets. The aim is to gain competitive advantage through such strategies as differentiating oneself from competitors and selecting segments of an industry in which one should compete (Porter, 1985). *Strategic issues management* focuses on identifying major issues that appear crucial to the organization's ability to achieve its objective and deciding how a working group in the organization will respond to these issues and resolve them. *Process strategies* and *strategic negotiation* approaches treat strategic decision making as a highly political process and prescribe ways of managing the constant bargaining required. Similarly, *logical incrementalism,* as described earlier, emphasizes the incremental nature of strategic decisions and ways to guide bargaining along a consistent path (for more detail, see Bryson, 1988).

Applications of Strategic Management in the Public Sector

Numerous frameworks for strategic management in the public sector are now available (Bryson, 1988; Bryson and Einsweiller, 1988; Backoff and Nutt, 1988). They focus on such procedures as strategic issue management, stakeholder analysis, environmental scanning, and SWOT analysis (described below). The procedures prescribed by scholars and consultants usually begin with a planning and organizing phase. A "strategic management group" (SMG) typically manages the process and must agree on who will be involved, how the strategic analysis will proceed, and what they expect to achieve. Usually the procedure requires a structured group process and a facilitator—a consultant skilled in helping groups make decisions. The facilitator often asks members of the group to list their views about important points, such as stakeholders, opportunities, and threats. Then the group follows a procedure for synthesizing their views, such as the nominal group technique described in Chapter Eight.

The SMG usually begins with a preliminary assessment of the history and current status of the organization to produce a general statement of the organization's mission, such as those provided in Table 4.1. Bryson (1988) suggests that for public organizations, this step requires a careful review of *mandates* for the organization—the requirements imposed by external authorities through legislation and regulations. This review can clarify what external authorities dictate and can also provide insights about new approaches. For example, representatives of a public hospital who interpret their mandate as forbidding competition with private health services may find upon review that they have the authority to do so.

Table 4.1. Mission and Value Statements of Public Agencies.

Social Security Administration

Mission. The mission of the Social Security Administration is to administer equitably, effectively, and efficiently a national program of social insurance as prescribed by legislation.

Operating Priorities. The mission translates into six operating priorities:

- Maintain the fiscal integrity of the Social Security trust funds.
- Improve public confidence in Social Security and how its programs are operated.
- Provide the best possible service to SSA's customers.
- Improve management to facilitate greater effectiveness, efficiency, and accountability.
- Use the best and most appropriate technology available to administer SSA programs.
- Continue to insure that SSA can count on a properly skilled and highly motivated workforce.

Two underlying principles guided the formulation of the strategic plan:

- Commitment to current beneficiaries of Social Security programs.
- Commitment to those who work for the Social Security Administration.

Strategic Recommendations: The plan presents 29 strategic recommendations for improvements in program simplification, service delivery, technology, and organization and human resources.

Internal Revenue Service

Mission. The purpose of the IRS is to collect the proper amount of tax revenues at the least cost to the public, and in a manner that warrants the highest degree of public confidence in our integrity, efficiency, and fairness. To achieve that purpose, we will:

- Encourage and achieve the highest possible degree of voluntary compliance in accordance with the tax law and regulations.
- Advise the public of their rights and responsibilities.
- Determine the extent of compliance and the causes of noncompliance.
- Do all things needed for the proper administration and enforcement of the tax laws.
- Continually search for and implement new, more efficient and effective ways of accomplishing our Mission.

Strategic Initiatives. The plan describes 55 strategic initiatives in the following areas:

- Balancing Efficiency and Effectiveness (Examples: Expand contracting of office automation and data processing services. Monitor public opinion. Identify and measure effectiveness goals.)
- Strengthening Voluntary Compliance (Examples: Establish a research project on withholding noncompliance. Conduct a survey of nonresponsive taxpayers. Strengthen training for IRS examiners.)
- Enhancing Recruitment and Retention of Employees. (Examples include initiatives in employee counseling, physical fitness, child care, rules of conduct, pride, involvement, and productivity, recruiting and training.)
- Developing an Information Management Strategy. (Examples: Establish an information resources management function. Establish an information systems planning process.)

Table 4.1. Mission and Value Statements of Public Agencies, Cont'd.

Alabama Division of Rehabilitation and Crippled Children Service
"Blueprint for the Future": Values and Goals

I. We value the worth, dignity, and rights of persons with disabilities.
  Goals:
  1. Provide quality services which lead to quality outcomes, giving priority to persons with severe disabilities.
  2. Involve advocates and persons with disabilities in agency planning and policy development.
  3. Advocate the rights of persons with disabilities.
II. We value the contribution of all staff in achieving our mission.
  Goals:
  1. Recruit, employ, and promote qualified staff.
  2. Establish open and honest communication.
  3. Provide staff opportunities for personal and professional growth.
  4. Establish realistic performance and productivity standards.
  5. Reward exemplary job performance.
  6. Encourage staff creativity and innovation.
III. We value an agency management style that provides opportunities for staff participation.
  Goals:
  1. Develop an agency management philosophy that promotes creativity and innovation.
  2. Provide management development opportunities for agency management staff.
  3. Promote an agency management style that encourages teamwork among all staff.
  4. Promote an agency management style that encourages greater staff participation in agency decision making.
IV. We value maximum acquisition and the efficient and effective management of resources.
  Goals:
  1. Acquire maximum financial and other resources.
  2. Increase legislative support.
  3. Develop a management information system to measure the effective and efficient use of our resources.
  4. Develop and use appropriate technological resources.
V. We value public support.
  Goals:
  1. Inform the public of our mission and our goals.
  2. Develop partnerships with business and industry.
  3. Encourage greater staff commitment to and responsibility for development of community-based agency support.

Sources: U.S. Department of Health and Human Services (1988); U.S. Department of the Treasury (1984); Stephens (1988).

Working toward the mission statement, the SMG typically reviews trends in the operating environment, using a framework like those described in Chapter Two. It may also conduct a stakeholder analysis at this point and develop idealized visions of how it wants the organization to be in the future. Ultimately, the mission statement expresses the general purpose of the organization and major values and commitments.

Next, the SMG members assess the strengths and weaknesses of the organization and look outward to the environment and to the future to identify opportunities and threats facing the organization. This assessment of strengths, weaknesses, opportunities, and threats is called a SWOT analysis. The SMG can choose from an array of techniques for this analysis (Backoff and Nutt,

1988). A typical approach involves the independent listing and nominal group technique described above. From the SWOT analysis, the SMG develops a list of *strategic issues*—conflicts among opposing forces or values that can affect the organization's ability to achieve a desired future (Backoff and Nutt, 1988). Then the group develops plans for managing these issues (Nutt and Backoff, 1987; Ring, 1988; Eadie, 1989). A wide variety of public-sector organizations now use this approach to strategic planning (Bryson, 1988; Boschken, 1988; Wechsler and Backoff, 1988).

Analytical Research on Managerial Strategy in the Public Sector

In addition to recommending procedures, researchers have studied the strategies that public organizations actually pursue and how strategic decisions actually develop. Some of these studies show the effects of government ownership on strategy. In their study of strategic decisions in thirty British organizations, Hickson and others (1986) found that strategic decision-making processes in public organizations, in both service and manufacturing functions, differed from those in private service and manufacturing firms. The public organizations follow a "vortex-sporadic" decision process. This involves more turbulence, more shifting participation by a greater diversity of internal and external interests, more delays and interruptions, and more formal and informal interaction among participants. The type of decision and the service-manufacturing distinction also made a great difference. The results, however, indicate that the public-sector context does impose on internal strategic decisions the sorts of interventions and constraints described in earlier chapters.

Mascarenhas (1989) studied 187 public and private offshore drilling firms in thirty-four countries to analyze their strategic domains (markets served, product type, customer orientation, and technology applied). The government-owned firms operated mainly in domestic markets, with narrow product lines and stable customer bases. Publicly traded private firms (those whose stock is traded on exchanges) are larger, operate in many geographical markets, and offer a wider range of products. Privately held private firms were more like the state-owned firms but had less stable customer bases. The nationality and size of the firms also made a big difference, but the ownership distinctions persisted even with controls for those factors. The results support the point mentioned in Chapter Two, that public organizations tend to have greater constraints on their strategic domains.

Other studies analyze important variations in strategy within the public sector. Wechsler and Backoff (1986) studied four state agencies in Ohio and found that they pursued four types of strategy. The Department of Natural Resources followed a *developmental* strategy. This agency had diverse tasks, constituency groups, and independent funding sources. The managers had relative independence to pursue a strategy of enhancing the capabilities, resources, and general performance of the organization. Stronger external forces shaped the *transformational* strategy of the Department of Mental Retardation. Professional experts and legal rights groups advocated deinstitutionalization of the mentally retarded — getting them out of large hospitals and into normal living conditions. The agency also faced constant budgetary pressures. It responded by transforming itself from a manager of hospitals to a monitor and regulator of client services delivered through community-based programs and contracts. The Department of Public Welfare received intense criticism in the media and from legislators and faced increasing human service needs and potential cutbacks in funding. The managers followed a *protective* strategy. They strengthened internal controls, lowered the agency's public profile ("getting the agency out of the newspapers"), mended relations with legislators, and worked to protect funding levels. The Public Utilities Commission, which regulates utility pricing decisions, adopted a *political* strategy. Nuclear energy issues and increasing fuel prices led to more political activity by consumer advocates. The agency's decisions became more favorable to consumers, reflecting a shift in response to changing configurations of stakeholders.

Boschken (1988) found that a private-sector model of strategic variations applied well to government enterprises. Miles and Snow's (1978) prominent typology suggests that *defenders* react to stable environments by trying to protect their hold on their markets and their customers, emphasizing efficiency and centralization. *Analyzers,* operating in moderately changing contexts, take a similar approach but seek to innovate moderately, allowing looser control of the innovative efforts. *Prospectors* in contexts of growth and dynamism seek opportunities and take risks, employing more decentralized and organic management. *Reactors* may appear in any context. They simply drift without clear purpose, responding to conditions as they arise. Boschken (1988) found this framework useful in analyzing the strategic behaviors of port authority organizations for various cities on the West Coast. Public authorities fall between public agencies and business firms. Nevertheless, the study suggests that the very general frameworks for the private sector can be useful in government.

These studies show that strategic orientation varies considerably among public organizations. Public managers, like private managers, engage in a variety of purposeful efforts to respond to their environments and to achieve objectives. This general perspective stands in sharp contrast to the negative stereotypes of public managers as passive and inattentive to long-term purposes that often get drawn into respectable academic theory. The research and writing also suggest that we can develop generalizations about power, decision, and strategy in the public sector.

Issues for Managers and Researchers

There are more observations about the general features of the public sector context than consensus about how to deal with the variations within it. The assertions about the general characteristics of public organizations that distinguish them from their private counterparts can be summarized as follows: There are more political intrusions into management in public organizations and a greater infusion of political criteria. A more elaborate overlay of formal, institutional constraints governs the management process, involving more formal laws, rules, and mandated procedures and policies. Goals and performance criteria are generally more vague, multiple, and conflicting for public organizations. Economic market indicators are usually absent, and the organizations pursue idealized, value-laden social objectives. The public sector must handle particularly difficult social tasks, often under relatively vague mandates from legislative bodies. Public organizations must jointly pursue all of the complex goals described earlier — accountability, responsiveness, representativeness, openness, efficiency, and accountability.

The literature on power in organizations reminds us that power is elusive and complex and that thinking too excessively in terms of power relations can be deluding. Yet the best intentioned of managers have to consider means of exerting influence for the good ends that they seek. We now have a considerable literature on the power of bureaucracies in general, with a growing set of case studies of effective public managers and how they gain and use influence within the political system (Olshfski, 1990; Doig and Hargrove, 1987; Allison, 1983; Lewis, 1980; Kotter and Lawrence, 1974). We do not, however, have many studies of large samples of public managers that analyze their power and influence within the system and what causes variations in it. Both managers and researchers, then, face the question of what to make of the current state of knowledge on this topic.

Pulling together the material from organization theory and political science allows for some suggestions. For one thing, public administrators apparently face relatively sharp constraints on their power and influence as a result of their particular context. High-level executives such as politically elected executives and appointed cabinet officers must share authority over their administrative units with legislators and other political authorities. Their authority over their subordinates and organizations is constrained by rules and procedures imposed by other units, such as those governing civil service procedures, purchasing, procurement and space-allocation decisions, and budgeting decisions. At lower managerial levels, managers' authority is further overshadowed by the stronger formal authority and resource control of the other institutional units. Kingdon (1984) reports a survey in which federal officials rated the president and Congress as having much more influence over the policy agenda than administrative officials.

Within this disadvantaged setting, however, officials have varying degrees of influence. Given the organizational power literature and the bureaucratic power literature, one would expect that administrative officials, although always subject to the shifting tides of political, social, and technical developments, have greater influence under the following conditions:

- When they play important roles in relation to major policy problems and issues related to obtaining resources for the agency — when they are in key budgetary decision-making roles and in policy areas central to the agency's mandates and to the support of major constituencies.
- When they have effective political support from committees and actors in the legislative branch, in other components of the executive branch, and in interest and constituency groups.
- When they have strong professional capabilities and credentials. Some agencies are dominated by a particular professional group, such as attorneys, foreign service officers, police officers, or military officers. Managers without strong credentials and abilities in these specializations will need other strengths, such as excellent preparation and reputation as generalist managers.
- When they have excellent substantive knowledge of government and its operations and institutions (for example, the legislative and administrative law processes) and of the policies and programs of the agencies in which they work.
- When they achieve or have the capacity to achieve a reputation for general stature and competence, including energy, intelligence, integrity, and commitment to serving the public.

Public managers have to consider these power and influence issues because they are directly related to the autonomy and authority that they exercise in decision processes and to the nature of the decision process itself. The debate over incrementalism in the public policy process, including the observations within that debate about vague legislative mandates to agencies, as well as the observation by the garbage can modelers about the application of that framework to public and educational organizations, suggests more political intrusions and institutional constraints on decisions in public organizations. Executives who have had experience in business and government echo these observations (Perry and Kraemer, 1983).

More explicitly, Ring and Perry (1985) synthesized literature and research on the context of management strategy for public organizations and came to a similar conclusion. They found that existing research and observation indicate that public-sector strategic decision making takes place under such conditions as the following:

- Policy ambiguity (policy directives are more ill-defined than for business firms).
- Greater openness to participation and influence of the media and other political officials and bodies and greater attentiveness from a more diverse array of them.
- More artificial time constraints due to periodic turnover of elected and appointed officials and mandated time guidelines from courts and legislatures.

- Shaky coalitions or relative instability of the political coalitions that can be forged around a particular policy or solution.

Besides the implications of the political science literature and these observations, recent research increasingly validates this general scenario. A number of studies show more constraints, interruptions, interventions, and external contacts in the public sector. Porter and Von Maanen (1983) compare city government administrators with industrial managers and find that the city administrators feel that they have less control over how they allocate their own time, feel more pressed for time, and regard demands from people outside the organization as a much stronger influence on how they manage their time. The study by Hickson and others (1986) described earlier emphasizes the more turbulent pattern of participation, delay, interruption, and participation in public sector decision making.

Ring and Perry (1985) also suggest some of the consequences of this context for strategic management. They say that in public-sector strategic decision processes, managers are more likely to have to follow incremental decision patterns, with strategies more likely to be emergent than intended — that is, these managers will have to shoot for more limited objectives, and strategic decisions and directions will more likely emerge from the process than follow some originally intended direction. More effective managers will maintain greater flexibility in their orientation toward staff assignments and controls and avoid premature commitments to a given set of objectives. They will have to straddle competing demands for efficiency, equity, high moral standards, and political responsiveness to constituent groups by showing open-mindedness, shunning dogmatism, and skillfully integrating competing viewpoints. They must effectively "wield influence rather than authority" and minimize discontinuities in the process. These suggestions from Ring and Perry are noticeably similar to suggestions about the nature of garbage can management but give more explicit attention to the external political context in which major decisions in public organizations are embedded.

The question of political influences on decisions raises one final implication of the organizational literature on decision making: the contingencies that determine whether decisions must be less structured and systematically rational. As illustrated in earlier examples, many decisions in public organizations are not pervaded with politics and institutional constraints but take place much as they might in a business firm. Yet researchers on public management have not clarified when such contingencies occur. A challenge facing practitioners and researchers alike is the clarification of where, when, and how deeply this political environment affects decision processes. Managers appear to have more encapsulated, internally manageable decision settings, where rational decision processes are often more appropriate, when tasks and policy problems are clear, routine, and tractable; at levels of the organization and in geographical locations that are remote from political scrutiny; when issues are minimally politically salient or enjoy consistent public support; when legislative and other mandates are clear as opposed to "fuzzy" (Lerner and Wanat, 1983); and when administrative decision makers gain stronger authority to manage a situation autonomously, without political intervention. Given the present state of research and knowledge, researcher and managers alike have to struggle to analyze such variations in decision contexts to determine the most appropriate approaches.

This theme of appropriately assessing and managing the political context in relation to other organizational contingencies comes up again in later chapters. In the next chapter, we address additional issues about structure and technology in public organizations, issues that are related to decision and influence processes within the political environment and that in turn relate to later questions about human behavior and performance in public organizations.

Chapter 5

Organizational Structure, Design, and Technology

Management researchers use the term *structure* to refer to the configuration of hierarchical levels and specialized units and positions, and the formal rules governing these arrangements. They use *technology* and *task* to refer to the work processes of the organization, especially in terms of their variability and certainty. The topic of structure has played a central role in organization and management theory from the beginning. Researchers also have analyzed technology and task as important considerations in finding the best structure. In spite of the constraints on them, public managers have considerable authority over structure and make many decisions in relation to tasks, so current thinking on these topics is important to effective public management.

This chapter first discusses the fascinating division of opinion about whether public organizations have distinctive structural characteristics, such as more red tape than experienced in private organizations. It then discusses the importance of structure and its relation to political power, strategy, and other topics. Next, it describes major concepts and points from the research on organizational structure, technology, and design by organization theorists. Organization theorists have done the most to analyze organizational structure, but they have usually addressed it from a generic perspective and devoted little attention to distinctive attributes of the structures of public organizations, even though some of their important studies concentrated on public agencies. Their general points apply to most organizations, however, and the discussion gives examples involving public organizations. The chapter concludes by turning more directly to the evidence about whether public organizations differ in structure and design.

Novelists, essayists, and popular stereotypes bemoan the absurdity and inhumanity of governmental bureaucracy, often focusing on structural matters such as rigid rules and hierarchy. More formal scholarship often agrees. In a virtual tradition among some economists, governmental bureaucracy plays the role of villain, sometimes as a threat to prosperity and freedom (Von Mises, 1944). In probably the most widely cited book on bureaucracy ever published, Downs (1967) argues that governmental bureaucracy inevitably moves toward rigidity and hierarchical constraint. He states a "law of hierarchy" that holds that large government organizations, with no economic markets for their outputs, have more elaborate and centralized hierarchies than do private business firms, which sell their outputs on economic markets. Downs's "law" represents a broad consensus that governmental bureaucracy has exceedingly complex rules and hierarchy, even as compared to large private-sector organizations (Dahl and Lindblom, 1953; Lindblom, 1977; Barton, 1980; Sharkansky, 1989). Yet, intriguingly, an opposite consensus also exists. While most organization theorists do not regard public organizations as distinctive, their research on structure offers the most specific and well-developed concepts. Much of the research that analyzes public organizations' structures and compares them to private organizations draws on these concepts and measures. We will first consider the generic ideas and how they apply to public organizations; we can then look at the comparative evidence with a clear sense of how this topic has developed.

The Development of Research on Structure

Although interest in the topic of structure has recently faded somewhat among organization theorists (Hall, 1987), structure has always played a major role in management because of its implications for power, authority, decision making, strategy, leadership, motivation, and efficiency and effectiveness.

We have already seen many examples of political actors' and governmental authorities' influence on the structures of public agencies: rules and clearances imposed on federal managers by oversight agencies; micromanagement by legislators who specify rules and organizational structure; legislators and interest groups jealously guarding the structural autonomy of an agency, preventing its reorganization under the authority of another; President Reagan demoting the federal career civil servants by creating new positions above them. Additional examples abound. The U.S. Department of Education was separated from the former Department of Health, Education, and Welfare in part because education interest groups wanted an independent agency over which they could exert more influence. Presidents have created new agencies and placed them outside of existing agencies to keep them away from the political and administrative coalitions of those agencies (Seidman and Gilmour, 1986). John Kennedy placed the Peace Corps outside the State Department, and Lyndon Johnson kept the youth employment training programs of the Office of Economic Opportunity away from the Department of Labor.

Interestingly, however, early in this century, public administration experts who helped lead the development of the field left political dynamics out of the analysis. Luther Gulick and others in the administrative manage-ment school advocated such administrative "principles" as highly specialized, clearly described task assignments (when people specialize, they become very well versed in what they have to do and therefore better at it); clear chains of command and authority relationships, with "unity of command" where each person has "one master"—one supervisor—so that each person has clear directions; a centralized authority structure, with authority residing mainly at the top of the organization; and narrow "spans of control" to help main-tain clear lines of authority (a span of control is the number of subordinates reporting to a superior, and a narrow span of control means relatively few people reporting to any given supervisor).

These principles were to guide decisions about structure that would maximize efficiency and performance. Although later criticized and aban-doned, this drive for principles of efficient, effective structure drew energy from important issues in government at the time. A reform movement in the later part of the nineteenth century and the earlier decades of the twen-tieth attacked governmental corruption and mismanagement, particularly at the urban level. Reformers saw principles to guide efficient structuring of organizations as a means of purging political patronage and slovenly man-agement (Fesler, 1975; Stone and Stone, 1975).

Later, governmental growth during the New Deal and after World War II brought a vast proliferation of governmental agencies. Gulick and other proponents of the principles influenced major proposals for reorganizing the sprawling federal bureaucracy and played an important role in major developments in the structure of the federal government in this century (Stone, 1990). For example, some of the reforms proposed grouping vari-ous federal agencies under larger "umbrella" agencies as a means of nar-rowing the chief executive's span of control. Some experts feel that many government officials still hold the general view of proper organization that the administrative management school espoused (Warwick, 1975; Seidman and Gilmour, 1986). Their proponents argued that the principles of adminis-tration applied equally well in government and in business organizations. After all, the object was to make government more efficient, more business-like, and less "political."

In spite of its prominent role and insights that later critics underesti-mated (Hammond, 1990), the classic approach to organizational structure came under criticism as research on organizations burgeoned during the middle of the twentieth century (see the Introduction and the Appendix for more detail). The major developments in the study of organizational struc-ture began to come from sociologists and business management research-ers. Many of them regarded political institutions as only one among many factors influencing organizations. The contingency perspective on organi-zational structure, based on studies such as those by Burns and Stalker (1961) and Lawrence and Lorsch (1967), held that organizations do not and should not all follow one model of organizational structure but that structure must be adapted to key contingencies facing the organization, such as environmental variation and uncertainty, the demands of the "technology" or production process, the size of the organization, and strategic decisions by managers and coalitions within the organization.

A profusion of empirical studies in the 1960s and 1970s added to this perspective, seeking to define and measure structural concepts (Hall, 1968; Hage and Aiken, 1969; Pugh, Hickson, and Hinings, 1969) and contingency concepts. Major studies attempted to develop typologies of organizations, emphasizing their structural characteristics (Haas, Hall, and Johnson, 1966; Pugh, Hickson, and Hinings, 1969) and analyzing such factors as the role of organizational size (Pugh, Hickson, and Hinings, 1969; Blau and Schoenherr, 1971), joint programs among government agencies (Hage and Aiken, 1969), and the strategic choices of managers (Child, 1972). Many of these studies focused on government agencies, although they gave virtually no attention to whether their governmental status had anything to do with their structural properties (Argyris, 1972). In the 1970s, research journals were filled with empirical studies analyzing these concepts and debates over their meaning and adequacy—and the adequacy of contingency theory itself. The activity led to the fairly typical version of contingency frameworks that we will examine next and to the topic of *organizational design,* which we will take up after that.

Structural Dimensions and Influences

Researchers trying to work out clear definitions and measures of structure have run into many complications. For example, you can measure structural features objectively, by counting numbers of rules, or subjectively, by asking people how strictly one must follow the rules. In addition, organizations can be very complex, with different units having markedly different structures, making it hard to develop an overall measure of structure for the organization.

Dimensions of Structure

While the issue is a complex one, research has produced concepts that help to clarify the topic of structure. Researchers typically use such dimensions as the following to define organizational structure.

Centralization. The degree of centralization in an organization is the degree to which power and authority concentrate at higher levels of the organization. Some researchers measure this with questions about the location of decision-making authority, such as whether decisions have to be approved at higher levels.

Formalization. This dimension is the extent to which the organization's structure and procedures are formally established by written rules and regulations. Some researchers have measured this with questionnaire items asking employees how much they have to follow established rules, whether they must go through "proper channels," and whether a rule manual exists (Hage and Aiken, 1969). Others determine whether the organization actually has organization charts, rule manuals, and other formal instructions (Pugh, Hickson, and Hinings, 1969).

Complexity. Organizational complexity is measured in terms of the number of subunits, levels, and specializations in an organization. Researchers break this dimension down into subdimensions (Hall, 1987). Organizations vary in *horizontal differentiation,* or the specialized division of labor across subunits and individuals. Some researchers simply count the subunits and individual specializations in the organization (Blau and Schoenherr, 1971; Meyer, 1979). *Vertical differentiation* refers to the number of hierarchical levels—the "tallness" or "flatness" of the organization's structure.

Influences on Structure

The research has also analyzed a number of factors that influence organizational structure, concentrating on the following ones.

Size. Various studies that have included public organizations show that larger organizations tend to be more structurally complex than smaller ones, with more levels, departments, and job titles (Pugh, Hickson, and Hinings, 1969; Blau and Schoenherr, 1971). Blau and Schoenherr also concluded, however, that the rate at which complexity increases with size falls off at a certain point, where organizations grow larger without adding new departments and levels as rapidly. In addition, this research indicates that larger organizations tend to have less administrative overhead. So, contrary to stereotypes and popular books about bureacracy (Parkinson, 1957), larger organizations often have smaller percentages of their personnel in administrative work.

Argyris (1972) criticized the findings of some studies of size as they are related to public organizations. He noted that Blau studied government agencies controlled by civil service systems and drew conclusions as if the results applied to *all* organizations. Civil service regulations may have caused the organizations to emphasize task specialization and narrow spans of control and thus grow in the patterns that Blau observed. Business organizations might not, however. In contrast to the findings of Blau and Schoenherr (1971) in a study of state employment agencies, Beyer and Trice (1979), studying a set of federal agencies, found no strong relationship between size and vertical and horizontal differentiation—the number of levels and divisions. Ultimately, they concluded that increased size increases the division of labor, which in turn increases vertical and horizontal complexity. In addition, these relationships were stronger in federal units doing routine work than in those doing nonroutine work. Thus, larger public organizations tend toward somewhat greater structural complexity (more levels and subunits, greater division of labor). Much larger organizations almost certainly show more complexity than much smaller ones, but the effects of size are not clear-cut.

Other researchers have reported further evidence that size has little clear influence on structure. Reviewing this research, Kimberly (1976) pointed out that size is actually a complex variable with different components, such as number of employees and net assets. Since different researchers use different measures of size, it is difficult to consolidate their findings and draw conclusions from them.

Environment. Chapter Two showed that the organizational environment dominates many of the current analyses of organizations and their structures, including the contingency perspective. One of the central arguments of this perspective is that a formalized, centralized structure may operate well enough in a simple, stable environment, where it can take advantage of specialization and clear patterns of communication and authority. As the environment presents more changes and more uncertainty, however, strict rules, job descriptions, and chains of command become more cumbersome, unable to change and process information rapidly enough. Therefore, rules and assignments have to become more flexible. Communication needs to move laterally among people and units, and not strictly up and down a hierarchy. People working at lower levels must be given more authority to decide, without having to ask permission up the chain of command. As the environment becomes more fragmented, the organization must reflect this complexity in its own structure, with people in units to confront these segments, who have the authority to respond to conditions there. Although somewhat outdated, this general perspective still exerts a great influence on current prescriptions for managers (Peters, 1988; Daft, 1989).

More recent approaches, such as institutionalization models, suggest that organizations adopt rules and structural arrangements because of prevailing beliefs about their appropriateness or because of influences from external institutions such as government. As we have seen, a number of researchers have advanced claims and evidence about the effects on structure of governmental ownership and funding.

Technology and Task. A number of studies indicate that structure also depends on the nature of the work processes, or the technologies and tasks, of the organization. Researchers use a wide variety of definitions of technology and task, such as the interdependence required by the work and the routineness of the work. The effects on structure depend on which of these definitions one uses (Tehrani, Montanari, and Carson, 1990).

In a much-respected book, Thompson (1967) analyzes technology in terms of the type of *interdependence* among workers and units that the work requires. Organizations such as banks and insurance companies have *mediating* technologies. They deal with many individuals who need largely the same set of services, such as checking accounts or insurance policies. Their work involves *pooled* interdependence because it "pools" together such services and sets of clients. They establish branches that have little interdependence with each other and formulate standardized rules and procedures to govern them. *Long-linked technologies,* such as typical assembly-line operations, have a *sequential* pattern of interdependence. One unit completes its work and passes the product along to a next unit, which completes another phase of the work, and so on. Plans and schedules become a more important form of coordination for them. Units with *intensive* technologies have a *reciprocal* pattern of interdependence. The special units in a hospital or a research and development laboratory need a lot of back-and-forth communication and adjustment in the process of completing the work. These units must be closer together and coordinated through more mutual adjustment and informal meetings. Analyzing many studies of structure, Tehrani, Montanari, and Carson (1990) found some support for Thompson's observations. The studies tended to find that organizational units with high interdependence were much less likely to have a lot of standardized work procedures.

Public organizations often follow these patterns. The Social Security Administration operates regional service centers around the country that take in claims from clients applying for their Social Security coverage— mediating technologies. For a long time, the agency also processed the claims through a long-linked technology. (Thompson points out that in many organizations, different units have different technologies.) When the service center forwarded the claim to the main installation in Baltimore, one large unit performed one phase of processing the claim (adjudication), then passed it to another (disbursement), and so on. As Social Security eligibility became more complex, however, the people working on different parts of the claim needed more and more communication about the cases. This created backlogs as they sent cases back and forth between units. As Chapter Ten describes, the agency reorganized to establish modular work units, which brought people from the different phases together in the same unit. They could communicate and adjust more rapidly—a more intensive technology. Other factors besides work processes influenced the reorganization, but Thompson's ideas about interdependence clearly apply.

Perrow's (1973) analysis of technology, the most frequently cited, argues that work processes vary along two main dimensions: the frequency with which exceptions arise and the degree to which these exceptions are analyzable (that is, can be solved through a rational, systematic search). If a machine breaks down, often a clear set of steps can lead to fixing it. If a human being breaks down psychologically, usually few systematic procedures lead as directly to diagnosis and treatment.

Organizational technologies can rank high or low on either of the two main dimensions. *Routine* technologies involve few exceptions and provide clear steps in response to any that occur (high analyzability). In such cases, the work is usually programmed through plans and rules, since there is little need for intensive communication and individual discretion in doing the work. For examples of routine technology, researchers usually point to the work of many manufacturing personnel, auditors, and clerical personnel. At the opposite extreme, nonroutine technologies involve many exceptions, which are less analyzable when they occur. Units and organizations doing this type of work tend toward flexible, "polycentralized" structures, with power and discretion widely dispersed and with much interdependence and mutual adjustment among units and people. Units engaged in strategic planning, research and development, and psychiatric treatment apply such nonroutine technologies.

Between these extremes, Perrow suggests two intermediate categories, *craft* technology and *engineering* technology. Craft technology involves infrequent exceptions but no easily programmed solutions when they occur. Government budget analysts, for example, may work quite routinely but with few clear guidelines on how to deal with the unpredictable variations that arise, such as unanticipated shortfalls. These organizations tend to be more decentralized than those with routine technologies. Engineering technology involves many exceptions but analyzable responses to them. Engineers may encounter many variations, but often they can respond in systematic, programmed ways. Lawyers and auditors often deal with this type of work. When an Internal Revenue Service auditor examines a person's income tax return, many unanticipated questions come up about whether certain of the person's tax deductions can be allowed. The auditor can resolve many of the questions, however, by reference to written rules and guidelines. Organizations with engineering technologies tend to be more centralized than those with nonroutine technologies but more flexibly structured than those with routine technologies. Tehrani, Montanari, and Carson (1990) also found support for Perrow's observations. The studies they analyzed found that organizational units with routine technologies had more formal rules and procedures and fewer highly educated and professional employees.

Perrow's analysis clearly has applications to public organizations. In a study of state employment agencies, Van de Ven, Delbecq, and Koenig (1976) used questionnaire items about task variability and task difficulty based on Perrow's work. The questions asked about how much the work involves the same tasks and issues, how easy it is to know whether the work is done correctly, and similar issues. The researchers found relationships between the structures and coordination processes in organizational units and the nature of their tasks. Some units, such as clerical claims-processing units, had tasks low in uncertainty (low in variability and difficulty), more plans and rules, fewer scheduled and unscheduled meetings, and relatively little horizontal communication among individuals and units. Units with high task uncertainty, however, such as employment counseling units, relied less on plans and rules and had more scheduled and unscheduled meetings and more horizontal communications. Units that were intermediate on the task dimensions fell in the middle ranges on the structural and coordination dimensions. So, in many government agencies, in spite of the external political controls, subunits tend toward more flexible structures when they have uncertain, nonroutine, variable tasks.

Yet Perrow himself pointed out that organizations doing the same work can differently define the nature of it. Job Corps training centers for disadvantaged youths in the 1960s were first operated by personnel from the U.S. Office of Economic Opportunity, who adopted a nurturant approach to running the centers. Serious disciplinary problems led to the transfer of some of the centers to the Department of the Interior. The centers more and more emphasized strict rules and discipline and highly structured routines and procedures. The same organization in effect altered its definitions of its task. Similarly, many organizations have purposely tried to transform routine work into more interesting, flexible work to better motivate and utilize the skills of the people doing it. The Social Security Administration changed to modular work units partly for such reasons.

Also complicating the analysis of technology, various studies found weak relationships between structure and technology, sometimes finding that size influences structure more than technology does. Recent studies also suggest that technology shows stronger effects on structure in smaller organizations than in larger ones (Tehrani, Montanari, and Carson, 1990). Similarly, the effects of task characteristics on structure are strongest within task subunits; that is, the task of a bureau within a larger organization has a stronger relationship to the structure of that bureau than to the structure of the larger organization. Size shows stronger effects on the structure of government agencies with routine technologies than on structures of agencies with nonroutine technologies (Beyer and Trice, 1979). In sum, size, technology, structure, and other factors have complex interrelationships.

Strategic Choice. As discussed in Chapters Two and Four, managers' strategic choices also determine structure. Managers may divide up the organization into divisions and departments designed to handle particular markets or products that have been chosen for strategic emphasis. Product divisions described below are one example. The Florida Department of Health and Human Services adopted a district structure, with district directors in charge of the department's activities in different geographic areas of the state. The aim, in part, was to create divisions which would be more responsive to the particular needs of the different parts of the state.

Organizational Design

The work on contingency theory led to the development of literature on organizational design and the structuring of organizations in which authors sought to develop guidelines for managers and others engaged in designing organizations (Galbraith, 1977; Khandawalla, 1977; Mintzberg, 1979, 1983; Daft, 1989). These authors usually treat public organizations as if they have no special distinctiveness, but many of their concepts apply in public management.

Design Strategies

Jay Galbraith (1977) proposes a set of design alternatives for coordinating activities in organizations that is based on an information-processing approach. Organizations face varying degrees of uncertainty, according to how much more information they need than they actually have. As this uncertainty increases, the organizational structure must process more information. Organizations employ a mix of alternative modes for coordinating activities. They first use *hierarchy of authority,* where superiors direct subordinates, answering their questions and specifying rules and procedures to reduce the information-processing load. As uncertainty increases, it overwhelms these approaches. The next logical strategy, then, is to set *plans and goals* and allow subordinates to pursue them with less referral up and down the hierarchy and with fewer rules. They can also narrow *spans of control,* so that superiors deal with fewer subordinates and can process more information and decisions.

Many contemporary organizations operate under such great uncertainty that these basic modes become overloaded, so that they must pursue additional alternatives. First, managers can try to reduce the need for information. They can engage in *environmental management* to create more certainty through more effective competition for scarce resources, public relations, and cooperation and contracting with other organizations. They can create *slack resources* (that is, create a situation in which they have extra resources) by reducing the level of performance that they seek to attain or create *self-contained* tasks, such as profit centers or groups working independently on individual components of the work. Alternatively, managers can increase information-processing capacity by investing in *vertical information systems,* such as better computerized management information systems, or by creating *lateral relations,* such as task forces or liaison personnel. Thus, managers have to adopt coordination modes in response to greater uncertainty and information-processing demands.

Mintzberg's Synthesis

Mintzberg (1979) presents one of the most comprehensive reviews of the literature on structure, summarizing the set of structural alternatives that managers can pursue. He begins by setting forth his own scheme for describing the major components of organizations. Organizations have an *operating core,* including members directly involved in the basic work — police officers, machine operators, teachers, claims processors. The *strategic apex* consists of the top managerial positions — the board of directors, chief executive officer, president, and president's staff. The *middle line* includes the managers who link the apex to the core through supervision and implementation — the vice-presidents down through the supervisors. Finally, two types of staff units complete the set of components. The *technostructure* consists of analysts who work on standardizing work, outputs, and skills — the policy analysts and program evaluators, strategic planners, systems engineers, and personnel training staff. The *support staff* units support the organization outside the work flow of the operating core — for example, mailroom, food service, and public relations.

Design Parameters. Organizations establish structures to divide and then coordinate the work within and among these units through four categories of design activity: designing positions, superstructures, lateral linkages, and decision-making systems.

   Design of Positions. Individual positions can be established through *job specialization, behavior formalization* (written job descriptions, written work instructions, general rules), and *training and indoctrination* in which individuals learn the skills that they will apply using their own judgment.

   Design of Superstructure. Then the different positions must be coordinated through the design of the superstructure. All organizations do this in part through *unit grouping,* based on any of a number of criteria: knowledge and skill (lawyers, engineers, social workers); function (police, fire, and parks and recreation employees, military personnel); time (night shift, day shift); output (product divisions of business corporations); clients (inpatients or outpatients, or survivors' insurance recipients or disability insurance recipients); or place (the regional structure of business firms, of the federal government, and of many state agencies; the precinct structure of the New York City Police Department).

   Managers choose among these bases or some combination of them. We have little conclusive scientific guidance for those choices, but Mintzberg offers suggestions about *criteria for grouping.* Choices about grouping can follow *work-flow interdependencies,* where natural phases in the work require certain people to closely communicate or to be located near each other. *Process interdependencies* make it useful to group together people doing the same type of work (attorneys, claims eligibility experts) so that they can learn from each other and share tools and materials. Because of *scale interdependencies,* certain units may become large enough to need their own members of the functional categories — their own attorneys, for example. Also, *social interdependencies* may make it useful to group individuals to facilitate social relations, morale, and cohesiveness. Military units often are trained and kept together for these reasons.

   Design of Lateral Linkages. Coordination also requires linking operations laterally, or across the barriers between units. Managers can design *planning and control systems* through either *performance-control systems* or *action-planning systems.* Performance-control systems specify general results. For example, the Social Security Administration sets objectives for reducing overpayments of claims by a certain percentage; the Internal Revenue Service sets goals for reducing the time a taxpayer must wait for help; the Forestry Service sets goals for timber sales. In spite of these examples, a common generalization about public organizations claims that they tend to use action-planning systems, in which the actions that people are to take are specified in detail.

Liaison Devices. A liaison position might involve having an "ambassador" from one unit assigned to track developments in another, and to facilitate communication. Task forces or standing liaison committees can also address problems of coordination.

Designing Decision Systems Through Decentralization. Organizations can also decentralize. *Vertical decentralization* involves pushing decision-making authority down to lower levels. *Horizontal decentralization* involves spreading authority out to staff analysts or experts or across individuals involved in the work.

Types of Organizational Structure. Mintzberg also proposes a topology of five types of structure, based on the employment of these design alternatives and shifts in the roles of the components described earlier. *Simple structures* are usually adopted by new, small government agencies, small corporations run by an entrepreneur, and other new, small, aggressive organizations headed by strong leaders. They tend toward vertical and horizontal centralization and coordination by direct supervision from a strong strategic apex. *Machine bureaucracies* include the prototypical large bureaucracies in the public and private sectors. They evolve from simple structures as growth, aging, or external control leads to more emphasis on standardizing the work process. The technostructure becomes more important as experts and staff specialists assume roles in this process. Mintzberg suggests a subcategory of *public machine bureaucracies* — government agencies that assume this form because they are required to standardize for political oversight. Alternatively, simple structures with a strong professional component (law firms, research organizations) evolve toward *professional bureaucracies,* with a profession that dominates their operating cores, coordination primarily through standardization of skills (through professional training) rather than standardization of tasks, and general decentralization. Machine bureaucracies may further evolve into *divisionalized forms* as further growth leads to economies of scale for product-oriented subunits. It becomes more cost effective to break the organization up into product divisions with their own versions of the various functional components — for example, their own manufacturing and marketing divisions. Mintzberg (1989) observes that public machine bureacracies cannot do this. Without profit and sales measures by which their general performance can be monitored, and under more intensive political oversight, public machine bureaucracies face more constraints than their private counterparts on their ability to decentralize to relatively autonomous divisions. Finally, an *adhocracy,* such as NASA or an innovation-oriented firm, has a very organic structure with great emphasis on fluid communication and flexibility, largely through decentralization to project teams.

Major Design Alternatives: Functional,
Product, Hybrid, and Matrix Structures

Management writers also contrast the pros and cons of major design alternatives from which organizations choose (Davis and Lawrence, 1977; Dessler, 1987; Daft, 1989). *Functional* structures, the classical prototype, organize by major functions — marketing and sales, manufacturing, finance, R&D. The advantages include economies of scale within the functional units (all the attorneys in the legal department can use the same law library; the manufacturing personnel share plants and machinery). Departments concentrate on their functions and enhance their specialized skills. Yet this may weaken coordination with other functions to ensure overall product quality and the implementation of needed changes.

As organizations grew and produced more diverse products, competing in more rapidly changing, diverse markets, the functional structure proved too slow in responding to changes and too hierarchical to allow rapid coordination across the functional divisions. Large corporations such as the major automobile manufacturers began to adopt *product* structures with divisions responsible for a product line. Each division contained its own units for major functions such as sales and manufacturing (for example, the Oldsmobile, Chevrolet, and Buick divisions of General Motors). This sacrifices some of the advantages of the functional form but provides for more rapid responses to environmental changes (in product technology, customer demands, competitors) and more concentration on the quality of the products rather than on individual functions. In fact, many corporations actually employ *hybrid* structures, with major product divisions (for example, chemicals, fuels, lubricants; Daft, 1989) but also some major functional units (finance, human resources).

Some firms have developed the *matrix* structure in response to demands for both high-quality products in highly technical areas (product emphasis) and rapid and reliable production (functional emphasis). Military weapons manufacturers, for example, face pressure to produce highly technical weapons systems according to high quality standards and to do so within sharp time constraints. Matrix structures purposely violate the classic prescriptions about "one master" and clear chains of authority. High-level managers share authority over the same activities, with some exercising functional authority (vice-presidents for product development, manufacturing, marketing, procurement) and others having responsibility for the particular products or projects that cross all those functions. Thus, one manager may have responsibility for pushing the priorities for a particular aircraft project, while others share responsibility for the particular functions. The authority of the product executives crosses all the functions, while the functional executives have authority over their functions across all the products. Diagrammed, this appears as a matrix of two sets of executives with cross-hatched authority. This offers the advantage of the ability to rapidly share or shift personnel or other resources across product activities and to coordinate the response to the dual pressures from the environment. Yet it requires a heavy investment in coordination, liaison activities, and conflict resolution. Successful matrix designs often require a good deal of training and good interpersonal skills on the part of managers and typically produce high levels of stress and conflict that must be resolved.

Some structures in the public sector have been equated with matrix structures. Simon (1983) describes the use of a matrix management arrangement at the U.S. Consumer Product Safety Commission. The commission had been organized into functional bureaus, such as the Bureau of Engineering, Bureau of Economics, Bureau of Biomedical Science, and so on. Each bureau had partial responsibility for developing regulations issued by the commission, but none had overall responsibility. The matrix arrangement involved establishing six functional directorates and an Office of Program Management. The Office of Program Management had a program manager for each of a set of new product-oriented programs, including a chemical products program, electrical products program, and children's products program. These program managers chaired program teams that were made up of representatives from the various functional directorates. The teams managed the overall development of regulations for the products their programs were responsible for and coordinated the work of the functional directorates pertaining to those programs. The commission's executives felt that the matrix arrangement improved productivity, morale, effective use of resources, communication, and accountability. As matrix arrangements usually do, it also increased stress and turf battles, and evoked some resistance.

The executive director of the commission observed that public managers face particular challenges in adopting matrix designs. He felt that private executives have more authority over rewards and have profit objectives to use as incentives for cooperation. Public executives have fewer sanctions and weaker authority to reassign those who resist a new design. Here again we see that a design developed in industry has potential value in government, but requires skillful implementation within the constraints imposed by the public-sector context. Swiss (1991) provides examples of the use of matrix organization in city governments.

Actually, structure in industrial organizations shows a great deal of variation, and managers apply heavy doses of pragmatism in working out structures (Webber, 1979). Some large corporations, for example, appoint staff vice-presidents to act as the eyes and ears of the presidents of the various divisions. Complexity and even conflict are built into many contemporary corporate structures. Management experts currently propose that many organizations should adopt highly adaptive permeable, fluid, loosely arranged structures (Peters, 1988).

The function-versus-product distinction is not always clear in government. Are the military, police, firefighters, public works programs, youth services, elderly services, and family services functions or products services?

Generally, however, government agency observers remain wedded to the functional form (Golembiewski, 1987b). Before its reorganization, the Social Security Administration, for example, followed the typical structure of organization by functions—claims intake, claims adjudication, claims disbursement. Demands for accountability, absence of profits and sales measures, and officials' adherence to the old principles of administration (clear chain of command, unity of command, and so on) drive this functional emphasis (Warwick, 1975, Golembiewski, 1987b; Mintzberg, 1989). Golembiewski calls for more efforts to organize around *purpose* in public organizations, through such designs as variants of the matrix form. For example, the Florida Department of Health and Rehabilitative Services established district directors who shared authority over programs in their districts with program officials in the central headquarters. In addition, functions can be organized around a purpose, such as service to clients as individuals. The new modular work units in the Social Security Administration brought the functions together in the units, so that each processes an individual client's claim from beginning to end. The Florida Department of Health and Rehabilitative Services set up service units with representatives of each of the agency's programs—youth services, family counseling, drug treatment programs—in the same location. Developing and assessing such alternatives remain a challenge for public managers and researchers.

Organizational Structure in Public Organizations

The question of alternative designs for public organizations brings us back to whether public organizations have distinctive structures. As mentioned earlier, some academic theories and observations suggest that they inherently differ from private organizations, since governmental oversight and the absence of performance indicators such as sales and profits cause them to emphasize rules and hierarchy. If true, this suggests that public organizations cannot adopt some structural forms, such as decentralized and flexible designs, or that they can do so only with great difficulty. On the other hand, many organization theorists regard government auspices as unimportant, in part because their research has often found little evidence that public organizations have distinctive structures. Pugh, Hickson, and Hinings (1969), for example, predicted that government organizations in their sample would show higher levels of formalization (they used a measure called "structuring of activities") but found that they did not. Over the years, additional studies concurred. Buchanan (1975) also sought to test the proverbial red-tape differences by comparing federal managers to business managers on a "structure salience" scale. Unexpectedly, the public managers reported *lower* perceived salience of structure. Bozeman and Loveless (1987) found that public-sector research and development units differed only slightly from private-sector units on a measure of red tape.

Yet other evidence suggests that public organizations do differ. Although Pugh, Hickson, and Hinings (1969) did not find greater "structuring of activities" in government organizations, those organizations had more concentration of authority at the top of or outside the organization, especially authority over personnel procedures. The researchers concluded that size and technological development act as the main determinants of structuring of activities, and that government ownership exerts an influence independent of size and technology, causing concentration of authority at the top of the organization or with external authorities, especially authority over personnel procedures. The study included only eight public organizations, all local government units with tasks similar to those of many business firms, such as a local water department and a manufacturing unit of a government agency. This might explain why they did not show as much bureaucratic structuring as anticipated. It also indicates, however, the effects of government ownership even on organizations much like business firms. A public manager would probably comment that the researchers simply observed the effects of civil service systems.

Mintzberg (1979) cited this evidence from Pugh, Hickson, and Hinings when he designated public machine bureaucracies as a subtype within the machine bureaucracy category in his typology of structures. He argued that many public bureaucracies tend toward the machine bureaucracy form because of external governmental control. Other studies come to similar conclusions. Warwick (1975) concluded from his case study of the U.S. State Department that public bureaucracies inherently incline toward elaborate hierarchy and rules. Meyer (1979) analyzed a national sample of state and local finance agencies and found their vertical hierarchies very stable over time. Political pressures forced frequent changes in their subunit composition, however, and pressures from the federal government led to formalization of their personnel systems. He concluded that public bureacracies have no alternative to elaborate hierarchy. Their managers' political strength and skill, however, determine how well they can defend their organizations from external forces that can strip away subunits for assignment to some other department.

Holdaway, Newberry, Hickson, and Heron (1975) found that in Canadian universities, higher degrees of public control are related to higher levels of formalization, standardization of personnel procedures, and centralization. Chubb and Moe (1990) reported that public school employees perceive more externally imposed formal constraints on personnel procedures and school policies than do private school employees. Rainey's (1983) sample of middle managers in state agencies perceived more organizational formalization, particularly on items pertaining to going through channels and standard operating procedures, than did middle managers in business firms. This study and a number of others found that government managers report much stronger constraints on administration of extrinsic rewards such as pay and promotion under the existing personnel rules for their organizations than do business managers. Chapter Six cites various studies that have found this difference at all levels of government. Also indicating the effects of government auspices on personnel procedures, Tolbert and Zucker (1983) showed how federal pressures influenced the diffusion of civil service personnel systems across governments in the United States.

Studies by professional associations and government agencies, and the testimony of public managers paint a similar picture. The National Academy of Public Administration (1986) report laments the complex web of controls and rules governing federal managers' decisions and their adverse effects on the managers' capacity and motivation to manage. The report complained that managers in charge of large federal programs often face irritating limits on their authority to make even minor decisions. The head of a program involving tens of millions of dollars might have to seek approval of the General Services Administration before he or she can send some assistants to a short training program. Very large surveys of federal employees find that a large percentage of the managers and executives say that they do not have enough authority to remove, hire, promote, and determine the pay of their employees. Large percentages also feel that personnel and budgeting rules create obstacles to productivity (U.S. Office of Personnel Management, 1979, 1980, 1983). Executives who have served in business and government say similar things about the constraints on their authority in government positions resulting from overarching rules and oversight agencies (Allison, 1983; Blumenthal, 1983; Chase and Reveal, 1983).

These studies and reports provide increasing evidence that government auspices influence structure in a number of ways, particularly regarding rules and structural arrangements over which external oversight agencies have authority, such as personnel and purchasing regulations. Bozeman and Bretschneider (1989) provide explicit evidence of these patterns. They analyzed research and development laboratories on the basis of public and private ownership and amount of government funding. The government labs had highly structured personnel rules. The private labs did not, even when they received high levels of government funding. They did, however, receive more contacts and communications from government officials when they received more public funding. This suggests that governmental funding brings with it a different pattern of governmental influence than does governmental ownership. Ownership brings with it the formal authority of oversight agencies to impose rules of the jurisdiction, usually governing personnel, purchasing, and accounting and budgeting. Bretschneider (1990) provided more evidence in an analysis of decisions about computer systems in public and private organizations. Managers in the public organizations experienced longer delays in getting approval to purchase computer equipment and in the processing of those purchases. The delays apparently reflect the procurement rules supervised by central procurement agencies such as the General Services Administration. In sum, these studies provide evidence, consistent with the pattern that began to emerge with the Pugh, Hickson, and Hinings (1969) study, that government ownership often subjects organizations to central oversight rules over such matters as personnel, purchasing, and budgeting and accounting.

Researchers also find structural features of public organizations that are not tied to rules imposed by oversight agencies. Tolbert (1985) found differences in subunit structures of public and private universities that are related to external influences from public and private institutions and the universities' dependence on them for resources. Crow and Bozeman (1987) and Emmert and Crow (1987, 1988) report that public research and development units differ from private units on such structural features as administrative intensity and research team organization. The public labs actually had more team-based organization. This again emphasizes that government organizations vary a great deal, and by no means do they all follow a rigid bureaucratic pattern. In fact, these government labs appear to respond more directly than the private labs to task contingencies of the sort discussed earlier.

The Macrostructure of Public Organization

The evidence of governmental influences on the structures of public organizations also brings up a structural topic that needs much further development in our body of knowledge, among both researchers and managers. Structure *within* public organizations does not easily separate from governmental structure *outside* the organization. The structures of agencies reflect, in part, *jurisdictional structures,* or the structural characteristics of the government under whose auspices the agency operates. Legislatures, oversight agencies, and other institutions impose systemwide rules and configurations on agencies within their jurisdiction (Warwick, 1975; Meyer, 1979; Hood and Dunsire, 1981).

The examples above show that external authorities often directly impose rules and structural configurations on agencies. Federal managers point out, however, that the oversight structures influence their own decisions about structure. When they start a new venture or unit, they often have to fit the new positions into the federal job classification system maintained by the U.S. Office of Personnel Management. They must assign each new person within one of those classifications, even if that person does not fit any of the categories very well. Similarly, at one point in Florida, bureaus — relatively small units — proliferated rapidly within state agencies. Apparently to escape the constraints of the state's pay system, managers got raises for their assistants by creating bureaus and appointing the assistants as bureau chiefs. To curb this tendency, the Department of Administration, the agency in charge of personnel systems, adopted regulations governing when an agency could establish a bureau. This instance illustrates a constant tension in governments at all levels between the oversight agencies and the operating agencies. The former emphasize relatively uniform rules, often for good reasons, such as fairness and equal treatment (such as preventing unequal pay for the same work in different agencies). Yet this imposes on other agencies overarching structures that dominate their own and constrain their managers in their efforts to respond to their own problems.

In addition, different units of government differ in the structural arrangements of their major institutional entities, such as their formal, constitutional powers (Abney and Lauth, 1986). In some states, the governor has less formal power than in others, and the legislature has more formal authority. The governor of Florida, for example, appoints fewer of the cabinet officers of the state government than do governors in other states. Instead, some run for independent election, and the agencies that they head tend to have more independence from the governor than in other states. Similarly, Meyer (1979) found that independently elected heads of finance agencies more effectively defend the structures of their agencies against the loss of subunits than do political appointees. At local levels, different cities have different structures for the authority of mayors, city councils, and city managers. In strong-mayor forms, the mayor is elected by the citizens, appoints department heads, and has veto power over some of the actions of the city council. In weak-mayor forms, the mayor may appoint few of the department heads, have no veto over the council, and share authority for the administration of the city with the council. In the council-manager form, there may not even be a mayor; if there is, he or she is not elected by the people but is rather a member of the council serving on a rotating basis with other council members, with the city administrative duties largely under the authority of the city manager who is accountable to the council. Macrostructural arrangements such as these shape the capacity of the authorities in a jurisdiction to impose structure on particular agencies.

Another important macrostructural dimension involves structural relations between jurisdictions. Different units at the same level may engage in joint activities or agreements. For example, large federal and state agencies share responsibility for programs and have joint policy-making committees. Local units of government now engage in elaborate relationships with other units of government through regional councils, areawide planning agencies that link a number of counties, and service agreements and contracts between local governments for provision of services such as police and water. In addition, special districts for services such as these, like the traditional school districts, are proliferating rapidly around the country, operating within and between other jurisdictions, such as counties. The field has no term for these structural arrangements, but we might call them *lateral interjurisdictional structures*. Similarly, the complex relations among levels of government, well recognized under the topic of *intergovernmental relations,* involve structural issues that need better development. The federal government implements many programs through state and local governments. Federal rules, grants, or other funding patterns essentially pay the states and localities to hire people and establish offices to run the programs under federal guidelines. Thus, the structure of many federal agencies meshes with other agencies at so-called lower levels of government. We might refer to these structural arrangements as *vertical interjurisdictional structures*.

Complications such as these have been recognized in a large body of work on intergovernmental relations, public policy implementation (for example, Lester, Bowman, Giggin, and O'Toole, 1987), and interorganizational relations (Whetten, 1987). Yet we need to know much more about how these macrostructural complexities are related to the structures of particular agencies and to many other topics in public management. Even pending that, however, the obvious characteristics of this complex macrostructural terrain support the observation that public organizations operate in larger structures that heavily influence their own.

Summing Up the Structural Literature

The researchers on organizational structure who reject a public-private distinction have shown us that structure is multidimensional and that both types of organization vary widely on different structural dimensions. Often these variations are related to the major contingencies of size, strategy, technology and task, and environmental uncertainty and complexity. Obviously, technological similarities cause government-owned electric utilities, hospitals, railroads, airlines, R&D labs, and manufacturing units to show stronger structural similarities to private or nonprofit versions of the same types of organizations than to other types of government organizations. The same holds true for internal offices and units in public, private, and hybrid organizations engaged in a particular task, such as internal research and development labs or legal offices. Their general structures often resemble those of private-sector counterparts more than those of other units in the same parent organization. Also, relatively small, independent organizations usually have simpler structures (Mintzberg, 1979), so that a smaller unit of government may have quite a bit less red tape or hierarchical complexity than a large private firm. Obviously, government agencies respond to environmental complexities and uncertainties as well, as reflected in district structures. Thus, we can see that it is dangerously oversimplifying to treat all public organizations as a uniform mass, inherently subject to intensive red tape and bureaucracy. These researchers rightfully condemn such stereotypes.

Other research, including that on macrostructure and governmental environments, supports a balanced conclusion. This research suggests that public organizations generally tend toward higher levels of internal structural complexity, centralization, and formalization than do private organizations. Size, task, technology, and environmental contingencies make a difference, often figuring more importantly than public or private auspices. Within given task categories, however, public versions tend toward more stable hierarchies and more centralized and formalized rules, especially rules pertaining to the functions governed by oversight agencies—personnel, purchasing and procurement, and budgeting and accounting. Very general measures of red tape and complexity may not reflect large differences between public and private organizations because of the multidimensionality of structure. Government organizations may not have more formalized and elaborate rules than private organizations of similar size, but they often have more centralized, formalized rules for functions such as personnel and procurement. Comparisons of governmental and nongovernmental organizations engaged in the same type of work tend to support such conclusions.

Still, wide variations are likely — R&D labs or other special units may have even more general structural flexibility under government auspices. In addition, governmental ownership and influence are multidimensional, in that hybrid organizations such as public enterprises may be owned by government but privately funded and exempt from some central rules and controls. Privately owned organizations with extensive public funding often show heavy governmental influences on certain aspects of their structures; for example, defense construction firms have small armies of governmental auditors located within them, applying governmental regulations to their spending and record-keeping patterns. Here again, governmental rules tend to flow with governmental ownership or funding.

Finally, researchers point out that typical government agencies that are fully owned and funded by government (as opposed to public enterprises or other hybrids), especially at the federal level, often engage primarily in administrative functions — making and enforcing regulations, administering grants, contracts, and transfer payments, administering programs actually provided at other levels of government or in the private sector. Others point out that the absence of fairly concrete or quantifiable performance measures for many public and nonprofit activities makes governmental managers and officials rely more on rules as means of managing their organizations. Also, this inclines public and nonprofit organizations to adopt particular forms and structures because they represent the widely accepted way of doing the work or the way authorized by higher levels of government or professional associations, and this becomes more influential where technologies and performance measures are vague.

All managers must deal with structural complexity and with external influences on their authority. Public managers, however, usually face more elaborate structural arrangements and constraints and must learn to work with them. Their understanding of the elaborate macrostructural patterns in government, of the structures of their own agencies, and of the origins and purposes of these arrangements can serve as a valuable component of their professional knowledge as public managers. Among other challenges, they must find ways to reward and encourage people working with these complex structures, even when personnel systems do not readily provide much flexibility. The next chapter further considers that topic. They need to understand the sources and nature of these constraints, not only as part of their own adjustment to them but also as ways of considering the useful changes that they can hope to make. Later chapters discuss how public managers can and do make valuable changes, in part through effective knowledge of the structure of government and its agencies and in part through effective applications of the general body of knowledge on organizational structure that we have just covered.

Chapter 6

The Individual
in the Organization:
Values, Motivation,
and Work Attitudes

Motivation is the central topic in the field of organizational behavior and one of the most sensitive challenges facing public managers. Many organizational behavior researchers treat motivation as an internal organizational matter, influenced by such factors as supervisory practices, pay, and the nature of the work. Such factors figure very importantly in public organizations. Motivation in public organizations, however, opens interesting issues about the effects on organizational behavior of the political and nonmarket environment discussed in earlier chapters.

Many surveys find that citizens regard public employees and organizations as inefficient and wasteful (Volcker Commission, 1989). Politicians, editorialists, and cartoonists repeatedly echo this impression. In 1990, Gary Larson's popular cartoon "The Far Side" depicted a government employee who made civil service history by going to work for a couple of hours on a holiday. A manager with the U.S. Drug Enforcement Administration mentioned in an interview the following day that the cartoon really bothered him, since he felt that he and others in his office worked very hard. Such reactions are not isolated. Many surveys of government managers find that their perceptions of the public image of government influence their motivation and thoughts on leaving the public service (U.S. Merit Systems Protection Board, 1987; Volcker Commission, 1989; Perry and Miller, 1990).

More tangible impacts occur as well. Chapter Three described the public outcry that halted the proposed pay increase for federal executives and officials, and recent reforms of civil service systems at all levels of government. Those reforms sought to correct allegedly weak linkages between

119

performance and pay, promotion, and discipline in government — these weak linkages allegedly weaken motivation. Yet these reforms came about not just because of public attitudes but because government managers for years have complained about their weak authority over their subordinates' pay, promotion, and discipline (Macy, 1971; U.S. Office of Personnel Management, 1983). The reforms also reflect, then, the constraints on public managers that earlier chapters have described. The fact that such reforms have foundered or backfired (Sherwood and Wechsler, 1986; Perry, Petrakis, and Miller, 1989), raises the possibility that these constraints are inevitable in the public sector. Many analysts and experienced practitioners regard the constraining character of governmental personnel systems as the critical difference between managing in the public and private sectors (Thompson, 1989).

As with other topics in this book, however, another side argues that government differs little from business in matters of motivation. Businesses also have problems motivating managers and employees, including union pressures, selfish and unethical behaviors, and ineffective bonus and merit-pay systems. In addition, there are indications of high motivation in many government organizations. Executives coming to government from business typically mention how impressed they are with how hard government employees work (Volcker Commission, 1989). In surveys, government managers mention frustrations of the sort mentioned above but also report high levels of work effort and satisfaction.

This chapter takes the position that both sides are right, in a sense. Public managers often face unique motivational challenges, but those of us interested in public management can apply a great deal from the general motivation literature. This chapter first reviews claims that the public sector is a distinct context for motivation. As with previous topics, the management and organizational behavior literature offers the most careful analyses of motivation and related topics. From that perspective, many of the claims about motivation in public management appear oversimplified and need clarification. The chapter therefore reviews the coverage in the organizational behavior literature of individual motives and values, theories and techniques of motivation, and topics such as work satisfaction, role perceptions, organizational commitment, and professionalism. The coverage of these topics considers how they apply in public organizations. It shows that we now have a good deal of evidence about the effects on motivational issues of the governmental context, as well as some studies that fail to support some of the claims about those effects. The chapter then examines what we know about some special issues for public management, such as public-service motivation, as well as what we do *not* know.

The Context of Motivation in Public Organizations

Previous chapters presented observations and research findings that suggest a unique context for motivation in public organizations (Perry and Porter, 1982). The chapters on environments described external influences on public organizations that can affect motivation:

- The absence of economic markets for outputs of the organizations and the consequent diffuseness of incentives and performance indicators.
- The multiple, conflicting, and often abstract values that public organizations must pursue.
- The complex, dynamic political and public-policy processes in which the organizations operate, involving many actors, interests, and shifting agendas.
- The external oversight institutions and processes that impose structures, rules, and procedures on the organization. These include civil service rules governing pay, promotion, and discipline and rules that affect training and personal development.
- The external political climate of attitudes toward taxes, government, and government employees, which turned sharply negative during the 1970s and 1980s.

The earlier chapters have also related these conditions to characteristics of public organizations that in turn influence motivation:

- Sharp constraints on leaders and managers that limit their motivation and ability to develop their organizations. Politically elected and appointed top executives and their appointees turn over rapidly. Institutional oversight and rules limit their authority. People at lower levels can develop external political alliances with interest groups and legislators, which can enhance their independence.
- The relatively turbulent, sporadic decision processes in public organizations that can influence managers' and employees' sense of purpose and impact (Hickson and others, 1986).
- Relatively complex and constraining structures in many public organizations, including constraints on administration of incentives.
- As a result of the preceding factors, greater vagueness of goals for individual jobs and for the organization, weakened sense of personal significance within the organization, more unstable expectations, and less cohesive collegial and work groups (Buchanan, 1974, 1975; Perry and Porter, 1982). Many observers argue that people at the lower and middle levels of the organization often become lost in the elaborate bureaucratic and public-policy system. They work under elaborate rules and constraints, which paradoxically fail to hold them highly accountable (Warwick, 1975; Barton, 1980; Lipsky, 1980; Michelson, 1980; Lynn, 1981).
- Differences in the type of people who choose to work in public management, in view of the constraints on pay and the performance of public services.

Some of these observations are difficult to prove or disprove. For others, we have increasing evidence. When we examine the evidence, however, it is important to consider how organizational researchers have treated motivational issues.

The Concept of Work Motivation

These observations about the public sector often seem facile to people familiar with the topic of motivation. A substantial body of theory, research, and experience provides a wealth of insight into motivation in organizations. Yet, in scrutinizing the topic, scholars have more and more shown its complexity. Everyone has a sense of what we mean by *motivation*. The term derives from the Latin word for *move*, as do the words *motor* and *motif*. We know that forces move us, arouse us, direct us. Work motivation refers to a person's desire to work hard and work well. Managers in public, private, and nonprofit organizations use motivational techniques all the time. Yet debates about motivation have raged for years, because the simple definition just given actually leaves many questions about what it means to work hard and well, how one measures such behavior, and what determines a person's effort to do so.

Researchers have found many determinants and dimensions of motivation, to the point where it now serves more as a general topic with many subtopics than as an individual concept. In an authoritative review, Campbell and Pritchard (1983) point out that among organizational psychologists, *motivation* increasingly serves as a general label for determinants of the choice and direction of work efforts and their amount and persistence. They also point out that motivation serves as one among many determinants of performance, which also depends on ability, leadership, work-group influences, knowledge of the task, and other factors. For a long time, they have distinguished between the motivation to join and stay in an organization and the motivation to work hard and well within it (March and Simon, 1958). The former often depends more on work satisfaction, the latter on whether rewards depend on performance. (This distinction becomes important when we interpret findings about public organizations below.)

Measures of Motivation

Another reason that motivation serves more as a broad topic than a precise variable is that researchers have great difficulty measuring it, especially through questionnaire items. Given the importance of motivation, researchers have developed surprisingly few measures of it. Patchen (1965) developed a scale of motivation that has been used in some of the research on public organizations described later. The scale contains questions about how often time seems to drag on the job, how often employees do some extra work that is not really required, and whether they work harder, less hard, or about the same as others doing the same type of work in the organization. Landy and Guion (1970) developed scales on which a person's peers in an organization rate that person on various dimensions of motivation: team attitude, task concentration, independence and being a self-starter, organizational identification, job curiosity, persistence, and professional identification. These measures require a lot of time and resources if many peers are to rate each person, and they show the multidimensional complexity of motivation. Cook, Hepworth, Wall, and Warr (1981) review 249 different measures of work experiences, only a few of which pertain to motivation. Most of those concern internal or intrinsic work motivation, involving questionnaire items asking people to report on how much satisfaction, pride, and enjoyment they get from doing their work. In sum, there are no conclusive measures of motivation, and this complicates interpretation of findings on public organizations.

What Do People Want?
Needs, Values, Motives, and Incentives

An important dimension of motivation is the internal impetuses and external attractions that arouse and direct effort — what needs, motives, and values push us and what incentives, goals, and objectives pull us. Every theory of work motivation, including those we discuss below, refers to these factors in some way. Classic debates have raged, however, over what to call them, what the proper set includes, and what roles they play (Staw, 1984).

Motivation theorists use a variety of terms to refer to human purpose, such as *need, value, motive, incentive, objective,* and *goal.* Different writers define these terms in overlapping ways, but one can suggest definitions that distinguish among them. For example: A *need* is a resource or condition required for the well-being of the individual. A *motive* is a force acting within an individual that causes him or her to seek to attain or avoid some external object or condition. An *incentive* is an external object or condition that evokes behaviors aimed at attaining or avoiding it. A *goal* is a future state that one strives to achieve, and an *objective* is a more specific, nearer-term goal, a step toward a more general, longer-term goal. Rokeach, an authority on human values, defines a *value* as "an enduring belief that a specific mode of conduct or end-state of existence is personally or socially preferable to an opposite or converse mode of conduct or end-state of existence" (Rokeach, 1973, p. 5).

Many people would disagree with these definitions and switch some of them around. The challenge for public managers, however, is to develop a sense of the range of values, motives, incentives, and goals that influence employees, even in view of all the quandaries that researchers raise. The research on motivation tells us to expect no simple list, since goals, needs, values, and motives always occur in complex sets and relationships. They are linked together in time, generality, and significance — one value takes on importance as a means to a more general or important other one. They are also embedded in sets, where one pursues all members of the set simultaneously. Herbert Simon (1973) pointed out years ago that any particular goal always comes as a member of a set of goals, all of which we try to optimize concurrently. We want more pay, but not if it costs us our friends, damages our health, and so on. These complications leave motives, needs, and so on full of ongoing riddles for everyone, managers included, but they cannot be ignored. Critics of the civil service reforms described earlier claim that the reforms failed because they treated too simplistically the complex of motives and incentives in the public service and concentrated too narrowly on material incentives and control-oriented management.

Attempts to Specify Needs, Values, and Incentives

Tables 6.1 and 6.2 present some of the prominent lists and typologies of needs, motives, values, and incentives. These lists illustrate the complexities and diversity among theorists and provide some of the most useful enumerations ever developed.

Murray's Typology of Human Needs, for example, provides one of the more elaborate inventories of needs ever attempted but still fails to exhaust all possible ways of expressing human needs and motives.

Maslow's Need Hierarchy, one of the most prominent theories of human needs, has significantly influenced the field of management. Maslow proposed five categories of need, arranged in a "hierarchy of prepotency." This means that certain needs take precedence until satisfied to an acceptable level. Then the individual concentrates on the next higher level of need, and so on. *Physiological needs* for relief from hunger, thirst, and sleepiness and for defense from the elements dominate behavior if they are not satisfied. Next are *safety needs,* which include the need to be free from the threat of bodily harm. *Social needs* include love, affection, and belongingness. *Esteem needs* include the need for a sense of achievement, confidence, recognition, and prestige. The highest order of needs, the *self-actualization* needs, involve the desire to become everything that one is capable of becoming, to achieve self-fulfillment. According to Maslow, ths type of need leads individuals to seek fulfillment in a particular role or life goal, such as through excellence as an executive, a professional, or an artist.

Researchers trying to determine whether individuals rank their needs as the theory predicts have found that Maslow's five-level hierarchy does not hold (Campbell and Pritchard, 1983). The evidence indicates a two-step hierarchy: Lower-level employees show more concern with material and security rewards, while higher-level employees place more emphasis on achievement and challenge (Lawler, 1973; Pinder, 1984). Alderfer's (1972) typology of existence, relatedness, and growth (ERG) needs comes closer to the more limited categories supported by research.

This distinction between higher- and lower-order motives holds in public organizations. Surveys show that public employees attach more importance to job security and benefits, while public managers and executives say that they consider these factors less important than accomplishment and challenging work. Managers coming into government often say that they are attracted by the opportunity for public service and for influence on significant events. At the same time, as described below, prominent motiva-

As of Fall 2000,
the Riverside Community College
Library/Learning Resources will
charge fines for overdue materials!

Riverside City Campus Library
(909) 222-8651

Norco Campus Library
(909) 372-7019

Moreno Valley Campus Library
(909) 485-6112

Fines
General collection and Daily Reserve
20 Cents per day, per item

Hourly reserves
$1.00 per hour, per item

Maximum overdue fine
$20.00 per item

Library Privileges will be suspended
When a patron owes $25
Or a replacement bill is issued

Renewals
Bring books to circulation desk,
in person with library card
No phone renewals!

Patrons **must** have library card
To check out library materials
Or use Internet PC's!

Access the library's web page at:
http://rcclamp.rccd.cc.ca.us

Table 6.1. The Complexity of Human Needs and Values.

Murray's (1938) List of Basic Needs	Maslow's (1954) Need Hierarchy	Alderfer's (1972) ERG Model	Rokeach's (1973) Value Survey — Terminal Values	Instrumental Values
Abasement	Self-actualization needs	Growth needs	A comfortable (prosperous) life	Ambitious (hard-working, aspiring)
Achievement	Esteem needs	Relatedness needs	An exciting (stimulating, active) life	Broadminded (open-minded)
Affiliation	Belongingness social needs	Existence needs	A sense of accomplishment (lasting contribution)	Capable (competent, effective)
Aggression	Safety needs		A world at peace (free of war and conflict)	Cheerful (lighthearted, joyful)
Autonomy	Physiological needs		A world of beauty (of nature and the arts)	Clean (neat, tidy)
Counteraction			Equality (brotherhoood, equal opportunity for all)	Courageous (standing up for one's beliefs)
Defendance			Family security (taking care of loved ones)	Forgiving (willing to pardon others)
Deference			Freedom (independence, free choice)	Helpful (working for the welfare of others)
Dominance			Happiness (contentedness)	Honest (sincere, truthful)
Exhibition			Inner harmony (freedom from inner conflict)	Imaginative (daring, creative)
Harm avoidance			Mature love (sexual and spiritual intimacy)	Independent (self-reliant, self-sufficient)
Nurturance			National security (protection from attack)	Intellectual (intelligent, reflective)
Order			Pleasure (an enjoyable, leisurely life)	Logical (consistent, rational)
Play			Salvation (eternal life)	Loving (affectionate, tender)
Rejection			Self-respect (self-esteem)	Obedient (dutiful, respectful)
Sentience			Social recognition (respect, admiration)	Polite (courteous, well-mannered)
Sex			True friendship (close companionship)	Responsible (dependable, reliable)
Succorance			Wisdom (a mature understanding of life)	Self-controlled (restrained, self-disciplined)
Understanding				

Table 6.2. Types of Incentives.

Incentive Type	Definitions and Examples
Barnard (1938)	
Specific incentives	Incentives "specifically offered to an individual"
Material inducements	Money, things, physical conditions
Personal, nonmaterialistic inducements	Distinction, prestige, personal power, dominating position
Desirable physical conditions of work	
Ideal benefactions	"Satisfaction of ideals about nonmaterial, future or altruistic relations" (pride of workmanship, sense of adequacy, altruistic service for family or others, loyalty to organization, esthetic and religious feeling, satisfaction of hate and revenge)
General incentives	Incentives that "cannot be specifically offered to an individual"
Associational attractiveness	Social compatibility, freedom from hostility due to racial, religious differences
Customary working conditions	Conformity to habitual practices, avoidance of strange methods and conditions
Opportunity for feeling of enlarged participation in course of events	Association with large, useful, effective organization
Condition of communion	Personal comfort in social relations
Simon (1948)	
Incentives for employee participation	Salary or wage, status and prestige, relations with working group, promotion opportunities
Incentives for elites or controlling groups	Prestige and power
Clark and Wilson (1961) and Wilson (1973b)	
Material incentives	Tangible rewards that can be easily priced (wages and salaries, fringe benefits, tax reductions, changes in tariff levels, improvement in property values, discounts, services, gifts)
Solidary incentives	Intangible incentives without monetary value and not easily translated into one, deriving primarily from the act of associating
Specific solidary incentives	Incentives that can be given to or withheld from a specific individual (offices, honors, deference)
Collective solidary incentives	Rewards created by act of associating and enjoyed by all members if enjoyed at all (fun, conviviality, sense of membership or exclusive-collective status or esteem)

Table 6.2. Types of Incentives, Cont'd.

Purposive incentives	Intangible rewards that derive from satisfaction of contributing to worthwhile cause (enactment of a law, elimination of government corruption)
Downs (1967)	
General "motives or goals" of officials	Power (within or outside bureau), money income, prestige, convenience, security, personal loyalty to work group or organization, desire to serve public interest, commitment to a specific program of action
Niskanen (1971)	
Variables that may enter the bureaucrat's utility function	Salary, perquisites of the office, public reputation, power, patronage, output of the bureau, ease of making changes, ease of managing the bureau, increased budget
Lawler (1971)	
Extrinsic rewards	Rewards extrinsic to the individual, part of the job situation, given by others
Intrinsic rewards	Rewards intrinsic to the individual and stemming directly from job performance itself, which satisfy higher-order needs such as self-esteem and self-actualization (feelings of accomplishment and of using and developing one's skills and abilities)
Herzberg, Mausner, Peterson, and Capwell (1957)	
Job "factors" or aspects. Rated in importance by large sample of employees.	In order of average rated importance: security, interest, opportunity for advancement, company and management, intrinsic aspects of job, wages, supervision, social aspects, working conditions, communication, hours, ease, benefits
Locke (1968)	
External incentive	An event or object external to the individual which can incite action. (Money, knowledge of score, time limits, participation, competition, praise and reproof, verbal reinforcement, instructions)

tion theorists argue that employees at all levels can be motivated by higher-order motives and should be treated accordingly. Chapter Ten describes how that philosophy played a role in a reorganization of the Social Security Administration.

Another application of Maslow's theory in public organizations comes from researchers using measures of need satisfaction based on Maslow's hierarchy. Comparing public and private managers, they found the public managers somewhat lower on many of the need categories. The samples were limited and the interpretation complicated, as described below.

Human values are also basic components of motivation. Rokeach (1973) developed two corresponding lists of values — instrumental values and terminal values (see Table 6.1) — and designed questionnaires to assess a person's commitment to them. Sikula (1973a) compared government and business executives using the Rokeach instrument, and he compiled responses from twelve occupational groups. Six of the groups consisted of managers from industry, education, and government, including fifty-four executives in the U.S. Department of Health, Education and Welfare (HEW). The value profile of the HEW executives was similar to that of the other managerial groups; they all placed a higher priority on values related to competence (being wise, logical, and intellectual) and initiative (imagination, courage, sense of accomplishment) than did the other groups. Among all the groups, the government executives placed the highest priority on being responsible, honest, helpful, and capable. They rated higher than any other group on the terminal values of equality, mature love, and self-respect but lower than the other groups on the terminal values of happiness, pleasure, and comfortable life. Sikula's limited sample leaves questions about whether the findings apply to all public managers. Yet the emphasis on service (helpfulness) and integrity and the deemphasis on comfort and pleasure conforms with other findings about public managers.

Incentive Theories of Organization

Some very prominent theories about organizations have depicted them as economies of incentives. Organizational leaders must constantly maintain a flow of resources into the organization to cover the incentives that must be paid out to induce people to contribute to the organization (Barnard, 1938; Simon, 1948; March and Simon, 1958; for more detail, see the Appendix). In analyzing these processes, these theorists developed the typologies of incentives outlined in Table 6.2, which provide about as thorough an inventory as anyone has produced (although Barnard used some very awkward terms). The typologies reflect the development, earlier in the century, of an increasing emphasis in management theory on incentives besides material ones, such as personal growth and interest and pride in the work and the organization. Barnard, March, and Simon, of course, implied that all executives, in public or private organizations, face these challenges of attaining resources and providing incentives.

Clark and Wilson (1961) and Wilson (1973b) followed this lead in developing a typology of organizations based on the primary incentive offered to participants — material, solidary, and purposive (see Table 6.2). Differences in primary incentives force differences in leadership behaviors and organizational processes. Leaders in solidary organizations, such as voluntary service associations, face more pressure to develop prestige and worthy service projects to induce volunteers to participate. Leaders in purposive organizations, such as reform and social protest organizations, must show accomplishments in relation to the goals, such as passage of reform legislation. Subsequent research on this typology concentrated on why people join political parties and groups and did not specifically address public agencies. The concept of purposive incentives, however, has great relevance for government.

For many public managers, a sense of valuable social purpose can serve as a source of motivation, although in many agencies, they appear to face impediments in fulfilling this motive. In the survey of the U.S. Merit Systems Protection Board (1987), only 20 to 40 percent of the respondents from most federal agencies agreed that "opportunity to have an impact on public affairs" provides a good reason to stay in government service. In the Environmental Protection Agency, however, more than 65 percent of the employees identified this as a reason to stay.

Extrinsic and Intrinsic Incentives. The distinction between extrinsic and intrinsic incentives figures importantly in current research on motivation in organizations. Since the days of Frederick Taylor's pay-them-by-the-shovelful approach to rewarding workers (see the Appendix), management experts have increasingly emphasized the importance of intrinsic incentives in work.

What Are the Most Important Incentives? The variety of typologies in Table 6.2 show why we can expect no conclusive rank-ordered list of the most important needs, values, and incentives in organizations. There are too many ways of expressing the incentives, and preferences for them vary according to many factors, such as age, occupation, and organizational level. Herzberg, Mausner, Peterson, and Capwell (1957) compiled the rankings shown in Table 6.2 from sixteen studies including 11,000 employees. Other studies have come to different conclusions, however. Lawler (1973), for example, disagrees with the Herzberg ranking, indicating that a wider review of research suggests that people rate pay much higher, averaging about third in importance in most studies. He argues that management scholars underestimated the importance of pay in reaction against managerial approaches that rely excessively on pay as a motivator. He points out that pay often serves as a proxy for other incentives, because it can indicate successful achievement, recognition by the organization, and other valued outcomes.

Motives and Incentives in Public Organizations. In spite of these complications, there are some useful theories and research about the importance of certain motives and incentives in public organizations. Downs and Niskanen, two economists who developed theories about public bureaucracy, proposed the inventories of public managers' motives described in Table 6.2. They make the point that for public managers, power in the political system, serving the public interest, and serving a particular government bureau or program become important potential motives. Downs (1967) developed a typology of public administrators on the basis of such motives. Some administrators, he argued, pursue their own self-interest. Some of these are *climbers,* who seek to rise to higher, more influential positions. *Conservers* seek to defend their current positions and resources. Other administrative officials have mixed motives, combining a concern with their own self-interest with concerns for larger values, such as public policies and the public interest. They fall into three groups, who pursue increasingly broader conceptions of the public interest. *Zealots* seek to advance a specific policy or program. *Advocates* promote and defend an agency or more comprehensive policy domain. *Statesmen* pursue a more general public interest. As public agencies grow larger and older, they fill up with conservers and become rigid, since the climbers and zealots leave for other opportunities or turn into conservers. Among the mixed-motive officials, few can maintain the role of statesmen, and most become advocates. In the absence of economic markets for outputs, the administrators must attain resources through budget allocation and have to develop constituencies and political supports for their agency. This pushes them toward the advocate role and discourages statesmanship.

Downs's (1967) is almost certainly the most widely cited book ever written on government bureaucracy, but researchers have virtually never tested his theory in empirical studies. Its accuracy remains uncertain, then, but it does make the important point that commitments to their agencies, programs, and the public interest become important motives for many public managers. They also face difficult decisions about the relative importance of these motives and the relationships between them.

Niskanen (1971) was also interested in how bureaucrats "maximize utility," as economists put it. He theorized that, in the absence of economic markets, bureaucrats pursuing any of the incentives listed in Table 6.2 do so by trying to attain larger budgets. Even those with public service and altruistic motives have the incentive to ask for more staff and resources and hence larger budgets. Government bureaucracies therefore tend to grow inefficiently. Although this theory, too, has received scant empirical testing, public managers clearly defend their budgets and usually try to increase them. Yet many exceptions occur, in which the budgets for agencies increase because of legislative decisions about formulas and entitlements that the agency administrators have not requested. Some agencies also undertake cuts in funding or personnel or accept them fairly readily (Rubin, 1985). In 1986, the Social Security Administration launched a project to reduce its work force by 17,000, about 21 percent of its staff (U.S. General Accounting Office, 1986). For reasons such as this, apparently, Niskanen's more recent work focuses on discretionary budgets — those parts of the budgets over which administrators have some discretion.

Both of these theories reflect the tendency of some economists to argue that public bureaucracies incline toward dysfunctions because of the absence of economic markets for their outputs. These theories may accurately depict problems to which public organizations are prone. Later chapters, however, discuss the ongoing controversy over the performance of public organizations and point out that they often perform very well.

Attitudes Toward Money, Security and Benefits, and Challenging Work. Government does not offer the large financial gains that some people make in business, although civil service systems have traditionally offered job security and well-developed benefit programs. One might expect these differences to be reflected in public employees' attitudes about such incentives. We have increasing evidence that they do, although with many complications. Numerous surveys have found that government employees place less value on money as an ultimate goal in work and in life than do employees in business (Kilpatrick, Cummings, and Jennings, 1964; Lawler, 1971; Rawls, Ullrich, and Nelson, 1975; Rainey, 1983; Siegel, 1983). Yet such attitudes vary by time period, organizational level, geographical area, occupation, and type of agency. Below the highest levels of the organizations, pay levels are often fairly comparable in the public and private sectors. A federal study in 1989 found federal white-collar salaries about 22 percent lower than private-sector salaries for similar jobs (U.S. General Accounting Office, 1990). The federal government and many state and local governments conduct pay-comparability studies, however, and try to keep their pay levels competitive with those of the private sector. Different localities also vary widely in public-private pay differentials. The federal government and other units of government pay well relative to the private sector in some locations around the country, although federal salaries for professional, technical, and administrative positions fall behind in most areas. Federal personnel specialists have been working toward proposals to allow more variations around the country in federal white-collar pay.

At the highest executive levels, of course, and for advanced professions such as attorneys or doctors, the private sector offers vastly higher financial rewards, and these differences have been increasing (Volcker Commission, 1989). The massive earnings differentials for top executives and some attorneys and other professionals lead newspapers to carry stories questioning why anyone with these credentials works for government (Kelman, 1989). Studies of high-level officials who entered public service find that most of them took salary cuts to do so, saying that compensation did not influence their decision and that challenge and desire to perform public service provided the main attractions (Hartman and Weber, 1980).

In sum, many people choosing to work for government do not emphasize making a lot of money as a goal in life, although at lower organizational levels many public employees do not work at markedly lower pay than in similar private-sector jobs. At top executive and professional levels, government employees work at much lower salary levels than private-sector counterparts and have to pursue motives other than high earnings. Pay issues can still have very strong influences on motivation, however. As pointed out above, pay can have symbolic meaning, as a recognition of performance (Lawler, 1971). Studies with limited samples have also found that some public managers attach higher importance to increases in their pay than do private-sector managers. Apparently, these middle-level public managers felt that they had little impact on their organizations and turned to pay rather than responsibility as a motive (Schuster, 1974).

Research also indicates that security and benefits serve as important incentives for many who join and stay with government. A major survey by Kilpatrick, Cummings, and Jennings (1964) found that vast majorities of all categories of public employees, including federal employees, cited job security and benefit security (retirement, other protective benefits) as the motives causing a person to become a federal civil servant. Sixty-two percent of their sample of federal executives (GS-12 and above) held this view. A survey of about 17,000 federal employees by the U.S. Merit Systems Protection Board (1987) found that 81 percent of the respondents considered annual and sick leave benefits a reason to stay in government, and 70 percent saw job security as a good reason to stay. A rough version of the Maslow need hierarchy tends to apply, however. Smaller percentages of the executives and managers attached importance to benefits and job security.

Managers and executives report more attraction to opportunities for challenge and significant work (Hartman and Weber, 1980). Rawls, Ullrich, and Nelson (1975) found that students headed for the nonprofit sector—mainly government—showed higher "dominance," "flexibility," and "capacity for status" in psychological tests and a lower valuation of economic wealth than students headed for the for-profit sector. The nonprofit-oriented students also played more active roles in the program. Guyot (1960) found that a sample of federal middle managers scored higher than business counterparts on a need-for-achievement scale and about the same on a measure of need for power. We have some evidence, then, that government managers express as much or more concern with achievement and challenge than private managers.

Public executives and managers also tend to express a higher motive to serve the public, as shown by Sikula's (1973a) survey. Similarly, Kilpatrick, Cummings, and Jennings (1964) found that federal executives, scientists, and engineers gave higher ratings than did their counterparts in business to work-related values such as the importance of doing your best, even if you dislike your work; the importance of doing work that is worthwhile to society; and helping others as the main satisfaction from work. Rainey (1983) found that state agency managers rated the "opportunity to engage in meaningful public service" as a more important work reward to them than it was to managers in large business firms. Findings such as these suggest the form that service motives in government may take—a high value on work that helps others and benefits society as a whole, on a degree of self-sacrifice, and on responsibility and integrity. Public managers often mention such motives (Hartman and Weber, 1980; Lasko, 1980; Kelman, 1989; Sandeep,

1989). Later, however, we discuss some evidence that such motives often encounter frustrations and the imperative that public managers better understand and nurture service motives.

These studies suggest that challenging, significant work and opportunity for public service often provide the main attractions for public managers, but perceptions of public service vary over time, with changes in the political climate. A recent survey of career preferences among top students at leading universities found that they placed high priority on challenging work and personal growth, and low priority on salary. They saw government positions, however, as less likely to provide challenging work and personal growth than positions in private industry (Sanders, 1989). They saw government as providing superior opportunities for service to society but rated that opportunity as intermediate in importance. Their attitudes may reflect the antigovernment climate of the 1980s, and general perceptions about government may change. For public management, however, these findings raise the continuing issue of how to provide challenging work in government. They also raise questions about what we mean by public-service motives, to which later sections return.

Theories of Motivation

The discussions of incentives and motives provide only one component of the topic of motivation. Responses to incentives depend on many factors, such as their relation to performance and whether people perceive them as fair. Organizational researchers have developed numerous theories to draw together some of these additional factors. None has ever proved fully adequate, but they all add insights about particular factors and processes in motivation. Most of them apply to public employees. Some have implicitly provided the basic theory for reforms in government and some of the concepts and methods used to evaluate those reforms.

McGregor's Theory X and Theory Y

Reflecting the influence of Maslow's theory of human needs, Douglas McGregor (1960) advanced one of the most influential arguments in contemporary management thought (for more detail, see the Appendix). He described two alternative views of employees that guide managers. Theory X managers, whom he saw as predominant in industry, view workers as lazy and in need of direction and control. Theory Y, which McGregor wanted to see more widely accepted, drew on Maslow's ideas about higher-order needs and self-actualization. Theory Y holds that workers can enjoy working, be highly motivated, and handle self-direction and the assumption of responsibility. McGregor called on managers in industry to adopt Theory Y approaches by specific steps, such as decentralized decision making, participative management, and enlarging jobs to make them more interesting and responsible. Chapter Ten describes two federal agencies that reorganized to try to adopt approaches of this sort. In both cases, executives cited McGregor's ideas as important influences on the reorganizations.

Herzberg's Two-Factor Theory

With a similar message, Frederick Herzberg (1968) proposed one of the best-known analyses of motivational issues in his two-factor theory. On the basis of a number of studies involving about two thousand respondents in numerous occupational categories, he and his colleagues concluded that two major factors influence the motivation of workers—"motivators" and "hygiene factors." Hygiene factors are aspects of work that contribute to dissatisfaction with the job if not adequately supplied but do not themselves cause high levels of satisfaction. They include company policy and administration, supervision, interpersonal relationships, working conditions, salary, status, and security. Motivators, on the other hand, produce high levels of satisfaction. While hygiene factors can only prevent dissatisfaction, motivators actually produce an extra impetus, which provides high levels of job satisfaction. Motivators, intrinsic to the job, include achievement, recognition, the work itself, responsibility, growth, and advancement.

Herzberg argued that his findings showed that managers must avoid negative techniques of controlling and directing employees and must arrange job settings to provide the motivators—growth, achievement, recognition. This requires careful job enrichment programs that design jobs to make the work itself interesting and to give the worker the sense of control, achievement, growth, and recognition that produces high levels of satisfaction.

Herzberg's work sparked controversy among experts and researchers. His research methods drew criticism; Herzberg and his colleagues asked the people that they studied to describe events on their jobs that led to feelings of extreme satisfaction and events that led to extreme dissatisfaction. Most of the positive reports involved the intrinsic and growth factors later labeled motivators. Research using other methods, however, did not reproduce this breakdown between the two types of factors. Other researchers felt that when people were asked to describe an event that made them feel high satisfaction, they might hesitate to report that they felt great because they got more money or got a new air conditioner in the office. These concerns and the inability to reproduce the two factors with alternative methods have led researchers to search elsewhere for a more complete theory. Still, Herzberg added another influential voice to the calls for more emphasis on intrinsic rewards through enriched jobs, participation, and recognition, which has influenced the adoption of such approaches in many public organizations (Martin, 1983). In addition, studies adhering to Herzberg's methods find that his conclusions apply to public organizations. Park, Lovrich, and Soden (1988) asked administrators and white-collar personnel in a variety of government organizations in the United States and Korea to describe favorable and unfavorable job situations. In both countries, respondents most often cited recognition and achievement in describing favorable situations and extrinsic factors such as company policies in describing unfavorable ones.

McClelland and the Need for Achievement

As mentioned above, Guyot (1960) found that a sample of government managers scored higher than a group of business managers in need for achievement. The need-for-achievement measure stems from McClelland's theory that individuals have varying degrees of need to feel a sense of achievement, improvement, and mastery in their work. Individuals with high levels of need for achievement (NAch) seek situations where they receive concrete information on how well they perform. Many successful business executives have high NAch. Successful research scientists may not, since they must go for long periods without concrete results to indicate success. In various studies of the psychology of high-NAch types, McClelland found that they emphasize themes concerning improvement and success. In goal-setting situations, they set moderately difficult but achievable goals. McClelland also developed questionnaire measures of NAch and studied the development of NAch in children. He argued that the economic prosperity of nations depends on how much parents encourage it. He developed training courses to increase it in managers, claiming that such courses improved the performance of factories in underdeveloped countries.

McClelland's theory has not remained as prominent as it once was, in part because theorists searched for a more complete theory of motivation. His theory, however, emphasizes an important point about motivation. Managers often find that individuals simply differ in internalized motivation. Some people simply carry with them higher levels of determination and desire to excel and perform well. In addition, although Guyot's finding draws on a limited sample, it contrasts with the frequent claims that caution abounds among public managers (Downs, 1967; Warwick, 1975). The question of whether they show great caution is complex, as discussed later. Guyot's findings, however, and those of others, such as Rawls, Ullrich, and Nelson (1975), suggest that public managers vary widely and that overgeneralized claims about their cautiousness have little validity.

Equity Theory

J. Stacy Adams (1965) argued that a sense of equity in contributions and rewards has a major influence on work behaviors. A sense of inequity brings discomfort, and people act to reduce or avoid it. People judge the balance between their inputs to an organization and the outcomes or rewards that they receive from it, and feel inequity if their balances differ from those of other employees. For example, if another person and I receive the same salary, recognition, and other rewards, yet I feel that I make a superior contribution (such as working harder, producing more, having more experience), I experience inequity. Conversely, if the other person makes superior inputs but gets lower rewards than I get, I experience inequity in the opposite sense, of feeling overcompensated.

In either case, according to Adams, a person tries to eliminate the inequity. If people feel overcompensated, they may try to increase their inputs or reduce their outcomes to redress the inequity. If they feel undercompensated, they will do the opposite, slowing down or reducing their contributions. How workers will react depends on factors such as whether they receive hourly pay or pay according to rate of production.

The theory received some confirmation in laboratory experiments. The theory proves difficult to apply because of problems in defining and observing inequity in realistic settings. Still, concern about the equity of contributions and rewards plays a significant role in the working lives of many people. Equity perceptions have become components of many more recent theories. Equity issues also play a role in debates about civil service reforms and performance-based pay plans in the public sector. Some people argue for an equality principle, in which everyone gets the same raise. Supporters of performance-based pay plans, on the other hand, often cite equity principles akin to those in this theory. They argue that people who perform better than others but receive no better pay experience inequity and loss of morale and motivation (Schay, 1988).

Expectancy Theory

The expectancy theory of work motivation has been the most promising theory yet proposed and has had the most important applications in public organizations. Expectancy theory holds that an individual considering an action sums up the values of all the outcomes that will result from the action, with each outcome weighted by the probability of its occurrence. The higher the probability of good outcomes and the lower the probability of bad ones, the stronger the motivation to perform the action. In other words, the theory draws on the classic utilitarian idea that people will do what they see as *most likely* to result in the *most good* and the *least bad*.

Vroom (1964) stated the theory formally, with algebraic formulas. He put it this way: The force acting on an individual to work at a particular level of effort (or choose to engage in a particular activity) is a function of the sum of the products of (1) the perceived desirabilities of the outcomes associated with working at that level ("valences") and (2) the "expectancies" for the outcomes. Expectancies are the person's estimates of the probabilities that the outcomes will follow from working at the level. In other words, multiply the value (positive or negative) of each outcome by the expectancy (perceived probability) that it will occur and sum these products for all the outcomes. A higher sum reflects higher expectancies for more positively valued outcomes and should predict higher motivation.

Researchers originally hoped that this theory would provide a basis for systematic research and diagnosis of motivation. Ask people to rate the positive or negative value of important outcomes of their work and the probability that desirable work behaviors would lead to those outcomes or avoid them, and use the expectancy formula to combine these ratings. They hoped that this approach would improve our ability to predict motivational levels and analyze good and bad influences on them, such as problems due to beliefs that certain outcomes were unattainable or that certain rewards offered little value. A spate of empirical tests soon followed, with mixed results. Some of the studies found that the theory failed to predict effort and productivity. Critics soon began to point out weaknesses in the theory (Behling and others, 1973; Campbell and Pritchard, 1983; Connolly, 1976). They complained that it does not accurately represent human mental processes because it assumes that humans make exhaustive lists of outcomes and their likelihoods and sum them up systematically. Researchers found it difficult to list on a questionnaire all the possible outcomes important to people in the organization and to measure their valences (Connolly, 1976).

Nevertheless, expectancy theory still stands as one of the most prominent work motivation theories, and researchers continue to propose various improvements in it (Kopelman and Thompson, 1976; Pinder, 1984; Staw, 1984; Evans, 1986). More recent versions relax the mathematical formula and simply state that motivation depends generally on the positive and negative values of outcomes and their probabilities, in ways that we cannot precisely specify. In addition, more recent forms of the theory have broken down the concept of expectancies into two types. Expectancy I (EI) perceptions reflect the individual's beliefs about the likelihood that effort will lead to a particular performance level. Expectancy II (EII) perceptions reflect the perceived probability that the particular performance level leads to a given level of reward. The distinction helps to clarify some of the components of motivational responses. For example, the Performance Management and Recognition System (PMRS), one of the many pay-for-performance plans adopted by governments during the 1980s, applied to middle managers in federal agencies (GS 13-15). Under PMRS, a manager's superior would rate the manager's performance on a five-point scale, and the manager's annual salary increase was to be based on that rating. PMRS, however, got off to a bad start in many federal agencies. In some agencies, the vast majority of the managers received very high performance ratings, and their EI perceptions strengthened—it became clear that they had a high likelihood of performing well enough to receive a high rating. Yet about 90 percent of the managers in some agencies received pay raises of 3 percent or less, and fewer than 1 percent of them received pay raises of as much as 10 percent. EII perceptions, then, naturally weaken. One may expect to perform well enough to get a high rating (EI), but performance at that level may not lead to a high probability of getting a significant reward (EII). PMRS, like many other performance-based pay plans in government, implicitly applies expectancy theory but so far fails to do so adequately (Perry, 1986; Perry, Petrakis, and Miller, 1989). The more recent formulations of the theory provide useful frameworks for pinpointing the sources of failure.

The more recent versions of the theory also draw in other variables. They point out, for example, that a person's self-esteem can affect EI perceptions. Organizational characteristics and experiences, such as the characteristics of the pay plan, can influence EII perceptions — as in the PMRS case. Some of the most recent versions bring together expectancy concepts with ideas about goal setting, control theory, and social learning theory (Evans, 1986; Klein, 1989).

Expectancies as Dependent Variables. In spite of the controversies over the theory, researchers and management consultants regularly use expectancy-type questions as *dependent variables*. Individuals' beliefs about the relationship between performance and pay, job security, promotion, and other incentives often show significant relationships to other important attitudes, such as work satisfaction and self-reported work effort. Researchers use Expectancy I scales with items concerning beliefs about the relationship between effort and performance, asking whether effort will lead to high-quality and high-quantity output (House and Dessler, 1974). For example, one item asks for agreement or disagreement with the statement "Trying as hard as I can leads to high-quality output." Expectancy II items ask about the linkage between performance and rewards: "Producing a high-quality output increases my chances for promotion." Other EII items ask about the relationships of quantity, quality, and timeliness of output to rewards such as promotion, higher pay, job security, and recognition from the company.

Expectancy Theory and Public Organizations. The PMRS and pay-for-performance examples show why expectancy theory has had important applications in the public sector. It has served as the implicit theoretical underpinning of many reforms of civil service and other government pay systems. In addition, expectancy questions of the sort described above have been used in major surveys of government employees that were intended in part as means of evaluating some of the reforms (U.S. Office of Personnel Management, 1979, 1980, 1983). As described below, these and other surveys using expectancy items have found some consistent distinctions between public-sector and private-sector incentive structures.

Skinnerian Psychology, Operant Conditioning, and Behavior Modification

Another recent approach, with implications similar to those of expectancy theory, applies operant conditioning and behavior modification concepts to the management of employees. This approach draws on theories by psychologists such as B. F. Skinner. Skinner argued that we can best analyze behavior by studying the relationships between observable behaviors and contingencies of reinforcement. A reinforcement is an event that follows a behavior and changes the probability that the behavior will recur. (We might call this a reward or punishment, but Skinner felt that the term *reinforcement* was a more objective one, since it assumes less about what goes on inside the subject.) Learning and motivation depend on schedules or contingencies of reinforcements, such as how regularly they follow a particular behavior. For example, a manager can praise an employee every time he or she engages in a desirable work behavior, such as completing a particular task on time, on a constant reinforcement schedule. Or the manager can follow a variable-ratio reinforcement schedule, praising the behavior once out of every several times it occurs.

Skinner analyzed such relationships — although he studied laboratory animals, not managers — and proposed principles of reinforcement about various types and schedules of reinforcement. For example, he pointed out that a subject more rapidly acquires a behavior under a constant reinforcement schedule but that the behavior will extinguish (stop occurring) faster than one brought about using a variable-ratio schedule. Behaviorists also point out that positive reinforcement works better than negative reinforcement.

Behavior modification refers to techniques that apply principles of operant conditioning to modifying human behaviors. Behavior modification practitioners claim successes in psychological therapy, educational settings, supervision of mentally retarded patients, and rewarding attendance by custodial workers. Many organizations, including public ones such as garbage-collection services, have adopted variants of these techniques to improve performance and productivity. Emery Air Freight applied one of the most widely publicized programs, involving production goals coordinated with praise from supervisors and financial incentives when the workers met the goals (Kreitner and Luthans, 1987; Gordon, 1990).

Some critics argue that many behavior modification programs in organizations offer no great theoretical breakthrough but amount to programs that set goals and tie rewards to their accomplishment. Others complain that the techniques can be manipulative, oversimplified, and applicable only to low-level, simple situations in organizations. Yet some of the more interesting recent discussions of the approach bring it together with social learning theories and claim progress in developing insights for managers. Proponents argue that the behavior modification approach strengthens emphasis on behavior (as opposed to having the right attitude, for example) by attaching rewards and consequences to performance, with emphasis on positive reinforcement. One can distinguish between behavior modification and expectancy theory in many ways, but they share this emphasis on the importance of connecting rewards to performance. This seems obvious enough, but tying rewards to performance and desirable behavior always presents ongoing challenges for every manager. Organizations typically have at least some problems with dysfunctional incentives, which reward the wrong behaviors and discourage desirable ones — they very frequently reward one thing while hoping for another (Kerr, 1989).

Incentive Structures and Reward Expectancies
in Public Organizations

The challenge of tying rewards, especially extrinsic rewards, to performance is even greater in many public organizations than in private ones. As we have shown, there are now a number of studies that demonstrate that organizations under government ownership usually have more highly structured, externally imposed personnel procedures than private organizations have (Pugh, Hickson, and Hinings, 1969; Holdaway, Newberry, Hickson, and Heron, 1975; Meyer, 1979; Tolbert and Zucker, 1983; Bozeman and Bretschneider, 1989; Chubb and Moe, 1990). These studies include comparisons of central government agencies, schools, universities, and government organizations with private organizations that have comparable tasks. The civil service systems and centralized personnel systems in government jurisdictions apparently account for these effects.

Of course, public organizations also vary among themselves in how much such systems affect them. The U.S. General Accounting Office, for example, has a relatively independent personnel system, with a pay-for-performance system. Government enterprises often have greater autonomy in their personnel procedures than typical government agencies. In demonstration projects, some federal units have adopted pay-for-performance plans with apparent success (Schay, 1988). Debate continues over whether pay constraints are an inherent feature of government (Sherwood and Wechsler, 1986; Gabris, 1987; Siegel, 1987). At present, public organizations more often have more formalized, externally imposed personnel systems than do private organizations.

This evidence of more formalized personnel rules does not in itself prove that people in public organizations perceive them as such. Numerous surveys now show that public managers, as compared to private sector counterparts, report more formalized personnel procedures, and greater structural constraints on their authority to administer extrinsic rewards such as pay, promotion, and discipline and to base these on performance (Rainey, 1983; Baldwin, 1990; Coursey and Rainey, 1990; Powell and Ogilvie, 1990). Some of these surveys ask managers from all levels of government and different regions of the country whether the personnel rules governing the organization facilitate tying a person's pay, promotion, and discipline to his or her performance or make it more difficult. They find the public managers much more likely to say that the rules make it hard to tie pay, promotion, and discipline to performance. In a survey of state government administrators from ten major states around the country, Elling (1986) found that high percentages of them rated such constraints as serious. The responses varied from state to state, but very large percentages rated rewarding outstanding employees, civil service procedures for recruitment and selection, and dismissing and disciplining incompetent employees as the most serious problems among a set of personnel issues. In the surveys of thousands of federal employees conducted by the U.S. Office of Personnel Management (1979, 1980, 1983), large percentages (50 to 70 percent) of the federal executives and managers said that they had too little authority to remove poor performers, hire competent people, promote people, and determine their employees' pay.

The feelings of the public managers in all these studies may reflect shared stereotypes. Perhaps business managers have problems just as serious but have stereotypes about rewards being strongly related to performance in the private-enterprise system. Even if that is the case, these findings indicate that these perceptions on the part of public managers currently form part of the culture at all levels of government in the United States.

The existence of formalized personnel systems and the managers' perceptions of constraints under them does not prove that public employees see no connection between extrinsic rewards and performance. For years, expert observers (Thompson, 1975) have pointed out that some public managers find ways around formal constraints on rewards by isolating poor performers, giving them undesirable assignments, or in other ways establishing linkages between rewards and performance. Nevertheless, a number of surveys now indicate that public employees perceive weaker relationships between performance and pay, promotion, and disciplinary action than do private employees (Porter and Lawler, 1968; Rainey, 1979, 1983; Lachman, 1985; Rainey, Traut, and Blunt, 1986; Solomon, 1986; Coursey and Rainey, 1990). These studies use expectancy-theory questionnaire items about such relationships and find that public-sector samples rate them as weaker. Similarly, the U.S. Office of Personnel Management (1979) surveys found that sizable percentages of federal employees feel that pay, promotion, and demotion do not depend on performance. Again, these results may reflect shared stereotypes. In fact, there are some conflicting findings. Analysts in the Office of Personnel Management compared results on their survey question about pay and performance to results for a similar item on a large survey of private-sector workers. They found little difference in the percentages of employees who expect to get a pay raise for good performance.

Self-Reported Motivation Among Public Employees

The reforms of the civil service systems and numerous writers on public organizations assume that these differences in incentive structure diminish motivation among public employees. One can more readily make that claim than prove it. As noted earlier, organizational researchers have difficulty measuring motivation. A few studies have compared public and private managers and employees on scales of self-reported motivation, however, and have found no large differences. Rainey (1979, 1983), using the Patchen scales described earlier, found no differences in self-reported motivation between middle managers in public and private organizations. Virtually all of the public and private managers said that they work very hard. Baldwin (1987, 1990) also found no difference in self-reported motivation between groups of public and private managers, and Rainey (1983) found no difference in responses to expectancy items about the connection between performing well and intrinsic incentives such as the feeling of accomplishing something worthwhile, although the public managers perceived stronger connections between performance and the sense of "engaging in a meaningful public service." Bozeman and Loveless (1987) report somewhat higher levels of positive work climate in public research and development labs than in less public, more private labs.

Similarly, in spite of the many assertions about cautious government bureaucrats (Downs, 1967; Warwick, 1975), public managers claim in response to surveys that they feel openness to change and to new ways of doing things (Rainey, 1983). Many federal employees express skepticism about prospects for changing their organizations, but most federal managers and executives (65 to 75 percent) see change as possible (U.S. Office of Personnel Management, 1979). Bellante and Link (1981) report a study showing that more risk-averse people join the public sector. Their measures of risk aversion, however, included smoking and drinking less, using automobile seat belts, and having higher medical and automobile insurance coverage. These could just as well serve as indicators of the sort of dutiful, public-service-oriented, somewhat ascetic individuals suggested in the studies of work-related values (Kilpatrick, Cummings, and Jennings, 1964; Sikula, 1973a) and do not themselves indicate aversion to professional and managerial risks. Golembiewski (1985; Golembiewski, Proehl, and Sink, 1981) reviews 270 organizational development efforts in public organizations and concludes that more than 80 percent of them were apparently successful. Roessner (1983) notes scant evidence on the comparative innovativeness of public and private organizations but finds no indication of private-sector superiority in rates of diffusion of technological innovations.

In addition, the very large surveys of public employees and managers mentioned earlier find that they report high levels on measures related to motivation. They report very high work effort, strong sense of challenge, strong sense of the importance to them of their organizations, high ratings of the effectiveness of their organizations, and high general work satisfaction (National Center for Productivity and Quality of Working Life, 1978; U.S. Office of Personnel Management, 1979; U.S. Merit Systems Protection Board, 1987).

Self-reports about one's effort and about these other factors have obvious limitations. The research indicates, nevertheless, that although many public employees and managers perceive relatively weak connections between performance and extrinsic rewards such as pay and promotion, they report high levels of attitudes and behaviors related to high motivation.

Methods of Motivating People in Organizations

Public and private managers and employees show many similarities in motivation in part because they use generally similar techniques for motivating employees. In spite of academic controversies over motivation theories, managers in organizations have to go ahead with plans to enhance motivation. They use such methods as the following.

Improved Performance-Appraisal Systems. Although performance-appraisal systems are standard in most organizations now, the literature generally laments the weaknesses of these systems in all settings — public, private, wherever — and calls for reforms involving the use of group-based appraisals (ratings for a work group rather than an individual), appraisals by a member's peers, and other approaches.

Merit Pay and Pay-for-Performance Systems. Governments at all levels have tried approaches that link a person's pay to measure of performance, with dubious success to date except in certain demonstration projects.

Bonus and Award Systems. These systems offer one-time awards for instances of excellent performance or other achievements. Business organizations typically have more flexibility in adopting financial bonus systems than do government organizations, and they abound in some industries, especially for managers. The federal government initiated such a system for higher executives in the Civil Service Reform Act of 1978. Many organizations, including public ones, regularly operate award systems of various types, such as programs in federal, state, and local governments to provide financial awards to people who make money-saving suggestions (Florkowski and Lifton, 1987); Delta Airlines has a program to recognize and reward employees for incidents of excellent customer service.

Profit-Sharing and Gain-Sharing Plans. A related approach, involving sharing profits with members of the organization, is usually possible only in business organizations, for obvious reasons. Employee stock ownership plans are one of the means used to reward employees when the organization does well. Public enterprises and corporations may have some prospects for using profit sharing or employee stock schemes. Government agencies increasingly try gain-sharing schemes, where employees receive a share of the money saved through productivity (Florkowski and Lifton, 1987).

Management by Objectives and Other Performance-Targeting Procedures. Organizations of all types have tried management by objectives (MBO) programs, which involve evaluating people on the basis of stated work objectives (Swiss, 1991). Superiors work with subordinates on developing objectives for their work, thus enhancing communication, and the subordinates' performance appraisals then concentrate on those objectives. This focuses an employee's attention on the most important outcomes of work, gives the employee more say in what he or she does, and enhances decentralization and autonomy, since agreement on the objectives provides a basis for allowing the employee to go ahead and work in his or her own way, rather than through constant directions by the boss. The most elaborate MBO programs involve mapping broad organizational objectives down through more specific objectives at the different levels of the organization. Organizations also use a wide variety of "performance-targeting" procedures (Greiner and others, 1981) emphasizing productivity or performance targets for groups.

Participative Management and Decision Making. These approaches involve a sustained commitment to engage in more communication and sharing of decisions, through teams, committees, task forces, general meetings, open-door policies, and one-to-one exchanges.

Work Enhancement: Job Redesign, Job Enlargement, and Job Rotation. Job redesign usually means changing jobs to enhance control and interest for the people doing the work (Greiner and others, 1981). Job enlargement, or "horizontal loading," involves giving a person more different tasks and responsibilities at the same skill level. Job restructuring, or "vertical loading," involves giving a person more influence over decisions normally made by superiors, such as work scheduling, or more generally enlarging employees' sense of responsibility by giving them control of a more complete unit of work output (work teams who build an entire car as a team or caseworkers who handle all needs of a client). These approaches may involve job sharing and rotation among workers and various team-based approaches. The change in the Social Security Administration (discussed in Chapter Ten) applied elements of job redesign.

Quality-of-Work-Life Programs and Quality Circles. Organizations of all types have tried quality-of-work-life (QWL) programs, which typically involve efforts to enhance the general working environment of an organization through representative committees, surveys and studies, and other procedures improving the work environment. Quality circles, used successfully in Japanese companies, are teams that focus more directly on improving the quality of work processes and products.

Organizational Development Interventions. Organizational development (OD), employed widely in the public and private sectors, applies behavioral science techniques to improving communication, conflict resolution, and trust. (Chapter Ten describes OD in detail.)

Transformational Leadership, Cultural Enhancement, and Excellence Campaigns. Chapters Eight and Twelve describe the recent trends towards development of these approaches.

Other Motivation-Related Work Attitudes

The use of these techniques is also part of the reason that public employees express favorable attitudes on an array of motivation-related variables: work satisfaction, the importance of the organization, and sense of challenge, for example. These concepts return us to the point that motivation as a general topic covers numerous dimensions. Motivational techniques often aim at enhancing these attitudes as well as work effort. Researchers have developed many of these, often distinguishing them from motivation in the sense of work effort. These distinctions have importance in their own right, but researchers have also used some of them to compare public and private managers.

Job Satisfaction. Thousands of studies and dozens of different questionnaire measures make job satisfaction the most intensively studied variable in organizational research. Job satisfaction is a measure of how an individual feels about his or her job and various aspects of it (Gruneberg, 1979), usually in the sense of how favorable — how positive or negative — those feelings are. Job satisfaction often shows relationships to other important attitudes and behaviors, such as absenteeism, the intention to quit, and actually quitting.

Years ago, Locke (1976) pointed out that researchers had published about 3,500 studies of job satisfaction without coming to any clear agreement on its meaning. Job satisfaction nevertheless continues to play an important role in the most recent research (Shore, Thornton, and Newton, 1989; Griffin, 1989). The different ways of measuring job satisfaction illustrate different ways of defining it. Some studies use only two or three summary items, such as the following:

- In general, I like working here.
- In the next year, I intend to look for another job outside this organization.

General or global measures ask questions about enjoyment, interest, and enthusiasm to tap general feelings in much more depth. They often employ multiple-item scales with responses to be summed up or averaged, such as the following from the Minnesota Satisfaction Questionnaire (Weiss, Dawis, England, and Lofquist, 1967):

- I definitely dislike my work [reversed scoring].
- My job is pretty uninteresting [reversed scoring].
- I feel happier in my work than most other people.
- I find real enjoyment in my work.
- Most days I am enthusiastic about my work.

Specific, or facet, satisfaction measures ask about particular facets of the job, such as the following examples from Smith's (1976) Index of Organizational Reactions:

Supervision
- Do you have the feeling you would be better off working under different supervision?

Company identification
- From my experience, I feel this organization probably treats its employees [five choice responses, from "poorly" to "extremely well"].

Smith also includes scales for kind of work, amount of work, co-workers, physical work conditions, financial rewards, and career future. Porter's (1962) Need Satisfaction Questionnaire asks respondents to rate thirteen statements describing fulfillment of a particular need, rating how much of each factor there is now and how much there should be. The degree to which the "should be" rating exceeds the "is now" rating measures need dissatisfaction, or the inverse of satisfaction. The following are examples of the items included:

Security needs
- The feeling of security in my management position.

Social needs
- The opportunity, in my management position, to give help to other people.

Self-actualization needs
- The opportunity for personal growth and development in my management position.

Porter's questionnaire, which is not used very frequently any more, employs categories based on Maslow's need theory. Some of the research on public-sector work satisfaction described below used this method.

Determinants of Job Satisfaction. Different measures imply different meanings of job satisfaction, and this complicates the research on the topic. Different studies using different measures — and hence different meanings — often come to conflicting conclusions about how job satisfaction is related to other variables. Partly because of these variations, researchers do not agree on a coherent theory or framework of what determines job satisfaction. Research generally finds higher job satisfaction associated with better pay, promotional opportunities, consideration from supervisors, recognition, working conditions, and utilization of skills and abilities (Staw, 1984). Even so, some studies report contradictory findings for almost any possible determinant.

This situation actually makes sense, because it is obviously unrealistic to try to generalize about how much any single factor affects satisfaction. Any particular factor in any given setting contends with other factors as they exist in that setting. Various studies suggest the importance of *individual differences:* level of aspiration, comparison level for alternatives (whether the person sees better opportunities elsewhere), level of acclimation (what a person is accustomed to), educational level, level in the organization and occupation, professionalism, age, tenure, race, gender, national and cultural background, and personality differences (values, self-esteem, and so on). Yet the influence of any one of these depends on other factors. For example, tenure and organizational level usually correlate with satisfaction. Those who have been longer in the organization and are at higher levels report higher satisfaction. This makes sense. Unhappy people leave; happier people stay. People who get to higher levels should be happier. Yet some studies find the opposite. In some organizations, longer-term employees feel undercompensated for their long service. Some people at higher levels may feel the same way or that they have hit a ceiling on their opportunities. Career civil servants sometimes face this problem (Rainey, 1983).

Researchers also look at *job characteristics* and *job design* as determinants of job satisfaction. The most prominent recent approach, by Hackman and Oldham (1980), also draws on Maslow's need-fulfillment theory. These researchers report higher job satisfaction for jobs higher on the dimensions measured by their Job Diagnostic Survey, which includes the following subscales: skill variety, task identity, task significance, autonomy, feedback from the job, feedback from agents, and dealing with others. Critics find some faults (Staw, 1984), but Hackman and Oldham's findings conform with a typical position among management experts, that more interesting, self-controlled, significant work, with feedback from others, improves satisfaction.

Besides looking at the person and the job, researchers have analyzed factors extrinsic to the work itself: pay, promotion, job security, supervision, work-group characteristics, participation in plans and decisions, and organizational structure and climate. These factors often influence satisfaction but depend on the other factors in a given setting.

Consequences of Job Satisfaction. Controversy also persists regarding the consequences of job satisfaction. For years, authors regularly pointed out that job satisfaction showed no consistent relationship with individual performance (Pinder, 1984). They typically cite Porter and Lawler's (1968) interpretation of this disappointing evidence, which pointed out that good performance can lead to higher satisfaction just as well as satisfaction might lead to performance. A good performer who gets better rewards feels greater satisfaction. Yet a good performer who gets no better rewards as a result experiences dissatisfaction, thus dissolving any positive link between satisfaction and performance. The link between performance and rewards, they concluded, plays a key role in determining the performance-satisfaction relationship. Studies continue to report weak relationships between satisfaction and performance (Shore, Thornton, and Newton, 1989), although recent meta-analytical studies — analyses of many studies to look for general trends in their results — suggest that the relationship of job satisfaction to performance is generally stronger than this typical interpretation suggests (Petty, McGee, and Cavender, 1984).

While the relationship with performance seemed dubious, researchers have pointed out that satisfaction shows fairly consistent relationships with absenteeism and turnover. These behaviors cost organizations a lot of money, so since satisfaction helps to explain them, they are important variables.

Although fairly consistent, these relationships have not proved extremely strong either. Obviously, practical factors such as health and family problems influence these behaviors. Satisfaction shows a stronger relationship with the expressed *intention* of turnover, but this does not always predict turnover very well.

In spite of these complexities, job satisfaction figures very importantly in organizations. Distinct from motivation and performance, it can nevertheless influence them as well as other important behaviors, such as turnover and absenteeism. Some studies have found work satisfaction to be related to life satisfaction and physical health (Gruneberg, 1979). In addition, measures of satisfaction have proved valuable in assessing attitudes in public organizations (Volcker Commission, 1989). As described below, studies find public-sector respondents to be somewhat lower on such measures than private business employees. We know a good deal about influencing satisfaction and motivation, and we need to put that knowledge to better use in public organizations.

Role Conflict and Ambiguity. In an influential book published some years ago, Kahn and others (1964) argue that characteristics of an individual's "role" in an organization determine the stress that the employee experiences in his or her work. A number of "role senders" impose expectations and requirements on the person through both formal and informal processes. If these expectations are ambiguous and conflicting, the stress level increases. Other researchers later developed questionnaire items to measure role conflict and role ambiguity (Rizzo, House, and Lirtzman, 1970; House and Rizzo, 1972). *Role ambiguity* refers to the lack of the necessary information available to a given organizational position. The role ambiguity questionnaire asks about clarity of objectives, responsibilities, amount of authority, and time allocation in the person's job.

Role conflict refers to the incompatibility of different role requirements. A person's role might conflict with his or her values and standards or with his or her time, resources, and capabilities. Conflict might exist between two or more roles that the same person is expected to play. There might be conflict among organizational demands or expectations or conflicting expectations from different role senders. The survey items on role conflict ask whether there are adequate labor and other resources to carry out assignments, whether others impose incompatible expectations, and whether the respondent has to buck rules in order to carry out assignments.

The two role variables consistently show relationships to job satisfaction and some similar measures, such as "job-related tension" (Miles and Petty, 1975; Miles, 1976; Szilagyi, Sims, and Keller, 1976), but are not so consistently related to measures of job performance (Schuler, 1977, p. 164). They also show relationships to a number of other organizational factors, such as participation in decision making, leader behaviors, and formalization. Individual characteristics such as need for clarity and perceived locus of control (whether the individual sees events as under his or her control or as controlled externally) also influence how much role conflict and ambiguity a person experiences. These concepts have importance in themselves, since managers increasingly concern themselves with stress management and time management. Managing one's role can play a central part in these processes. In addition, however, research on public managers has also employed role questionnaires.

Job Involvement. In observing increasingly technical, professional, and scientific forms of work, researchers find differences among individuals in their involvement in their work. For some people, especially advanced professionals, work plays a very central part in their lives. Researchers measure job involvement by asking people whether their major life satisfactions come from their jobs, whether their work is the most important thing in their lives, and similar questions. Job involvement is distinct from general motivation and satisfaction but resembles intrinsic work motivation (Cook, Hepworth, Wall, and Warr, 1981). It figures importantly in the work attitudes of highly professionalized people who serve in crucial roles in many organizations. The concept has also played an interesting role in the research on public managers reviewed below.

Organizational Commitment. Individuals vary in their loyalty and commitment to the organizations in which they work. Certain people may consider the organization itself to be of immense importance to them, as an institution worthy of service, as a location of friends, as a source of security and other benefits. Others may see the organization only as a place to earn money. Professionals such as doctors, lawyers, and scientists often have loyalties external to the organization — to the profession itself and their professional colleagues. Currently, management experts in the United States show great interest in the excellent competitiveness of Japanese corporations. One explanation for this excellent performance is higher levels of organizational loyalty among the Japanese.

Scales for measuring organizational commitment ask whether the respondent sees the organization's problems as his or her own, whether he or she feels a sense of pride in working for the organization, and similar questions (Mowday, Porter, and Steers, 1982). Studies also show the complex, multidimensional nature of commitment. For example, Angle and Perry (1981) show the importance of the distinction between calculative commitment and normative commitment. One form of organizational loyalty can be calculative, based on the perceived material rewards that the organization affords. Another basis for organizational loyalty is normative: The individual is committed to the organization because he or she sees it as a mechanism for enacting personal ideals and values. As we will see later, researchers have raised some interesting issues about organizational commitment in the public service.

Professionalism. For years, sociological researchers have studied the way in which highly trained specialists control complex occupations. Technological advances have made certain valuable types of work increasingly complex and difficult to apprehend. Specialists in these areas must have advanced training and must maintain high standards. Only specialists, however, have the qualifications to establish and police the standards. From the point of view of society and of large organizations, these factors raise problems of monopoly, self-interest, and mixed loyalties. Government and business organizations also face challenges in managing the work and careers of highly trained professionals.

Researchers have offered many definitions of *profession,* typically including these elements: (1) application of a skill based on theoretical knowledge, (2) requirements for advanced education and training, (3) testing of competence through examinations or other methods, (4) organization into a professional association, (5) existence of a code of conduct and emphasis on adherence to it, and (6) espousal of altruistic service. Occupational specializations that rate relatively highly on most or all of these dimensions are highly "professionalized." Medical doctors, lawyers, and highly trained scientists are usually considered advanced professionals without much argument. Scholars usually place college professors, engineers, accountants, and sometimes social workers in the professional category. Often they define less developed specializations, such as librarians and computer programmers, as semiprofessions, emerging professions, or less professionalized occupations.

In turn, management researchers analyze the characteristics of individual "professionals," because they play key roles in contemporary organizations. They point out that, as a result of their selection and training, professionals tend to have certain beliefs and values (Filley, House, and Kerr, 1976): (1) belief in the need to be expert in the body of abstract knowledge applicable to the profession, (2) belief that they and fellow professionals should have *autonomy* in work activities and decision making, (3) identification with the profession and fellow professionals, (4) commitment to the work of the profession as a calling, or life's work, (5) a feeling of ethical obligation to render service to clients without self-interest and with emotional neutrality, and (6) a belief in self-regulation and collegial maintenance of standards; that is, a belief that fellow professionals are best qualified to judge and police each other. Members of a profession vary on these dimensions. Those relatively high on most or all are highly professional by this definition.

The characteristics of professions and professionals may conflict with characteristics of large bureaucratic organizations. Belief in autonomy may conflict with organizational rules and hierarchy. Emphasis on altruistic service to clients can conflict with organizational emphasis on cost savings and standardized treatment of clients. Identification with the profession and desire for recognition from fellow professionals may dilute the impact of organizational rewards, such as financial incentives and organizational career patterns. Professionals might prefer professional reputation to salary increases and prefer their professional work to moving up into "management." Without moving up, however, they hit ceilings on pay, promotion, and prestige. Studies have found higher organizational formalization associated with higher alienation among professionals (Hall, 1987).

Conflicts between professionals and organizations do not appear to be as inevitable as once supposed, however. Certain bureaucratic values, such as emphasis on technical qualifications of personnel, are compatible with professional values (Hall, 1987). For example, professionals may approve of organizational rules on qualifications for jobs. Professionals in large organizations may be isolated in certain subunits, such as laboratories, where they are relatively free from organizational rules and hierarchical controls (Larson, 1977; Bozeman and Loveless, 1987; Crow and Bozeman, 1987). Certain professionals, such as engineers and accountants, may want to move up in organizations in nonprofessional roles (Schott, 1978; Larson, 1977). Some empirical results indicate that, for some professionals, professional commitment is positively correlated with organizational commitment (Bartol, 1979).

Management writers offer some useful suggestions about the management of professionals. They prescribe *dual career ladders,* which add to the standard career path for managers another for professionals, so that professionals can stay in their specialty (research, legal work, social work) but move up to higher levels of pay and responsibility. This relieves the tension over deciding whether one must give up the profession and go into management. Some organizations rotate professionals in and out of management positions. The U.S. Geological Survey has a policy of rotating geologists in administrative positions back into professional research positions after several years. Some organizations also allow professionals to take credit for their accomplishments. For example, they allow them to claim authorship of professional research reports rather than requiring that they publish them anonymously in the name of the agency or company. Organizations can also pay for travel to professional conferences and in other ways support professionals in their desire to remain excellent in their professions.

Researchers have not reported much comparative research on professionals in the public and private sectors. Typically, they treat the issues as very generic, crossing the sectors. Government agencies have many professional employees, however, and a particular profession dominates many government agencies (Mosher, [1968] 1982), so the issues figure importantly in public management. Recently, the Volcker Commission (1989) reported that the federal government faces grave difficulties in attracting highly qualified professionals because the private sector offers them so much higher salaries. On the other hand, work settings for some professionals in government appear to offer equal or superior intrinsic incentives for professionals. As noted earlier, Bozeman and Loveless (1987) found that public-sector research and development labs have more positive work climates than private labs. Many public managers face a challenge of doing all they can to provide those intrinsic incentives to compete with the superior salary levels for some professionals in the private sector (Romzek, 1990).

Motivation-Related Variables in Public Organizations

Researchers have made comparisons on a number of these variables between public and private samples, which shed some light on how the two categories compare. Although far from complete, the evidence suggests that public managers and employees express somewhat lower levels of favorable work attitudes.

Comparisons on Scales of Role Ambiguity, Role Conflict, and Organizational Goal Clarity. For some work-related attitudes, researchers have found few differences between managers in public and private organizations. This has been the case with the most frequent observation in all the literature on the distinctive character of public management: Public managers confront greater multiplicity, vagueness, and conflict of goals and performance criteria than do managers in private organizations (Rainey, 1989). Executives often mention this distinction (Allison, 1983), and researchers refer to it in interpreting their findings (Buchanan, 1975; Boyatzis, 1982). These observations about vague, multiple goals in the public sector bear on classical questions about social controls through politics or through markets (Lindblom, 1977), yet there is a fascinating divergence between the political economists and organization theorists on the observations' validity. Political scientists and economists tend to regard this goal complexity as an obvious consequence or determinant of governmental (nonmarket) controls, while many organization theorists tend to regard it as a generic problem facing all organizations.

Beyond the observations of experienced executives, however, strikingly little comparative research directly addresses this issue. Rainey (1983) compared middle managers in government and business organizations on the role conflict and role ambiguity items described earlier, which contain questions about the clarity of one's goals in work, conflicting demands, and related matters. The government and business managers showed no differences on these questions, nor on additional questions about whether they regarded the goals of their organizations as clear and easy to measure. Baldwin (1987) also found private managers only slightly more likely to report high organizational goal clarity than public managers. One explanation for these results may be that public managers clarify their roles and objectives by reference to standard operating procedures, whether or not the overall goals of the organization are clear and consistent (Perry and Porter, 1982). In addition, when researchers ask managers to describe their decision criteria, private managers mention financial performance criteria much more frequently than do public managers (Solomon, 1986; Schwenk, 1990).

The real issues, then, may not be whether managers perceive that goals are clear, but rather what criteria and processes they use to clarify their goals, as well as just how valid those criteria are as sound measures of performance.

Whatever the explanation, these limited findings point to important challenges for both researchers and practitioners in further analyzing such issues as how managers in various settings that span public, private, and hybrid auspices perceive objectives and performance criteria; how these objectives and criteria are communicated and validated, if they are; whether these objectives and criteria do in fact coincide with the sorts of distinctions between public and private settings assumed to exist in our political economy.

Work Satisfaction. On other work-related attitudes and perceptions, many studies find differences between respondents from the public and private sectors. Public employees and managers express high levels of general work satisfaction, usually comparable to private-sector counterparts (Kilpatrick, Cummings, and Jennings, 1964; U.S. Office of Personnel Management, 1979). Numerous comparisons of work satisfaction of public and private respondents, however, especially at managerial levels, report somewhat lower satisfaction for the public-sector respondents on various more specific facets of work (Paine, Carroll, and Leete, 1966; Rhinehart and others, 1969; Buchanan, 1974; Hayward, 1978; Rainey, 1983; Lachman, 1985; Solomon, 1986; Baldwin, 1989; Kovach and Patrick, 1989). These studies use different measures of satisfaction and varied samples, and this makes it hard to generalize about them. For example, Paine, Carroll, and Leete (1966) and Rhinehart and others (1969) found that groups of federal managers showed lower satisfaction than business managers on all categories of the Porter scale. Smith and Nock (1980), analyzing results of a large social survey, found that public-sector blue-collar workers show more satisfaction with most aspects of work than their private-sector counterparts, but public-sector white-collar workers show less satisfaction with co-workers, supervision, and intrinsic aspects of work. Hayward (1978) compared employees and managers from a diverse group of public and private organizations and found satisfaction ratings generally high among both groups. The public respondents, however, gave somewhat more unfavorable ratings of their jobs, abilities to make necessary decisions, adequacy of supplies, duplication, and being expected to do too much. Rainey (1983) found that state agency managers scored lower than business managers on satisfaction with promotion and with co-workers.

The findings of these studies vary a great deal and are not easily summarized. The public and private respondents often do not differ greatly, yet one finds it hard to dismiss as accidental the consistent tendency for public managers and employees to score lower on various satisfaction scales. Taken together, these studies reflect a somewhat lower satisfaction with various intrinsic and extrinsic aspects of work in many public organizations than in many private ones. Some of the findings appear to reflect the sorts of administrative constraints described earlier — personnel system constraints (promotion) and purchasing constraints (supplies). Others appear to reflect related frustrations with administrative complexities and the complex political and policy process that diminishes some intrinsic rewards — problems of duplication and lack of authority to make decisions and lower satisfaction of higher-order needs on the part of managers (Rhinehart and others, 1969).

Organizational Commitment and Job Involvement: In Search of the Service Ethic. These suggestions of some particular frustrations of public service also show up in research on public employees' organizational commitment and job involvement. This evidence in turn raises important questions about how public managers and researchers can better understand and reward public-service motives.

Buchanan (1974, 1975) found that groups of federal executives expressed lower organizational commitment and job involvement than executives from private firms. He concluded that the public managers felt less commitment because they did not feel as strong a sense of impact on the organization, because the organization did not expect as much commitment, and because their work groups were more diverse and less of a source of attachment to the organization. He also suggested that the lower involvement scores indicated a frustrated service ethic. His evidence showed that the involvement responses resulted from a sense of less challenging jobs, less cohesive work groups, and more disappointing experiences with organizational reality in relation to what the public managers expected. These disappointments, he thought, might arise when idealistic, service-oriented entrants confronted the realities of large government agencies where they feel they have little impact. Boyatzis (1982) draws a similar conclusion from his comparisons of public and private managers. And Chubb and Moe (1990) find generally lower perceived sense of control and commitment among staff members and teachers in public schools than among their private school counterparts.

Case observations paint a similar picture. Michelson (1980) describes examples of hardworking bureaucrats in nonworking bureaucracies. They work hard, but the diffuse goals and haphazard designs of some programs make their efforts futile. Cherniss (1980) observes that many public-service professionals experience stress and burnout as a result of their frustrated motivation to help their clients and the bureaucratic systems that aggravate their frustrations. Downs's observations about discouraged statesmen and increasing conservatism and Warwick's description of the State Department have similar implications.

The large federal surveys also found a combination of indications of positive attitudes and expressions of frustration or discouragement. The overwhelming majority of respondents to the federal employee attitude survey (U.S. Office of Personnel Management, 1979) said that they feel that they do meaningful work, that what happens in their organization is important, and that their organization performs effectively. Yet high percentages of employees (more than 45 percent), managers (35 percent), and executives (25 percent) express concern that employees feel that they cannot trust the organization. Many employees expressed a sense of powerlessness, a lack of influence and participation in decision making (U.S. Office of Personnel Management, 1979, p. 36). In another large survey, only a limited number of respondents felt that opportunity to have an impact on public affairs represents an important reason to stay in public service (U.S. Merit Systems Protection Board, 1987).

Taken together, these contributions suggest that the majority of public employees and managers have many positive work attitudes and feel that they work hard. Yet a particular problem in public management appears to result from many employees' and managers' lack of a sense of impact and consistent direction, including a feeling of weak impact on public service. This appears to reflect the effects of political and administrative constraints and complexities in the context for motivation in public organizations.

In turn, however, this interpretation raises questions about what we mean by service motivation and impact. Rainey (1982) asked middle managers in state agencies and business firms to rate the values of various rewards from work, including "the opportunity to engage in a meaningful public service." The public managers rated this item much more highly than the business managers, and their ratings were strongly related to their job satisfaction but only weakly related to their scores on job involvement. Maybe job involvement does not capture public-service motivation. Public-service motivation apparently differs from job involvement, organizational commitment, and other generic concepts developed in organizational behavior research, in ways that we need to better understand.

Studies so far have suggested the general nature of the public-service motive (Kilpatrick, Cummings, and Jennings, 1964; Sikula, 1973a). Both managers and researchers need to develop a better understanding of its dimensions and their dynamics. For example, Perry and Wise (1990) suggest that public-service motives can fall into three categories: *instrumental motives,* including participation in policy formulation, commitment to a public program because of personal identification, and advocacy for a special or private interest; *norm-based motives,* including desire to serve the public interest, loyalty to duty and to government, and social equity; and *affective motives,* including commitment to a program based on a conviction about its social importance and the "patriotism of benevolence." They draw the term *patriotism of benevolence* from Frederickson and Hart (1985), who define it as an affection for all people in the nation and a devotion to defending their basic rights, as granted by enabling documents such as the Constitution.

Yet public-service motivation involves additional dimensions. It appears to vary over time, with changes in the public image of government service, and to take different forms in different agencies and service areas. It presents an elusive topic for analysis. Sociologists studying the altruistic commitments of civil rights workers found that they have trouble putting into words their motives for their sacrifices and risks (Demerath, Marwell, and Aiken, 1971). Public managers' references to their own service motives often take a similarly diffuse form. Although complex, these motivations need more attention from managers and researchers. The constraints on extrinsic incentives in government make intrinsic and public-service incentives even more important, in part because managers have some influence over them (Cohen, 1988; Romzek, 1990). Research shows that highly committed employees in government feel that their jobs are compatible with their ethics, values, and professional standards and that their families and friends support their affiliation with the organization (Romzek, 1990). Although the studies reviewed above indicate difficulties in establishing such conditions in some public organizations—probably very complex, controversial, and highly politicized ones with diffuse mandates—public managers can often overcome those problems. As the research also shows, the challenges in the public sector may not be so much more severe than those in the private sector as simply somewhat different (Golembiewski, 1985, 1990a). Public managers can effectively apply techniques and approaches described in this and other chapters: motivational techniques; strategic management and mission setting; transformational leadership and the management of organizational culture, including a culture of excellence; and organization development and planned change. Descriptions and examples of these approaches in the following chapters show that public managers can effectively utilize them.

Chapter 7

Leadership, Managerial Roles, and Organizational Culture

The challenges of leadership in public organizations should be evident. Observers and experienced executives claim that performance indicators and goals evade clarification. Civil service systems, other institutional controls, and the political environment weaken the authority of leaders. Again, experts differ as to how much of this picture is attributable to stereotype and how much to valid observation. Recently, however, a countertrend has begun to emphasize effective and entrepreneurial public leadership. In addition, a long tradition in management looks at leadership as a generic topic, with leadership in public organizations differing little from that in other settings.

This chapter reviews theories of leadership and managerial roles developed in the generic literature and assesses the research on leadership in public organizations. A major recent trend in management literature emphasizes the way in which effective executives, usually business executives, exercise leadership by influencing organizational culture through transformational leadership, or leadership through vision. This trend raises important points about how and when active public managers can use such approaches (Romzek, 1990).

Leadership Theories in Management and Organizational Behavior

An immense body of research has examined leadership in organizational settings. By *leadership,* most people mean the capacity of someone to direct and energize the willingness of people in social units to take actions to achieve goals. The issues raised in the discussion of power and authority in earlier chapters serve as part of the discussion of leadership. Leadership in one sense can draw mainly on blunt power, but usually the term implies legitimate authority. Some people interpret leadership as one of the functions of management—directing and energizing people, in addition to discharging all the other functions of management. Others treat management as the subordinate function. In this usage, leadership involves the crucial functions of championing goals and values, setting direction, and inspiring, while management involves housekeeping functions, such as watching the budget and making sure that the work gets done. Faced with the challenges of understanding this paradoxical topic, how have management researchers attacked the problem?

Trait Theories

First, researchers have tried to determine those characteristics that make a person an effective leader. The research on leadership during mid-century concentrated on this trait approach. They tried to identify the traits of effective leaders—physical characteristics such as height, intellectual characteristics such as intelligence and foresight, personality characteristics such as enthusiasm and persistence. They identified many important traits such as these, which have often shown relationships to effective leadership, and leadership characteristics of various sorts have remained an important element of leadership research. No one, however, has ever identified a common set of traits for excellent leaders. Leaders come in a variety of sizes, shapes, talents, and dispositions. The quest for universal traits has been replaced by other approaches.

The Ohio State Leadership Studies

The social sciences developed rapidly during the middle of this century, with more and more studies using new techniques such as questionnaires and computer analysis and increasing emphasis on systematic observations of human behavior. Drawing on samples from the military, schools, and other organizations, researchers at Ohio State University developed questionnaires that asked people to report on the behaviors of their superiors. In repeated analyses of the questionnaire results, they found that observations about leaders fell into two dimensions that under various names would become central issues in much of the work on leadership to follow—consideration and initiating structure. *Consideration* refers to the leader's concern for relationships with subordinates. Questionnaire items pertaining to consideration ask whether the leader is friendly and approachable, listens to subordinates' ideas and makes use of them, cares about the morale of the group, and otherwise deals with subordinates in an open, communicative, concerned fashion. *Initiating structure* refers to the leader's emphasis on setting standards, assigning roles, and pressing for productivity and performance. The two dimensions tend to be related to each other, but only to a limited extent, which suggests that they are somewhat independent.

This research played a pivotal role in moving the field into empirical research on leadership. It drove the trait approach into disrepute by showing that leaders vary on these dimensions. It also set the dimensions in place in the literature as two key aspects of leader behaviors. Yet the reviewers also raised questions about the adequacy of the scales and the dimensions, and the two dimensions do not make for a complete picture of leadership practice and effectiveness. Researchers have moved off in search of more complete models.

The Blake and Mouton Managerial Grid

The Ohio State leadership studies had a significant impact on Blake and Mouton's (1984) "managerial grid" approach to improving managerial practices. Blake and Mouton characterized organizations according to two dimensions that had clear roots in the earlier studies — *concern for people* and *concern for production*. Organizations low on the former and high on the latter have "authority-obedience" management. Those high on concern for people and low on concern for production have "country club management." Those low on both have "impoverished management." This approach sought to move organizations toward high levels of both factors, or to *team management,* through open communication, participative problem solving and goal setting, confrontation of differences, and teamwork. This framework supported Blake and Mouton's popular organization development consulting, which they applied in a broad range of government, business, and third-sector organizations.

Fiedler's Contingency Theory of Leadership

Researchers still sought more complete theories, especially those that would better account for the variations in situations facing the leader. Fiedler's (1967) contingency theory received a lot of attention because at the time it offered one of the best frameworks for examining relationships between leadership style and the leadership setting and, in turn, how the fit between those two factors is related to the effectiveness of the leader. Fiedler used a "least-preferred co-worker" (LPC) scale to distinguish between types of leadership styles. The LPC scale asked a leader to think of the person with whom that leader could work *least well* and then to rate that person on about twenty numerical scales of personal characteristics, such as pleasant or unpleasant, tense or relaxed, boring or interesting, and nasty or nice. Through repeated studies, Fiedler and his associates felt that they had discovered that leaders' responses on this LPC scale break down into two types: A *high-LPC* leader gives relatively favorable ratings to this least-preferred associate, and *low-LPC* leaders rate the associate much more unfavorably. The responses of high-LPC leaders show that they have more favorable dispositions toward co-workers and thus are *relationship-oriented.* Low-LPC leaders are *task-oriented;* they concentrate on task accomplishment over relationships with co-workers and find less desirable co-workers more irritating because they hinder successful work.

Fiedler's theory holds that either type of leadership style can be effective, depending on whether it properly matches the contingencies facing the leader. According to the theory, the key contingencies, in order of their importance in determining effective leadership, are *leader-member relations,* the degree of friendliness, trust, initiative, and cooperativeness of the subordinates; *task structure,* the clarity and specificity of what must be done; and *position power of the leader,* the amount of formal power that the leader has.

Leadership situations vary from favorable to unfavorable on each of these dimensions. Obviously, the leader enjoys the most favorable setting where all three are favorable and the least favorable setting where all three are bad. Moderately favorable settings have a mixture of good and bad conditions, such as good leader-member relations but an unstructured task setting and weak position power. Fiedler contends that low-LPC (task-oriented) leaders perform most effectively in the very favorable or very unfavorable settings, while high-LPC (relations-oriented) leaders do best in the intermediate settings.

Fiedler's rationale for these interesting relationships evades easy explanation, but the logic appears to go like this: Low-LPC leaders do well in the best situations because everything is in place and the subordinates simply need to be given direction, and they accept the leader as authorized to give such direction. The leader of an airplane crew who has power, clear structure, and good relations does best if he or she concentrates on giving orders to best accomplish the task. The low-LPC type also does well in very bad situations that have so much potential disorder and disaffection anyway that worrying about establishing good personal relations wastes time. The leader might as well go ahead with pressing for structure, order, and output. The high-LPC leader does best in the intermediate situations, because emphasis on good relations can overcome the one or two bad dimensions and take advantage of the favorable aspects. For example, a weakly empowered chair of a newly formed, poorly structured interdepartmental committee who has good relations with the members can take better advantage of those good relations through participation and opinion sharing to overcome the other problems.

Fiedler argued that his theory showed that, rather than trying to fit leaders to fit the settings that they would face, organizations must match the right type of leader to the setting. He and his colleagues developed a "leader match" procedure, in which leaders use questionnaires to assess their own style and their leadership situation and then consider ways of changing the situation to make it better fit their own style.

Fiedler has continued to report studies supporting the theory, but critics question the adequacy of the evidence and the methods used. Clearly, the theory includes a very limited picture of the possible situational factors and variations in leadership styles. Still, it raises key issues about leadership processes and has advanced the effort to develop more complete theories. House and Singh's (1987) authoritative review describes it as the most substantiated theory in recent research.

The Path-Goal Theory of Leadership

The most comprehensive theory to date, the path-goal theory, draws on the expectancy theory of motivation described in the last chapter. Expectancy theory treats motivation as arising from expectations about the results of actions and the value of those results. Similarly, path-goal theory holds that effective leaders increase motivation and satisfaction when they help subordinates pursue important goals and see how to achieve them — that is, to see the goals and the paths to them and to follow those paths effectively. Leaders must do this by showing subordinates the value of outcomes over which the leader has some control, finding ways to increase the value of those outcomes, using appropriate coaching and direction to clarify the paths to those outcomes, and removing barriers and frustrations.

The theory also considers a variety of leadership styles, subordinate characteristics, and situational factors that affect the proper approach to the leader's path-goal work (House, 1971; House and Mitchell, 1974; Filley, House, and Kerr, 1976). House and Mitchell considered four leadership styles: *directive,* where the leader gives specific directions and expectations; *supportive,* involving encouraging, sympathetic relations with subordinates; *achievement-oriented,* where the leader sets high goals and high expectations for subordinate performance and responsibility; and *participative,* where the leader encourages subordinates to express opinions and suggestions.

Which is the best style depends on various situational factors: task characteristics such as whether the task is structured and provides clear goals, whether subordinates have well-developed skills and sense of personal control over their environments ("locus of control"), how much formal authority the leader has, and whether the work group has strong norms and social relations. Where factors such as these already provide weak path-goal indications and incentives, the proper leadership style can enhance them. The leader, however, must also avoid behaviors that impose redundancies and aggravations.

Researchers have predicted and tested relationships such as these: Directive leadership enhances satisfaction and expectancies if the task is ambiguous but hurts them if the task is well structured and clear. Clear tasks already provide clear paths to goals, and subordinates may see more directions from a leader as redundant and irritating. Supportive leadership enhances satisfaction when tasks are frustrating and stressful but can be inappropriate under conditions where the task, the work group, and the organization provide plenty of encouragement and subordinates need the leader to clarify directions and set high standards. Achievement-oriented leadership increases performance of ambiguous tasks, because those conditions make the leader more able to encourage high goals or because achievement-oriented subordinates tend to select such tasks. Participative leadership works best for ambiguous tasks in which subordinates feel that their self-esteem is at stake, since participation allows them to influence decisions and to work out solutions to the ambiguity. For clear tasks, however, participative leadership will be effective only if subordinates value self-control and independence.

As these examples show, the theory weaves together leadership styles and situational factors to make sufficiently subtle predictions to capture some of the complex variations in real leadership settings. A lot of research, however, has produced mixed results and much debate. Some research continues to find support for some variant of the theory, although it has not received much research attention recently (House and Singh, 1987).

The Vroom-Yetton Normative Model

Vroom and Yetton (1973; Vroom and Jago, 1974) propose an elaborate framework for leaders to use in deciding how and how much to involve subordinates or subordinate groups in decisions. The framework takes the form of a decision tree that guides the leader through a series of questions about how important the quality of the decision will be, whether the leader has the necessary information to make a high-quality decision, whether the problem is well structured, whether acceptance of the decision by subordinates is important, and whether conflict among them is likely. The decision process guides the leader in selecting from various ways of handling the decision, such as delegating it and making it after consulting subordinates.

Attribution Models

Social psychologists have developed a body of theory about how people make attributions about one another, or how they attribute characteristics to others. Some leadership researchers have applied this perspective to leadership and produced useful insights. They look at how leaders draw conclusions about how and why their subordinates are behaving and performing and how subordinates form impressions about leaders. Leaders interpret the apparent causes of subordinate behavior and performance in deciding how to respond. They take into account how unique to a particular task the performance happens to be, the consistency of the behaviors, and how they compare to those of other subordinates. Some of the research shows that, when a subordinate performs poorly, leaders tend to attribute the problems to the subordinate if he or she has a bad record. If the person has a good record of past performance, however, leaders often conclude that the problems result from the situation surrounding the person and are not his or her fault. For their part, subordinates often attribute the lion's share of credit or blame for the group's performance and characteristics to their leader. If the group has performed well in the past, they tend more readily to give the leader credit for current successes, even rating him or her more highly on certain leader behaviors and interpreting these as causes.

   Attribution theories obviously offer partial approaches that do not cover the full topic of leadership, but they clearly point to important processes for leaders to keep in mind. Leaders always face the challenge of managing the impressions that others form of them and trying to form valid impressions of those with whom they work. These attribution processes pertain to problems in public management, where political appointees come in at the tops of agencies and must establish relations with career civil servants in the agencies. Frequently, the political appointees anticipate resistance and poor performance from the careerists. The careerists sometimes anticipate amateurishness from the political appointee. When problems come up, the two types tend to attribute the problem to their preconceptions about each other, aggravating the problem of developing working relations. The careerists and appointees often come to respect each other, but the attribution processes often slow this process (Heclo, 1978; Light, 1987; Ingraham, 1988).

Life-Cycle Theory

Hersey and Blanchard (1982) offer another form of contingency theory. Their life-cycle theory suggests that leadership styles must fit the level of maturity of the group being led. Mature groups have a higher capacity to accept responsibility because they are well educated, experienced, and capable in accomplishing the group tasks and have well developed relationships with each other and the leader. With groups that are very low on these dimensions, however, leaders must engage in *telling,* emphasizing task directions over developing relationships with the group, to move the group toward better task capabilities. As the group moves higher on those dimensions of maturity but remains at a low level of maturity, the leader must do more *selling,* or heavily emphasizing both tasks and relationships. As the group moves to moderately high maturity, *participating* becomes the most effective style. The leader relaxes emphasis on task direction but still attends to relationships. Finally, for a very mature group, *delegating* becomes the effective approach. The leader deemphasizes his or her own role in directing tasks and maintaining relationships and shifts responsibility to group members.

Loosely defined concepts plague the theory, but it makes important points. Leaders often face the challenge of assessing just how much the group can accept delegation and how much it needs someone to take charge and set directions, as well as determining how to move the group toward greater capacity to handle its tasks and relations independently.

Operant Conditioning and Social Learning Theory Models

The operant conditioning and behavior modification perspectives described in the last chapter have found their way into the search for leadership theories. Some early behavior modification approaches emphasized reinforcement of outcomes over concern with internal mental states. Proponents argued that these approaches offered significant improvements for leadership techniques, for several reasons. They stressed observations of behavior, rather than dubious inferences about what happens in a person's head. For example, they said that managers should look at behaviors and performance outcomes, rather than whether a person has a "good attitude." They called for close attention to the consequences of behavior, saying that leaders must attend to the behaviors that they reinforce or extinguish by associating consequences with those behaviors. They emphasized positive reinforcement as most effective.

Later approaches, however, began to take into account the developments in social learning theory in psychological research. Albert Bandura (1978) and other psychologists demonstrated that operant theory models needed expansion to include the forms of learning and behavioral change that are not tied tightly to some reinforcement. People learn by watching others, through modeling and vicarious learning. They use mental symbols, rehearsal, and memorization techniques to develop their behaviors. Taking these insights into account, more recent social learning theory models of leadership have added internal mental states and social learning to their analyses of leadership (Kreitner and Luthans, 1987). This has led to additional suggestions about leadership practices. Accepting that internal mental states and social learning affect behavior, in addition to emphasizing feedback and after-the-fact reinforcement, leaders can use "feedforward" influences. They can anticipate problems and actively avoid them by clarifying goals and enhancing their acceptance through participative development of the goals, using social cues such as providing good role models. They can also emphasize self-management for themselves and their subordinates. This involves managing one's own environment by recognizing and working with the way environmental cues influence one's behavior and through personal goal setting, rehearsal, and self-instruction.

Cognitive Resource Utilization Theory

Researchers continue to work on additional theories. Among very recent ones, Fiedler's cognitive resource utilization theory has received the most validation in supporting studies (Fiedler and Garcia, 1987; House and Singh, 1987). It extends the Fiedler contingency theory, specifying when directive (low-LPC) behaviors affect group performance but also drawing in the role of the leader's intelligence, competence, and stress level. Fiedler and Garcia report that research had unexpectedly shown that considerate (high-LPC) leader behavior had little effect on group performance. For such leaders, if the group supports them and the task requires cognitive abilities, then the cognitive abilities of the group determine performance. If the group does not support them, then external factors, such as task difficulty, determine performance.

For directive leaders, with much control over the situation, performance depends on whether the leader is free of stress, whether the task requires cognitive abilities, and whether the group supports the leader. If these conditions hold, the leader's intelligence strongly predicts performance. If the leader is under stress, however, the leader's experience becomes the best predictor of performance, because the stress prevents the effective use of intelligence and brings background experience more strongly into play. Also, if the task does not require cognitive skill or the group does not support the leader, then the leader's intelligence has little or no effect on performance. As the authors state, their theory and research suggest the "not surprising conclusion that directive leaders who are stupid give stupid directions, and if the group follows these directions, the consequences will be bad" (Fiedler and Garcia, 1987, p. 199). Directive leader behaviors result in good performance only if linked to high leader intelligence in a supportive, unstressful setting. The theory offers useful new insights into such variables in the leadership process as stress, which leaders can strive to manage (House and Singh, 1987).

Other theories, such as social information-processing theory and dyadic linkage theory, also receive attention, but probably the most striking departure in recent leadership research concerns transformational leadership. Before covering that approach, however, it is useful to review a body of research on managerial roles and behaviors to which the transformational leadership research reacts.

The Nature of Managerial Work and Roles

As the research on leadership developed, there also emerged a body of work on the characteristics of managerial work, roles, and skills. This literature actually involves something of a trait approach. It seeks to develop general conceptions of managerial activities and competencies. Ever since the classical theorists began trying to define the role of the administrator, the approach of "planning, organizing, staffing, directing, coordinating, reporting, and budgeting" (PODSCORB; see the Appendix) or some variant of it has served as a guiding conception of what managers must do. Often coupled with this view is the constantly repeated view that managers in all settings must do pretty much the same general types of work. Graham Allison (1983) illustrated the prevalence of the PODSCORB conception of managerial responsibilities when he used a form of it in one of the most widely reprinted and circulated articles ever written on public management (see Table 7.1).

Not so preoccupied with what managers must do as with what they actually do, Henry Mintzberg (1972) produced *The Nature of Managerial Work*, which now stands as a classic in the field. He did something that, remarkably, was considered quite original at the time: He closely observed the work of five managers by following them around and having them keep notebooks. He concluded that their work falls into the set of roles listed in Table 7.1.

Mintzberg also reported that when one actually watches what managers do, one sees the inaccuracy of some popular beliefs about their work. Managers do not play the role of systematic, rational planners but rather emphasize action over reflection. Their activities are characterized by brevity,

Table 7.1. Managerial Roles and Skills.

Allison (1983): Functions of General Management

Strategy
    Establishing objectives and priorities
    Devising operational plans
Managing internal components
    Organizing and staffing
    Directing personnel and the personnel management system
    Controlling performance
Managing external constituencies
    Dealing with external units subject to some common authority
    Dealing with independent organizations
    Dealing with the press and the public

Mintzberg (1972): Executive Roles

Interpersonal
    Figurehead
    Leader
    Liaison
Informational
    Monitor
    Disseminator
    Spokesperson
Decisional
    Entrepreneur
    Disturbance Handler
    Resource Allocator
    Negotiator

Cameron and Whetten (1983): Management Skill Topics

Self-awareness	Effective delegation and joint decision making
Managing personal stress	Gaining power and influence
Creative problem solving	Managing conflict
Establishing supportive communication	Improving group decision making
Improving employee performance, motivating others	

The Benchmarks Scales (McCauley, Lombardo, and Usher, 1989)

1a. Resourcefulness
1b. Doing whatever it takes
1c. Being a quick study
2a. Building and mending relationships
2b. Leading subordinates
2c. Compassion and sensitivity
3. Straightforwardness and composure
4. Setting a developmental climate
5. Confronting problem subordinates
6. Team orientation
7. Balance between personal life and work
8. Decisiveness
9. Self-awareness
10. Hiring talented staff
11. Putting people at ease
12. Acting with flexibility

variety, and discontinuity. While managers are often told to plan and delegate and avoid regular duties, in reality they handle regular duties such as ceremonies, negotiations, and relations with the environment, such as meeting visitors and getting information through the sources to which they have the best access of anyone in the organization. Managers meet visiting dignitaries, give out gold watches, talk with managers and officials from outside the organization, hobnob at charitable events, and preside over the annual banquet. While managers are sometimes told that they need aggregate, systematically analyzed information, they actually favor oral media, such as telephone calls and face-to-face talks and meetings. While management increasingly has scientific supports and processes, managers still rely a great deal on intuition and judgment. A good deal of research now supports Mintzberg's observations about management and his typology of managerial roles (Kurke and Aldrich, 1983). Generally, the research finds his typology widely applicable to managers in many settings. Yet Mintzberg also found some particular characteristics of the public-sector setting, and these, too, have been supported in recent research, as discussed later.

In addition, experts on management have developed a wide variety of concepts and measures of management skills for use in evaluation and development of managers. Cameron and Whetten (1983), for example, classify important skills under the topics shown in Table 7.1. McCauley, Lombardo, and Usher (1989) report the use of a "benchmarks" instrument for assessing managers' development needs. Based on studies of the development of executives, the scales (see Table 7.1) assess both skills and managerial values and perspectives. Boyatzis (1982) reports a study of the primary competencies of managers in federal agencies and large private firms, discussed later.

Transformational Leadership

Interest in transformational leadership has burgeoned recently. During the 1970s, researchers in the field expressed increasing concern about the inadequacy of their theories. Leadership theorists began to argue that research had concentrated too narrowly on the exchanges between leaders and their subordinates in task situations and on highly quantified models and analyses. Some researchers called for more attention to larger issues and other sources of leadership thought, such as political and historical analysis and more qualitative research using interviews and case studies. A political scientist, James MacGregor Burns (1978), exerted a seminal influence on leadership thought in the management field. Concerned with major political and social leaders such as presidents and prime figures in social movements, Burns distinguished between *transactional* leadership and *transformational* leadership.

Transactional leaders motivate followers by recognizing their needs and providing rewards to fulfill those needs in exchange for their performance and support. Transformational leaders raise followers' goals to higher plains, to a focus on transcendental, higher-level goals akin to the self-actualization needs defined by Maslow. In addition, they motivate followers to transcend their own narrow self-interest in pursuit of these goals, for the benefit of the community or the polity. Martin Luther King provides an example of a leader who did not simply offer to exchange benefits for support but called for a new order of existence, a society of greater justice, and he inspired many people to work for this vision. Many others refrained from opposing it because of its moral rightness.

Management experts found these ideas provocative. Uncharitably, Bennis and Nanus (1985, p. 4) say of the body of research on leadership, "Never have so many labored so long to say so little." They argue that our institutions and their leaders face increasing complexity and challenges to their credibility, requiring new conceptions of "transformative" leadership. This type of leadership relies on power, but not in a controlling, centralized way. These leaders use extraordinary talents for coupling visions of success and directions to them and the "empowerment" and motivation of others to contribute.

Bennis and Nanus report on their interviews with ninety outstanding leaders from business and the "public sector" (for example, a federal agency director, an orchestra leader, a football coach). They draw a sharp distinction between leadership and management. The latter, they say, involves conducting, taking charge, accomplishing goals with efficiency, and "doing things right" (p. 21). Leadership involves guiding directions, actions, opinions, or, as they put it, "doing the right thing" (p. 21). Excellent leaders, they conclude, lead others in large part by carefully managing *themselves,* through such strategies as the following:

- *Attention through vision:* They effectively create visions of successful futures, which focus their attention and that of their followers, in part by transactions with followers that bring out the best in both leader and followers (Tichy and Ulrich, 1984).
- *Meaning through communication:* They effectively transmit this vision to others in ways that give meaning to their work and their quest. Bennis and Nanus describe examples of even very taciturn leaders who got across their points and purposes through symbols and drawings. The communication transmits not simply facts but, more importantly, reasons why and ways of learning and problem solving.
- *Trust through positioning:* The outstanding leaders show particular skill at choosing the best course, at knowing what is right and necessary. They choose directions and themes and adhere to them with constancy in ways that induce trust in their identity and integrity.
- *The deployment of self through positive self-regard:* They have high regard for their own skills and utilize them effectively. Yet they also remain aware of their own limitations and work to overcome them, often by attracting people who compensate for those limitations. They work with those people with respect, courteous attention, trust, and the ability to do without constant approval from them.

- *The Wallenda factor:* Bennis and Nanus describe one way that leaders pursued this deployment of self by pointing to the example of the famous tightrope walker Karl Wallenda. Wallenda put great energy and focus into his work; he did not obsess himself with past problems or prospects of failure. Wallenda finally lost his life in a major appearance before which he had been utterly preoccupied with *not* falling. The outstanding leaders encourage in themselves and others a spirit of development, experimentation, reasonable risk-taking and adventure, and even tolerance for well-intentioned mistakes that lead to learning. They concentrate on succeeding rather than becoming obsessed with the possibility of failure.
- *Empowerment:* Successful leaders also expand their own capacity by empowering others, making them feel a sense of significance, community, competence, and even fun. Thus, the others strive to contribute not because of close direction and control by the leader but through empowerment.

Bass (1985) presents a much more systematic analysis of transformational leadership, which adds too many additional points to be covered here. Like Burns, he sharply distinguishes transactional from transformational leadership. Burns, however, sees transformational leadership as uplifting. It shifts followers' focus from lower- to higher-order needs. It motivates them to sacrifice their own self-interest by showing followers that their self-interests are fulfilled or linked to community or higher-order needs. Bass agrees that there must be a shift in needs, but he points out that major leaders — Hitler, for instance — can have a transforming influence through a *negative* shift. Bass argues that the wrong kind of transformational leadership can damage followers and other groups.

Bass's analysis of transformational leadership is so careful and elaborate that any summary does injustice to it. Generally, however, he points out that this form of leadership involves an emotional and intellectual component. The emotional component involves charisma, an inspiring influence on followers. The intellectual component involves processes of careful attention to individual followers, often of a benevolent, developmental, mentoring nature, as well as intellectual stimulation. The intellectual aspects can take various forms, such as manipulating symbols, rational discourse, or evocation of ideals, and involves cognitive stimulation as much as intellectual teaching. Bass emphasizes that leadership research has often underrated the importance of the technical competence of the leader as a basis for the leader's influence and effectiveness. Followers often admire and follow primarily because the leader is very good at what he or she does.

While Burns treats transactional and transformational leadership as two polar extremes, Bass argues that transformational leaders also engage in varying degrees of transactional relations with followers. They have to provide rewards and reasonable clarity of goals and directions. Yet overemphasis on exchange and direct reward, especially when negative and punishing, can be harmful. The significance of transformational leadership derives from its capacity to lift and expand the goals of individuals, not by overemphasizing direct, extrinsic returns to self-interest but rather by inspiring new, higher aspirations. Hence comes the emphasis on relatively intangible and idealized influences through vision, empowerment, charisma, inspiration, individual consideration, and intellectual stimulation. Transformational leaders do not directly control their subordinates but rather seek to influence the climate in which they work. Thus, this view of leadership has connections with another recent trend, the emphasis on managing organizational culture.

Leadership and Organizational Culture

Transformational leaders avoid closely "managing" their subordinates and organizations. Rather, they work their influence through "social architecture," the basic symbols and core values, or *culture,* of the organization. Writers on organizational culture describe the key roles that leaders play in forming, maintaining, and changing those cultures (Schein, 1985).

As with the transformational leadership topic, the interest in organizational culture grows out of a disenchantment with the way that organizational research has been going. Many writers on culture complain that researchers have worried too much about testing highly structured conceptual models of the sort we reviewed earlier for motivation and leadership, with tightly quantitative procedures. This provides only crude, static snapshots of reality, they argue, which do not explain the phenomena very well. Ott (1989) mounts this criticism and ties the interest in culture to a growing interest in more qualitative research methods. These often involve going into organizations without preconceived ideas and carefully observing events and behaviors. This allows for more attention to the whole picture and to dynamic processes. Culture theorists argue that this approach more accurately analyzes organizational reality and prevents misconceptions and inaccuracies that arise out of the use of standard surveys and other heretofore conventional techniques. One cannot genuinely understand organizations and their successes and failures, they contend, without effective analysis of their cultures.

Analysts now offer many different definitions of organizational culture, referring to the climate, the basic values, symbols, and myths, the norms of appropriate behavior, and other elements. In a prominent book, Schein (1985) argues that culture incorporates all of these but that none of these factors captures the basic idea. Culture exists on various levels, he says. The most basic and least observable level, often overlooked in other conceptions of culture, is the *basic assumptions* on which the organization operates. Often invisible and unconscious, these concern the relationship with the environment (for example, highly active and manipulative or passive and reactive), the nature of reality, time and space (for example, orientation toward rapid action), and the nature of humans and their activities and relationships (for example, does knowledge arise from the individual, from scientific authority, or from experienced leaders?). The next level involves more overtly expressed *values* about how things ought to be and how one ought to respond in general (for example, always try to keep debt low, always have strong relationships with key members of Congress, always develop the careers and skills of young managers). Finally, the most observable level includes *artifacts and creations,* such as actual technological processes (purposely designed work processes and administrative procedures and instructions), art (symbols, logos, creations), and behaviors (words used, communication patterns, significant outbursts, rituals and ceremonies).

Schein attaches great significance to the roles of founders and leaders of organizations. Founders have a formative influence on the culture, setting basic directions, orientations, and assumptions. Subsequent leaders must maintain and, as needed, transform these cultural orientations. They can embed cultural elements through a variety of mechanisms. One of these is what they pay attention to and measure. A leader who says that henceforth she will evaluate how well managers develop their subordinate managers sends a powerful message about priorities. Another is responding to significant instances and crises. A major outburst can send strong signals. Reacting sharply in a meeting to mistreatment of an employee transmits strong messages about the leader's assumptions and values. Bennis and Nanus report the interesting incident of a manager who lost a lot of money through aggressive actions in a project for a computer company. When he offered his resignation, his superior asked, "How can we fire you when we have just spent ten million dollars educating you?" A powerful message about reasonable risk taking and aggressiveness comes across. Additional mechanisms are deliberate role modeling and coaching, reward and status criteria, and criteria for recruitment, selection, promotion, and removal. Mechanisms of somewhat less importance include organizational structures and procedures, design of physical space and buildings, stories and legends, and formal statements of organizational philosophy.

The topic of organizational culture has been very popular recently, but the topic remains elusive. Authors tend to illustrate its importance by pointing out a single element of what they call culture and showing how mismanagement of it causes problems. Schein gives an example of cultural mismatch: A food services company created problems when it bought out a video games company and instituted individual performance incentives in the video games company. Since the games were designed by teams, the individual incentive system did not work out. Does this really reflect the clash of corporate cultures or just poor planning and implementation of an incentive system?

Despite such questions, the topic of organizational culture, like the work on transformational leadership, reflects important developments in management thought. Studies of organizational culture offer insights into the dynamics of public organizations. For example, Maynard-Moody, Stull, and Mitchell (1986) provide a rich description of the development and transformation of culture in the Kansas Department of Health and Environment. Early in the century, an influential secretary of the department had instituted a culture that emphasized professional expertise in defense of public health, with relative autonomy from political intrusion, strict rules, adherence to the budget. Through slogans, pamphlets, symbolic political actions, and publicity campaigns, he led the development of a well-established culture that predominated for decades. Much later, the governor and legislators, to bring the department under stronger political control, brought in an outsider as secretary. He and his followers led a reorganization that reduced the status of the adherents of the old culture and their beliefs and values, in part through constant denunciations of the old ways of doing things. The new culture, which emphasized different basic beliefs, such as the importance of political responsiveness and adherence to strict operating procedures, clashed with and supplanted the older culture.

These ideas about managing culture have pervaded management practice. More and more, analysts characterize successful organizations and leaders, especially in private corporations, as responding to current conditions of high flux and complexity by seeking to foster an encouraging environment in which people can work, rather than through directly manipulating and directing people. Paradoxically, they extend control by relaxing control in certain ways. They gain power by sharing power. Public managers have increasingly adopted some of these approaches. The development of strategy and mission statements (see Chapter Four) often draws on ideas about vision and culture. Chapter Four also described how Robert Dempsey tried to manage aspects of the culture of a Law Enforcement agency, including basic decision premises about communicative leadership. Chapters Ten and Eleven describe examples of these approaches in the public and private sectors. Such approaches often address factors that public managers can influence even when legislative mandates and administrative constraints tie down many extrinsic rewards (Romzek, 1990). In the discussion of effective public managers below, we see many features of transformational leadership and the management of culture. Chapter Ten provides further examples of the part such orientations have played in campaigns to revitalize troubled government agencies. Chapter Eleven gives examples of excellent public agencies, many of which appear to emphasize such orientations.

Leadership and Management in Public Organizations

A review of the literature shows that researchers in the management field have treated leadership and management in the public sector as essentially the same as in other settings, including business. Many of the major contributions, such as the Ohio State leadership studies and Fiedler's theories, developed in part out of research on military officers or governmental managers. Bennis and Nanus (1985) included public-sector leaders, such as the head of the Securities and Exchange Commission and the city manager of

Cincinnati, and emphasized the similarities among all the leaders that they studied. Mintzberg's (1972) study included a public manager (a school system superintendent) and a quasi-public manager (a hospital administrator). Additional studies find that Mintzberg's role categories apply to managers in government agencies (Lau, Pavett, and Newman, 1980). While Mintzberg and later researchers (Kurke and Aldrich, 1983) found some special features of public managers' work, still others find that even these few distinctions do not always hold for all types of public managers (Ammons and Newell, 1989). Small wonder that leadership researchers typically regard a public-versus-private distinction as rather inconsequential. Leaders in all settings face the challenges and general tasks suggested in the theories that we have reviewed.

Generalizations About the Distinctive Context

Although virtually everyone accepts the premise that executives and managers face very similar tasks and challenges, a strong and growing body of evidence suggests that public managers also operate within contexts that require rather distinctive skills and knowledge. For years, political scientists writing about public bureaucracy argued that the political processes and governmental institutions in which governmental managers work made their jobs very different from those of business executives. Those writers did not, however, do as much empirical research on leadership as the organizational behavior and management researchers did. Clear evidence of differences remained rather scarce, and many management scholars noted the evidence of similarity among all managerial roles and rejected such notions as crude stereotypes.

   More recently, however, more attention to the topic of public management brought out some additional evidence. One form of evidence about the nature of public management comes from executives who served in both business and government and wrote about the differences that they saw between the two roles (Allison, 1983; Blumenthal, 1983; Cervantes, 1983; Chase and Reveal, 1983; Rumsfeld, 1983). Although diverse, the executives agree that the constraints, controls, and processes described in earlier chapters bore heavily on their managerial behaviors:

- Jurisdiction-wide rules for personnel, purchasing, budgeting, and other administrative functions, usually with an oversight agency administering them, which limit executive authority
- Legislative and interest-group alliances with subgroups and individuals within the organization that dilute the executive's authority over those groups or individuals
- Control by legislatures and chief executives over resource and policy decisions and the strong demands from legislators for strict accountability of the agency head for all matters pertaining to the agency

- The influence of the press and the imperative that executives concern themselves with media coverage
- The short tenure of many top executives, which limits their time horizons and weakens their influence over careerists
- The absence of clear and accepted performance measures for their organizations and the activities within them

Federal executives report from a very special perspective, of course. Although we have more than a dozen such reports (Allison, 1983), this still includes only a small sample. Yet more structured academic research paints a similar picture. Various studies of public managers show a general tendency for their roles to reflect the context of political interventions and administrative constraints.

Much of this evidence comes not from studies of leadership practices per se but from analyses of managerial roles. In his seminal study, Mintzberg (1972) found that the work of all the managers fell into his now well-known role categories. Yet the public manager in the sample (a school administrator) and the quasi-public manager (a hospital administrator) spent more time in contacts and formal meetings with external interest groups and governing boards and received more external status requests than did the private managers. More recently, Kurke and Aldrich (1983) replicated the study, including the findings about public management; they point to public-versus-private comparisons as an important direction for future research on managerial roles. Lau, Pavett, and Newman (1980), also using a technique based on that of Mintzberg, find the roles of civilian managers in the U.S. Department of the Navy comparable to those of private manufacturing and service firm managers. Yet they also add a role of "technical expert" to the role categories for the navy managers and note that they spend more time in crisis management and "fire drills" than the private managers. Ammons and Newell (1989), on the other hand, conducted a survey of mayors and city managers using Mintzberg's categories and found somewhat different results. Comparing their sample of mayors and city managers to private-sector samples from previous studies, they found that these city officials spent no more time in formally scheduled meetings than did the private-sector managers. This contradicts the findings of Mintzberg and of Kurke and Aldrich in general. Yet a closer look shows that the mayors and city managers did spend more time in phone calls and in conducting tours than did the private-sector managers. Ammons and Newell note that they cannot really say what the phone calls involved, and they may well represent contacts with external groups and political actors.

A study by Porter and Von Maanen (1983) supports this interpretation. They compare city government administrators to industrial managers and find that the city administrators feel less control over how they allocate their own time, feel more pressed for time, and regard demands from people outside the organization as a much stronger influence on how they manage their time. At the level of state government, Weinberg (1977) reports a case study of the management of New Jersey state agencies by the governor and concludes that "crisis management" plays a central role in shaping public executives' decisions and priorities.

In an observational study of six bureau chiefs of large federal bureaus, Kaufman (1979) found that they spend much of their time in classic, generic management functions such as motivating employees, communicating, and decision making. The political environment figures crucially in their roles, however. Relations with Congress outweigh relations with the higher executives of their departments. Clearly, they operate within a web of institutional constraints on organizational structure, personnel administration, and other matters. Aberbach, Putnam, and Rockman's (1981) study of legislators and administrators in six countries (described in Chapter Three) supports this depiction of congressional influence as stronger than that of agency heads.

Boyatzis (1982) conducted a study of managerial competencies and compared managers in four federal agencies and twelve large firms. He found that private managers were higher on "goal and action" competencies, and he attributed this to clearer performance measures, such as profits, in the private sector. The private managers also scored higher on competencies in "conceptualization" and "use of oral presentations." Boyatzis suggests that more strategic decision making in the private firms and more openness and standard procedures in the public sector account for this. Interestingly, Boyatzis's findings correspond to those of earlier studies. Like Guyot (1960), he finds that public managers show *higher* levels of need for achievement and need for power. Yet their lower scores on goal and action competencies reflected less ability to fulfill such needs. Boyatzis's interpretation agrees with that of Buchanan (1975). They both regard this as evidence that fairly ambitious and idealistic people come to managerial work in government but appear to experience constraints within the complex government agencies and policy processes.

Chase and Reveal (1983) discuss the challenges of public management on the basis of Chase's extensive experience in government, especially in large urban agencies. Their depiction of the key challenges in managing a public agency concentrates on managing the external political and institutional environment — dealing with elected chief executives who have shorterterm, more election-oriented priorities and competing for a place on their agenda; coping with overhead agencies such as civil service commissions, budget bureaus, and general service agencies (travel, purchasing, space allocation); dealing with legislators (including city councils); and managing relations with special-interest groups and the media.

While these studies differ among themselves in findings, types of managers studied, and other important ways, they confirm the general observations that public managers carry out their work under conditions of constraint and intervention from the political and administrative environment.

The form of influence or constraint may vary between mayors, public school superintendents, governors, and middle managers in federal agencies, but it shows up consistently in one form or another, in reference to formal meetings with controlling groups, fire drills, crisis management, phone calls, external demands on time and priorities, the crucial role of legislators, media, and interest groups, and other indications of the openness of the managerial role to the political process and the governmental administrative structure.

Does the Context Affect Performance and Behavior?

Clearly, the executives who report on their experiences in both sectors do not regard themselves as inferior managers. They agree that managing in the public sector is *harder* (Allison, 1983) and in this sense acknowledge that a public executive has more trouble exerting a great impact.

　　　Yet sharper critiques raise crucial questions about whether the public-sector context simply penalizes or prevents excellence in leadership. From his case study of the U.S. State Department, Warwick (1975) concludes that federal executives and middle managers face strict constraints on their authority. Goals are vague. The Congress and other elements of the federal system — including many politically appointed executives themselves — adhere to an "administrative orthodoxy" akin to the old principles of administration. They hold top executives accountable for all that happens in the agency and expect agencies to show clear lines of authority and accountability through their ranks, and narrow spans of control. The executives and middle managers have little control over career civil servants, yet they feel intense pressure to control them to avoid bad publicity or political miscues. Because of vague performance criteria, they try to control behavior rather than outcomes through a profusion of rules and required clearances. Paradoxically, this fails to exert real control on the lower levels and further complicates the bureaucratic system. Warwick refers to this drawing upward of authority as "escalation to the top" and says that an "abdication at the bottom" mirrors it at lower levels, where careerists emphasize security and accept the rules. When they disagree, they simply "wait out" the executives' short tenure. Top executives also preoccupy themselves with external politics and public policy issues, abdicating any role in developing human resources or organizational support systems and processes and otherwise developing the organization itself. Warwick cites Downs (1967) pointedly, and his view accords with Downs's and Niskanen's views described in Chapter Six.

　　　Lynn (1981) and Allison (1983) express much less pessimism but nevertheless a similar concern about a performance deficit. Lynn, too, laments the tendency of many federal executives to emphasize political showmanship over substantive management. He refers to the problem of "inevitable bureaucracy," in which higher levels try to control lower levels through disseminating rules and directives, which add to the array of them without really exerting influence. Similarly, the report of the National Academy of Public Administration (1986) laments the complex web of controls and rules over managerial decisions in federal agencies and the adverse effect on federal managers' capacity and motivation to manage their units.

In addition, the Volcker Commission (1989) reports a quiet crisis at the higher levels of the federal career service. The poor image of the federal service, pay constraints and higher pay levels in the private sector, and pressures from political executives and appointees have damaged morale among these executives and increased their likelihood of leaving the federal service. Recruitment to replace them is hampered by the same factors that discourage them. The loss and demoralization of experienced executives and difficulties in finding high-quality replacements will likely diminish effective leadership practices.

Surveys Concerning Leadership Practices

Several surveys of employees' ratings of their supervisors provide mixed evidence about the quality of leadership in government organizations. The large survey by the U.S. Merit Systems Protection Board (1987) found that only 49 percent of the respondents agreed that "my supervisor has good leadership qualities." Also, bare majorities agreed that they have trust and confidence in their supervisor and that the supervisor does well at organization of the work group and encouragement of suggestions. Just over 60 percent agreed that the supervisor is fair, communicative, and technically skillful. The even larger federal employee attitude survey (U.S. Office of Personnel Management, 1979) found more favorable ratings. Sixty to 75 percent of the respondents agreed with statements that their supervisor deals well with subordinates, handles the technical and administrative parts of the job well, encourages the respondent's help in developing work methods, and asks the respondent's opinions about work-related matters. Yet sizable percentages did not feel that their supervisor encouraged their participation in important decisions. The managers and executives responded to a series of questions about whether top executives got their appointments through skill and merit, whether top executives express dissenting views and try new ideas, and whether there are good provisions for developing executives. Sizable percentages (20 to 40 percent) gave unfavorable responses to these questions.

Responses such as these admit to no easy interpretation. Should we rejoice that 60 percent respond favorably about some aspect of leadership or worry that 40 percent disagree or say that they are undecided? In addition, a comparison with the private sector might reveal that government experiences no greater problems than other domains. We do have some comparative evidence. The National Center for Productivity and Quality of Working Life (1978) analyzed a large data set compiled from surveys in ten public and eleven private organizations, where thousands of employees had responded to the same survey questionnaire. The public organizations included state and city governments and federal agencies, and the private organizations included private manufacturing, food-service, and banking firms. The private respondents generally gave more favorable ratings about their organizations, work, and supervision. The private-sector managers and employees were 10 to 15 percent more likely to agree that their supervisors do a good job and show technical competence, and that their supervisors' supervisors do a good job. The public managers gave slightly higher ratings of their supervisors' human relations skills. Ten percent more of the public employees, however, disagreed with a statement that their supervisors had good human relations skills.

The most reasonable conclusion from these surveys resembles the general conclusion about differences between the sectors in satisfaction ratings. In general, with the exception of current problems at the higher levels of the federal career service, the public sector does not show problems of crisis proportions or of markedly greater severity than the private sector. Generally, public-sector employees and managers express favorable impressions of leadership practices in their agencies. Yet the evidence also indicates some public-sector problems and a degree of private-sector superiority in developing leaders, the participativeness of leaders, and some other leadership practices in government. These results coincide generally with some of the concerns expressed by the authors cited above about constraints on leadership in government. Yet they also place those concerns in perspective by showing the inaccuracy of overstatements of the problem. While governments probably do face constraints in encouraging and developing excellent leadership practices, many excellent leaders and managers serve in government.

Attention to Management and Leadership

Although many observers claim that public managers pay scant attention to leading and managing their organizations, the evidence clearly shows otherwise, at least in many specific cases. Saying what we mean by managing and leading is part of the problem. The complaints say that public managers show too little attention to long-range objectives and to internal development of the organization and human resources. Critics of business management, especially in recent years, complain that similar problems plague industry in the United States. Business firms place too much emphasis on short-term profit, while foreign competitors such as the Japanese outcompete them by emphasizing longer-term strategies for enhancing product quality. Also, they point out, business leaders concentrate on achieving huge financial returns for themselves, even where the performance of their firms lags. During the takeover boom of the 1980s, when many firms were purchased or merged, experts on business worried that these purchases created a moutainous burden of debt for the companies, since the purchases often involved leveraging through "junk bonds" on the company being purchased.

In this period, experts also noted that large segments of the financial and industrial sectors in the United States concentrated on such machinations rather than on engineering and product quality. Others argued that the pressures were good for American industry, forcing improvements. Yet even this position implies shortsighted, lethargic management. Under what definition of management and leadership can we depict government as inferior?

Moreover, abundant evidence shows that many governmental managers work very hard. Ammons and Newell (1989) report that mayors, city managers, and their immediate executive assistants say that they work about sixty to sixty-six hours per week. Executives from the private sector who have served in Washington regularly report their impressions of how hard the staff members and executives in the federal government work (Volcker Commission, 1989).

Do they spend much of this time working on political gamesmanship, as some of the critiques of federal executives suggest? At the city level, several surveys have asked city officials to report on the time that they spend in managerial roles (staffing, budgeting, evaluating, directing, and so on), in policy roles (forming policy about the future of the city, meeting with other city officials, and so on), and in political roles (dealing with external political groups and authorities, such as state and federal officials and active community groups, and engaging in public relations activities such as speeches and ceremonies). Ammons and Newell (1989) found that the mayors, city managers, and executive assistants in their survey reported, on average, devoting 55 percent of their time to managerial roles, 28 percent to policy roles, and 17 percent to political roles. Mayors ranged above these averages in concentration on the political role, and the assistants paid more attention to the managerial roles, as might be expected.

Ammons and Newell asked questions about the importance of the various roles to success. Most mayors placed greatest importance on the political role, although 23 percent still emphasized the managerial role as most important. The city managers emphasized the policy role more frequently, but in both the Wright and the Ammons and Newell studies, about 40 percent rated the managerial role as most important. The executive assistants overwhelmingly rated the managerial role as most important. In sum, city officials see themselves as devoting substantial amounts of time to managerial roles.

Similarly, the Kaufman (1979) study noted earlier found that the respondents in their small sample of federal bureau chiefs spent much of their time in typical managerial activities. Later chapters on effective management in the public sector report on some of their techniques for motivating the people in their bureaus, a challenge to which they devoted extensive time and attention. This orientation does not square with the complaints that public managers do not manage very conscientiously. What explains this distance between various observers and researchers on a key point such as this?

Contingencies and Variations

Obviously, many variations in context and in the individual officials surveyed account for these different views. The bureau chiefs that Kaufman
studied tended to be longer-term career civil servants, at levels lower than
the short-tenure political appointees at the tops of diverse agencies. The level
of the manager and the institutional context make a lot of difference. As
pointed out earlier, officials vary by elected versus appointed status, level
in the agency hierarchy, distance from the political center (such as Washington, D.C., versus a district office, the state capitol versus a state district
office), political and institutional setting of the agency (such as executive
and legislative authority in the jurisdiction; weak-mayor, strong-mayor, and
council-manager structures at the local level), level of government, and other
factors.

    We realize that these variations have great significance. We know that,
at virtually all levels and in virtually all settings, public managers must in
some degree balance managerial tasks with policy making and handling the
political and institutional environment (oversight agencies, legislative and
other executive authorities, clients and constitutents as individuals or organized groups, and the media). Yet some managers in public and private
nonprofit agencies face intense challenges of the latter sort, while others operate in virtual isolation from political intrusions. At present, however, the
field lacks a coherent model of all these variations. Development of better
conceptions of such variations represents a challenge for practitioners and
scholars in the field.

    Despite these deficiencies, there is available a good deal of relevant
research and thinking, including the previously described studies by Aberbach, Putnam, and Rockman (1981), Abney and Lauth (1986), and Brudney and Hebert (1987). Meyer (1979) concludes from a large study of heads
of state and local finance agencies that those in stronger positions politically —
who are elected or career civil servants instead of political appointees — show
more ability to defend their agencies against pressures for change in structures and loss of units to other agencies, apparently because of greater ability to draw on support from political networks.

    Even more research and thinking have focused on officials in cities,
probably because city management has developed as one of the more professionalized areas of public management and has attracted more systematic
research and theorizing as a result. Kotter and Lawrence (1974) reported
one of the most elaborate analyses, in which they argued that effective mayors
must effectively "coalign" major components of their context. These include
the mayor's own personal characteristics (cognitive and interpersonal skills,
needs, and values), their agendas (tasks and objectives in the short and long
run), their networks (the resources and expectations of the members and
their relations to the mayor), and characteristics of the city itself (such as
size and rate of change). For example, they argue that the mayor's cogni-

tive style must align with the variety and variability of information about the city that must be processed. A *technician* orientation, emphasizing analysis of discrete amounts of information, best aligns with a small, homogeneous, stable city, where information varies little and can be analyzed relatively easily. A *professional* orientation fits a large heterogeneous city with unstable, hard-to-analyze information. The more professional mayor emphasizes using professional judgment to apply professional guidelines and knowledge. Between these extremes, an *engineering* mayor works best in a large, diverse, stable city, where information is highly varied but analyzable. A *craftsman* most effectively deals with the less varied but less analyzable information in a small but unstable city. This typology draws on Perrow's ideas about information contingencies of tasks (see Chapter Five). Kotter and Lawrence also discuss ways in which the mayor's network must coincide with the agenda and the agenda with city characteristics in an analysis of how these components must coalign.

Anderson, Newland, and Stillman (1983) also propose a typology, based more on a framework akin to the managerial grid described earlier in this chapter. They argue that cities have varying levels of demand for the city officials to display people orientations and technical orientations. *Growth communities* create high demands for both and for a chief executive type of manager who works for change within regular organizational structures. *Caretaker communities* demand maintenance of existing services and an administrative caretaker. *Arbiter communities* require much conflict resolution and therefore more of a people orientation than a technical one; a community leader mode of management best satisfies these requirements. A *consumption community* demands the most public services at the least cost and hence provides a context appropriate for an administrative innovator, who follows the direction of the elected council members and seeks innovations for the sake of efficiency and service delivery; that is, less emphasis on people, more on technical skill.

Entrepreneurship in Government

Recent studies of entrepreneurial leaders and policy innovators in government also break away from overgeneralizations about ineffectual managers struggling with an overwhelming political and administrative system (Roberts and King, 1988; Roberts, forthcoming). Much of this work consists of case studies about major executives, but it suggests general conclusions.

For example, Lewis (1980) studied Hyman Rickover's development of the "nuclear navy," J. Edgar Hoover's impact on the FBI, and Robert Moses's transformation of the New York Port Authority. He observed a common developmental pattern in the three cases. In each case, he found an organization that was ineffective in achieving the major goals for which it presumably existed until it experienced a process of mentoring by an effective superior. In this process, the superiors developed appropriate goals and learned how to get things done. Then they engaged in an "entrepreneurial leap" that changed the organization and its resource allocation in unforeseen ways, and they created an "apolitical shield" that defended their work from political intervention by casting it as nonpolitical and objectively necessary. Later phases involved struggling for autonomy, reducing environmental uncertainty, expanding the organization's domain, and fully institutionalizing the new organization, with consequent problems of "ultrastability."

Lewis's subjects stand as controversial titans who, through exceptional ambition, energy, and political and technical skill, took advantage of key political and technological developments to build major organizations. Other writers have described executives who played major roles in the development of the National Aeronautics and Space Administration, the Tennessee Valley Authority, major Department of Defense policies, the Social Security Administration, and the Forestry Service. Much of the work continues to consist of case discussions and anecdotes, but general conclusions emerge. Doig and Hargrove (1987) conclude from a set of such studies that entrepreneurial leaders in the public sector display certain general patterns. They identify new missions and programs for their agencies. They develop external and internal constituencies for these new initiatives, identify areas of vulnerability, and neutralize opposition. For their new missions, they enhance the technical expertise of the agency and provide motivation and training for organizational members. The leaders tend to follow some mixture of rhetorical strategy, involving evocative symbols and language, and coalition-building strategy, emphasizing the development of political support from many groups. Some leaders rely on both strategies; some emphasize one over the other.

External conditions set the stage for these activities, according to Doig and Hargrove. The entrepreneurs actually take advantage of the diverse and fragmented governance structures often cited as reasons why public managers accomplish little. The difficulties of strong central control in such a system provide the entrepreneurs opportunities to forge their own directions. They also take advantage of patterns of potential public support (for example, changing public attitudes during the 1930s supported a more active role for the federal government) and new technologies and alliances with elected political officials.

In their personalities and skills, the leaders display an "uncommon rationality," a remarkable ability to perceive effective means to ends. They are able to see the political logic in an emerging historical situation and link their initiatives to broader political and social trends. Doig and Hargrove also stress the individual's motivation to "make a difference," coupled with a sustained determination and optimism. Success depends, however, on the association of personal skills with organizational tasks and with favorable historical conditions, such as public and political support and timely technological possibilities.

Another important point about the ability of public managers to influence important developments is revealed in studies of policy entrepreneurs (Roberts and King, 1988; Roberts, forthcoming). This conception of entrepreneurship analyzes people who influence policy, often from outside formal positions, by pressing for innovations in policies and programs. Some develop public support for the innovations, press legislators and administrators for support, and otherwise move the system by sustained roles as policy champions. Others may play roles as policy intellectuals, providing innovative ideas. As described above, public executives and managers can play such roles, but they sometimes face constraints on their independence to do so. They can also, however, act as catalysts and sponsors, who provide support, listen, and respond when policy champions with good ideas press for a hearing.

All these studies of entrepreneurship suggest ways in which we might reconcile the broad observations about indifferent public management with the evidence that many public managers have hammered out so much change that they raise controversies about their proper role in a democratic republic (Lewis, 1980). Marmor and Fellman (1986; Marmor, 1987), for example, offer a typology of public executives that is akin to many previous typologies, such as that of Downs. It concentrates more directly on the issue of internal program management in the direction of program accomplishment, however, and therefore suggests key distinctions in motivation and objectives. They argue that public executives vary in managerial skills and commitment to program goals. Among those with low managerial skills are the *administrative survivors,* who also have low commitment to program goals and provide little effective leadership. *Program zealots* have high programmatic commitments but weak skills and also tend to be unsuccessful administrators. The Reagan administration provided numerous examples of this pattern, since political ideology often served as a major criterion for executive appointments. As for those with high managerial skills, *generalist managers* show low commitment to program goals. The executive elite at the federal level has included highly respected executives such as Eliot Richardson and Donald Ruckleshaus, who developed excellent reputations for effective management in a variety of agencies. Yet Marmor and Fellman suggest that this dilutes their commitment to the long-term care and feeding of particular programs.

Program loyalists, highly skilled managers with strong programmatic commitments, serve as the most likely candidates for entrepreneurial impact. Their commitment focuses on the program as their personal business and concern, with deemphasis of personal fame or recognition for influence. Thus, they tend to have the longevity and sustained commitment to hammer out substantial, long-term, original changes. Marmor and Fellman point to Robert Ball, an influential leader in the development of the Social Security Administration, as a prime example of their category of program loyalist.

Interestingly, in a footnote they indicate that Ball himself suggested that they missed an important category, the dedicated career administrators at the second, third, and fourth levels, the mid-level managers at the central office or the heads of district offices. Marmor and Fellman label these "competent loyalists" and locate them between program zealots and program loyalists, because they competently manage only one part of a general program. Ball's tendency to remember these people, however, and to emphasize their significance reflects a sustained commitment to competent management in general as well as to the management of the particular program.

Later chapters continue the discussion of effective public leadership and management, so efforts to summarize are better left until later. The theories and studies reviewed here provide valuable contributions to that analysis and to the long-term challenge of developing a conception of public management that recognizes the skills and practices of the many effective public managers and organizations.

Chapter 8

Teamwork: Understanding Communication and Conflict in Groups

Some of the very good books on public management pay far too little attention to groups in organizations. The human group served as one of the founding topics in the social and administrative sciences. Large portions of our lives are spent in groups, which exert powerful influences on the people in them and play important roles in numerous human activities. Teams, committees, task forces, staffs, work units, and other groupings make up the structure and activity of organizations. Many organizational change and improvement efforts revolve around group processes, such as quality circles, and organizational development interventions, such as team-building exercises, problem-solving groups, and sensitivity sessions. Social scientists studied groups so intensively for many years that, as with other important topics, such as motivation, the research seems to have played out by discovering more and more complexities. For example, so many kinds of groups operate under so many different conditions that researchers strain to understand all the variations. Groups also incorporate so many internal variations that some group researchers have moved off to look at component topics, such as communication and perception between individuals. Yet some of the classic issues about groups never lose their significance for managers. New insights, such as those about a malady called *groupthink,* continue to emerge.

Organizational communications and conflict do not have to occur in and between groups, but they often do. Much of the research on groups came about because people realized that groups influence communication and conflict among their members and between themselves and other groups.

In addition, communication and conflict often intertwine. Members of the department of human services of a large state communicate to members of the state's department of labor that labor's opposition to a program to aid migrant laborers simply reflects the labor department's subservience to certain wealthy fruit growers. The labor department officials communicate back that human services is proposing an incompetently designed program just to build its own empire. A skillful, highly trained social scientist may have the ability to detect the presence of conflict! Conflict may cause or result from bad communication, and the way out of conflict usually emphasizes establishing effective communication. Of course, these topics are closely related to ideas discussed in earlier chapters on power, behavior, structure, and other topics, but they also fit together well.

While researchers have examined many dimensions of group processes, this chapter concentrates on certain fundamental insights that figure importantly in discussions of organizational change and improvement. In addition, as usual, we need to examine the application of these topics to public organizations.

Groups

Research has demonstrated that while groups often create strong pressures on their members for conformity with others in the group, they also represent arenas for sharing and communicating. They affect the way we view ourselves and others in and out of the group and the way we behave toward those people. They influence our attitudes, including acceptance or rejection of new ideas. They affect work habits and productivity.

During this century, research on group dynamics flowed along a number of avenues and became richly elaborated. Yet some of the pioneering studies in this area illustrate many of the central themes mentioned above (the Appendix describes some of these developments in more detail). One of the Hawthorne Experiments found that the work group played a major role in shaping the work behavior of the members. The members of a department had come to some implicit agreements about how much each member should produce, and they put pressure not only on individuals who fell too far below this mark but also on those who produced too much. Much research would follow on how work groups in industry pressured "rate busters."

Kurt Lewin fled Hitler, came to the United States, and virtually founded the group dynamics movement. Having observed the traumatic shifts of opinion and behavior in the rise of Hitler, he pursued his interest in how attitudes form and shift and how social forces figure in these changes. Lewin developed concepts of *force-field analysis,* such as the distinction between forces that drive a person toward some new attitude or behavior and restraining forces that press against the change, as well as between *induced* forces, which press on a person from outside, and *own* forces, which press for or against change from within. Lewin saw groups as powerful media for such forces. He typically applied his simple framework for analysis of change — *unfreezing, moving, refreezing* — in group sessions. Trying to help the war effort with research on how to change housewives' resistance to serving their families less popular foods and thus ease the burdens of food rationing, he assembled housewives in groups where they discussed the possibility of changing. The discussion and camaraderie served to unfreeze their resistance and move them toward a new attitude. Lewin asked some of the women to declare before the rest of the group that they would try the new foods. Those who did so were more likely to carry out the change. The sense of having committed themselves before the group more effectively refroze their position in the new attitude.

In these and other studies, Lewin demonstrated the significance of group effects. People who worked with him typically depict him as a founding influence on group research and on developments that led that research along two diverging streams. One stream concentrated on theory and experimental research on groups, based largely at universities. The other emphasized actively applying group processes to individual and organizational development, with bases in such training and consulting organizations as the National Training Laboratories. This latter stream involved something of a movement, leading to proliferation of such practices as sensitivity sessions, and played a key role in the burgeoning field of organization development.

Other examples of influential studies add fundamental insights and reflect the stream of group research that Lewin helped to set in motion. Muzafir Sherif (Sherif and Sherif, 1953) conducted experiments with groups of boys in a camp setting and found that when they worked at tasks in competition with each other, the groups formed stronger internal bonds and more hostility toward the other groups. When the same groups worked in cooperative tasks, they developed more friendly attitudes and communication across group lines. In another field experiment, this one in a factory, Lester Coch and John R. P. French (1948) studied the adoption of new procedures by work groups and found that groups that participated in the decision to make the change adopted the new procedure more effectively than did groups simply told to adopt it.

Laboratory researchers have conducted experiments showing that *cohesive* groups, whose members have strong attraction or valuation of the group and each other, usually exert more influence on members' task performance than less cohesive groups. Stanley Schachter (1951) conducted experiments on communication in groups making decisions, which indicated that when the groups discussed an issue, a coalition rapidly formed among a subgroup who agreed on a particular position and would try to persuade other members to join their position. As the coalition grew, its members bombarded with persuasion attempts the holdouts who would not agree. Over time, however, they increasingly isolated the dissenters by breaking off communications with them. When asked how they felt about others in the group, participants expressed least respect and liking for the dissenters. These and innumerable additional studies have analyzed many important dimensions of groups. This complicated fund of research evades brief description, but we can summarize some of the points most relevant for managers.

Formation, Norms, and Roles

The question of why and how groups form invites simple answers, such as "The assistant secretary appointed a representative of each major division in the agency." Yet in every group, unique informal patterns emerge. Groups may form as they do through official appointments by leaders or under official rules or as a result of task imperatives such as the need for certain specializations. Some groups form entirely voluntarily, and even in formally established groups, members may decide how much to contribute or hold back, how much to cooperate or conflict, and so on. Groups vary in their attraction for members and their influence over them. Members move into roles and levels of influence that may correspond little to those formally designated.

Earlier chapters provided some of the reasons for these variations, including French and Raven's (1968) typology of power bases—reward, coercive, expert, referent, and legitimate. French and Raven were group theorists and intended their typology for analysis of why groups vary in power and in attractiveness to their members and power over them. Psychological experiments have shown that people often have fundamental impulses to group together with others. Schachter (1959) performed experiments which found that people expecting a painful experience chose to wait for it in the presence of others facing a similar fate, even if prohibited from talking to them. Psychologists interested in *social comparison processes* have pointed out that people often lack clear information about how they are doing and what they should do and draw on others as referents for their own behavior. Groups have strong referent powers in these processes. Also, then, groups gain this power and attractiveness as referents partly by dint of the other bases of power, such as their control of rewards, their expertness, and so on.

The controls that groups exert over members have received much attention because of their obvious importance. As groups form, norms and values develop. Some researchers find the concept of norms, or standards of behavior and attitude shared by the group, elusive and vague. Whether or not that concept perfectly captures the phenomena, however, groups clearly display patterns of conformity to certain behaviors and beliefs.

Researchers have also analyzed the elaboration of various roles in groups, especially the psychological and social roles that may not follow formal assignments. Leadership obviously figures very importantly, and much of the work reviewed in Chapter Seven, such as Fiedler's theory, pertains to group leadership. While leadership obviously may follow formal assignments and rank, informal leaders often in fact emerge. Researchers who have intensively studied the development of leadership in newly formed groups report such findings as the importance of participation: Those who participate most actively most often become the leader in the eyes of other members. Researchers have also discovered, however, that sometimes a long-winded assertive type comes to be regarded as the leader early on but the group later turns more and more to a less outspoken, more competent person. In fact, multiple roles can emerge, with one or several people taking the lead in social and emotional matters, such as maintaining morale and harmony, and another pressing for effective group structure and task accomplishment.

Context, Structure, and Outcomes

The generalizations about groups, particularly from research on experimental groups, provide insights, but very diffuse ones. Researchers have worked on the implications of variations in group settings and characteristics to try to understand the effects of such contingencies as group size, task, communication pattern, and composition. Groups often have advantages over individuals and smaller groups because of the availability of more talents, ideas, viewpoints, and other resources. Groups often outperform individuals at certain decision-making and problem-solving tasks. Yet larger groups can often raise problems of unwieldiness, diffusion of responsibility, and free-rider effects. Some research has also suggested that social relations tend to become more formal in larger groups and that their members tend to tolerate more impersonal, task-oriented behaviors by leaders.

Researchers have also intensively examined variations in group tasks, such as variations between individual and collaborative tasks and structured and unstructured tasks. Some researchers have produced evidence of social facilitation of individual tasks, where the mere presence of another person enhances task performance on familiar tasks. For more collaborative or group tasks, researchers and theorists have woven a complex array of concepts and relations among group size and such task characteristics as homogeneity and heterogeneity, and disjunctiveness and conjunctiveness. The material on contingency theories of organization provides some of the most important implications for managers in relation to this topic, such as the need for subunits with more complex and variable tasks to have more flexible, interactive processes.

The structure and composition of groups also influence their processes, of course. Highly diverse groups whose members represent many different backgrounds and goals face particularly severe challenges in establishing smooth working relations. Examples include groups with an appointed member for each department in an organization or each of a set of interest groups (such as a community advisory group for a government agency) and groups for negotiations between labor and management. The communication structure imposed on a group can also determine many important outcomes. For example, Leavitt (1951) conducted research on communication networks for groups, comparing communication processes and outcomes in groups required to communicate in different patterns. In one pattern, the circle, members communicated only with two adjacent members, so that information had to move around the group in a circle. In a chain pattern, members were arranged in a line along which communications had to flow back and forth. In a wheel pattern, all communication had to flow through one member occupying the center, hublike position. Other patterns included a fully interconnected group with all members able to communicate directly with all others. The patterns determined numerous outcomes for the groups. The wheel produced the fastest transmission of information and good accuracy but low overall satisfaction, except for the person in the middle, who had a great time, usually emerging as the leader of a centralized process. The chain and circle produced slower communication, with less accuracy; nobody liked the chain very much, but members expressed high satisfaction with the circle. In both the circle and the completely interconnected group, communication was often slow, but everyone got the word more effectively than with the other forms, and members felt higher satisfaction. The research thus dramatizes a trade-off faced by managers and groups, also suggested in contingency theory. Many of the human relations–oriented models prescribe participation, and these experiments demonstrate that when people more actively participate, they understand more and feel better about the process. Yet the research also shows that such processes often move slowly, and a more centralized structure has some advantages in speed, accuracy, and leadership impact. Managers and groups have to choose the most important outcome.

Advantages and Disadvantages of Groups

These sorts of findings from research and experience have made it clear that groups can serve as media for good and bad, depending on many factors. Managers must consider when and how groups can operate with most value. Maier (1967) provided a list of pros and cons of using groups for problem solving to which people often refer. Groups can often bring in more knowledge, information, approaches, and alternatives. The participation of more people in group settings increases understanding and acceptance of decisions; members have a better idea of what the group decided and why, and they can carry this information back to others in units or other groups that they represent. Yet the social pressures in groups can bolster majority opinions regardless of their quality. Aggressive individuals or subgroups may stifle more capable members. As indicated by research described above, groups may press for conformity and move toward solutions too rapidly by stifling dissent. Some members may concentrate simply on winning, from their own or their unit's point of view.

Maier also points out that other factors can be good or bad, depending on the skill of the leader. Effective leaders can manage conflict and disagreement constructively and turn the relative slowness of group decision making to advantage, to achieve good outcomes such as conflict resolution and more carefully discussed decisions. Groups may also sometimes make riskier decisions. While exerting pressures for conformity, they often paradoxically reflect a diffusion of responsibility, where individuals shirk or evade responsibility for the group's action or take social cues from others in the group that lead them to mistakenly underestimate the significance of a problem. Individuals may outperform groups where creativity and efficiency are paramount, where acceptance of the decision is less crucial, where the most qualified person is easy to identify, where individuals are very unlikely to cooperate, or where little time is available (Gordon, 1990).

Groupthink

Irvin Janis's (1971) work on groupthink reflects many of the elements of this body of research with particular significance for managers. Janis says that he has discovered groupthink not just in many organizational decision processes but in some of the most immensely significant decisions, such as major strategic decisions by firms and public-policy decisions such as the bombing of North Vietnam during the Johnson administration and John Kennedy's decision to carry out the Bay of Pigs invasion. Janis argues that groups under the stress of making major decisions often take on the symptoms of groupthink. They need consensus and commitment to the course of action they choose, and the pressures for conformity lead members to display such tendencies as these: They see the group as invulnerable to opponents. They develop rationales to explain away or avoid serious consideration of apparent problems and threats. They see themselves as morally right and stereotype their opponents as incapable or immoral. Pressure for agreement and unanimity falls on members who dissent, as others press them to agree and to support the group and its leader. Members sometimes adopt roles as "mindguards," withholding information that might shake the group consensus, and engage in self-censorship, stifling their own impulse to disagree.

Janis describes groupthink at lofty levels of authority, but managers encounter it in many settings. At the annual meeting of the county commissioners' association of a large state, when the governing council of the association convened, council members expressed outrage over new environmental protection regulations that the state legislature was imposing on counties. Members of the council fulminated against the regulations, charging that they usurped the rightful authority of the counties. As the discussion continued, members increasingly characterized the state legislators and agency executives behind the changes as tyrants and empire builders and depicted themselves as noble defenders of their constituents' rights to govern themselves. They boldly proclaimed their intention to write a strong letter of protest to the legislators and agency officials (a step likely to prove very ineffectual). Members reacted fairly scornfully to suggestions that a more reasonable and moderate discussion of the situation would be more productive, as if those making such suggestions lacked courage. The council members thus displayed groupthink symptoms, such as stereotyping the opposition, overestimating one's own postition, and stifling dissent.

For avoiding groupthink, Janis prescribes a number of steps: The leader should encourage members to act as critical evaluators and impartial decision makers and accept criticisms of his or her own actions; invite outside experts to join the discussion; require members to discuss the matter with others outside the group; assign two or more groups to work on the problem separately; assign a member to play devil's advocate; break the group into two subgroups at key points; assign time to review threats and weaknesses; and at points of major decisions, hold "last chance" sessions where members air their reservations. Later in this chapter, we will consider an abundance of additional advice and procedures for managing groups. Before turning to those, however, it is useful to cover some basic ideas about communication and conflict.

Communication

Besides communication in and between groups, other forms and channels of communication play crucial roles in organizations. The ideas about power, strategy, structure, and leadership considered earlier are relevant here as well, since communication can be implemented through rules and other structures themselves, through formal written channels, in one-on-one exchanges with a superior, and so on. Later sections of this chapter discuss some economists' sharply negative assertions about the capacities of public bureaucracies to communicate through such channels.

Discussions of organizational communication typically begin with a very general model of the communication process. According to such models, communication begins with a source from which a message originates. A transmitter encodes the message and sends it to a receiver, who decodes it and moves it to a destination. Noise influences the accuracy of the transmission. Other general conceptions depict a person as both a sender of messages through particular channels to another person and a receiver of messages back through channels from that other person. Both people also communicate with other recipients and senders concomitantly. These fairly obvious models show what the research and theory emphasize—the nature of sources, senders, and recipients; of channels along which messages flow; and, in particular, the problem of noise or distortion that impedes accurate transmission of information (Downs, 1988).

Typical discussions also distinguish among horizontal communication, vertical (upward and downward) communication, and external or outward communication with environmental components. Horizontal communications encounter difficulties as a result of conflict, competition, or other differences between subunits and groups. Vertical communications encounter difficulties as a result of hierarchical filtering and superior-subordinate relations such as resistance, inattentiveness, misunderstanding and reticence or withholding of information by lower levels. The distinction between formal and informal communications processes, already familiar by now, receives due notice, as does the research on communication networks described above.

Communication Roles

Analysts of organizational communication have drawn on concepts from other areas of the social sciences to distinguish roles in the communication process (Rogers and Argawala-Rogers, 1976). *Gatekeepers* occupy positions where they can control the flow of information between units and groups. Others around them look to *opinion leaders* for information about the form that their own opinions should take. People in *liaison* roles transmit information between two or more units or groups. *Cosmopolites* have many contacts outside the organization and bring a lot of external information into the organization.

Communication Assessments and Audits

Beyond these generalizations, obviously, myriad dimensions of communication receive attention from researchers, as illustrated by now numerous survey instruments and other procedures for assessing communication in organizations (Downs, 1988). Most of these ask individuals about their perceptions and evaluations of the information that they receive and the communication process. For example, the communications audit questionnaire of the International Communications Association asks about the amount of information that the respondent sends and receives on an array of topics — job performance, pay and benefits, relationship of one's own work to the overall organization, new procedures, organizational problems and policies, and so on. It also asks about the amount that the respondent *needs* to send and receive. It asks similar questions about the amount of information sent to and received from various sources, such as top management, middle management, immediate supervisors, co-workers, and the grapevine. Other questions ask about satisfaction with the information received about such topics and from such sources and with the organization and extent of communication processes; with how much follow-up on communications respondents receive and need; and with the quality of the organizational and work climate. Other communication assessment procedures track specific messages through the organization and map the dissemination of the information. Still others map actual communication networks in organizations, analyzing who communicates with whom about what.

Communication Problems

Obviously, the main issue in communications is getting it right, so the discussion often turns rapidly to what goes wrong. Table 8.1 provides a description of two representative lists of communication difficulties. Gordon (1990)

Table 8.1. Communications Problems and Distortions.

Gordon (1990)

Barriers to Effective Communication

Lack of feedback: One-way communication in which the receiver provides no return of information about whether and with what effect the information came across

Noise in communication: Interference with the message during transmission of it, ranging from actual physical noise or distortion to interruptions or biases that result from the presence of others who distract attention or from past experiences

Misuse of language: Excessively vague, inaccurate, inflammatory, emotional, positive or negative language

Listening deficiencies: Receivers listening inattentively, passively, or not at all

Barriers to Effective Communication Between Groups

When two groups define a conflict between them as a win-or-lose conflict

When one or both groups seek to aggrandize their own power and emphasize only their own goals and needs

When they use threats

When they disguise their true positions and actively distort information

When they seek to exploit or isolate the other group

When they emphasize only differences and the superiority of their own position

Gortner, Mahler, and Nicholson (1987)

Communication Distortions in Public Bureaus

Distorted perceptions: Inaccurate perceptions of information that result from preconceived ideas or priorities or from strivings to maintain self-esteem or cognitive consistency

Erroneous translation: Interpretation of information by receivers in ways not intended by the senders

Errors of abstraction and differentiation: Transmission of excessively abstract or selective information; underemphasis of differences in favor of similarities or excessive polarization of fairly similar positions

Lack of congruence: Ambiguity or inconsistency between elements of a message or between the particular message and other sources of information, such as conflicts between verbal and nonverbal cues or between officially communicated values and policies and other communications indicating that these policies and values do not hold

Distrusted source: Failure to accept an accurate message because of suspicions about bias or lack of credibility of the source

Jargon: Communications difficulties that result from highly specialized professional or technical language which confuses those outside the specialization (and often those within it). Some jargon has value, but officials may use inflated and pretentious language to appear knowledgeable or important, to intimidate or impede clients, to distort true intentions, or to evade accountability and scrutiny

Manipulating and withholding information: Senders' active distortion or withholding of information in line with their own interests and related influences that they seek to impose on the receiver

---

Sources: Adapted from Johnson and Johnson (1975), Gortner, Mahler, and Nicholson (1987), and Gordon (1990).

presents a list that represents a typical treatment of such problems in the general management and organizational behavior literature. Gortner, Mahler, and Nicholson (1987) list categories that apply more directly to some of the problems typically regarded as most serious in public bureaucracy, such as jargon, inflated prose, and the manipulation of information for political or bureaucratic purposes.

Some of the greatest literary and journalistic figures of the last two centuries have poured their talents into ridiculing and decrying these tendencies in government and governmental bureaucracies. Some of these critiques have become embodied in academic theories that posit that public bureaucracies and their bureaucrats distort and manipulate information more aggressively than their counterparts in business. Before examining these and some other theories and evidence about communication in public management, it is useful to cover the concept of conflict in organizations, which often intermingles with communication processes.

Conflict

Although conflict obviously presents major challenges for managers, the literature on organizational conflict has not developed as elaborately as has the body of research and theory on many of the other topics in organizational studies. Conflict receives attention in work on other major topics, however. Frederick Taylor said that he pursued the principles of scientific management in part because he wanted to diminish the conflicts between workers and managers by providing scientific solutions to the questions that they regularly disputed (see the Appendix). Lawrence and Lorsch (1967), in their seminal study of organizational design processes, found high levels of conflict in very effective organizations and very high investments in managing rather than avoiding it. Some of the most recent developments in organizational design, such as matrix designs and ideas about fluid and duplicating structures, intentionally design conflicts into the structure. Research shows that well-managed conflict often improves decision making in organizations. Research also shows, however, that managers, especially in business organizations, tend to dislike conflict and seek to avoid it, even though such conflict avoidance may lead to less effective decision making (Schwenk, 1990).

In public and nonprofit organizations, one expects and even hopes for intense conflicts, although preferably not destructive ones. As noted earlier, public organizations often represent organizational manifestations of the unceasing political competition and public-policy dilemmas of the nation. Government agencies and their subunits and managers compete for resources, executive and legislative attention, and turf. They share responsibilities for programs and policies, but often with differing points of view and priorities. New administrations and newly elected and appointed officials enter the picture regularly and rapidly, claiming new mandates and often the need to forget or freeze programs into which people have poured their working lives or to do ongoing things differently and better. Ombudsmen, examiners, auditors, oversight agencies, and legislative committees and hearings have the assigned duty of taking a sharply questioning and often conflicting view of an agency's operations. Often at issue are the very lives or the major conditions of life of many people and massive amounts of money, power, and influence. The principle of separation of powers that the founders designed into the governance structure of the United States actually calls for conflicting interests and authority as checks against each other. Yates (1985) observes that "Madisonian systems" with built-in contentions and divided authority abound in public and private organizations. Schwenk (1990) finds that executives in nonprofit organizations see a positive relationship between conflict in the decision-making process and the quality of the decisions, while executives in for-profit organizations regard conflict as damaging to the quality and clarity of decisions. The nonprofit executives, which included executives from government agencies, had to consider the needs of diverse constituents and groups. They found conflict unpleasant, but regarded it as useful in clarifying the needs and goals of diverse groups.

One must expect conflict, then, and try to make a healthy form of it flow in government and its agencies. Keeping it healthy represents the key challenge. For managers in organizations, the research in organizational studies has focused on what types of conflict occur, what brings them about, how conflict proceeds, and, as this chapter covers somewhat later, how to manage it constructively.

Types of Conflict

Experts on organizational conflict point out that numerous types and forms of conflict occur in organizations. Conflict can exist within a person (as the role conflict and ambiguity concepts emphasize), between people, and within and between groups and organizational departments or divisions. Conflict can rage horizontally, across levels of an organization. It can occur vertically, between higher and lower levels in a hierarchy, as in the classic disputes between management and labor; or, as occurs frequently in geographically dispersed government agencies and business firms, the people at headquarters may do battle with the field or district personnel.

Bases of Conflict

All types of conflict can originate in or be aggravated by organizational or subunit culture, values, goals, structures, tasks and functions, authority and leadership processes, and environmental pressures, as well as demographics and the individual personalities of members. You name it and it can provide reasons for a flare-up.

Researchers provide useful lists of some of the most frequent sources of strife, which help us to sort through some of the complexity. They cite differences in goals, values, cultures, and priorities, of course. The sociologists who began emphasizing the dysfunctions of bureaucracy around mid-century (see the Appendix) pointed out that the specialization of work and responsibility that bureaucracy involves, with emphasis on reliable adherence to the rules and goals for those specialized units, virtually ensures conflicts among units. Differences in power, status, rewards, and resources among people and groups can lead to feelings of inequity or simply to the obvious need to compete with the others and, in turn, to conflict. Where two groups' tasks or decision processes overlap, are intensely interdependent, or naturally compete, tensions can boil over. Not always mentioned in these lists but quite obvious are the surprisingly frequent instances of very significant conflict among high-level officials based simply on clashes of personal style and ego.

Conflict Stages and Modes

Analysts of conflict also note what they call the phases of conflict episodes. Pondy's (1967) frequently cited classification, for example, includes five stages: *Latent* conflict exists when conditions set the stage for conflict, though it has not yet simmered to the surface. *Perceived* conflict begins when the people involved begin to sense that conflict exists, even though they may attempt to downplay it or deny it. *Felt* conflict emerges when individuals begin to feel its effects in tension, anxiety, anger, or practical problems resulting from the conflict. *Manifest conflict,* figuratively or actually, involves open warfare. People or groups try to frustrate, harm, or defeat each other. Either one group must win or lose, the conflict must continue with destructive effects, or managers and members must effectively channel and manage the conflict toward constructive ends. The *conflict aftermath* is the stage after the outbreak of conflict, when some form of the alternatives and their results becomes evident.

As people and groups respond to the onset of conflict, their responses can take various forms. Thomas (1983) points out that people can respond through *avoidance* (trying to ignore or withdraw from the conflict). They can try *accommodation,* in which they cooperate and make concessions to the other party's demands or needs. *Compromise* involves an exchange of concessions and cooperative responses, without the implication that one side behaves more accommodatingly than the other. *Competing* involves simply trying to force, outdo, or defeat the other party without any appreciable accommodation or concern for its goals and needs. *Collaborating* occurs when two parties work together to meet both parties' needs mutually; it differs from compromise in implying that the two parties do not simply give up on certain goals and values, but rather both work to find ways to maximize returns for both.

Yates (1985) also offers useful suggestions about strategies and tactics for managing conflict. He describes methods of fostering a competitive debate among conflicting parties, using neutral language to avoid escalating hostilities, and behaving with civility and mutual respect. He suggests approaches that involve identifying mutual problems and avoiding development of enmities, win-or-lose situations, and long-term resentments. One does this partly through including all affected parties, providing complete information, and keeping communication channels open. Yates proposes a process of conflict management that has many similarities to the management of culture and transformational leadership described in Chapter Seven. The conflict manager must understand the people involved, establish a sense of shared mission to give the parties incentive to resolve the conflict, and adopt an incremental approach, focusing on winning concrete issues.

Conflict Outcomes, Suppression, and Escalation

Experts also detail the outcomes and effects of conflict, but those are fairly obvious in much of the rest of the organizational behavior literature. Excessive conflict can induce stress, frustration, dissatisfaction, turnover, absenteeism, and poor performance among employees. When poorly managed, it can damage organizations. The discussion of types and modes of conflict provides a useful reminder that suppressed or poorly handled conflict can hurt, in part because conflict can escalate. Researchers point out that conflict can feed on itself, aggravating the sorts of barriers to communication described earlier—use of charged language, bias in sending and receiving information, a tendency to interpret neutral statements from the other party as negative or aggressive, reduction of communication, and formation of we-they, win-lose perceptions of the relationship. Severely entrenched, intense conflict can make an organization sick, like a mentally disturbed person doing irrational, self-destructive things.

Managers have to work with organizations facing severe challenges to effective communication containing people and groups that have many reasons to come into conflict. Researchers and consultants have developed a fairly rich fund of prescriptions for managing and improving group processes, communication, and conflict-resolution processes. After we look at these, the discussion returns to special considerations about public organizations.

Managing Groups, Communication, and Conflict Resolution

Earlier chapters have covered much of what we know about managing groups, communication, and conflict, and later chapters cover still more. The discussion of leadership described the propositions from Fiedler's contingency theory, path-goal theory, life-cycle theory, and other approaches to understanding how leaders do and should behave toward the groups that they lead. These theories emphasize the many variations in leadership settings and leadership styles and the need for the setting and style to mesh. While recognizing these many variations, group theorists suggest numerous general considerations about groups. The prescriptions for avoiding groupthink provide one example. Leaders also have to try to enhance the attractiveness of group membership to increase group harmony, cohesiveness, and motivation (Zander, 1977). The typology of power sources — reward, coercive, expert, referent, and legitimate power — serves as a guide to some of the types of incentives that leaders can enhance and draw on to make groups effective. That typology implies additional incentives for group membership and motivation, such as prestige, sense of impact or importance, conviviality, specialness of membership, and so on, that group theorists advise leaders to utilize. Many group theorists have a greater human relations orientation than do leadership theorists. Prominent group theorists typically argue that, in general, effective work groups require participative leaders who respect the dignity of the members and maintain harmony in the group (Zander, 1977).

This human relations emphasis probably comes from the close connections between group theory and the field of organization development (OD). Chapter Ten describes OD and some of the specific group techniques used to improve organizations, such as *team building* and *T-group* procedures, and to enhance effectiveness, communication, and conflict resolution in work groups. OD consultants also use a variety of techniques to enhance communication and resolve conflicts between different groups (Gordon, 1990). For example, they might use an *organizational mirror* procedure, in which other groups in the organization report their views of a particular group or unit to that group so that it can better assess its impact and relations with others. A *confrontation meeting* brings two or more warring groups together to analyze and resolve the conflicts between them. *Third-party interventions* and *interpersonal facilitator* approaches have a person from outside the groups, and often outside the organization, come in to help with the conflict-resolution process. The latter approach involves a more central role of the facilitator in transmitting the communications between the two groups (Blake and Mouton, 1984).

Most of these techniques involve ways of controlling the expression of hostility and aggression to prevent the conflict from escalating. They usually try to provide systematic ways of drawing out the nature of conflicts and bases for resolution, through such procedures as *image exchanges,* in which members of the groups relate their views of the other group, *sharing appreciation* procedures, which call on the members to express appreciation for good things about the other group, and having the members list their expectations about the outcomes of the process. Management consultants may propose the use of a *dialectical inquiry* technique for managing and encouraging conflict in strategic decision-making processes. In this technique, the development of a strategic plan is followed by the development of a counterplan that questions the assumptions of the original plan. A *devil's advocacy* approach involves a critique of the basic assumptions of the strategic plan, but does not propose a specific alternative as in the dialectical inquiry approach (Schwenk, 1990).

Numerous other group procedures or techniques, not necessarily connected to OD practices, abound in organizations. The success of *quality circles* in Japan has led to their proliferation among organizations in the United States and other countries. A quality circle brings the members of a work group or organizational unit together for special group sessions on how to improve the quality of the unit's work and products. Organizations also typically employ special task forces, venture groups, policy committees, and other group-based approaches seeking explicitly to take advantage of group capacities. Several group decision procedures, such as the *nominal group technique, brainstorming,* and the *Delphi technique,* can facilitate communication and management of potential conflict (Gordon, 1990). In the nominal group technique, each group member makes a list of responses to a focal question or issue; for example, what are the most important goals? Then one by one each group member reads aloud the first item on his or her list, then each reads the second item, and so on through the lists. As the lists are read, the items are recorded and displayed for the group to see. The group then discusses the set of items—goals, in this example—to clarify them, discuss disagreements, and combine similar ones. Then they follow any of several possible ways of voting on the final set of goals. The procedure thus allows each person to contribute, minimizes digression, and channels conflict into constructive patterns. Brainstorming sessions invite members to suggest all alternatives or possibilities about an issue or problem. The group records all suggestions, and then evaluates them and works toward a conclusion. In the Delphi technique, a smaller group prepares a questionnaire about a topic and circulates it to a larger group, and then uses the latter's responses to prepare a revised questionnaire. This second questionnaire is circulated along with information about results of the first, and the process is repeated until a consensus of the larger group develops.

In addition, communications experts commonly stress the usefulness of conducting organization-wide communications audits of the sort described above. They point to the crucial role of the climate or culture of the organization in fostering or stifling communication and in determining whether and how well people manage conflicts.

Special Considerations for Public Organizations

The preceding review illustrates the ways in which researchers have treated these topics as generally applicable across organizations, with no need for any particular distinction among public, private, and nonprofit organizations. The review also indicates why they take this posture. They state the models and propositions at a high level of generality to make them applicable across groups and organizations. They see that managers in government, business, and nonprofit settings face common challenges in dealing with these dimensions of their work and can apply many of the proposed responses just as well in any of the so-called sectors.

Still, some of the time-honored observations about governmental bureaucracy claim sharp distinctions between that domain and business firms in matters pertaining to groups, communication, and conflict. Many of these virtually classic views echo throughout some of the most prominent recent theoretical efforts. In many governmental settings, for example, an elaborate, diverse configuration of groups and authorities contests over organizational policies and decisions. As noted earlier, inside and outside government organizations, "Madisonian systems" operate under formal law that establishes multiple authorities or arise as a result of the activities of groups and individuals seeking to influence government policies—the pluralistic governmental processes long discussed by political scientists. Complex groups and interests outside the organization often mirror a corresponding complexity within, according to many people who write about government organizations. Interest groups, congressional committees, and elements of the executive branch form alliances with units and individuals inside a particular agency and jealously defend these relations. Consequently, many large government agencies become highly diverse confederations of groups and units, whose relative independence weakens the authority of the politically appointed executives at the top (Warwick, 1975; Seidman and Gilmour, 1986).

Observers also say that the fact that the goals of public agencies are multiple, hard to specify and measure, and conflicting adds to this complexity. Often, two government agencies or two bureaus within a particular agency pursue diametrically conflicting goals—stop smoking but support the tobacco farmers, enhance international trade relations but defend the security of the nation by preventing the sale of sensitive technology—or have sharply differing priorities for a program for which they share responsibility.

For all these reasons, government often involves a particularly high frequency of power-sharing situations (Bryson and Einsweiller, 1991). Many commentators note that government managers need a particularly high level of tolerance for ambiguity and diversity and must deal frequently with conflicts among diverse groups.

Public managers also deal with particularly diverse work groups in many cases. Buchanan (1974, 1975) felt that his findings of lower organizational commitment among public managers resulted in part from his concurrent finding that they felt less encouragement from their work group to perform well and form strong commitment to the organization. He noted the sources of diversity mentioned above. He added, however, that government has proceeded more rapidly than industry in employing minorities and women. Buchanan suggested that these trends have led to more diversity within working groups and organizations in government. They simply employ more different types of people from different backgrounds and perspectives, which in turn leads to more diversity of perspective within the groups.

People who know government well also point out that the diversity plays a role in a paradox. Government heavily emphasizes control and accountability, but within a context where clear performance measures such as profits and sales are not available to aid in assessing accountability and performance. The greater diversity, they say, aggravates a conflicting tendency to emphasize reporting, record keeping, and requests for clearances from higher hierarchical levels. Even smaller units in government face intense requirements to report to higher levels of the larger institutions in which they are embedded as a result of the federal system of grants and contracts, larger agencies and jurisdictions, and so on. The system has become an elaborate array of "centrifugal and centripetal" forces (Warwick, 1975) and of "inevitable bureaucracy" (Lynn, 1981). More and more diversity, coupled with pressures for accountability but with few clear performance measures, breeds a profusion of rules, regulations, clearances, and reporting requirements.

While media commentators and the general public typically interpret these conditions as the results of bureaucratic bungling and officiousness, careful examinations show that a great many of these forms of red tape have a very reasonable background and rationale (Kaufman, 1976), and intense efforts to reduce federal paper work and red tape have not made a great deal of headway. All this implies that public management typically involves a great deal of information intensity and traffic. The tasks that public organizations carry out, of course, tend to be service oriented and information intensive. Careful studies of information handling in the public and private sectors show that public organizations do in fact involve greater information intensity, with private service organizations such as banks and insurance companies coming close to resembling them but actually falling in an intermediate range between industrial firms and public agencies (Bretschneider, 1990).

Tullock (1965) developed theoretical arguments that foreshadowed these observations about the paradox of many control efforts coupled with weak controls. He argued that the size and complexity of governmental bureaus create information leakage as lower-level officials communicate up the hierarchy. The officials must summarize the information that they report upward and screen the information that they receive from lower levels before transmitting it upward. This process deletes much of the information. In addition to simply boiling the information down, moreover, they report information most favorable to them and screen out unfavorable information. This leads to substantial distortions in upward communications in public bureaucracies, according to Tullock. He argued that private firms are better able to avoid such problems because higher levels use such measures as sales and profits to prevent the lower levels from inaccurately reporting favorable information about their activities.

Downs (1967) elaborated Tullock's observations into a more complex set of hypotheses. According to Downs, most communication in bureaus is "subformal." Subformal communication increases with more interdependence among activities, uncertainty, and time pressure but decreases between subunits in sharp conflict with each other. Newer, fast-growing, and changing bureaus have less effective communication networks than older, more stable ones. Information moving up the hierarchy becomes distorted for the reasons that Tullock described, and successful high-level officials use various strategies to counteract this distortion. They develop informal channels of information outside the bureau and set up overlapping responsibilities inside the bureau to create redundant internal channels. They employ "counterbiasing," which means that they adjust their own reactions to information from lower levels in ways that counter the biases that they know the reports contain. For example, they reduce reliance on information about future events or qualitative factors. In agencies with many crises and much specialization, they bypass levels to get "straight scoops" from lower levels. They seek to develop distortion-proof message systems, especially when precise accuracy and rapid transmission are very important and when there is a "tall" hierarchy and important variables are quantifiable. This characterization of the public-sector setting, together with preceding ones, if correct, depicts communications in the public sector as more intensive and difficult, with conflicts more likely and more difficult to manage.

Yet little explicit comparative research has assessed this view. While researchers have examined communications in public agencies (Warwick, 1975), such studies cannot resolve the question of whether large private firms would show the same characteristics and processes. Besides the Buchanan studies mentioned above, searches for this book located few public-private comparative studies explicitly dealing with groups, communication, and conflict. In one, Boyatzis (1982) found that his sample of public managers showed lower levels of skill at managing group processes than did the private-sector managers. In another, Baum and James (1984) compared the responses of 2,300 employees from nine "clearly public" and five "clearly private" organizations to the International Communications Association (ICA) communications audit survey questionnaire. On most of these questions, the respondents in the public organizations scored less favorably than the private-sector employees. On almost every item about information received and sent, they felt that they received and sent less and needed to send and receive more than the private-sector respondents. They also scored lower on each of thirty-two questions about organizational climate (about relations with co-workers, supervisors, and subordinates; about satisfaction with work, pay, communication, and other factors; about quality of products and services). As with the satisfaction studies discussed in Chapter Six, the public-sector respondents expressed reasonably high satisfaction on many of these items but scored lower than private-sector respondents. Baum and James concluded that public managers face greater challenges in establishing effective communications and must work harder at it.

Schwenk (1990) compared forty executives from for-profit (FP) and not-for-profit (NFP) organizations on their perceptions of conflict in decisions in their organizations. All the executives found conflict unpleasant, but the FP executives felt that conflict diminished the quality and clarity of decisions, and they found it more unpleasant than did the NFP executives. The NFP executives, however, reported a positive association between conflict and the quality and clarity of decisions. In describing their decisions, the FP executives much more frequently mentioned criteria related to financial performance — a finding consistent with that of Solomon (1986) — while NFP managers more often mentioned needs of constitutents and speed and effectiveness of service delivery. Schwenk also analyzed the executives' descriptions of their decisions using the decision framework of Mintzberg, Raisinghani, and Theoret (1976) described in Chapter Four. He found that conflict in the NFP organizations more often occurred in the early phases of the decision-making process (the phase concerned with problem recognition and diagnosis) and that NFP decision processes involved more steps and more "recycles" in which the decision process cycled back to an earlier phase. In the FP decision processes, conflict tended to occur later, in the phase involving evaluation and choice of alternatives. The NFP executives apparently regarded conflict as useful in clarifying diverse criteria and the demands of diverse interests and constituencies, particularly in the recognition and diagnosis of problems. While the sample for the Schwenk study is not large, the findings tend to reflect the organizational context for public organizations described earlier in this and other chapters. They also tend to concur with other researchers' findings about decision processes in public organizations as compared to private ones (Hickson and others, 1986; Solomon, 1986).

In sum, much theory and some expert observation hold that public organizations face greater complexity and more potential problems in group relations, communication, and conflict resolution. Little direct comparative evidence supports these observations, but the few studies that provide evidence about them tend to show greater complexity and problems. This rather gloomy picture should not be overstated and overgeneralized, however. The interpretation that the private sector performs better on these dimensions is too simple and easy. The public sector may face greater challenges precisely because of the nature of government as an arena for the complex policy decisions and political choices of an advanced political economy. Yet the review shows that for managers, the literature phrases the issues and prescriptions at a high level of generality, applicable to public, private, and non-profit organizations. Public managers may not need significantly different knowledge and skills from those covered here, but they do need particularly well-developed knowledge and skills in this area.

PART 3

Strategies for Managing and Improving Public Organizations

Chapter 9

Understanding and Measuring Organizational Effectiveness

Organizational effectiveness is the fundamental issue in the analysis of organizations although it is often dealt with only implicitly (Goodman, Pennings, and Associates, 1977). Virtually all organizational and management analysis in some way pertains to whether organizations do well. Obviously, public managers and public organizations face crucial and controversial questions about their effectiveness, for reasons discussed from the outset in this book. We have depicted public organizations as distinctive largely because of the goals that they must pursue and how they must pursue them, because of the ways in which other elements of the society want them to perform. We have also seen how beliefs about the performance of public organizations influence their funding, legal authorization, and oversight in ways that affect the behaviors of their members and the structures and operations of the organizations. Yet these beliefs also spark continuing controversy. Beliefs about the efficacy and legitimacy of government action and of the agencies of government play a key role in basic ideological divisions in the United States and other countries, between liberals and conservatives, socialists and capitalists. These beliefs have figured in some of the most significant political changes in recent history. They played a part in efforts in the United States and other countries in the 1980s to curtail the role of government in the society through "privatizing" government functions and limiting government. In Great Britain and other countries, the belief that government cannot effectively carry out various services and functions led to sustained efforts to sell off or otherwise devolve state-owned enterprises and other government activities. Change in the socialist and communist countries during this period shook the world. Those changes developed in part out of the spreading conviction that the socialist economies foundered as a result of the ineffectiveness of their basic organizing principles, such as government control of production, and in turn the performance of their government-controlled organizations and the people in them.

Here the frequently repeated point about the generic nature of research on organizations and management becomes most fascinating of all. When one turns to the literature on organizational effectiveness, one finds something of a muddle, although a very insightful one. Experts there emphasize the difficulty of defining and determining organizational effectiveness. They also argue forcefully or at least clearly imply that governmental ownership and control make little difference in the analysis of effectiveness. They have good reasons for doing so. They can point to clear evidence that business firms have malfunctions as severe as any faced by public agencies, and often of the same type that stereotypes impute to government, such as excessive red tape, lack of innovativeness, and motivational problems among the managers and workers. In effect, these experts pay a compliment to government by condemning crude stereotypes about the poor performance of public bureaucracy.

In addition, those who set out to study effectiveness soon realized that assessing whether an organization does its job well involves numerous complex technical, economic, ethical, and ideological issues. Their use of the somewhat unusual-sounding concept *organizational effectiveness* attests to this. If they refer to organizational success or performance, that bears less of a semantic implication that the activities of the organization brought about the success. Effectiveness suggests not only that the organization had good results but that it brought these results into effect through its management, design, and other features.

Many other terms for doing well also have limitations. In assessing business firms, most investors look carefully at profitability. Yet they also realize that short-term profitability may mask long-term problems. In addition, consumer advocates and environmental groups object to conceptions of business performance that leave out concerns for the environment and ethical concern for the consumer. A subfield concerned with corporate social responsibility has grown up to address the increasing pressures on business to respond to social and environmental needs. In addition, profitability does not apply to a vast population of government and nonprofit organizations that either generate no profits or have objectives that make profits completely insufficient to express their purpose. As with the generic approach in general, researchers have to consider the need for a general body of knowledge on organizational effectiveness, not one restricted to certain sectors or industries. As is made clear in other chapters in this book, much of what we can say about making organizations work applies about equally well in business, government, and nonprofit organizations. Thus, there is a need to develop general frameworks for analyzing organizational effectiveness and a general body of knowledge that we can broadly apply.

Models for Organizational Effectiveness

The people who study organizational effectiveness agree on many of the preceding points, but they cannot agree on one conclusive model or framework (Goodman, Pennings, and Associates, 1977; Cameron and Whetten, 1983). The complexities just mentioned, as well as many others, have caused them to try—and find inadequate—many approaches.

The Goal Approach

At the outset, it appeared obvious that one should determine the goals of the organization and assess whether it achieves them. As suggested already, however, organizations have many goals, which vary along many dimensions and often conflict with each other. Herbert Simon once pointed out that a goal is always embedded in a set of goals which a person or group tries to maximize simultaneously—achieve excellence in delivery of services to clients but keep the maintenance schedule up, keep the members happy and motivated, maintain satisfactory relations with legislators and interest groups, and so on. Many different coalitions or stakeholders associated with an organization—managers, workers, client and constituency groups, oversight and regulatory agencies, legislators, courts, people in different subunits with different priorities for the organization, and so on—can have different goals for the organization.

One can also state goals at different levels of generality, in various terms, and in various time frames (short-term versus long-term). Goals always link together in means-ends chains, where an immediate objective could be expressed as the goal, although ultimately it serves as a means to a more general or longer-term goal. In addition, researchers and consultants can have a hard time specifying an organization's goals because people in the organization have difficulty stating or admitting the real goals. Organizations have not only formal, publicly espoused goals but also actual goals. In their annual reports, public agencies and business firms often make glowing statements of their commitment to the general welfare as well as to their customers and clients. An automobile company might express commitment to providing the American people with the safest, most enjoyable, most efficient automobiles in the world. A transportation agency might state its determination to serve all the people of the state with the safest, most efficient, most effective transportation facilities and processes possible. Yet their actual behavior may indicate more concern with the security of the organization than with the clients and the general public. The goal model, in simplified forms, implies a view of management as a very rational, orderly process. Earlier chapters have described how management scholars increasingly depict managerial decisions and contexts as more turbulent, intuitive, paradoxical, almost accidental, and emergent than a rational goal-based approach implies.

All these complications caused organizational effectiveness researchers to search for alternatives to a simple goal model. The discussion of strategy in Chapter Four demonstrated, however, that experts still exhort managers to identify missions, core values, and strategies. This may depart from a strict goal-based approach, but when you tell people to decide what they want to accomplish and to design actions to achieve those conditions, you are talking about goals, even if you devise some other names for them. Goal clarification also plays a key role in managerial procedures described in earlier chapters, such as MBO.

Experts continue to suggest various terminologies and procedures for identifying organizational goals, and the goal model has never really been banished from the search for effectiveness criteria. These prescriptive frameworks, however, illustrate many of the complexities of goals mentioned above. Morrisey (1976), for example, illustrates the multiple levels and means-ends relationships of goals. He suggests a framework for public managers to use in developing management by objectives programs, which he describes as a funnel, in which the organization moves from greater generality to greater specificity by stating goals and missions, key results areas, indicators, objectives, and finally action plans. Gross (1976) suggests a framework involving seven different groups of goals — satisfying interests (such as those of clients and members), producing output, making efficient use of inputs, investing in the organization, acquiring resources, observing codes (such as laws and budgetary guidelines), and behaving rationally (through research and proper administration). Under each of these general goals he lists multiple subgoals. Obviously, managers and researchers have difficulty clearly and conclusively specifying an organization's goals.

For similar reasons, researchers have grappled with complications in measuring effectiveness. As usual, they encounter the problem of choosing between subjective measures and objective measures. Some have asked respondents to rate the effectiveness of organizations, sometimes asking members for the ratings, sometimes comparing members' ratings of their own units in the organization with the ratings that other members (such as top managers or members of other units) give them. Sometimes they ask people outside the organization for ratings. Others develop more objective measures, such as profitability and productivity indicators, from records or other sources. Some researchers develop both types of evidence, but they find this expensive. They also find sometimes that the two types of measures may not correlate with each other. In one frequently used variant of the goal approaches, researchers do not seek to determine the specific goals of a specific organization; rather, they measure ratings of effectiveness on certain criteria or goals that they assume all organizations must pursue, such as productivity, efficiency, flexibility, and adaptability. Mott (1972), for example, studied the effectiveness of government organizations (units of NASA, the State Department, the Department of Health, Education, and Welfare, and a state mental hospital) by asking managers in them to rate the quantity, quality, efficiency, adaptability, and flexibility of their divisions.

The Systems-Resource Approach

Partly because of difficulties with goal models, Yuchtman and Seashore (1967) developed a systems-resource model. They concentrated on whether an organization can attain valued resources to sustain itself from its environment. They placed effectiveness criteria in a hierarchy, with the organization's ability to exploit external resources and opportunities as the ultimate criterion, but an unmeasurable one. The next highest, or *penultimate,* criteria, they measured in a study of insurance companies. These criteria included such factors as business volume, market penetration, youthfulness of members, and production and maintenance costs. They developed these factors by using statistical techniques to group together measures of organizational activities and characteristics such as sales and number of policies in force. Drawing on a survey that they conducted in the same companies, they also examined the relationships between lower-order *subsidiary* variables, such as communication and managerial supportiveness, and the penultimate factors.

Not many researchers followed this lead with subsequent research efforts. Critics raised questions about whether the approach confuses the conception and ordering of important variables. Some of the penultimate factors could just as well be called goals, others seem to represent means for achieving goals, and some of the factors seem more important than others. Critics have complained that the analytical techniques bunched unlike factors together inappropriately. Others pointed out that the criteria represent the interests of those in charge of the organizations, even though others, such as customers and public-interest groups, might have very different interests.

Still, insights from the study influenced later developments in thinking about effectiveness. The study found that some subsidiary variables were related to *later* readings on penultimate variables. This shows that effective procedures now can lead to effective outcomes later and emphasizes the importance of examining such relationships over time. Some subsidiary measures are linked strongly to certain penultimate factors but not to others. This shows that one can point to different dimensions of effectiveness, with different sets of variables linking with them.

Also, while few researchers have reported additional studies following this model, at least one such study applied it to public agencies. Molnar and Rogers (1976) analyzed county-level offices of 110 public agencies, including various agricultural, welfare, community development, conservation, employment, and planning and zoning agencies. They argued that the resource-dependence model applied to business firms needs modification for public agencies for reasons similar to those discussed earlier in this book —

absence of profit and sales in markets, which blurs the link between inputs and outputs, consequent evaluation by political officials and other political actors, and an emphasis on meeting community or social needs that rivals the emphasis on internal efficiency.

Rogers and Molnar had people in the agencies rate their own organizations' effectiveness and the effectiveness of other organizations in the study. To represent the systems-resource approach for public agencies, they examined how many resources (equipment, funds, personnel, meeting rooms) an agency provided to other agencies in the study ("resource outflow") and how many they received from other agencies ("resource inflow"). They also calculated a score for how much resources flowing in exceeded resources flowing out. They found that the higher the level of resources flowing into an agency, the higher the level of resources flowing out. The more effective agencies thus appeared better able to develop effective exchanges with other agencies, using their own resources to attract resources from other agencies. Of course, effectiveness of public agencies involves many additional dimensions, but this study offers an interesting analysis of one means of examining effectiveness.

Participant Satisfaction Models

Another approach involves asking participants about their satisfaction with the organization. Many versions of this approach focus on whether the members of the organization feel that it fulfills their needs or that they share its goals and work to achieve them (Steers, 1977). This approach can figure very importantly in managing an organization, but it has serious limitations if participation is conceived too narrowly. One of the oldest debates about public organizations concerns whether their members serve their own interests instead of those of clients, the general public, and elected representatives. As described in Chapter Six, Barnard, Simon, March, and others (Georgiou, 1973) have analyzed organizations as coalitions of interested parties, held together by incentives for participating. These participants include not just employees but suppliers, customers, regulators and external controllers, and allies. Some of the more recent studies of effectiveness ask many different participants from such categories for ratings of the organization (Cameron, 1978). Others have tried to build in more ethical and social justice considerations by examining how well the organization serves or harms the most disadvantaged participants (Keeley, 1984). The participant satisfaction approach thus adds crucial insights to our thinking about effectiveness, but even these elaborated versions of the approach encounter problems in handling the general social significance of the organization's performance. Organizations affect the interests of the general public or society and of individuals not even remotely associated with the organization as participants.

Human Resource and Internal Process Models

Many approaches to management assume that the key to effectiveness lies in smooth internal functioning and essentially assess effectiveness by referring to such factors as internal communications, leadership style, motivation, interpersonal trust, and other internal states assumed to be desirable. Rensis Likert's four-system typology follows this pattern, assuming that as one enhances open and employee-centered leadership, communication, and control processes, one achieves organizational effectiveness. Blake and Mouton's (1984) managerial grid involves similar assumptions, as do many organization development approaches.

Some who take positions quite at odds with the human relations orientation nevertheless share this general view. Management systems experts who concentrate on whether the accounting and control systems work well or emphasize a particular approach to shaping up internal management or strict external accountability follow similar assumptions. These orientations have played an important role in the debate over what public management involves. Some writers see inadequacies in public management and a greater need for it primarily because of weak management systems and procedures of the sort that purportedly exist in superior form in industry (Crane and Jones, 1982; Steiss, 1982). They call for better accounting and control systems, better inventory controls, better purchasing and procurement, better contracting procedures, and so on.

These human resource and internal process approaches do not involve complete conceptions of organizational effectiveness, but public managers often employ them. In interviews, managers in state agencies of Florida, chosen because they had reputations as excellent managers, gave very high ratings of the effectiveness of their own organizations (Sherwood and Rainey, 1983). When asked how they knew that the organization was effective, they often mentioned internal processes or characteristics. They would point out that their staff and the subordinate managers got along very well, and things seemed to run smoothly. When they referred to external factors, they noted that they received few complaints from legislators, clients, or the press, which they took as evidence that things were running smoothly. Some mentioned that members of their organization received invitations to speak at professional conferences, which they took as evidence that they have an expert staff in place. Few referred to output indicators, systematic program or policy assessments, or other more performance-oriented measures. They may have interpreted the questions as asking how the organization achieved such results rather than how they knew that it did, but they showed a striking tendency to concentrate on internal processes and characteristics. Alimard (1987) replicated the study with state agency managers in Virginia and found very similar results, especially on the tendency for the managers to give very subjective impressions of the effectiveness of their agencies. Whether managers in private industry would refer more frequently to bottom-line criteria is an interesting question. A study by Gold (1982), described in the next chapter, found that both public and private managers mentioned the sorts of criteria described above but that the private managers more often mentioned profit as a basic goal.

Toward Diverse, Conflicting Criteria

Increasingly, researchers try to examine multiple measures of effectiveness. Campbell (1977) and his colleagues, for example, reviewed various approaches to effectiveness, including those described above, and developed a comprehensive list of criteria (see Table 9.1). Obviously, *many* dimensions figure into effectiveness. Even this elaborate list, however, does not capture certain criteria, such as effectiveness in relation to the general public interest or contribution to the general political economy (Nord, 1983). Item 25 refers to general public support, but even this does not suffice. Consider an economist who argues that even though the Social Security program has broad political support, privatizing the program would improve management and the economy of the country. Or consider the citizens who call for sharp cuts in military spending, even though military spending usually receives strong popular support. Right or wrong, these positions dramatize the quintessential difficulties of evaluating governmental organizations and the tendency of even comprehensive views of organizational effectiveness to take a relatively limited managerial perspective.

As researchers try to incorporate more complex sets of criteria, it becomes evident that organizations pursue diverse goals and respond to diverse interests, which impose trade-offs. Cameron (1978) reported a study of colleges and unversities in which he gathered a variety of types of effectiveness

Table 9.1. Organizational Effectiveness Dimensions and Measures.

Campbell (1977): Comprehensive List of Effectiveness Criteria

1. Overall effectiveness	16. Planning and goal setting
2. Productivity	17. Goal consensus
3. Efficiency	18. Internalization of organizational goals
4. Profit	19. Role and norm congruence
5. Quality	20. Managerial interpersonal skills
6. Accidents	21. Managerial task skills
7. Growth	22. Information management and communication
8. Absenteeism	23. Readiness
9. Turnover	24. Utilization of environment
10. Job satisfaction	25. Evaluations by external entities
11. Motivation	26. Stability
12. Morale	27. Value of human resources
13. Control	28. Participation and shared influence
14. Conflict/cohesion	29. Training and development emphasis
15. Flexibility/adaptation	30. Achievement emphasis

measures. Reviewing the literature, he noted that effectiveness studies had used many types of criteria, including organizational criteria such as goals, outputs, resource acquisition, and internal processes. They also vary in terms of universality (whether they use the same criteria for all organizations or different ones for different organizations), whether they are normative or descriptive (describing what an organization should do or what it does do), and whether they are dynamic or static. He also noted different sources of criteria. One can refer to different constituencies, such as the dominant groups in the organization, many constituencies in and out of the organization, or mainly external constituents. The sources also vary by level, from the over-all external system, to the organization as a unit, to subunits, or to individuals. Finally, one can use organizational records or individuals' perceptions as sources of criteria.

In his own study of educational institutions, Cameron (1978) drew on a variety of criteria—objective and subjective; measures reflecting the interests of students, faculty, and administrators; participant criteria and organizational criteria (see Table 9.2). Cameron developed profiles of different educational institutions according to the nine general criteria and found them to be diverse. One institution scored high on student academic and personal development but quite low on student career development. Another had the opposite profile—low on the first two criteria, high on the third. One institution scored high on community involvement, the others relatively low. This shows that even organizations in the same industry or service sector often follow different patterns of effectiveness. They may choose different strategies, involving somewhat different clients, approaches, and products or services. In addition, it shows that effectiveness criteria can weigh against each other. By doing well on one, the organization may show a weaker performance on another. Cameron points out that a university aiming at distinction in faculty research may pay less attention to the personal development of undergraduates than a college more devoted to attracting and placing undergraduates.

The Competing Values Approach

Quinn and Rohrbaugh (1983) draw this point about conflicting criteria into their competing values framework. They had panels of organizational researchers review the criteria in Table 9.1, to distill the basic dimensions out of the set. The panels' responses indicated that the criteria grouped together along three value dimensions (see Figure 9.1). An *organizational focus* dimension ranges from *internal* emphasis on the well-being of members of the organization to an *external* focus on the success of the entire organization. A second dimension concerns *control* as opposed to *flexibility*. The third involves relative concentration on *means* (such as doing good planning) or *ends* (such as achieving productivity goals). Quinn and Rohrbaugh point out that these dimensions reflect fundamental dilemmas that social scientists have debated

Table 9.2. Effectiveness Dimensions for Educational Institutions.

Perceptual Measures	*Objective Measures*
1. Student educational satisfaction	
Student dissatisfaction	Number of terminations
Student complaints	Counseling center visits
2. Student academic development	
Extra work and study	Percentage going on to graduate school
Amount of academic development	
3. Student career development	
Number employed in major field	Number receiving career counseling
Number of career-oriented courses	
4. Student personal development	
Opportunities for personal development	Number of extracurricular activities
Emphasis on nonacademic development	Number in extramurals and intramurals
5. Faculty and administrator employment satisfaction	
Faculty and administrators' satisfaction with school and employment	Number of faculty members and administrators leaving
6. Professional development and quality of the faculty	
Faculty publications, awards, conference attendance	Percentage of faculty with doctorates
Teaching at the cutting edge	Number of new courses
7. System openness and community interaction	
Employee community service	Number of continuing education courses
Emphasis on community relations	
8. Ability to acquire resources	
National reputation of faculty	General funds raised
Drawing power for students	Previously tenured faculty hired
Drawing power for faculty	
9. Organizational health	
Student-faculty relations	
Typical communication type	
Levels of trust	
Cooperative environment	
Use of talents and expertise	

Source: Adapted from Cameron (1978). The original table contains numerous additional measures for each dimension. See Cameron (1978) for complete listing.

for a long-time—means versus ends, flexibility versus control and stability, internal versus external orientation.

The dimensions combine to represent the four models of effectiveness mentioned in Figure 9.1. The *human relations model* emphasizes flexibility in internal processes and improving cohesion and morale as a means of developing the people in the organization. The *internal process* model also focuses internally, but with emphasis on control, through maintaining sound information, auditing, and review systems as means to stability and con-

Figure 9.1. The Competing Values Framework.

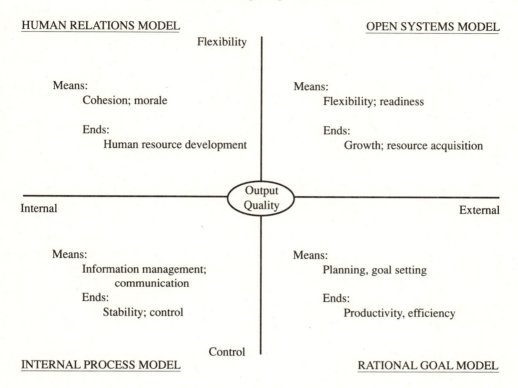

HUMAN RELATIONS MODEL   OPEN SYSTEMS MODEL

Flexibility

Means: Means:
    Cohesion; morale   Flexibility; readiness

Ends: Ends:
    Human resource development   Growth; resource acquisition

Internal   Output Quality   External

Means: Means:
    Information management;   Planning, goal setting
        communication
Ends: Ends:
    Stability; control   Productivity, efficiency

Control

INTERNAL PROCESS MODEL   RATIONAL GOAL MODEL

Source: Quinn and Rohrbaugh (1983). Reprinted by permission of the authors. Copyright 1983, the Institute of Management Sciences.

trol. At the external end, the *open-system* model emphasizes responsiveness to the environment, with flexibility in structure and process as means to achieve growth and to acquire resources. The *rational goal* model emphasizes careful planning to maximize efficiency.

    Quinn and Rohrbaugh recognize the contradictions among the different models and values. They argue, however, that a comprehensive model must retain them all, because organizations constantly face such competition among values. Organizations have to stay open to external opportunities yet must have sound internal controls. They must be ready to change but maintain reasonable stability. Effective organizations and managers balance conflicting values. They do not always do so in the same way, of course. Quinn and Cameron (1983) draw amoeba-like shapes on the diagram in Figure 9.1 to illustrate the different emphases that organizations place on the values. An organization that most heavily emphasizes control and formalization would have a profile illustrated by a roughly circular shape that expands much more widely on the lower part of the diagram than on the upper part. For an organization that emphasizes innovation and informal teamwork, the figure sweeps more widely around the upper part of the chart, showing higher emphasis on control and efficiency. This again underscores the point that different organizations may pursue different conceptions of effectiveness.

Quinn and Cameron also point out that the effectiveness profiles apparently shift as an organization moves through different stages in its life cycle. In addition, major constituencies can impose such shifts. They describe how a unit of a state mental health agency moved from a teamwork and innovative profile to a control-oriented profile because of a series of newspaper articles criticizing the unit for lax rules, records, and rule adherence.

Still, the ultimate message is that organizations and managers must balance or concurrently manage the competing values. Rohrbaugh (1981) illustrates the use of all the values in measuring the effectiveness of an employment services agency. Quinn (1988) has developed scales for managers to conduct self-assessments of their own orientations within the set of values for use in training them to manage the conflicts. The competing values framework expresses the values in highly generalized form and does not address the more specific substantive goals of particular agencies or the explicit political and institutional values imposed on public organizations. Nevertheless, it provides valuable insights into effectiveness of public organizations, especially on the point that the criteria are multiple, shifting, and conflicting.

Organizational Effectiveness and Public Organizations

As noted earlier, it is interesting that many organizational researchers regard public organizations as analyzable with the same effectiveness models as one would use for other organizations (with exceptions, such as Molnar and Rogers, 1976). Whether public organizations perform as well as private organizations has been a fundamental issue in the relevant literature for at least a century. Interest has increased recently, with more attention to the pros and cons of privatizing government activities in many countries of the world as ideologues voice foregone conclusions about the inferiority of government organizations.

Although not implying inferiority, many observers do note some ways in which effectiveness for public organizations involves even greater complexity than for private firms. Although all organizations pursue vague, multiple, conflicting goals, effectiveness researchers sporadically observe that the goals of public organizations seem particularly complex in these ways (Hannan and Freeman, 1989). This certainly agrees with the long list of authors that public organizations have goals of this nature.

In addition, the literature on public policy and public program evaluation, which developed during the 1970s and 1980s, characterizes governmental activities as channeled through policy subsystems and governmental programs. A given agency may carry out a diverse combination of programs or link into diverse policy subsystems. The effectiveness of a conglomerated agency such as the Department of Defense, the Department of Health and Human Services, or a state health and human services agency becomes an even more elusive abstraction than usual, since various programs may perform at different levels of impact or proficiency.

This last point raises still another complication. The literature on the evaluation of public programs points out a distinction between program failure and theory failure. This distinction refers to the problem that a program may achieve ineffective results because of weaknesses in the basic theory underlying the design of the program. For example, designers of the Job Corps youth training program assumed that disadvantaged young men benefit from leaving the rough areas of cities and going to work in wilderness areas—or at least program officials said so in testimony before Congress. The Job Corps trainees, however, showed a troublesome tendency to *like* the places they came from and to want to go back to them—it was home! The people in the program may be working as hard as they can, and with considerable effectiveness in many ways, but the basic theory does not work. Similarly, the program evaluation literature distinguishes between measures of *outputs* (such as number of tickets issued by police officers or number of arrests) and measures of *impact* (such as reductions in crime). Public programs and agencies often are assigned goals that involve changing complex, intransigent societal conditions. Public schools, police departments, and other public organizations often face an array of social conditions that can dampen the effect of their efforts. The organization may operate well but show little impact on the complex social conditions that it seeks to alter. These complications can produce a situation that Michelson (1980) depicts as "the working bureaucrat in the nonworking bureaucracy," the problem that employees may work quite hard in programs that nevertheless falter. Indeed, the public-policy literature includes discussions of programs that are designed to fail—established as ploys by political officials seeking to gain favor with certain constituencies but then underfunded or undersupported.

In addition, with many public organizations, it is not clear where the organization begins and ends (Kettl, 1988). During the savings and loan association scandal that erupted just as George Bush entered office, prominent news media such as the *Wall Street Journal* and the national television news programs announced that the failure of numerous savings and loan institutions around the country was largely the fault of the government. A major part of the problem, according to this analysis, arose because government raised the level of insurance on deposits with the institutions, thus inducing many people to invest indiscriminately in poorly run thrifts. In addition, regulatory actions by the FSLIC had been lax. Yet further revelations indicated that senators and members of Congress had played instrumental roles in the decision to raise the insurance level and had pressured agency officials to relax some of their oversight over prominent owners of savings and loans who had contributed to their campaigns. The agency was seriously ineffective in regulating the savings and loan industry, but the openness of a public agency means that the ineffectiveness may have its source in officials who might normally be considered outside the organization.

In spite of all the complications, however, the concern about governmental performance during the last several decades has produced a flood of productivity indicators and initiatives and evaluation criteria for public programs. There are now numerous examples of productivity and program performance indicators and frameworks, models, and programs for their use (National Commission on Productivity and Work Quality, 1975; Wholey, 1979). Interestingly, however, the debate over whether this produces effective performance in government continues.

Innovativeness in Public Organizations

As noted earlier, one time-honored assertion, advanced repeatedly by prominent authors, characterizes public bureaucracies as more rigid and change resistant than private firms (Dahl and Lindblom, 1953; Downs, 1967; Warwick, 1975). Some case analyses of public organizations support such assertions (Warwick, 1975).

Yet, in attitude surveys, public employees and managers report an interest in change and openness to it (U.S. Office of Personnel Management, 1979; Rainey, 1983). Golembiewski (1985; Golembiewski, Proehl, and Sink, 1981) reviews 270 organization development efforts in public organizations and concludes that more than 80 percent of them were apparently successful. Roessner (1983) notes scant evidence on the relative innovativeness of public and private organizations but finds that available evidence (for example, diffusion rates for new technologies in the public and private sectors) indicates no particular superiority on the part of the private sector. Evidence reviewed in earlier sections suggests that governmental, nonmarket organizations have a *tendency* (not an absolute imperative) toward elaborate constraints. Yet examples of successful innovation or change in public organizations (Rainey and Rainey, 1984; Golembiewski, 1985; Poister, 1988b) and of innovative behaviors on the part of governmental executives (Doig and Hargrove, 1987) show that many assertions about rigidity in the public sector overgeneralize harmfully.

Efficiency of Public and Private Organizations

The relative efficiency of public and private organizations attracts even more attention. Researchers have conducted numerous comparisons of public versus private provision of services, including studies of solid-waste collectin, fire protection, transportation, health care, custodial services, landscaping, data processing, and legal aid (Spann, 1977; Perry and Babitsky, 1986; Savas, 1987; Wolf, 1988). Most find the private form of provision more efficient. Some studies, however, particularly of hospitals and utilities, show no difference. Studies of utilities most often find that public utilities operate more efficiently (Atkinson and Halversen, 1986). Methodological problems with some of the studies complicate their interpretation (Parker, 1985). Some-times they fail to account for important control variables, such as size and age of the organization.

Simple efficiency studies may beg or confuse many of the questions about the role and nature of government (Downs and Larkey, 1986). Govern-ment activities may be less efficient because they serve different mixes of clients, follow more open and participative procedures, or in other ways serve such goals as openness, accountability, fairness and distributional equity, or stability (Kelman, 1987). Assessing these often abstract and value-laden goals can be very difficult.

The weight of the comparative evidence suggests that public organi-zations do face greater challenges in operating efficiently than do private organizations. Downs and Larkey (1986), however, describe several forms of evidence that many government agencies do not show drastically lower levels of efficiency. They point out that the National Commission on Produc-tivity appointed by President Nixon conducted a study of productivity in samples of activities in seventeen federal agencies. The study found that, between 1967 and 1971, productivity increased in these federal activities at a rate of 1.9 percent per year. The productivity increase in the private sec-tor during the same period was lower, at 1.5 percent. The much-maligned U.S. Postal Service has a level of productivity per worker 44 percent higher than the second best on this measure, the Japanese postal service. The cost of mailing a first-class letter in the United States is lower than in all but two of the other major nations—Switzerland and Belgium.

In addition, much evidence reflects serious, recurrent problems of efficiency and effectiveness in private firms. In 1982, the failure rate for pri-vate firms was 5,000 per week (Downs and Larkey, 1986). The *Wall Street Journal* (1990) reported that General Electric, arguably one of the best-managed large corporations in the world, lost $450 million because of a bad decision to produce and install compressors in its refrigerators. Tests had shown that the compressors were likely to fail, as they did, but the results of those tests never made it to the higher-level managers who controlled the decision to go ahead.

Another of the best-managed large corporations, Coca-Cola, introduced its *New Coke* product after one of the most extensive product-development campaigns for such a product in history. The product essentially failed. Coca-Cola is hardly alone, since 80 percent of the new products introduced into retail grocery stores fail to sell and have to be withdrawn. The expense of carrying so many unsuccessful products has led store operators to seek ways of imposing some of the costs back on the producers (Shapiro, 1990). The massive compensation packages for top executives in industry bear so little relation to performance that *Fortune* magazine ran an article on "The Mad-ness of Executive Compensation" (Downs and Larkey, 1986). The business press regularly carries such reports of fraud, waste, incompetence, and blun-dering by business firms and business executives. If anything, the discussion of market failures by economists understates the inability of markets to induce many business firms to engage in efficient and effective behaviors.

These weaknesses on the part of business firms severely undercut any claims for their great superiority over government agencies. In addition, a number of authors mount strong defenses of the general performance of government organizations. They muster various kinds of evidence, such as client satisfaction surveys and some of the studies mentioned in earlier chapters, to argue that government agencies often perform quite well and at least as well as private firms (Goodsell, 1985; Kelman, 1987; Tierney, 1988).

In addition to the simple efficiency studies, some researchers report more comprehensive comparative studies related to performance. Following a prominent study that indicated that private schools perform better, Chubb and Moe (1990) surveyed a very large sample of members of public and private schools. They found that public school members perceived stronger external influence from outside authorities, weaker parental involvement, less professional and more managerial orientations of the principals, less emphasis on academic excellence, less clarity of goals and disciplinary policy, and weaker faculty influence on the curriculum than reported by members of private schools.

This study appears consistent with much of what earlier chapters have had to say about the nature of public organizations. Their public character often subjects them to more external intervention and constraint. In turn, this often imposes on them greater challenges in trying to perform efficiently and effectively. The weight of the evidence indicates that public managers and organizations do face disadvantages in achieving efficiency and effectiveness. Yet it also indicates that many public organizations operate very well, often better than many business firms. In the next chapters, we turn to the problem of changing and developing public organizations to make them better and to examples of excellent management in the public sector.

Chapter 10

Organizational Change and Development

If organizational effectiveness serves as the fundamental issue in organizational analysis, then the challenge of changing organizations stands as a strong candidate for second place. A sprawling literature addresses organizational change and innovation, with much of it, including the elaborate subfield of organization development, focused on how to change organizations for the better. As we have pointed out, controversy simmers over whether public organizations and their employees resist change. As with all other topics taken up in this book, however, careful research uncovers many more dimensions and issues than popular discussions and some economic theories consider.

In fact, researchers and experts note a paradoxical aspect of change in public organizations. Far from being isolated bastions of change resistance, they change constantly (Meyer, 1979). This pattern may even impede substantial long-term change. In many public organizations, the politically appointed top executives and their own appointees come and go fairly rapidly. In federal agencies, the agency heads stay less than two years on average. Shifts in the political climate cause rapid shifts in program and policy priorities. This can make it hard to sustain implementation of major changes. This chapter also shows, however, examples of beneficial change in public organizations.

Relatively Natural Change: Organizational Life Cycles

Members of organizations plan and carry out some changes very purposefully. Other changes occur more spontaneously or naturally, as organizations pass through phases of development or respond to major shifts in their

223

environments. The two types of change intermingle, of course, as managers and other members respond to shifting circumstances. In the last two decades, scholars have turned more attention to the externally imposed or naturally evolving processes in writing and research on organizational life cycles, birth, and decline (Kimberly, Miles, and Associates, 1980; Cameron, Sutton, and Whetten, 1988).

Much of this work concentrates on business firms but also applies to public organizations (for example, Van de Ven, 1980; Quinn and Cameron, 1983). Years ago, Simon, Smithburg, and Thompson (1950) noted that public organizations become distinct by the nature of their birth. An influential set of interests must support the establishment of a public organization as a means of meeting a need that they perceive. They must express that need politically. Public agencies are born of and live by satisfying a sufficiently influential set of interests to maintain their political legitimacy and the resources that come with it.

Downs (1967) later suggested a more elaborate set of ways in which a public bureau can form. For one of these, Max Weber coined the term *routinization of charisma.* People devoted to a charismatic leader can press for an organization that pursues the leader's goals. Alternatively, as Simon, Smithburg, and Thompson (1950) pointed out, interested groups cause the formation of a bureau to carry out a function for which they see a need. A new bureau can split off from an existing one, as did the Department of Education from what used to be the Department of Health, Education, and Welfare. Also, entrepreneurs may gain enough support to form a new bureau. Admiral Hyman Rickover became a virtual legend by building an almost autonomous program for development of nuclear propulsion in the Nuclear Power Branch of the navy's Bureau of Ships and the Nuclear Reactor Branch of the Atomic Energy Commission (Lewis, 1987).

The Stages of Organizational Life

Downs also said that once a bureau comes into existence, it begins a three-stage life cycle. The earliest stage involves a struggle for autonomy. "Zealots" and "advocates" dominate young bureaus, and they struggle to build political support for its legitimacy and resource requests. Having established itself and ensured its survival, it enters a stage of rapid expansion, in which its members emphasize innovation. Ultimately, it enters a deceleration phase, in which the administrators concentrate on elaborating rules and ensuring coordination and accountability. Downs associated this process with what he called the rigidity cycle for bureaus. He said that as bureaus grow older and larger and enter the deceleration stage, the zealots and advocates either depart for more active, promising programs or settle into the roles of "conservers." Conservers come to dominate the bureau, and it ossifies. Others have pointed out that over time, many bureaus form strong alliances with interest groups and legislators — especially those on committees with oversight responsibilities for the agency. These allies guard their access and influence and stave off many change attempts (Warwick, 1975; Seidman and Gilmour, 1986).

Yet Downs oversimplifies about the foot-dragging bureaucracy. Large, old organizations change markedly, as recognized in recent life-cycle models. Quinn and Cameron (1983) developed a framework based on similarities among models that others had proposed. Their framework conceives four stages of development—the entrepreneurial, collectivity, formalization, and elaboration stages.

In the *entrepreneurial* stage, members of the new organization concentrate on marshaling resources and establishing the organization as a viable entity. An entrepreneurial head or group usually plays a strong leading role, pressing for innovation and new opportunities, with less emphasis on planning and coordination. Quinn and Cameron illustrate this stage by describing a newly created developmental center for the mentally disabled in a state department of mental hygiene (DMH). The energetic center director led a push for new treatment methods that involved deinstitutionalizing clients and developing their self-reliance. The center began to receive expanded support from federal grants, the DMH, and the legislature. In this stage, the center emphasized the open-systems model of effectiveness.

Out of the first stage developed the second, *collectivity* stage, in which members of the center developed high cohesion and commitment. The center staff operated in a flexible, team-based mode, with high levels of effort and zeal for the center's mission. In the competing values framework, this expands the emphasis to include the human relations model as well as the open-systems model.

The research on life cycles points out that crisis sometimes pushes organizations into new stages. About six years after the formation of the center, a major newspaper ran articles attacking the DMH for inefficiency, poor treatment of clients, and loose administrative practices. The articles cited critical reports from oversight agencies concerning inadequacies in such control mechanisms as organization charts, records, job descriptions, policy manuals, and master plans. The DMH conducted a special investigation and instructed the center director to move toward more traditional organizational structure and controls. The director left, and the new director emphasized clear lines of authority, rules, and accountability. Staff commitment fell, and many staff members left. The center had clearly moved into the *formalization and control* stage. In competing values terms, the rational control model predominated, with the importance of open systems and human relations criteria declining.

The case ended at this point, but the life-cycle framework includes a fourth stage, involving *structural elaboration and adaptation*. Confronting problems of extensive control and bureaucracy that develop during the third stage, the organization moves toward more elaborate structure to allow more decentralization but also corresponding coordination processes (Lawrence and

Lorsch, 1967). The organization seeks new ways of adaptation and renewal and expansion of its domain. A large corporation may move to a more conglomerate, profit-center design or a matrix design (Mintzberg, 1979). It appears difficult for public agencies to decentralize in these ways (Mintzberg, 1989). They have no sales and profit indicators to use in establishing profit centers, and they face stronger external accountability pressures. Note that in the DMH case, the press and the oversight agencies both pressed for traditional bureaucratic structures — charts, manuals, job descriptions. Some public agencies, however, also reconfigure in later stages, as described below.

Organizational Decline and Death

Many older, supposedly entrenched organizations face intense pressure to renew themselves. During the 1970s and 1980s, such pressures rose to particular intensity in the United States. Businesses faced surging international competition and swings in prices of oil and other resources. Government agencies faced tax revolts and skepticism about government. This bolstered the Reagan administration's efforts to cut the federal budget, including funding for many agencies and for federal support to state and local governments, many of which also faced state and local initiatives to force tax cuts (Levine, 1980a). Nonprofit organizations struggled to respond to changes in the tax laws that reduced tax incentives for charitable donations, as well as cuts in federal grants and contracts.

Organizational researchers realized that while such pressures may have intensified during the period, they actually reflected ongoing processes of decline and demise that had received little attention in organizational research (Kimberly, Miles, and Associates, 1980; Cameron, Sutton, and Whetten, 1988). Bankruptcy rates among business firms have always been very high, and all organizations, including public ones, tend to have low survival rates (Starbuck and Nystrom, 1981). Organizations may decline at various rates and in various patterns, for a number of reasons (Levine, 1980b). They may undergo atropy, or declining performance due to internal deterioration. They may become rigid, inefficient, and plagued with overstaffing and ineffective structure and communication. As described below, the Social Security Administration once became so overloaded with backlogs in processing client requests that everyone involved agreed that something had to be done.

Vulnerability and Loss of Legitimacy. Organizations, especially new ones, can also be quite vulnerable to losing resources or support from their environments. Shifts in consumer preferences can undercut businesses. The cutbacks in the public sector show that government organizations can face analogous problems when voters resist taxes. This is related to another reason for decline, the loss of legitimacy. Private firms, such as tobacco companies, can suffer when the public or public officials question the legitimacy of their products or activities. Legitimacy figures even more crucially for public organizations. Public and oversight authorities often impose stricter criteria on public organizations for honest, legitimate behaviors, as in the example of the HUD scandals described in Chapter Four.

Environmental Entropy. The environment can simply deteriorate in its capacity to support the organization. Resources may dry up. Political support may wane. Public organizations often lose support because of the waning of the social need that they address (Levine, 1980a).

Responses to Decline. Organizations respond with more or less aggressiveness and more or less acceptance of the need for change. Whetten (1988) characterizes several patterns of response. Some organizations take a *negative, resistant disposition* toward the pressures for change. They may aggressively strike a *preventive* posture or more passively react in a *defensive* mode. They may try to prevent pressures for change by manipulating the environment. Public agencies may try to develop or maintain legislation that rules out competition from other agencies or private providers of similar services. Public employee unions aggressively attack privatization proposals because they threaten public employees. On the other hand, organizations may adopt a less proactive defense against cuts, citing statistics showing the need for their programs and working to persuade legislators that their programs meet important social needs.

Other organizations take a more *receptive approach* to the need for change but approach change either *reactively* or by *generating* change and adaptation. Many public agencies react with across-the-board cuts in subunit budgets, layoffs, or reductions in force. On the other hand, a growing literature discusses ways in which organizations seek to adapt through very flexible, self-designing structures and processes. They allow lower-level managers and employees to redesign their units when they feel the need. The work on this topic concentrates on private firms and usually treats public organizations as less capable of making independent, aggressive responses to pressures for change (Whetten, 1988).

The pressures for reduced governmental taxing and spending have led to a rich discussion of tactics for responding to funding cutbacks. Table 10.1 summarizes Charles Levine's (1980b) description of some of those tactics. Rubin (1985) analyzed the Reagan administration's cutbacks in five federal agencies. She found that the responses in some ways matched what one would expect from the public administration literature and in some ways differed markedly. The president was fairly successful in achieving cutbacks in the agencies. His strong popular support blunted interest-group opposition to the cuts in the early phases. Still, agencies with interest-group support more effectively resisted cutbacks. Interest groups and congressional supporters do fight for their programs. Yet Rubin found no evidence of strong "iron triangles" (see Chapter Three) protecting the agencies. Sometimes

Table 10.1. Organizational Decline and Cutback Management:
Tactics for Responding to Decline and Funding Cuts.

	Tactics to Resist Decline	*Tactics to Smooth Decline*
External political (problem depletion)	1. Diversify programs, clients, and constituents 2. Improve legislative liaison 3. Educate the public about the agency's mission 4. Mobilize dependent clients 5. Become "captured" by a powerful interest group or legislator 6. Threaten to cut vital or popular programs 7. Cut a visible and widespread service a little to demonstrate client dependence	1. Make peace with competing agencies 2. Cut low-prestige programs 3. Cut programs to politically weak clients 4. Sell and lend expertise to other agencies 5. Share problems with other agencies
External economic/ technical (environmental entropy)	1. Find a wider and richer revenue base (for example, metropolitan reorganization) 2. Develop incentives to prevent disinvestment 3. Seek foundation support 4. Lure new public- and private-sector investment 5. Adopt user charges for services where possible	1. Improve targeting on problems 2. Plan with preservative objectives 3. Cut losses by distinguishing between capital investments and sunk costs 4. Yield concessions to taxpayers and employers to retain them
Internal political (political vulnerability)	1. Issue symbolic responses, such as forming study commissions and task forces 2. "Circle the wagons"—develop a siege mentality to retain esprit de corps 3. Strengthen expertise	1. Change leadership at each stage in the decline process 2. Reorganize at each stage 3. Cut programs run by weak subunits 4. Shift programs to another agency 5. Get temporary exemptions from personnel and budgetary regulations that limit discretion
Internal economic/ technical (organizational atrophy)	1. Increase hierarchical control 2. Improve productivity 3. Experiment with less costly service-delivery systems 4. Automate 5. Stockpile and ration resources	1. Renegotiate long-term contracts to regain flexibility 2. Install rational choice techniques such as zero-base budgeting and evaluation research 3. Mortgage the future by deferring maintenance and downscaling personnel quality 4. Ask employees to make voluntary sacrifices such as taking early retirements and deferring raises 5. Improve forecasting capacity to anticipate further cuts 6. Reassign surplus facilities to other users 7. Sell surplus property, lease back when needed 8. Exploit the exploitable

Source: Levine (1980b). Reproduced by permission of Chatham House Publishers, Inc.

agencies worked with congressional supporters, or Congress with interest groups, or agencies with interest groups, but not usually in some well-developed version of the iron-triangle notion.

The agencies were not nearly so self-directed and uncontrollable as sometimes claimed. Agency heads tended to comply with the president's cutback initiatives and usually did *not* work aggressively to mobilize interest-group support. Career personnel carried out many of the cuts, as part of their responsibility to serve the president. Rubin even suggests that one of the agencies behaved like a self-destroying agency that will not fight for itself. Some of the agencies, particularly housekeeping and regulatory agencies, had no strong interest-group support and were more vulnerable to cuts. In fact, such agencies might be cut back even if they are effective because they have no natural group support or even because they have made enemies of some interest groups.

Because of congressional and interest-group opposition to some of the cuts, the president relied on internal reorganizations and personnel cuts that did not require congressional approval. This damaged management and reduced productivity in some of the agencies. In the short term, the agencies suffered bad morale, lower productivity, bad decision making, and general disruption. The cutback process increased polarization of blacks versus whites, labor versus management, and career civil servants versus political appointees. The cuts reduced the attractiveness of federal employment and increased political influence over the federal agencies. Rubin's appraisal of these effects was made during the middle of the Reagan administration, and their duration remains to be seen. The analysis, however, does make some important points: Agency responses to decline are more complex and perhaps less politically resistant than depicted in the general literature. Agencies *do* change and do not necessarily resist change as forcefully as stereotypes and some theories suggest. Still, politics figures very importantly in change and cutback attempts and can severely impede them. Understanding when and how one can effect change becomes the major challenge, to which we return below.

The Ultimate Decline: Organizational Death. A conclusion similar to that of Rubin comes from a debate over whether public agencies can "die." Kaufman (1976) investigated the question of whether government organizations are immortal, in view of the many assertions about their staunch political support and intransigence against pressures for change, reduction, or elimination. He noted many threats to an agency's survival. They face competition from other agencies, loss of political support, or the constant reorganization movements that keep officials hunting for ways to reshape government, especially ways that appear more efficient. In reviewing evidence about death rates for federal agencies, he concluded that such rates are not negligible. Generally, however, federal agencies have a very strong tendency to endure. Of the agencies existing in 1923, he said, 94 percent had lineal descendants in 1974.

Later, Starbuck and Nystrom (1981) mounted a fascinating challenge to this conclusion. They pointed out that Kaufman classified agencies as lineal descendants even if they had changed organizational locations, names, or personnel or had substantially different functions. When agencies merged, he treated the new agency as a descendant of both of the former ones. Starbuck and Nystrom pointed out that studies of death rates of industrial organizations typically treat mergers between corporations as resulting in only one existing organization. When a corporation goes bankrupt and employees start a very similar new one, analysts do not count this as a continuation. Difficult issues exist, then, in defining organizational death. When Starbuck and Nystrom reanalyzed the data that Kaufman had used with criteria more akin to those used in studies of industry, they found that government agencies and industrial corporations have very similar death and survivial rates. Large proportions of government agencies and business firms do not survive very long. The analysis turns on whether one uses criteria biased toward organizational change or biased against it. Peters and Hogwood (1988), however, also report finding a great deal of organizational change in the U.S. federal bureaucracy. Their analysis shows, however, what other organization theorists have seen when they study public organizations (Meyer, 1979). Public organizations may be quite change resistant and intransigent in some ways, and controlling them in new and innovative directions may be a major challenge for contemporary societies. Yet they do, in fact, change a great deal, including the ultimate change of passing out of existence. As described in later sections, they can also revitalize themselves after periods of decline.

Innovation and Organizations

Innovations in society figure so importantly in social progress that a body of research on such processes developed in the last several decades. Some of it focused on the broad topic of diffusion of innovations in societies and across levels and units of government. Numerous studies analyzed such topics as adoption of birth control methods in overpopulated countries, of new agricultural methods in less developed countries and of different fire-fighting, garbage-collection, and teaching techniques across governments in the United States. Some studies also analyzed general measures of innovativeness, such as the number of health-related innovations adopted by county health departments. According to Rogers and Kim (1985), the vast majority of these innovation studies focused on public organizations or public programs, and the applications to business organizations still remain open to question. They also point out that many of these studies followed what they called the classical diffusion model, involving the following components: (1) characteristics of the innovation (see Table 10.2), (2) communication channels, (3) time (for example, rate of adoption of innovations), and (4) members of the social system (including characteristics of individuals and groups that affect their responses to innovations).

This work provides useful insights. Analyses of the attributes of innovations (Table 10.2), for example, provide useful guides for thinking through

Table 10.2. Attributes of Innovations That Affect Their Implementation.

1. Cost—initial and continuing; financial and social
2. Returns on investment
3. Efficiency—improvements in efficiency offered by innovation
4. Risk and uncertainty
5. Communicability—clarity of the innovation and its results
6. Compatibility—similarity to existing product or process
7. Complexity
8. Scientific status
9. Perceived relative advantage—whether potential advantages can be demonstrated or made visible
10. Point of origin—from inside or outside the organization; from what person, unit, or institution
11. Terminality—whether the innovation has a specific end point
12. Reversibility and divisibility—whether the innovation can be reversed or divided into steps or components so that the organization can return to the status quo if necessary
13. Commitment—the degree of behavioral and attitudinal commitment required for success
14. Interpersonal relations—how the innovation influences personal relations
15. Public- versus private-good attributes—whether the innovation provides public benefits or restricts benefits to a smaller set of individuals
16. Gatekeepers—how the innovation is related to various influential persons or groups that can block or initiate the innovation
17. Adaptability—whether users can modify and refine the innovation
18. Successive innovations—prospects for leading to additional innovations

Source: Adapted from Zaltman, Duncan, and Holbek (1973).

the prospects for a particular innovation. Yet studies following this general model fell under criticism for too much concentration on relationships between such factors. Researchers argued for more attention to processes involved in the flow of innovations from their initiation to their implementation and to how particular organizations respond to particular innovations (Downs and Mohr, 1976). Rogers and Kim argue that this trend moves toward a newer model of innovation, involving these components: `

I.   Initiation process
     A.   *Agenda setting.* Members of the organization perceive a performance gap or deficit (Zaltman, Duncan, and Holbek, 1973) that requires attention. This perceived problem leads to an agreement on the need for innovation.
     B.   *Matching.* A solution—the innovation—is matched to the problem.
II. Implementation process
     A.   *Redefinition.* The members of the organization modify the innovation for their organization. This involves some "reinvention" of the original innovation.
     B.   *Structuring.* Members modify the organization's structure to accommodate the innovation.
     C.   *Interconnecting.* Also called *institutionalization* or *routinization,* this phase involves establishing permanent relationships between the innovation and other elements of the organization.

Planned Change

Changes in organizations commonly involve purposeful, planned changes, initiated by their members. External or internal pressures usually press them into it, but managers and other members come together to plan and carry out changes.

Resistance to Change

From the beginning, management and organization theorists recognized the problem of resistance to change in organizations. Many authors have argued that traditional bureaucratic forms of organization inhibit change. They assign people to positions and departments on the basis of rules and job descriptions, and they require that people adhere to them and reward them for doing so. This aggravates the normal human tendencies to resist change for all the reasons implied by Zaltman, Duncan, and Holbek's analysis (1973) of the characteristics of innovations (Table 10.2): Change can be costly, troublesome, unfamiliar, threatening, and difficult to understand and accomplish.

Good Reasons to Resist Change

Human resistance to change can be one of the most destructive, dangerous tendencies in life, but managers and researchers often appear to forget that people have good reasons to resist change. Life involves balancing openness to the environment with reasonable consistency and stability of behavior. People without reasonably clear direction and consistency make bad leaders. People with too little of those properties end up in mental institutions (or, under deinstitutionalized programs, wandering the streets). Many intellectuals have shared with the uninformed the tendency to deride and belittle human conservatism about change because of the damage that it does. Managers often share this perspective. Fairly typically, a new manager enters an organization with a desire to have an impact and not simply to serve as a caretaker. Employees throw objections and obstacles in the way of the new manager's proposals. Quite often, the new manager expresses frustration with longer-term subordinates' commitment to the status quo.

Certainly, the new manager may have good reason to complain, but he or she may cripple effective change and innovativeness by too readily assuming that resistance means laziness, selfishness, or stupidity. People may have well-justified reasons to resist. Some ideas are simply bad ideas, and the people with the most experience realize it. The *New Yorker* magazine once ran a cartoon in which two employees of a fast-food restaurant watched a family stopped in their car at the drive-through window of the restaurant. The family members were leaning out of the car with tongs in hand, struggling to serve themselves out of a large salad bowl perched on the windowsill of the drive-through window. Cherry tomatoes bounced like Ping-Pong balls on the pavement. Lettuce floated in the wind like autumn leaves. One employee was saying to the other, "Well, it looks as if the drive-through salad bar is an idea whose time has not yet come." Some ideas are bad ideas. They deserve to be resisted.

Unsuccessful ideas abound in government and industry. As one prominent example, Lyndon Johnson directed that the planning, programming, and budgeting system (PPBS) be adopted in all federal agencies. Within a few years, the directive was withdrawn. Many elected officials and politically appointed executives at all levels of government initiate new programs, reforms, or legislation but show a disinclination to become too deeply involved in implementing them. Often, they feel that their duty involves setting policy and directing the bureaucracy rather than closely following its management. Many of them do not stay very long in their positions. Often their mandate is far from clear, however much they claim that it is. This can deprive the change process of essential elements.

The point is not to defend the prerogatives of the public bureaucracy to resist change but rather to emphasize a dilemma about organizational change in government. As described below, successful organizational change requires sustained support from higher levels, participative planning, and flexible implementation. Government managers achieve these conditions more often than many people suppose, but much of the literature nevertheless suggests their scarcity in the public sector. What we learn from the managerial literature on change makes the point that, in the example just above, the reason for the failure of PPBS was not necessarily that it was a bad idea. It was a well-intentioned innovation advocated by many experts on public administration. Good ideas are not simply born, however, they are made — developed and nurtured — through appropriate change processes. Too negative a view of resistance to new initiatives and ideas can cloud the message that people may have reasonable objections that can make a dubious idea into a better one. The challenge for public managers is to find ways to overcome obstacles to such participation and flexibility amid the political complexities and accountability pressures in government.

Types of Change

Many types, levels, and degrees of change complicate the discussion of the change process. Researchers have not incorporated these variations into their models very thoroughly; instead, they have moved to highly general frameworks that broadly cover many types of change. Still, the variations bear noting and have implications taken up in later sections. Daft (1989) points out that organizations undergo at least four types of change: (1) Technology changes occur in production processes and equipment, as in the installation of computerized client information systems or word-processing systems. (2) Administrative changes involve new performance-appraisal systems, such as the Performance Management and Recognition System for all middle-level managers in the federal civil service, pay-for-performance systems that state and local agencies have tried to implement, or affirmative action programs. (3) Changes in products and services abound in all types of organizations. As described below, the Social Seurity Administration struggled for the last several decades with steady increases in the number and nature of services that Congress mandated for the Social Security system. (4) Human resources changes occur as a result of training, development, and recruitment efforts aimed at improving leadership and human relations practices or upgrading employee skills.

While limited change may occur relatively independently in these different domains, they frequently intertwine. In fact, for major changes, the challenge is to coordinate them. Tichy (1983) argues that most of the approaches to organizational change have concentrated on one of three primary dimensions of organizational change: the political, technical, or cultural aspects. Strategic change, as Tichy calls it, involves moving beyond these more fragmented approaches to effect large-scale transformations in the organization's relations to its environment and the coordination of the three dimensions in this new orientation.

Golembiewski (1986) introduces further complexities by arguing that at least three types of change can occur in individual responses in organizations. *Alpha* change involves the change from one level to another along a measure of some dimension, such as job satisfaction. *Beta* change involves a similar change in degree, except that the significance that people attach to intervals on the measure may change as well. *Gamma* change, however, involves a general change in state, rather than just in degree. A person may shift to a redefinition or new conception of reality such that the meaning of the dimension fundamentally changes for that person. In their research, Golembiewski and colleagues find that virtually all the people in the most advanced stages of "burnout" fall at a point on a measure of work satisfaction almost diametrically opposite to the point at which virtually all of those who were in the earliest phases fall. This suggests that once a person moves into the more serious phases of burnout, he or she also moves to a fundamentally different state, in which the meaning and nature of job satisfaction change radically for that person. Differences in responses to job satisfaction measures do not fully capture this shift. This raises major issues for both research and practice pertaining to organizational change, since it complicates the measurement and assessment of change in very challenging ways.

As noted, research and theory have not yet accounted for these complexities and variations. The organizational literature does, nevertheless, provide useful, meaningful insights about change in organizations.

Organization Development

A well-established subfield of organization theory concentrates on changing organizations for the better. Writers and practitioners in organization development (OD) work to improve the functioning of organizations, especially along human relations and social dimensions, by applying social scientific theory and techniques. OD consultants or "change agents" work with people in organizations to improve communication, problem solving, renewal and change, conflict airing and resolution, decision making, and trust and openness. They often go into organizations to help them diagnose and overcome problems that they have along these lines. Ideally, they seek to leave the organization better able to manage such processes effectively. A mountain of books, articles, and professional journals, as well as a number of professional associations, deliberate about OD, and large corporations or government agencies sometimes have OD offices or bureaus that minister to the other parts of the organization.

As this description suggests, OD has firm roots in the human relations orientation in organizational studies and in the group dynamics movement. It also draws on various elements of social science and organizational behavior, such as theories of motivation, leadership and systems, and techniques such as survey research. OD theory and practice vary widely, but they tend to have common basic values and assumptions about organizations and the people in them. French and Bell (1978) point out that OD involves common assumptions about people, groups, and organizations:

- People have drives to grow and develop, especially if provided an encouraging environment. They want to make a greater contribution to organizations than most organizational settings permit.
- For most people, the work group is a very important factor. People value acceptance and cooperation in it. Leaders cannot provide for all leadership needs, so members of groups must assist each other.
- Suppressed feelings are detrimental to satisfaction, trust, and cooperation. Most groups and organizations induce suppressed feelings more than they should. Solutions to most problems in groups must be transactional, involving changes in the relationships among people.
- The leadership style and culture at higher levels tend to pervade the organization, shaping levels of trust and teamwork throughout.
- Win-lose conflict-management strategies among groups and individuals usually do harm in the long run.
- Collaborative effort has value. The welfare of all members of the system is important and should be valued by those most powerful in the system.

OD practitioners tend to value personal growth of people in organizations; a richer, more meaningful, more enjoyable, more effective life for people in organizations, especially through allowing feelings and sentiments to have a legitimate value; a commitment to both action and research; and democratization and power equalization in organizations. One can begin to guess some of the controversies that these assumptions and values engender among management experts. Before looking at those, however, it is useful to consider how OD interventions in organizations tend to proceed.

OD Interventions and Change Processes

OD consultants take a variety of approaches, but the action-research model shown in Table 10.3 illustrates a typical pattern. Key executives perceived a problem or performance gap. They bring in a consultant, who conducts a diagnosis of the organization and the problem, often using interviews, surveys, and group meetings. The consultant feeds the results back to the clients and works with them in interpreting the results and developing plans for the OD program, including objectives, problems to be addressed, and techniques to be used. The consultant continues gathering information for use in the activities, such as group problem-solving or team-building sessions. Further planning takes place as new ideas arise from the activities, and the consultant continues to gather information for assessment of the newly planned activities and their effects. This developmental process continues until the consultant leaves the people in the organization to continue it on their own. Similar models include an ultimate phase of institutionalizing the changes that the OD project has developed and terminating the relationship with the consultant (Burke, 1982).

OD Intervention Techniques

OD consultants draw from an array of responses to the problems that they help an organization identify. The literature in the field provides a variety of models, typologies, and tables suggesting the types and levels of intervention from which the people in the organization and the consultant might

Table 10.3. Phases of an Action Research Model for Organizational Development.

1. *Performance gap:* Key executives perceive problems.
2. Executives confer with an organizational consultant.
3. *Diagnosis:* The consultant begins a process of diagnosis and data gathering.
4. *Feedback:* The consultant feeds back the results to key clients and client groups.
5. *Joint action planning:* The consultant works with client groups in planning the objectives and procedures (such as team building) for the OD program.
6. *Further data gathering.* Consultant continues to monitor perceptions and attitudes.
7. *Further feedback.* In team building sessions or other settings, the organizational members address the problems identified in the diagnostic work.
8. The client groups discuss and work on the data from the diagnosis and earlier sessions. New attitudes emerge.
9. *Action planning.* The groups set objectives for further development, and plans for getting there.
10. *Action.* The plans are carried out and new behaviors develop.
11. *Further data gathering.*
12. *Further feedback.*
13. *Further action planning.*
14. *Continuation and consultant departure.* The cycle of diagnosis, feedback, planning, and action continues until the appropriate point for the departure of the consultant.

Source: Adapted from Burke (1982) and French and Bell (1978).

select (Burke, 1982). For example, focusing on problems at the level of individuals, the organization might work on new approaches to recruitment and selection, training and development, counseling, and job design. At the broader organizational level, OD may involve organization-wide survey-feedback processes, grid OD projects, quality-of-work-life programs, management by objectives projects, intergroup conflict-management procedures, and so on.

For the development of group processes, an OD project might employ team-building techniques, with which work groups try to develop more effective relations. Team-building exercises typically focus on setting goals for the group, analyzing members' roles and responsibilities and the work processes of the team, and examining relationships among the members. The OD consultant might draw on various techniques to support these efforts, such as a role negotiation process in which members list the things that they feel that each other member should do more or should do less. Then the members negotiate agreements about changes and confirm these agreements in a written contract (Burke, 1982).

OD consultants also employ techniques they call *process consultation.* The consultant observes the work groups and other activities, gathers observations and information about key processes such as communication, teamwork, and interpersonal conflict handling, and consults with the members on interpreting and improving these processes.

OD projects in the past often employed T-groups or sensitivity sessions. Such groups engage in intensive discussions aimed at helping participants learn more about how other people see them and respond to them and how they perceive others. The sessions follow a diverse array of approaches, often involving such exercises as having members take turns expressing perceptions of other members. In some versions, these techniques become highly confrontational and emotional, and participants often find the experience exhilarating. These techniques were very widely used during the 1960s, but their use has dwindled, apparently because of controversy about whether they had much long-term impact and about evidence that when they did have an impact, it often appeared to be damaging to some participants (Back, 1972).

OD Effects and Controversies

Just how the consultant selects, combines, and uses all these procedures depends on the experience and skill of the consultant. No organizing theory links the aspects of OD or systematically guides its practice. OD consultants play a role much like that of clinicians in psychology or psychiatry, in that they have no clear, uncontested theory and guide for practice. They operate on the basis of experience and intuition in choosing from an array of loosely defined procedures. The complexity of organizations and their problems makes it hard for them to establish and prove clear successes. Critics sometimes attack OD for this lack of substantive theory and theory-based research. They say that OD's concentration on human relations issues can lead to misdiagnosis of an organization's problems when they involve other dimensions, such as the accounting system or production processes. Tichy (1983), for example, argues that OD concentrates on the human resources issues in organizations when large-scale strategic change requires coordinating those issues with strategies for improving technical and political dimensions of the organization. OD adherents respond that they know that their efforts are often valuable, even if they cannot always produce simple, clear evidence of marked improvements in profits or other performance criteria. They also argue that the theories in other areas of organization theory hardly provide managers with beautifully crafted guides to changing and improving organizations and that they are justified in trying to go out and do what they can to apply behavioral science knowledge to the problems that organizations face.

OD in the Public Sector

Still, OD remains a widely used approach to improving and changing public and nonprofit organizations. OD experts who work with public-sector organizations regularly discuss the issue of whether public and private organizations differ in ways that affect the application of OD, and that discussion has an interesting history.

In the leading article in this debate, Golembiewski (1969) cited greater challenges in the public sector as a result of factors much like those discussed in earlier chapters. He said that five primary structural constraints complicate the application of OD in government. First, multiple actors have access to multiple authorities, thus presenting a complex array of possible supporters or resisters for an OD project. For example, the State Department once began a Project ACORD (Action for Organizational Development) after a career official with a strong alliance with key members of Congress pushed for it. Yet the project stalled when other prominent actors — the department head and officials in the budget and personnel bureaus — attacked it. The newspapers even got into the act, Golembiewski reports, with editorials calling for the State Department to leave its long-term civil servants alone and not pester them with a dubious program. Second, different interests and reward structures complicate the problem. Different congressional committees and different legislators and administrators may pursue different incentives. For example, some actors may press for improved organizational operations, while others seek to defend political alliances. Third, the administrative hierarchy is fragmented and weakened by these competing affiliations, thus making it harder to sustain the implementation of OD projects. Administrative officials may have stronger ties to congressional allies and stronger commitments to their programs than to the top executives in their departments or to the president. Fourth, weak linkages between career civil servants and politically appointed executives produce a similar problem of diffuse authority. Fifth, Golembiewski agrees with Kaufman (1969) that the political system continually shifts its emphasis among several goals for the executive branch—representativeness, executive leadership, and politically neutral competence. During a period of emphasis on the first two, such as President Reagan's drive to master and reduce the federal bureaucracy, the climate for OD deteriorates.

Golembiewski argues that these factors interact with managerial "habits" in government in ways that hinder OD. Higher-level executives tend to avoid delegating authority and to establish multiple layers of review and approval because of their tenuous authority over lower levels. Legislative and legal strictures constrain many dimensions that OD often seeks to reform, such as reward systems and job classifications. Government agencies more often than business firms have secrecy and security requirements. People in government show more "procedural regularity and caution." The role of the professional manager is poorly developed in government as compared to business, according to Golembiewski. He suggests that this results in part from the difficulty of enhancing a sense of ownership of the organization's objectives and values because of the organization's public nature and hence poses greater challenges in enhancing managers' commitment to the agency.

Golembiewski concludes that these differences from business firms create differences in the culture that predominates in public agencies. They place more constraints on managers and offer fewer supports and rewards for inventiveness, risk taking, and effort. Some of the managers take a cautious orientation toward initiatives in their organization.

Most other authors who examine this issue agree with Golembiewski in general, but with variations in the analysis. Davis (1983), for example, offers a very similar analysis of the effects of the external political environment on the use of OD in the public sector. Yet he more heavily emphasizes the problem that most public programs pursue multiple goals with vague programs and performance criteria, perhaps because he draws on an OD project in a human services agency, an area of government where these challenges probably take the severest form.

Fascinatingly, however, these writers emerge from these discussions with the conclusion that OD certainly can succeed in the public sector. While their depictions of the public-sector environment make some of the economists' notions of bureaucratic rigidity sound positively optimistic by comparison, these OD experts treat the public-sector context as perhaps more challenging but ultimately as a set of conditions for which one can be prepared. Golembiewski (1985) reports evidence that OD projects in the public sector enjoy a relatively impressive success rate, apparently competitive with that of projects in the private sector. First, he and colleagues reviewed numerous published reports of OD initiatives in public organizations and classified the apparent difficulties that they encountered. They found that in 270 reports of OD applications, the writers frequently mentioned the sort of constraints that Golembiewski had described. They mentioned problems with external constraints such as procedural rigidity (mentioned in 124 cases), diversity of interests and values (111), public scrutiny (87), and the "volatile political/administrative interface" — the relations between legislative and administrative units and between career officials and political officials (62). They also mentioned internal constraints such as lack of professionalism (78), weak chains of command (70), complexity of objectives (61), and short time frame (52). Also, reports for urban government applications were generally similar to those for other levels of government. While the reports cited these complications, Golembiewski noted that the large number of initiatives reported, especially considering that agencies carry out many efforts that are not reported in the professional literature, suggests that "the constraints may be tougher in the public sector, but they are not *that* tough" (p. 67).

To add to the evidence, Golembiewski reports studies that have sought to assess the effectiveness of OD applications in both sectors. One of his students assessed the success of the 270 OD initiatives mentioned above, using procedures similar to those used in previous studies of OD success rates, and found that most of the reports indicated a balance of positive effects (43 percent) or highly positive effects (41 percent). The results also suggested that the initiatives in the public sector included a healthy percentage of the most demanding OD applications and did not indicate that the success rate resulted from a tendency to try more limited forms of OD intervention in government. Golembiewski also had independent observers do similar ratings of forty-four reports of OD applications in urban government and found even higher success rates. These success rates are very similar to those reported for the private sector, Golembiewski concluded, and indicate that despite the apparent constraints that the governmental context imposes, OD practitioners do fairly well at adapting to them.

Gortner, Mahler, and Nicholson (1987) raise some challenging issues about Golembiewski's conclusions. They argue that the methodology of the assessment has weaknesses because people report the successful cases and not the unsuccessful ones. When they write articles, they describe the project in the best possible light. In addition, the OD application may fade over time. Golembiewski's study does, however, provide evidence of the possibility of successful OD in government. Those who apply OD in public agencies face special challenges, but those applications continue with frequency and apparent success throughout government.

Success and Failure in Large-Scale, Planned Organizational Change

Organizations undertake many change processes other than OD initiatives. Tichy (1983) and others suggest elaborate guidelines for managing and assessing large-scale strategic changes. The literature on large-scale organizational change does tend toward general consensus about conditions necessary for success, however. The picture is consistent with the one painted by OD adherents.

Some time ago, Greiner (1967) provided a useful summary of these generalizations. He reported a survey of eighteen cases of major organizational change attempts to draw from them the patterns of successful change. He first noted that some frequently used approaches to change often seem to founder. Examples include unilateral actions, such as top-down decrees or commands for structural changes, limited attempts at power sharing through group decision making, and efforts to encourage delegation of authority through T-group training. The successful change efforts that Greiner observed involved much more comprehensive approaches, including the following conditions and steps:

- A pressure for improvement is felt widely among people within the organization and among relevant actors outside.
- A new person is brought in as head of the organization or as consultant to lead the change effort.
- Top executives involve themselves very heavily in beginning and sustaining the change process.
- The change agent (new head or consultant), with involvement of top executives, initiates a general diagnosis.
- The change agent leads this diagnosis in a multilevel, collaborative fact-finding and problem-solving process aimed at identifying and diagnosing the key problems. Representatives of many units and levels participate. The human resources or personnel unit is heavily involved.
- Participants develop solutions. The solutions are tested on a small scale, then implemented and tested on a wider scale.
- Participants use successes to reinforce results, and the results become widely accepted.

Greiner emphasizes the key role of power sharing in the successful patterns, concluding that success appears to require it and that it must occur through a developmental process. The failures that he observed involved more unilateral pressures for change, with an illogical sequence of steps.

Successful Revitalization in Public Agencies

Many of these conditions and steps, together with emphases on transformations of organizational culture, characterize successful revitalization efforts in public organizations that had declined. Poister (1988b) provides a compilation of case studies of such efforts. In one of these, Holzer (1988) describes a marked enhancement in the productivity of the New York City Department of Sanitation, with improved labor-management cooperation and teamwork, enhanced productivity measurements and management information systems, technical innovations in refuse collection, and upgrading of managerial talent and organization (which involved contending with stringent civil service regulations and trying to modify them).

Decker and Paulson (1988) describe the vastly improved performance of the Jacksonville Electric Authority through a multifaceted performance-improvement system. The system included efforts to improve work planning and information-system management and to transform the organizational culture to place more emphasis on consultative team management, strategic planning and identification of corporate goals, and well-developed management systems to achieve them. Stephens (1988) describes how a new director of the Alabama Division of Rehabilitation and Crippled Children Service led the division through a transformation from a troubled, control-oriented organization to a more quality-oriented, participative one. She led a widely participative process to develop the division's "Blueprint for the Future"and to improve agency policies, performance evaluation, quality assurance, and organization. The process also aimed to make supervisors more oriented to coaching and consultation and involved project teams in reviewing agency policies. The director used aspects of managing culture similar to those described in Chapter Four. She faithfully met and spoke with the teams. She posted the "Blueprint for the Future" on her office wall. She redesigned the organization chart, placing Alabama's disabled children and adults at the top of the chart, to dramatize emphasis on client service.

Poister and Larson (1988) describe the revitalization of the Pennsylvania Department of Transportation, which involved a reorganization to make the agency less top-heavy and a greater emphasis on merit selection to improve the professional capabilities and management capacities of the agency's personnel. The agency's leaders also mounted a campaign to build political support. They worked to improve financial and programmatic control and to develop the organization through quality circles, participative management, and identification of guiding values.

Poister (1988a) points out that all these efforts reflect multifaceted processes of strategic change, involving many policy, managerial, technological, and political initiatives and a series of strategies that developed over time. While diverse, they all emphasize developing a shared vision and mission, strategic planning, and developing the organization's leadership and culture. They involve redistributions of power toward more active involvement of the agency's members. Yet they also emphasize enhancements of management systems, such as financial, productivity-measurement, and mangement-information systems. Effective revitalization campaigns also required the agency managers to develop and maintain effective political support to provide resources and a mandate for the changes. Thus, successful revitalizations occur in different types of public organizations, often in patterns very similar to those in private firms. Yet success requires not just skillful employment of generic principles of organizational change. It requires skill in dealing with the political context and administrative features of public organizations. These skillful applications and the conditions supporting them can be further clarified by a comparison of a successful and an unsuccessful attempt at large-scale change in public agencies.

Failure and Success in Public Organizations: Two Contrasting Cases

Reviewing two cases of large-scale change in government agencies helps to clarify the applicability of Greiner's and Golembiewski's observations. Warwick (1975) reports a failed attempt in the U.S. State Department to do what everyone would love to do—reduce bureaucracy. The Social Security Administration (SSA), on the other hand, succeeded in a similar effort. When the SSA faced extreme problems with administrative foul-ups and delays in processing applications for benefits, the people in the agency responded with a successful redesign of the organization and work processes for processing claims and apparently improved performance. These cases illustrate the validity of the many observations about the ways in which the political and institutional context of government and the internal cultures of public agencies can impede change. Yet they also support the claim that, under the right circumstances, applying sound principles of change, skillful public managers and employees can carry out major changes very effectively.

The O Area Reforms in the Department of State. Warwick (1975) describes a fascinating case in which a well-intentioned undersecretary in the State Department initiated an unsuccessful effort to decentralize decision making and eliminate levels of hierarchy. An administrative area known as the O Area had become a complex array of hierarchical layers and diverse offices. The undersecretary's reforms eliminated six hierarchical levels (including 125 administrative positions) and started a process of "management by objectives and programs." The program managers at the levels below the eliminated layers would now manage more autonomously—without so many administrators above them and with more direct lines to the deputy undersecretary. They would also follow a management by objectives program in which they specified objectives, target dates, and needed resources.

Although the undersecretary's ideas for reform were heavily influenced by McGregor's (1960) concept of Theory Y management, other managers commented that he sought to apply Theory Y by Theory X methods. The undersecretary made the changes fairly unilaterally and then called together a large group of managers and employees to announce them. Rumors had gone around about the reforms, but the nature of them, according to Warwick (1975, p. 37), caught "even the most reorganized veterans off guard."

Yet Warwick devotes most of his analysis to the factors hindering change in the State Department, which he tends to generalize to all government agencies. Externally, congressional relations and related politics played a major role. Some of the administrators whose positions were targeted for elimination had strong allies in Congress and among interest groups that

opposed the changes. The State Department had several different personnel systems (foreign service officers and others), which complicated the change
process. A bill that would have unified the systems, however, did not pass
in Congress. A civil service union opposed it, a powerful senator felt that
it would dilute the foreign service, and the chair of the Senate Foreign Relations Committee gave it little support because he wanted better cooperation from the secretary of state on matters pertaining to the war in Vietnam. The secretary of state became concerned about the wide span of control
that the reduction in the hierarchy created (many program managers reporting to the undersecretary).

Warwick argues that an "administrative orthodoxy" prevails in Washington and elsewhere in government. Legislators and political executives
expect traditional chains of command and hierarchical arrangements and
worry that their absence means disorganization. The secretary of state faced
a great deal of political pressure from Congress and the public over decisions about the Vietnam War and did not want to waste political capital
through any controversy over administration of the State Department.

Warwick argues that career civil servants are accustomed to turnover
among the top political executives every two or three years. Motivated by
caution and security, they can easily build defenses against the repetitive
cycles of reform and change that the political executives attempt during their
short stays in the agencies. The careerists can simply wait out the top executives by doing nothing, or they can mobilize opposition in Congress and
the interest groups. Faced with this resistance, the top executives tend to
avoid delegating authority and to require many levels of review and approval
to ensure accountability of the lower levels. The lower-level people tend to
accept this because it provides them with security. Like many public agencies, the State Department also had internal conflicts among units and specialists, such as a tradition of rivalry between foreign service officers and
other types and between units organized by function versus units organized
by geographical regions of the world. These internal conflicts complicate
change efforts, especially because the participants often have external political allies.

The undecretary implemented his changes with some good effects. The
changes appeared to have beneficial effects on autonomy, experimentation,
and motivation of some of the units and managers. Yet coordination appeared to suffer, and internal and external resistance mounted. Not long
after attempting the changes, the undersecretary left the State Department.
His successor derided the reforms, and within about nine months after the
departure of his predecessor, he had eliminated most of them. Some useful
remnants endured, according to Warwick, and some of the lessons learned
proved valuable in later change efforts. Yet he concludes that the reforms
clearly failed.

More generally, Warwick suggests that the conditions that he found
in this case tend to sustain complex bureaucracy in government agencies.

Congress and interest groups often resist change because they develop alliances with agencies and their subunits. They jealously guard against reorganizations that threaten those arrangements. Rapid turnover at the tops of the agencies has the effects noted already. The diversity and interrelations of government agencies complicate change efforts. Many agencies tend to be involved in any particular public-policy arena (the Departments of Agriculture and of Commerce and many other agencies have involvements in foreign affairs). Since legislation and policy decisions may involve many of them, consensus and support become more elusive. Statutes and "systemwide rules" govern many aspects of organization and procedure, sometimes dictating the actual agency structure and placing constraints on job descriptions, purchasing, space procurement, personnel decisions, and many other processes. The administrative orthodoxy, coupled with diffuse agency goals, reinforces the tendency to impose classic bureaucratic control mechanisms.

Warwick notes conditions particular to the State Department that had a lot to do with the outcome of the reforms—the problems of the Vietnam War during this period, a history of complex political influences on the department, internal rivalries, the particularly great need for security of communications, and the worldwide scope of operations. Still, he moves toward very gloomy conclusions about prospects for changing public bureaucracies. Almost as if determined not to end on such a note, however, Warwick offers suggestions about reducing and changing bureaucracy that echo those of Greiner and the OD experts. He points out that facile prescriptions for participative management in public agencies face some sharp challenges. Many of the conditions described above weigh against prospects for highly participative processes. Conditions of complexity and shared power may be the conditions under which one *must* achieve some form of increased participation, however (Bryson and Einsweiller, 1991). Warwick encounters this imperative in suggesting how change might work out. He argues that one cannot eliminate bureaucracy by decimation—by firing people or merging or cutting units—or by top-down demands for reform. Effective debureaucratization, he concludes, must have strong roots within the agency. The people in the agency must see the changes as important and useful to them. All significant internal constituencies must participate in considering the problem. There must be a careful, collaborative diagnosis, followed by broad-based discussions about concrete alternatives for change. Then proponents of the change must seek support from external controllers and allies. To avoid the problems of rapid turnover among top executives, a coordinating body should monitor and sustain the change, and this body should include more than one senior politcal appointee.

Modularization of Claims Processing in the Social Security Administration.
While the very words *modularization of claims processing* summon up the impulse to doze off, this example represents an effective attempt to do some-

thing similar to what the State Department reforms failed to do—to reform bureaucracy in the direction of decentralized control over the work and an enriched work environment. In the 1960s, the Social Security Administration became overloaded and backlogged in processing claims for Retirement and Survivors' Insurance—that is, Social Security payments. Clients complained to the SSA and to members of Congress who passed the heat along to the agency. At one point, the SSA struggled with a backlog of one million claims. Something had to be done.

The problem had developed largely because Congress had added new programs and new forms of coverage to the original Social Security program, such as extending coverage to dependents, farmers, the self-employed, and the disabled. Together with population growth, this continually expanded the number of claims to be processed. In addition, with the different programs and the complications of individual cases, some of the claims could raise confounding difficulties. A claimant might have worked under multiple aliases and have a degenerative brain disease and no memory of his or her original name and birth date.

The organizational system for handling the claims proved more and more ineffective at responding to the load. The SSA had several major functional bureaus, for the Retirement and Survivors' Insurance (RSI) program, for disability insurance, for data processing and records, and for supervising the district offices. The district offices, located around the country, took in claims from clients applying for their benefits. For the RSI program, they then forwarded the claims to one of six program service centers (PSCs). These PSCs were located in six regions of the country. Each had around 2,000 employees. When a claim arrived at a PSC from the district office, a clerical support unit would prepare a folder for the claimant and forward it to a claims unit. There, a claims authorizer would determine the type and degree of eligibility for Social Security payments. Then the folder would be forwarded to a payments unit, where a benefit authorizer would compute the amount of the benefit payment and do some paper work necessary to begin processing the payments through the computer. Then the folder would go to an accounts unit, which assembled and coded information about the case, then to another unit for entry into the computer, then to a records maintenance unit for storage. In some of these units, hundreds of people worked at desks in long rows, receiving deliveries of stacks of folders from shopping carts, with coffee and lunch breaks announced by the ringing of bells. Control clerks and supervisors, emphasizing the technical issues and production rates of their unit, spot-checked the work for accuracy.

Any incomplete information or disagreements among the technical specialists would delay a claim, because it would have to be sent back to the earlier point in the process for clarification or correction. The communication about the problem usually had to be in writing. There was no provision for getting it back to the same person who had done the earlier work. The increasing numbers of claims and the complications of many of the claims increasingly clogged the system. The system created incentives for employees to "cream" the cases by avoiding the very difficult ones or even slipping them by to the next phase to get them off one's desk. Problem cases piled up.

Robert Ball, the long-term, highly respected commissioner of the Social Security Administration, appointed an experienced SSA official, Hugh McKenna, as director of the RSI bureau with a mandate to correct the problems. McKenna initiated an open-ended process of change, with some four years of research, development, experimentation, and morale building. Several task forces with internal and external representation studied management processes, case handling, and labor relations. A consulting firm analyzed the case-management process. Large team-building and morale-boosting meetings were held between managers and staff from PSCs, district offices, and the RSI central office. The office staff worked with PSCs to develop training courses on participatory management. Interestingly, some made a comment about McKenna similar to the one made about the State Department undersecretary — that he "*ordered* participatory management." He did, but obviously with crucial variations in the way that the order was imposed.

Out of these developments emerged a concept for a modular claims-processing unit. The planning staff in the central office suggested setting up a smaller unit of fifty employees, containing all the technical specialists needed to process claims, and let them handle the claim from beginning to end. Claiming to draw on the ideas of McGregor, Herzberg, Likert, and Maslow, the proponents of the module concept argued that it would provide job enrichment and participatory management. Individuals would have more identity with the task and the clients as individuals, easier access to supervisors and managers, and more control over the flow of the claims processing and their part in it.

One of the PSCs tried out such a unit on an experimental basis and then adopted a total of six modules. Problems arose. At one point, productivity had dropped in the modules, and termination of the experiment was seriously considered. However, the staff decided that the problems could be corrected. Managers apparently had some trouble adjusting to the new system. In one instance, two module managers tried to merge their modules to create combined functional units for files, accounts, claims, and so on. The central staff had to urge them back to the original concept. The blending of clerical staff and technical specialists in the modules caused some racial and status conflicts. Relations with other agencies, such as the Civil Service Commission (now the Office of Personnel Management), required skillful handling in attempts to obtain new space and receive approval of new personnel structures. Ultimately, other PSCs adopted the modules with some modifications. In one, the specialists involved in processing a claim sat around a desk together, working through the individual cases in direct contact with each other. The modular approach was also adopted by the Disability Insurance Bureau, although with more employees per module.

The modular concept became widely accepted in the agency as a success. At one point, processing time for new claims in the PSCs had dropped by 50 percent to an average of twenty days, and it later dropped further to an average of fifteen days, with very few long-delayed cases. Some employee surveys showed increased job satisfaction in the modules. The picture does not remain all rosy, however. Some longer-term employees disliked the change. Problems with computer systems complicated matters. Morale later suffered very badly when the agency began a process of eliminating 17,000 employees in the 1980s, which apparently made it difficult to properly staff some of the modules. Nevertheless, many people in the agency regarded the modular concept as successful.

The success may simply reflect proper application of some of the generic principles of change. The change involved widely shared recognition of the need for it, support from the top, flexible implementation with adaptation, feedback, and experimentation, and a realistic strategy for achieving the objectives of the agency. The change did, in a sense, have a top-down character, but this appears to illustrate what the experts mean by support from the top. There must be process sponsors and process champions with sufficient authority and resources. In addition, this change did not involve leadership by an outside consultant or change agent, although McKenna could be regarded as having played such a role.

Some particulars about the SSA case distinguish it from the State Department case. SSA had as chief executive a long-term career civil servant who had enjoyed trust and support from key congressional figures and thus could gain a grant of authority to solve the agency's problems without interference. SSA has strong support from a large clientele receiving a specific service, and the agency's tasks tend to be clear and mechanistic. The people in the agency were able to "encapsulate" their work processes and management and seal them off from political intervention.

While such factors, as well as the generic principles of successful change, may have provided SSA with advantages, the case suggests some key additional considerations about successful change in public organizations (G. W. Rainey, 1990). SSA had a durable, skillful power center, committed to successful change. Ironically, for all the stereotypes about career bureaucrats resisting change, in this case the long-term civil servants were the champions of change. As Warwick pointed out, the change must have strong roots within the agency. In one instance, they even had to outwit a conservative political appointee who sought to undercut the reforms because he thought that they would result in "grade creep." They hurried through an approval of the new personnel structure by the Civil Service Commission to prevent any blockage of the reforms. In this and many other ways, they utilized their knowledge of the political and administrative system to sustain the change. Also, they were not leaving soon. They had the career commitment to the agency to want the changes to succeed, and they and others knew that they would be there for the duration.

The SSA change took place at the appropriate time for collective support. (See Chapter Three, on environments and the policy process, for a
discussion of the concept of "windows of opportunity" in the political process.)
The reform at State was hindered by the Vietnam War and other problems
with the timing of the change. Of course, the SSA enjoys no inherent im-
munity from political intervention; many agencies doing mechanistic work
on clear outputs get buffeted by external political forces. The timing was
right for this SSA change, however, in that no distracting crises or controversies weighed against it. The need for change was widely recognized inside
and outside the SSA. In part, this reflects luck. In part, it reflects the skill
of experienced public managers and staff members who knew when and how
to work for better alternatives.

Indeed, they did develop a better alternative, one that was comprehensive, clear, and realistic. Rather vague, prepackaged models, such as
MBO, will fail if not adapted to fit structural and cultural conditions within
particular organizations. The sponsors and champions of the change in the
SSA applied relatively firm, consistent pressure for a reasonably clear, realistic
idea, while allowing a degree of experimentation and variation in its implementation.

Later events may have diminished the impact of the modular-claims-
processing reforms. Other aspects of the Social Security program and related
policies can be debated at length. Still, experienced career civil servants in
the Social Security Administration brought about an effective improvement
in the management of a process that represents one of the largest single
categories of disbursement from the federal budget of the United States, and
that very directly affects the lives of at least sixty million Americans. The public
will hear little about this. News reporters will overlook it. Indeed, it should
not receive heroic treatment. It represents only one of many instances of skillful
change and management that go on in government continually.

Chapter 11

Managing for Excellence in the Public Sector

Preceding chapters have described many possibilities for effective management of public organizations. This chapter first describes some studies of particularly effective business and government organizations and what they found about the management strategies in those organizations. Then it offers a number of suggestions and exhortations concerning public management, summarizing and adding to material from earlier chapters.

The management literature increasingly repeats refrains about complexity, flux, turbulence, paradox, conflicting values, and even chaos (Kiel, 1989). The mounting complexity raises the question of whether human organizations can manage to avoid abject failure and crisis (Lindblom, 1977). For public organizations, additional pressures from public and political hostility have created what many experts depict as a crisis, especially at the federal level (Volker Commission, 1989), although state and local governments face similar pressures (Beck, Rainey, and Traut, 1990).

At the same time, however, a growing literature concentrates on successful management. Peters and Waterman's (1982) description of excellent corporations became one of the best-selling popular books about management in history. It led to a profusion of similar books about successful corporate management. The success of Japanese corporations attracted much attention (Ouchi, 1981).

The attacks on the public sector during the 1970s and 1980s elicited a reaction from many authors and officials who mount strong defenses of the performance of government and public organizations (Milward and Rainey, 1983; Goodsell, 1985). Others describe effective public managers and organizations (Gold, 1982; Porter, Sargent, and Stupak, 1986; Doig and Hargrove, 1987; Poister, 1988b; Tierney, 1988; DiIulio, 1989; Wilson, 1989). Public organizations and their managers will continue to play crucial roles. The challenge now is to build, rather than belittle, their effectiveness.

Profiles of Corporate Excellence

Peters and Waterman's (1982) *In Search of Excellence* became so popular because it forges beyond the riddles about organizational effectiveness over which researchers puzzle and puts forth stimulating observations about management in excellent firms (although their conclusions actually echo much of the earlier literature on human relations in organizations and organizational responses to complexity). They used a set of performance and reputational indicators to choose the sixty-two best-managed American companies. From their observations and interviews in these companies, they found that the managers place a heavy emphasis on "productivity through people" (p. 14). They do not merely mouth that value, they "live their commitment to people" (p. 16), and they "achieve extraordinary results with ordinary people" (p. xxv). They definitely try to attract and reward excellent performers, but they also emphasize both autonomy and teamwork. According to Peters and Waterman, they reject a heavy emphasis on big raises for top performers and weeding out the poorest performers.

The firms devote careful attention to managing the culture of the organization. They develop coherent philosophies concerning product quality, business integrity, and fair treatment of employees and customers. Together with stories and slogans that flourish in the companies, these philosophies emphasize shared values that guide major decisions and motivate and guide performance. The firms nurture the philosophies through heavy investments in training and socialization, including out-and-out "hoopla." "Without exception," the authors note, "the dominance and coherence of culture proved to be an essential quality of the excellent companies" (p. 75). The firms behaved as if they accepted the principle that "soft is hard"; that is, that the intangible issues of culture, values, human relations—matters that many managers regard as fuzzy and unmanageable—can and must be skillfully managed.

The successful firms strive for coherence in their approach to management, with the shared values of the culture guiding the relations among staff characteristics, skills, strategies, structure, and management systems. In so doing, they accept ambiguity and paradox as part of the challenge. Organizing involves paradoxes, where one tries to do conflicting things at the same time, under conditions that often provide little clarity. The paradoxical aspects are evident in some of their approaches to management, which Peters and Waterman described in these terms:

- *A bias for action:* They tend toward an approach that one executive described as "ready, fire, aim." They avoid analyzing decisions to death and take action aggressively.
- *Close to the customer:* Deeply concerned about the quality of their products and services, people in the companies seek to stay both in close touch with their customers and aware of their reactions.

- *Autonomy and entrepreneurship:* Many of the companies try to provide autonomy in work and encourage people to engage in entrepreneurial behaviors. They often tolerate failure in well-intended, aggressive initiatives.
- *Productivity through people:* As noted above, the companies emphasize motivating and stimulating their people through respect, participation, and encouragement. They often use imagery, language, symbols, events, and ceremonies to do this.
- *Hands-on, value driven:* The people in the firms devote much attention to clarifying and stating the primary beliefs and values that guide the organization to clarify what the company "stands for."
- *Stick to the knitting:* While often very complex, the companies stay focused on the things that they can do well and avoid ill-advised forays into activities that dilute their efforts and goals.
- *Simple form, lean staff:* The companies often have relatively simple structures and small central staffs. Some massive corporations achieved this by decentralizing into fairly autonomous business units, each like a smaller company in itself.
- *Simultaneous loose-tight properties:* The companies balanced the need for direction and control with the need for flexibility and initiative. They might have "tight" general guidelines and commitments to certain values but allow considerable flexibility within those general values and guidelines. The approach that the Social Security Administration took when it adopted the modular work units (described in Chapter Ten) appears to fit this pattern. The change followed a clear general concept of the modules, with firm commitment to the concept from the top, yet units could adopt the concept experimentally and flexibly. They could make reasonable adaptations but not radically depart from the basic idea. This example suggests the ways in which many of these approaches mesh together. The relatively clear idea for the change, coupled with relatively clear and appealing values expressed as a part of the modular concept, provided sources of motivation and direction but also a reasonable framework that higher levels could firmly insist on, without being rigid or dictatorial.

At about the same time as Peters and Waterman's book appeared, Americans became increasingly interested in the success of Japanese firms, which competed so effectively against American companies in many key industries. These observations bear similarities to the depictions of the particularly successful American companies. In one of the prominent books on the topic, Ouchi (1981) says that many Japanese firms offer lifetime employment and seek to avoid layoffs in hard times. They express a holistic concern for employees. They move slowly in evaluating and promoting personnel. They use more implicit control mechanisms, such as social influences on employees. They practice collective decision making and collective responsibility and develop relatively nonspecialized career paths.

The Japanese companies strive for trust on the part of the employees so that they will have the confidence to contribute to the organization in many ways. They emphasize work groups as the basis for collective decisions and responsibilities. Through these collective activities, slow evaluations, and nonspecialized career paths involving reassignments and varied experiences, the system achieves subtlety and intimacy by encouraging detailed knowledge of the company and its employees. The companies emphasize the development of organizational philosophies or styles, which guides objectives, operating procedures, and major decisions such as new product decisions. They support these philosophies through extensive training programs. Ouchi notes that some successful American corporations, such as IBM, Proctor & Gamble, Hewlett-Packard, and Eastman Kodak (which were included in Peters and Waterman's study), have orientations similar to some of these aspects of Japanese management.

The appearance of books such as these, especially the Peters and Waterman book and several sequels and television programs on the same theme, produced something of a movement, or fad, within management circles in the United States. Numerous similar books appeared, and many corporations took steps to emulate the purported patterns of excellence. More and more annual reports proclaimed the company's philosophy, typically including sonorous expressions of devotion to employees, customers, and high-quality products. The annual report of one high-tech firm described the company as a closely knit family of 40,000 employees!

Predictably, some controversy has followed the material on corporate excellence and Japanese management. The very generalized observations about the characteristics of the firms leave some ambiguity about just how valid they are and how closely they apply to any particular organization. It is not always clear how one carries out some of the zenlike prescriptions, and especially how one weaves them all together. Some of the excellent companies that Peters and Waterman studied encountered some difficulties later. Peters and Waterman themselves noted that some managers told them that culture plays only one of many parts in the organization. Other features, such as sound technical and production systems, can figure just as crucially. Ouchi notes that the excellent American and Japanese corporations with their dominant cultures and familial orientations could imply that those who do not fit in need to leave or not to apply in the first place. Still, the trend raises some valuable and fascinating points in the literature. These include the importance of people, human relations, and organizational culture; the inevitability of paradox and ambiguity and the necessity to manage them; and the feasibility of managing complex organizations successfully.

The trend also raises questions about how it applies to public organizations. Certainly, some of the approaches and suggestions do apply. Many public agencies used the films that Peters produced in training sessions. Robert Dempsey, director of the Florida Department of Law Enforcement, found the Peters and Waterman material very attractive and successfully used his own versions of many of the ideas. He adopted an open-door policy and encouraged the managers below him to do so as well. He moved around the organization and visited and talked with employees. He conducted surveys, including invitations for employees just to write him about what they liked and did not like. He initiated many events aimed at stimulating the atmosphere of the department and making it an enjoyable place to work, including picnics, a departmental five-kilometer run for charitable purposes, and a fitness program. He worked to be sure that contractors responsible for keeping offices painted kept up with their contracts and generally emphasized cleanliness and pride in the appearance of the organization. He sought to encourage and develop his immediate staff by giving them more responsibility. He sought higher pay levels for the employees but openly pointed out to them that he could not control such factors, since the legislature had the ultimate authority. He would do what he could about pay, he told them, and they could all try to make the organization a better place to work in as many other ways as possible. Of course, he and others in the department also worked hard on more technical and policy-related issues, but the organization gained an apparently well-deserved reputation as a well-managed and increasingly effective organization.

Dempsey's success did not come easily. He would tell anyone who asked that it took him at least a year or two to convince some members of the organization that he sincerely wanted to hear their complaints and try to do something about them. He would also relate with pride his claims of success in helping some of his staff members markedly improve themselves and their outlook on the organization and their work. Thus, a dedicated manager can make use of the excellence literature, but the question remains whether the public-sector context makes it harder to apply ideas from it. Some more systematic evidence comes from a few studies that have followed the Peters and Waterman pattern of trying to locate and describe excellent organizations and leaders. (Also see Contino and Lorusso, 1982).

Effective Public Organizations

Strikingly, the corporate excellence literature turns on their heads some of the previous observations about problems of public organizations. The Civil Service Reform Act of 1978 institutionalized the belief that weak links between pay, firing, and performance cause public organizations to perform poorly. Yet the writers on corporate excellence say that the best of the profit-oriented firms do not worry too much about such tight linkages. They try very hard to recognize and reward excellent performers, but not in a harshly competitive way. They emphasize a culture of communication, shared values, and mutual loyalty and support between the organization and its employees. They also emphasize decentralization, flexibility, and adaptiveness. Can this strategy apply to the public sector, given the context and constraints that it faces? As with virtually all the issues taken up heretofore, the answer is yes, but with special considerations, and with a degree of inconclusiveness remaining in the research and thinking on the topic. Examples of public organizations achieving these conditions do exist and are even fairly common. Yet they also suggest some particular difficulties that public organizations face in achieving them and leave questions about whether the good examples are relatively exceptional.

Gold (1982) studied ten successful organizations, five public and five private. He chose healthy organizations with well-respected products that appeared to be good places for the employees to work. The public organizations included the U.S. Forest Service, the U.S. Customs Service, the U.S. Passport Office, and the city governments of Sunnyvale, California, and Charlotte, North Carolina. He found that the ten organizations had certain common characteristics:

- They emphasize clear missions and objectives, widely communicated and understood throughout the organization.
- The people in the organization see it as special because of its products or operations and take pride in this.
- Management places great value on the people in the organization, on treating them fairly and respectfully and on open, honest, informal communication with them.
- Managers do not see their organizations as particularly innovative, but they emphasize innovative ways of managing people.
- Management emphasizes delegation of responsibility and authority as widely and as far down in the organization as possible. They strive to involve as many people as possible in decisions and activities.
- Job tasks and goals are clear, and employees receive much feedback. Good performance earns recognition and rewards.
- The handling of jobs, participation, and personnel management aims at challenging people and encouraging their enthusiasm and development.

Gold also found distinctions among the public and private organizations, however. The public organizations did not articulate their missions as clearly and consistently as did the private ones. Apparently, the private organizations' focus on profit as an element of their objectives helped in this process. The studies described above cite Hewlett-Packard as a pioneer in issuing statements of corporate philosophy that express commitment to employees and customers. Yet Gold found that in that same corporation, the managers and the policy statements consistently cite profit as an indispensable objective. The managers in the public organizations, however, talked about excellence in professionalism of staff and smoothly run operations and processes. The public organizations also had a harder time promoting from within, an approach that the private firms emphasized as a way of building experience, knowledge, and commitment.

Porter, Sargent, and Stupak (1986) identified a set of federal agencies reputed for excellence, as well as some that had lost such reputations. For example, the Federal Executive Institute (FEI) developed a reputation for excellent training and development programs for federal executives. The FEI follows such principles as "intrapreneurship" (internal entrepreneurial activities), emphasis on process as much as product, and the value of interaction among the executives as part of their development. The Treasury Executive Institute within the Department of the Treasury also emphasizes interaction among participants and close attention to the needs of the executives and reputedly provides sophisticated executive training programs. The Naval Weapons Center at China Lake, California, encourages intrapreneurialism, team building, risk taking, and mentoring relationships and has earned a reputation as an innovative, effective research and development laboratory. (Significantly, this center is the site of the demonstration project on performance-based pay described in Chapter Six). The Office of the Comptroller in the Environmental Protection Agency initiated an ambitious, effective program for human resource development in the agency. The Office of Fusion Energy in the Department of Energy adopted a successful program for developing the skills of its scientists and technicians for working in teams and dealing with counterparts in other countries.

The agencies that Porter, Sargent, and Stupak (1986) found to have fallen from the highly effective status that they once had included the Internal Revenue Service. It once had an excellent reputation for client service and employee development but appears to have lost its emphasis on client service, they argue. NASA once had a strong reputation for participative management, encouragement of openness and honesty, and collegial and highly professional relations with contractors but appears to have moved to more operational, money-making objectives. The Federal Aviation Administration lost a reputation for effectiveness in the wake of President Reagan's firing of striking flight controllers early in his administration. The Social Security System lost some of its reputation, they conclude, when the agency's mission became diffused by the requirement that it administer the Supplementary Social Insurance program, which made it a welfare agency as well as a client service agency and severely overburdened the computer system and other management systems.

Whether or not these evaluations are correct, they do raise important observations about influences on the effectiveness of public agencies. They echo the fairly common observations about why it is harder to develop excellence in the federal government—sheer size and complexity of the system, fuzzy bottom line, greater difficulty establishing clear mission, openness to the political environment and multiple participants and consequent complications for decision making, inhibition of managers by the political scrutiny of decisions and by the "micromanagement" of oversight bodies, and difficulties in relations between career and politically appointed officials. Porter, Sargent, and Stupak argue, however, that excellence can prevail where agencies establish clear vision and mission, have effective top leadership, encourage idea champions and entrepreneurial behaviors, establish close involvement with employees and clients, develop the managerial capacities of the professional and technical experts who serve in management positions, and emphasize culture over structure and process over product.

Interestingly, all the excellent agencies that they describe are small, which raises further questions about how often one can achieve the conditions that they cite. Similarly, Brudney (1990), studying volunteer programs in the public sector, finds that smaller organizations appear to have advantages in developing an attractive culture for volunteer participation. Goodsell (1985) points out that most public organizations are small or are divided into relatively small units, so that such conditions prevail widely in the public sector. As Chapter Five describes, some evidence indicates that very large organizations perform better than often supposed, but managing the culture of a huge agency poses obvious difficulties. Dorcas Hardy, as director of the Social Security Administration, disseminated some strategic objectives for the agency. A survey later found that a large percentage of the agency's employees had no familiarity with the objectives. To better disseminate the objectives and to confront morale problems that the survey also uncovered, she held a series of meetings with employees in all regions of the country. Shaping the culture of a large agency obviously requires extensive resources and commitment.

These studies of excellent public organizations have a judgmental, subjective character, and their validity escapes easy assessment. They do find troubling indications of the effects of the relatively unique and difficult conditions under which public organizations operate. They also suggest, however, that effective public organizations have many similarities to private ones. This in turn suggests that many of them can be managed as well as or better than private ones and that many public managers perform very effectively and often more effectively than many managers in successful business firms. The challenge is to continue to develop our knowledge of how they do so and of how we can encourage them to keep doing so.

Management and the Public Purpose: Suggestions and Exhortations

The earlier chapters have provided many suggestions about handling the dimensions of public management. Since the studies of excellent organizations emphasize the ways those organizations use exhortations and expressions of values, they encourage some concluding exhortations and suggestions here. Making general suggestions is awkward. Management involves paradoxes and conflicting values and objectives. As we have seen, particularly high levels of value complexity and conflict envelop many public organizations. General statements about what to do usually cannot encompass all the possible contingencies that managers must take into account. The complexities of the public sector—its many levels, types of agency, various types of officials—raise questions about when, where, and to whom general suggestions apply. Budget constraints undercut the prospects for ideas about improving management. Public stereotypes may exaggerate the problems and dangers of public organizations—fraud, secrecy, waste, incompetence, mistreatment of individuals, self-aggrandizement—but they exist all too clearly. They make some proposals about decentralization and humanizing management sound naive. Paradoxically, however, a justification for some of these suggestions is that a number of public managers and officials do not need to hear some of them because they already carry them out effectively.

The Volcker Commission (1989) report proposes a series of steps to stem the crisis in the public service that it identifies and to rebuild the public service. The report calls for the president, other public officials, and other participants in public service to devote leadership to this effort. The report will not satisfy everyone concerned with public management, but supporting the spirit and substance of the commission's proposals can enhance effective public management. The proposals focus on improving leadership and the talent pool and establishing a "culture of performance."

The steps for improving leadership include efforts to enhance the public image of government. The report responds to the trends in recent years for presidents and other participants in the political system to berate public bureaucracies and their employees and, in the Reagan administration, to diminish their authority; it calls on the president and other officials simply to speak more favorably and respectfully about civil servants. Additional proposals outline steps for a better presidential appointments process, better relations between career civil servants and political appointees, and more higher-level positions being made available to career civil servants. Additional proposals call for reducing the complex administrative controls on managers in the federal government to provide them with more authority and incentive to manage their units. For improving the talent pool, the report calls for better recruiting practices and improved communications with students and others about working with the federal government. For developing the culture of performance, the report proposes enhancements in pay and incentive systems, a strengthened role for the Office of Personnel Management, and support of productivity improvement, training, and working conditions in the federal agencies.

Steps for Management Systems

The Volcker Commission report adds to the case that public management suffers from inattention and weak support. Sustained support for the commission's proposals and similar efforts to support management at state and local levels can strengthen the concept and practice of public management.

Make Management Matter. Observers say that politically elected officials do not concern themselves much about management of agencies and programs.

Experts also complain that politically appointed executives and their staffs do not nurture and build their agencies and the people in them. The news media treat management issues superficially and with emphasis on the negative, when they pay any attention to them at all. When these people do turn some attention to the issues, they apply an old-fashioned conception of management, demanding clear lines of command, complex reporting requirements, omniscience at the top of the organization, and getting tough with the employees. The truth of these criticisms and just how widely they apply is hard to assess. Clearly, many exceptions exist. Many elected officials and appointed executives pay very effective attention to management. Some newspapers and TV news shows cover the good work that government officials do. Yet the evidence covered in earlier chapters suggests that the problem is fairly pervasive.

One form of evidence comes from the poor management systems and infrastructure in many agencies at all levels of government. Peter Grace headed a commission that pursued federal waste during the Reagan administration and claimed to find an abundance of it (Downs and Larkey, 1986). Yet Grace himself frequently pointed out that government computer and information systems performed poorly. You cannot manage if you cannot get information, he argued. Implicitly, he was calling for more investments in management systems in the federal government. By 1989, major newspapers and network news broadcasts carried coverage of a government report criticizing the Internal Revenue Service for failure to collect billions of dollars in taxes. The headlines spoke of a management crisis in the IRS. The details indicated that an antiquated computer system created a major part of the problem. Management may well have failed in key ways, but underfunding of the infrastructure appears to be a central part of the problem. In interviews, state agency managers can list numerous examples of underfunded systems and problems in obtaining the equipment and materials that they need. The head of a consumer complaint division, for example, says that she cannot get funding for a word-processing system even though her unit does virtually nothing but word-processing.

Similarly, for a long time, government agencies have devoted much less funding and attention to management development and human resource development than do sucessful private firms (Malek, 1974; Volcker Commission, 1989). Budgets are low and policies weak for training, development, and recruiting. Many agencies at all levels of government and many governments, including the federal government, lack clear, coherent policies for human resource development and for management in general. Governments need to develop coherent management policies that strive for integrated strategies for developing and coordinating the various dimensions of management, including human resources, technical systems, and work processes.

Make Modern Management Matter. All those who are concerned with public management should increasingly point to the irony that management conceptions of public officials, presidential administrations, and the media stress accountability, rationality, control, and centralization, even as much of the popular literature on private-sector management more than ever prescribes looseness, participation, empowerment, sharing, respect, and so on. The conception of governmental accountability in the United States should incorporate two relatively new features. First, we must hold political officials more accountable for effectively managing and developing the human and organizational resources of the governmental units over which they have authority. Second, in consonance with the contemporary literature on successful management (which actually conveys a message that is decades old within the management literature), accountability must not be conceived in terms of simple cost cutting and control of the bureaucracy. Government officials must show their capacity to lead, motivate, empower, delegate, and listen participatively and to encourage innovative new structures and program designs that support these processes. Many candidates for political office call on one of the hackneyed phrases in the political lexicon when they promise to "run the government like a business." This usually means little, since many businesses are very badly run. In the view of the candidate, however, it usually means cost cutting and a narrow control orientation. Increasingly, all elements of the political system need to demand that public officials do indeed run government like a business—a successful, innovative, well-managed business, but with a complex, pluralistic board of directors. Some of the suggestions below draw on more specific examples of such approaches from preceding chapters.

Steps for Individual Leaders and Managers

Some additional suggestions focus more on the individual leader and manager in a public organization.

Know the System. The knowledge of the governmental systems with which he or she has experience constitutes one of the valuable resources that a public manager can contribute to the public interest. The vast complexity of the system overwhelms even experienced public officials. Elected and appointed officials often arrive in government in a surprisingly amateurish state, at an even greater disadvantage. Public managers commonly observe that many people get positions in public agencies because of their political ties or their professional knowledge or expertness in a particular policy area, without much preparation for management roles. Remember that the successful change in the Social Security Administration was effected by experienced career administrators who understood how to work with Congress, the personnel agency, and the general services agency and who understood the workings of their own agency. Public managers must know, rapidly learn about, or have help from people who know about at least the following: the organization itself and its policies and programs, legislative processes and structures, legal processes, including administrative law, and central management and oversight agencies responsible for governmental personnel, purchasing, budgeting, evaluation, and auditing.

Manage Transitions Well. Executive transitions that take place when an elected or appointed official replaces another or when a new administration takes office receive haphazard and even incompetent treatment in government (Rainey and Wechsler, 1988). Investments in better transition procedures can make it easier to know the system and prepare for politics. Knowing how to manage such transitions provides an example of the valuable administrative knowledge mentioned above.

Establish Effective Relations Between Careerists and Political Officials. Knowledge and experience in handling the relations between career civil servants and political appointees provide another specific example of valuable administrative knowledge that public managers can develop. Events during the Reagan administration suggest that decimation strategies and adversarial approches to career-political relations can backfire badly (Rubin, 1985). We have increasing attention to strategies for improving these relations (Ingraham and Rosenbloom, 1989; Volcker Commission, 1989). Ingraham's (1988) research on these relations in the Reagan administration suggests that often the greatest successes in making and sustaining changes in policies and programs came when the relations were sound. Managers and scholars need to continue work on ways of improving this crucial link in the public service.

Prepare for Politics. Knowledge and mature understanding of the political system constitute another valuable resource that the public manager can provide. Stories abound of business executives who take positions as political appointees and find the governmental context extremely frustrating (Bozeman and Straussman, 1990). Consultants or executives from business serving on state commissions to study compensation policies express surprise that a step that they consider obvious and automatic in industry cannot be taken without going to the legislature for a change in the statute. Many experienced public employees and managers work in technical positions at some remove from the political arena and sometimes forget its implications for the work that they do. They, too, express frustration that would sometimes be ameliorated by the realization that the problems arise from the playing out of processes necessary to our political system. They sometimes join in the stereotyping of public bureaucracy by attributing slow movement and complications to the bureaucratic sloth of some higher officials. They may be right in many cases, but some of the savvy public employees have an understanding of the complex nature of the system. Chapters Two and Three offered additional suggestions about dealing with the media, constituent groups, and political authorities. Innovative entrepreneurs become masters of such knowledge (Doig and Hargrove, 1987).

Prepare Your People for Politics. Leaders need to help people adjust to the political environment. For instance, staff members may object when the head of the organization or unit decides to accede to pressure from a legislator to provide funding for a project that, on the basis of professional or technical criteria, the staff does not support. Especially if the staff has been chosen according to professional or technical criteria and has little background in public management, managers will need to articulate their own ethical and political rationales, the relationships of such decisions to longer-term objectives, and the legitimacy of certain types of political responsiveness. Robert Dempsey, the director of the Florida Department of Law Enforcement, dealt with some of the political and institutional constraints that he faced by openly discussing with other members of the organization his inability to change those constraints.

Seek a Positive Form of Power and Influence Through Excellence and Integrity. Public managers often have to play politics, but simply buying support through political favors, especially unethical ones, can make you a danger to yourself and others. (Chapter Four summarizes prescriptions for attaining power and influence within organizations.)

Master Conflict Resolution and Group Decision-Making Strategies. Since decisions in public organizations are often more politicized or involve more actors and interests than decisions in private organizations, public managers should be expert at techniques for resolving conflicts and implementing decision-making strategies.

Empower People. Leaders should seek positive power in order to empower others. They should give people important, interesting responsibilities and encourage them to participate in decisions about what is important and interesting. One reason for working to develop strategy, mission, and culture and for locating points of discretion is to find opportunities for involving and stimulating people.

Prepare to Manage Complexity. Managers in all settings have to maintain a high tolerance for ambiguity and to learn to operate effectively in turbulent and paradoxical environments. As argued throughout this book, the public-sector context involves more conflict among goals, actors, and priorities than do other settings. The earlier chapters summarize much of what we are learning about the ways managers deal with such contexts. The "garbage can" model described in Chapter Four stresses the ambiguous and chaotic nature of most important decision processes, and recent studies find decisions in governmental organizations even more ambiguous and chaotic (Hickson and others, 1986). That chapter also described some of the prescriptions that authors have offered for managing in such circumstances. Additional books are appearing that offer guidance for managers in turbulent contexts facing conflicting pressures (Morgan, 1988; Quinn, 1988).

Set and Sustain Strategy. Chapter Four described procedures for developing management strategy in the public sector. Well-versed managers can respond to complexity in part by sustained investments in strategic management processes.

Clarify Missions and Goals. The descriptions of excellent public and private organizations emphasize management through vision, mission, culture, and the clarification of goals and values. This and earlier chapters offer examples of public agencies and leaders that have adopted this orientation.

Assess Autonomy and Discretion. Public managers may actually have considerable discretion, more than they sometimes assume. Chapter Four describes the examination of mandates as part of strategy development. Strategic management processes and assessment of culture and mission can help managers to locate points where they can be innovative.

Consider Structural Alternatives. Leaders in public organizations should decentralize as much as possible, and seek to create smaller units and search for ways to reduce rules and reporting requirements. Most of the descriptions that we have considered of the design of client-centered and purpose-centered units (Golembiewski, 1987b; G. W. Rainey, 1990) have drawn on examples from human service organizations. Yet the Social Security Administration provides an example of an application in claims processing. More mechanistic tasks in many government agencies should lend themselves even more easily to such designs. Wilson (1989) suggests greater efforts to decentralize authority in such areas as military weapons design.

Public managers must also understand the internal and external politics of organizational structure so as to analyze alternatives. They have to know the system (or have the help of people who do) to know the political forces acting for and against structural changes—how interest groups, legislators, oversight units, and chief executives can become involved in the politics of structure. Effective knowledge of these relations and how to handle them supports the public manager's capacity for change and innovation.

Of course, accountability demands almost always create problems for decentralization and delegation in government. Where they must impose or endure structural constraints and controls, public managers can sell the structure to the good employees, if not to the occasional rotten apples. That is, they can seek to justify and explain that the constraints serve important purposes. They can transmit an understanding of the nature and environment of public management. A well-developed strategic orientation and well-stated sense of mission can support this process. Selling the structure does not mean encouraging blind acceptance of it, and people should be encouraged to propose alternatives that allow them to display their performance and honesty without the rules and reporting requirements.

Studies of red tape and red-tape reduction efforts at the federal level have encountered the problem that most red tape has a fairly reasonable justification behind it (Kaufman, 1976). Yet many experts also point to a tendency for officials and managers to impose rules and requirements for reports and higher-level approvals, often with demands for elaborate quantification, all because they simply assume that sound management requires such controls. Alternatively, they may feel that they are supposed to be in control and they had better do something to control things (Lynn, 1981; Warwick, 1975; Mintzberg, 1989). As we have seen, legislators and media reporters sometimes interpret the presence of proper accountability structure as the essence of good management. The phenomenon occurs in many settings. A new member once came on the board of a local United Way agency and began pressing the staff to set up accounting records to keep track of the handling of the money from the soft drink machine in the agency's office. Everyone needs to search for ways to reduce unnecessary rules, reports, and structures, and managers should reward employees for suggesting useful alternatives.

Master Strategies for Planned Change, and Attempt Change Only with Sustained Commitment. Leaders should *not* reorganize just to show that they are boss, to express their preferences, or just to shake everyone up. Reorganizations are expensive and troublesome, seldom save money (Seidman and Gilmour, 1986), and can further demoralize public employees in organizations raked back and forth by successive political appointees. Major changes require sustained, reasonable, flexible commitment of resources and executive and managerial time and attention.

Take a Comprehensive Approach to Performance Management. Too much of the attention at the federal and state levels has focused on tying pay to performance, based on appraisals by superiors. It is better to invest in management and employee development through training, motivational activities such as organizational projects and recreation, promoting the success of employees and the organization, and participative management and communication between management and workers. Alternative motivational techniques, such as gain sharing, should be considered. Relative rigidities in public personnel systems are likely to remain. Still, it is important to recognize that the differences from industry are not all that vast. All managers face such problems. They should not give up on pay for performance and sound appraisals but should recognize the dangers of instituting them too bureaucratically. They should take developmental and experimental steps, such as decoupling pay raises and performance appraisals until the appraisal process is improved. They should consider alternative appraisal and compensation systems, such as team-based appraisals and incentives. Committees of managers and employees can consider candidates for performance bonuses, recommended by their superiors. An interest in total quality management systems in some agencies, such as units of the Defense Department, should be encouraged and evaluated. Such approaches downplay individual performance appraisals, because they focus attention on one's own performance rather than the quality of overall performance and output.

Humanize Public Organizations. Old-fashioned authoritarian management techniques should be discarded. Judis (1989) reports that in one U.S. Postal Service installation, where injuries from machinery and carts were common, managers installed a glass cage in the middle of the mail room. Injured workers had to spend the day in the cage, not even allowed to read. This was impractical, as well as inhumane. After union protests that the practice made workers reluctant to work hard for fear that they would be injured and have to spend the day in the cage, managers removed the cage. When Anthony Frank became postmaster general, he began programs to introduce new training techniques, management recognition of employee achievements, and discussion groups between workers and management. At some sites that implemented such programs, mail mishandling went down by 6 percent and delays by 14 percent (Judis, 1989).

The adequacy of these particular exhortations ultimately has less importance than the general determination to maintain and improve public management. The government of the United States, including all the levels and adjoining private activities, amounts to one of the great achievements in human history. Like private and nonprofit organizations, public organizations routinely provide beneficial services that would have been considered miracles a century ago. Yet they also have the capacity to do great harm and impose severe injustice. The viability and value of government depend on legions of managers, employees, supporters, and critics who share the determination that this great institution will perform well and that, through its performance, the nation will prosper and improve.

Appendix

```
┌┐┌┐┌┐┌┐┌┐┌┐┌┐┌┐┌┐┌┐┌┐┌┐┌┐┌┐┌┐┌┐┌┐┌┐
```

The Study of Organizations: A Historical Overview

Large, complex organizations have existed for many centuries but have expanded and proliferated tremendously within the last century. The extension of large government agencies, business firms, labor unions, churches, charitable organizations, voluntary associations, and other organizations into virtually all aspects of our lives has occurred largely within the last two centuries. There have been various forms of thought, writing, and training relevant to administration for many centuries, but, not surprisingly, research and writing on large organizations and their management, like the large organizations themselves, have proliferated only fairly recently. It is impossible to understand the developments in the fields of organization theory and organizational behavior without reviewing major contributions over the last century. As we will see, even the earliest of these contributions still have a significant bearing on the characteristics of present-day organizations and management.

The Systems Metaphor

There has been a flood of material on organizations and management in the last fifty years, and no brief overview can do it all justice. One major organizing theme for these developments, however, is that the field has moved from early, now-classical approaches that emphasized a single appropriate form of organization and management to more recent approaches which rejected this "one best way" concept. These more recent perspectives emphasize the variety of organizational forms that can be effective under different contingencies.

This trend in organization theory borrows from the literature on general systems theory, which is actually quite elaborate but which has sought

266

to develop the relatively simple idea that there are various types of systems in nature that have much in common. Analysis of their characteristics and the principles governing their operations is therefore valuable, according to systems theorists, as a source of insights about diverse phenomena and of a common language to facilitate communication among diverse specialists (Kast and Rosenzweig, 1973, pp. 37–56). By studying physical systems in humans and animals, social systems such as organizations and other human aggregates, and various other systemic processes in nature, they hope to develop knowledge useful for understanding all these different topics.

A system is an ongoing process that transforms certain specified *inputs* into *outputs,* which in turn influence the subsequent inputs into the system in a way that supports the continuing operation of the process. Obviously, such processes are all around us and even inside us. Our digestive systems transform food into bodily nutrients and waste. The nutrients fuel the activities of the body in acquiring additional food, and the waste fuels the activities of politicians and college textbook writers. Obviously, then, there are subsystems within the human system. There are also interdependencies among systems and hierarchial relations among systems, with certain systems serving as subsystems for others. For a specifically designated system, the basic elements also include the *throughputs,* a set of internal linkages and processes that make up the transformation process, and the *feedback,* the influences that the outputs have on subsequent inputs.

These terms are obviously quite general — some say too general to be meaningful as anything but a very rough guide for analysis. Still, a number of people have found these general concepts valuable at least as a way of organizing an analysis. A number of discussions of organizations have taken the systems approach in describing organizational characteristics and processes (Katz and Kahn, 1966). Some analysts have found that it is helpful to take this approach, beginning by listing inputs, outputs, feedback processes, and so on, when addressing a complex problem such as analyzing organizations or political processes. This approach is often applied to management problems as well (Kast and Rosenzweig, 1973), to the point that it has sometimes become part of the management jargon. During the Carter administration, a cabinet appointee was asked at her confirmation hearing how she would handle a certain administrative problem and she used systems terminology in making her response. According to a newspaper account, she was subsequently nicknamed the "input-throughput-output lady" by wags in the media and congressional staff. Systems language has gotten around.

The systems approach also provides the metaphor characterizing a major trend in this century: distinguishing between *closed, open,* or *adaptive systems.* Some systems are closed to their environments in the sense that the internal processes remain the same regardless of environmental changes. A thermostat is a system that transforms inputs in the form of room temperature into outputs in the form of responses by heating or air conditioning units. These outputs feed back by changing the room temperature. The system's processes are very stable and machinelike. It consistently responds in a programmed pattern. It may deteriorate or malfunction, but this is a dysfunctional change that is permanent until the system is repaired or discarded. In fact, closed systems are often defined as those that display *negative entropy,* a tendency toward disorganization or death of the system. The thermostat will eventually wear out.

A human being is an example of an open or adaptive system. Humans can learn and transform their behaviors to better adapt to their environments, especially when there are environmental shifts for which the system is not programmed. Thus, its internal processes are more open to the environment in that they are better able to adapt to shifts in it. Open or adaptive systems also achieve a *steady state, dynamic equilibrium,* or *homeostasis* (Kast and Rosenzweig, 1973, p. 40) in that they adapt to their environments in ways that make them more resistant to negative entropy than closed systems. They also reflect *equifinality,* the possibility that similar results can be achieved through different processes. This may seem a peculiar abstraction, but it will be clear later why this concept was very appealing to organizational researchers who were finding that organizations were successfully adopting a variety of forms.

Recently, organization theorists have been expressing more and more skepticism about the usefulness of the systems approach (Meyer, 1979). The systems metaphor has nevertheless been very influential in the development of organization theory. It was applied to those developments through the observation that the earliest, "classical" approaches to organizational and managerial analysis treated organizations and employees as if they were closed systems. Their approaches emphasized stable, clearly defined structures and processes, as if goals were fairly clear and the central problem was the design of the most efficient, repetitive, machinelike procedures for maximizing attainment of the goals. This is also the basis for the characterization of these approaches as emphasizing "one best way" to organize.

Classical Approaches to Organizations

Frederick Taylor and Scientific Management

Frederick Taylor (1919) is usually cited as one of the foremost of the early progenitors of organizational analysis. He was the major figure in the scientific management school, which in Taylor's own words involved the systematic analysis of "every little act" in tasks to be performed by workers. Taylor characterized scientific management as involving a division of labor that was relatively new in historical terms. Whereas work procedures had for centuries been the province of skilled crafts people and artisans, scientific management recognized a division of responsibility between a managerial group and a group that performed the work. The role of management was to gather detailed information on work processes, analyze it, and derive rules and guidelines for the most efficient performance of the tasks. Workers were then to be selected and trained in these procedures so that they could maximize their output, the quality of their work, and their own earnings.

Taylor and others developed procedures for analyzing and designing tasks that are still in use. They conducted time-motion studies, which involved detailed measurement and analysis of physical arrangements in the workplace such as the placement of tools and machinery in relation to the worker and the movements of the worker and time devoted to them. The objective was to achieve the most efficient pattern of motions and work arrangements for performance of the task.

Such studies are still in use. A federal client services agency, for example, recently introduced a computerized system for recording client interviews. Agency employees had formerly helped clients fill out forms by reading them the questions and filling in their responses. The forms were then entered into the agency's computer by other employees. Under the new system, the interviewer would sit at a terminal and punch the client's responses directly into the computer, through a process in which the form would appear on the computer screen. A time-motion study was conducted to determine the most efficient arrangements and procedures for the new interview method. Among other findings, the analysis revealed that original plans to place the client to the interviewer's righthand side were inefficient. The interviewers had a tendency to face the clients when asking them a question. The systematic observations of movements and time devoted to them showed that the interviewers were spending an inordinate amount of time turning from the computer screen in front of them to face the client to their right. The arrangements were altered to have the clients sit just to the right of the screen, where the interviewer had only to make a slight turn of the head to look at the client while asking a question. Over millions of interviews, such an alteration can be immensely valuable in time and energy saved. Another example of the present-day influence of scientific management is the surgical procedures and arrangements in hospital operating rooms, which are apparently still very similar to procedures developed years ago by members of this school.

Taylor's heavy emphasis on efficient programming of task and workers was fairly controversial even in its heyday and would be harshly criticized in later years for its apparent inhumanity and its underestimation of psychological and social influences on worker morale and productivity. Some of this criticism is overdrawn in that it fails to give Taylor credit for the positive aspects of his pioneering work. Taylor actually felt that his methods would benefit workers by allowing them to increase their earnings and the quality of their work. In his own accounts of his work he said that he originally became interested in ways of encouraging workers without supervisors having to place pressure on them. As a manager, he had been involved in a very unpleasant dispute with workers, which he attributed to the obligation to put them under pressure (Burrell and Morgan, 1980, p. 126). He wanted to find alternatives to avoid such situations.

Yet Taylor did emphasize pay as the primary reward for work. He stressed minute specialization of worker activities, as if the worker were a rather mindless component of a mechanistic process. He did not improve his image with later organizational analysts when he used as an illustration of his techniques a description of his efforts to train a Scandinavian worker, whom he described as dumb as an ox, in the most efficient procedures for shoveling pig iron. While the value of his contribution is undeniable, these aspects of his work make it clear that as a guiding conception of organizational analysis, scientific management severely oversimplified the complexity of the needs of humans in the workplace.

Max Weber: Bureaucracy as an Ideal Construct

While Frederick Taylor was an early influence on the development of industrial psychology, industrial and systems engineering, and business management, the growing influence of organizations in society was also attracting the attention of sociologists. Max Weber's discussion of bureaucracy as a social phenomenon provided the most influential early analysis of the topic (Gerth and Mills, 1946). Translations of his work were not widely available in the United States until the middle decades of the twentieth century, but they had an immense influence on the development of organizational sociology.

The proliferation of organizations with authority formally distributed among bureaus or subunits is actually a fairly recent development in human history. Max Weber, whose work is identified by virtually every text in organization theory and public administration as the origin of contemporary organization theory, undertook to specify the defining characteristics of the bureaucratic form of organizations, which he saw as a relatively new and desirable form that had appeared in society as a part of the movement of societies toward more legal and rational forms of authority, as contrasted with the traditional and charismatic forms of authority that had previously predominated. The bureaucratic form was distinct even from the administrative systems of the ancient Orient (such as Mandarin China) and other administrative systems regarded as having parallels with modern ones. In the more traditional feudal or aristocratic systems, he said, the functions were discharged by personal trustees or appointees of the ruler, and the offices were in the nature of avocations, with authority discharged as a matter of privilege and the bestowal of favor.

The bureaucratic form was distinct in its legalistic specification of the authorities and obligations of office. Weber wrote that the fully developed version of bureaucracy had the following characteristics:

1.   There are fixed and official jurisdictional areas, established by rules. The rules distribute the regular activities required by the organization as the official duties of these fixed positions. The rules also distribute in a fixed way the authority required to discharge the duties and strictly

delimit that authority, and there is provision for regular and continuous fulfillment of the duties by persons with specified qualifications.

2. There is a hierarchy of authority involving supervision of lower offices by higher ones.
3. Administrative positions in the bureaucracy usually require expert training and the full working capacity of the official.
4. Management of the subunits follows relatively stable and exhaustive rules, and knowledge of these rules and procedures is a special expertise of the official.
5. The position serves for the official as a full-time vocation, a career.

Weber regarded this bureaucratic form of organization as having distinct technical advantages, especially compared to administrative systems where positions were filled on an avocational basis, as a bestowal of favor by a ruler or some other superior, and discharged largely on the basis of the officials' personal discretion. In Weber's view, the provision for qualified career officials, the structured hierarchy, and the clear rule-based specification of duties and procedures made for precision, speed, clarity, consistency, and reduction of costs. In addition, the strict delimitation of duty and authority of career officials and the specification of rights and procedures by rules support the principle of objective performance of duties, "without regard for persons." Duties would be performed and clients treated with consistency and without favoritism or purely personal motives.

In comparison to the aristocratic and autocratic systems that had predominated in the past, Weber saw the bureaucratic form of organization as a vast improvement in organizational efficiency. With officials placed in positions on the basis of merit rather than birthright or political favoritism, constrained by rules defining their rights and duties, and serving as career experts as opposed to the casual avocations of aristocrats or their appointees, bureaucracies represented the most efficient organizational form yet developed, from Weber's perspective.

Weber expressed concern that bureaucratic routines could oppress individual freedom (Fry, 1989) as well as concern about the potential problems that can arise from having experts in the bureaucracy largely in control of major societal functions. Nevertheless, he sees bureaucracy as a desirable form of organization, especially for efficiency and fair and equitable treatment of clients and employees. He thus emphasized one model of organization, a model involving clear and consistent rules, hierarchy, and role descriptions. For this reason, Weber is often grouped with the other classic figures as a proponent of what later would be characterized as the closed-system view of organization.

The Administrative Management School: Principles of Administration

Somewhat later than the writings of Taylor, from the late 1920s into the 1940s, a number of writers published their efforts to develop the first theories of administration and management encompassing the full range of functions for those roles and the proper means of discharging them. Henry Fayol, Mary Parker Follett, James Mooney, Luther Gulick, Lundall Urwick, Ralph C. Davis, and others proposed conceptions of the role of management and, in particular, "principles" to govern the various administrative functions assigned to that role. This group has come to be referred to as the administrative management school (March and Simon, 1958) or the classical school of administrative theory.

The members of the administrative management school had in common an interest in developing general principles to guide such administrative functions as planning, organizing, supervision and control, and delegation of authority. They were the most direct and emphatic of these early theorists in espousing one proper mode of organizing. They either directly stated or implied that their principles were to be a generic set of guidelines as to how the effective organization is to be designed. From a later perspective, the sense of prescriptive optimism in their work is almost touching. They exuded a feeling that such principles were feasible and could be "scientifically" developed and disseminated to guide managers in the design of their organizations.

The flavor of the administrative management school and the principles that its adherents sought to develop are effectively represented in two prominent papers, the first by Gulick and the second by Mooney. In "Notes on the Theory of Organization," Gulick (1937) discusses what he regards as two fundamental functions of management, the division of work and the coordination of work. Concerning the division of work, he generally discusses the need to create clearly defined specializations. There is an immense amount of knowledge required in organizational work, and no one can know it all, so specialization allows the matching of skills to tasks and the clear, consistent delineation of tasks. He points to certain limits on specialization. No job should be so narrowly specialized that it does not take up a full workday of the worker's time, such that the worker will be idle. Certain technological conditions and traditions or customs may constrain the assignment of tasks; there are certain tasks, such as licking an envelope, that involve steps so organically interrelated that they should not be divided.

Concerning the coordination of work, once it has been properly divided, Gulick becomes clearer on the principles that he proposes. Work can be coordinated through organization or through a dominant idea or purpose that unites efforts. Coordination through organization should be guided by several principles. First is the *span of control*—the number of subordinates reporting to one supervisor. Gulick points out that previous authorities, such as Fayol, differ as to the proper span of control. Some say that a supervisor should have no more than six subordinates; others say no more than ten. Nevertheless, the span of control should be kept narrow; effective supervision requires that the supervisor's attention not be divided among too many subordinates. Another principle is *one master*—each subordinate should have only one superior. There should be no confusion as to who the supervisor is. A third principle is *technical efficiency through the principle of homogeneity* — tasks must be grouped into units on the basis of their homogeneity. Dissimilar tasks should not be grouped together. In addition, a specialized unit must be supervised by a homogeneous specialist. Gulick gives examples of problems resulting from violation of this principle in government agencies; in an agricultural agency, the supervisor of the pest control division must not be given the supervisory responsibility over the agricultural development division.

Also in this paper, Gulick sought to define the job of management and administration through what became one of the most widely cited and influential acronyms in general management and public administration: *POSDCORB.* The letters stand for planning, organizing, staffing, directing, coordinating, reporting, and budgeting. These are the functions, he said, for which principles needed to be developed in subsequent work.

In "The Scalar Principle," James D. Mooney (1930) presented a generally similar picture of the effort to develop principles. An organization must be like a scale, a graded series of steps, in level of authority and corresponding responsibility. The principle involved several component principles. The first of these was leadership, under which the "supreme coordinating authority" at the top projects itself through the entire "scalar chain" to coordinate the entire structure. This was to be accomplished through the principle of delegation, under which higher levels assign authority and responsibility to lower levels. These processes accomplished the third principle of functional definition, under which each person is assigned a specific task.

These two papers are representative of the characteristics of the administrative management school. If certain of the "principles" seem vague, that was typical, as critics would later point out. In addition, there is clearly an emphasis on formal arrangements in the organization and the formal hierarchical authority of administrators. There were variations among authors, and they often acknowledged complexities and conflicts that made application of the principles difficult.

While some of the principles were vaguely discussed, some of the precepts were quite clear. Tasks should be highly specialized. There should be clear lines of hierarchical authority, with clear delegation down from the top, and clear accountability and supervisory relations. Span of control should be narrow. There should be unity of command; a subordinate should be directly accountable to one superior. Again, consistency, rationality, and machinelike efficiency are stressed, as if organizations could operate most effectively as closed systems, designed according to the one proper form of organization.

The historical contribution of this group is undeniable; the tables of contents of contemporary texts in management continue to reflect the influence of their early efforts to conceive the role of management and administration. There are some highly successful corporations where the top executive passes around this literature to subordinates for their edification (Perrow, 1970b). Gulick and others played an important role in the Hoover commission on reorganization of the federal government, which had an immense impact on the structure of the federal government. That influence has continued across the years, and structural developments in public agencies and the attitudes of governmental officials about such issues still appear to reflect the influence of the administrative management school (Golembiewski, 1962; Warwick, 1975, pp. 69-71). Their influence on the Hoover Commission may well be the most significant direct influence on practical events that organization theorists, especially those oriented toward public administration, have ever had. Nevertheless, we will see that their approach came to be regarded as too limited for organizational analysis and that many successful contemporary organizations violate the principles so drastically and enthusiastically that one can imagine administrative management devotees having to cover their eyes.

Reactions, Critiques, and New Developments

The Hawthorne Studies: the Discovery of Human Beings in the Workplace

Even as the members of the administrative management school were writing, events were occurring that would ultimately represent a major reaction against Taylor's scientific management and the principles of the administrative management school. While Taylor was working, less heralded activity was being engaged in by researchers in the emerging area of industrial psychology. They emphasized psychological factors in work settings more than detailed analysis of tasks or principles of management. They were beginning to study such factors as fatigue and monotony and the relationship of these factors to productivity and were also beginning to analyze such working conditions as rest periods, hours of work, methods of payment, routineness of work, and the influence of social groups in the workplace (Burrell and Morgan, 1980, p. 129). This trend erupted into the organizational literature and the more popular discussion as a result of reports of a series of experiments at the Hawthorne plant of the Western Electric Company that began in the mid 1920s.

The Hawthorne Experiments were actually a complex series of experiments, elaborate exercises in data collection and analysis, and academic and popular reports of these activities over a number of years. There is a good deal of controversy about what actually happened at Hawthorne and what the implications and value of the studies actually are, but the general contribution usually attributed to them is clear. Social and psychological factors are very significant influences on work behavior, often more important than factors such as pay or physical conditions of work. An employee's work group, a sense of the importance of one's work, and attention and concern on the part of supervisors are among a number of important social and psychological influences on workers.

Principals in the project describe several major experiments and observations as the most significant in the study (Roethlisberger and Dickson, 1939). In one, the researchers lowered the level of illumination in the workplace and found that productivity nevertheless increased, because the workers responded to the attention of the researchers. In another, they improved the working conditions for the workers in a small unit through numerous alterations in rest periods and working hours. Increases in output were at first taken as evidence that the changes were influencing productivity. When the researchers tested that conclusion by withdrawing the improved conditions, however, they found that output, rather than falling off, remained high. In the course of the experiment, the workers had been consulted about their opinions and reactions and questioned sympathetically; their physical well-being was of obvious concern to the researchers. The so-called experiment on physical conditions of work had actually altered the social situation in the workplace, and that appeared to account for the high output.

In observing another work group, the researchers found that the group enforced strict norms regarding productivity by group members. To be a socially accepted member of the group, a worker had to avoid being a "rate buster" by turning out too much work, a "chiseler" by turning out too little, or a "squealer" by saying something to a supervisor that could be detrimental to another worker. This suggested to the researchers a distinction between the formal organization, as officially designed in organization charts and rules, and the informal organization. The informal organization develops through unofficial social processes within the organization but can involve norms and standards that are just as forceful as influences on the worker as the formal ones. In some cases, they are even more influential, and in directions contrary to the formal rules or objectives.

There has been controversy about whether the results of the studies actually supported some of the conclusions that the Hawthorne researchers drew. Critics have also pointed out various limitations of the procedures: the researchers were too subservient to management; they omitted major factors such as unions. Burrell and Morgan (1980, pp. 120–143) argue that the significance usually attached to the experiments—the social influences on work behavior—is oversimplified and that the real value of the work was in its recognition of the importance of sociotechnical systems; that is, that worker behavior is actually the product of complex interrelationships among social, technological, and other factors.

The general significance of the work is undeniable, however. Accurately or not, the Hawthorne studies have been widely regarded as the most significant demonstration of the importance of social and psychological factors in the workplace up to that time. As such, they are regarded as having contributed to a major shift in research on management and organizations. The *Hawthorne effect* became a term widely used in the social sciences to refer to a common problem in social research: The effort to observe human behavior can in itself alter the behavior, thus confounding the analysis of the actual influences on it. In organizational analysis, the emphasis on social influences in work groups, informal processes in organizations outweighing or opposing the formal arrangements stressed in the principles of administration, and the influences on workers of attention from others and of a sense of significance of their work constituted a major counterpoint against the principles of administrative management and scientific management.

Chester Barnard and Herbert Simon: The Inducements-Contributions Equilibrium and the Limits of Formal Rationality

Another development in the literature that weighed against the administrative management school and moved research in new directions was the work of an unlikely tandem, a successful business executive turned organization theorist and an academic who would become a Nobel laureate. Encouraged by members of the Harvard group who were responsible for the Hawthorne studies and related work (Burrell and Morgan, 1980, p. 148), Chester Barnard wrote *The Functions of the Executive* (1938), which became one of the most influential books in the history of the field. It was one of the first efforts at a fairly comprehensive theory of organizations, aimed at explaining organizational processes as opposed to stating prescriptive principles.

Barnard proposed a definition of organizations that is completely inadequate as a definition but does illustrate the sharp difference between his perspective and that of the classical theorists: an organization is "a system of consciously-coordinated activities or forces of two or more persons" (1938, p. 73). Barnard was interested in the process by which the cooperative activities fundamental to an organization are induced and coordinated. An organization is an "economy of incentives" in which individuals contribute their participation and effort in exchange for incentives that the organization provides. A major function of the executive cadre in an organization is ensuring the smooth operation of this economy. The executive must keep it in equilibrium by ensuring the availability of the incentives to induce the contributions from members that in turn earn the resources for continuing incentives, and so on. Barnard undertook an elaborate listing of the possible incentives, including not just money and physical and social factors but also power, prestige, fulfillment of ideals and altruistic motives, participation in effective or useful organizations, and many others. Different organizations, such as industrial organizations and political organizations, might differ in the extent to which they rely on the various incentives.

The operation of this economy of incentives was also complex. It was not, in Barnard's view, a system of simple, clear exchanges but was interrelated with processes of communication and persuasion that were also functions of the executive. The executive could use persuasion to alter the subjective perceptions and valuations of various incentives. The persuasion process requires a communication process, and Barnard discussed both at length. He also distinguished between formal and informal organizations, but not as much in the sense of conflicting sets of norms and influences as the Hawthorne researchers had pictured them. Barnard saw them as interrelated and necessary to each other and even asserted that the formal organization developed out of the informal one. Clearly, he thought of the informal organization as the embodiment of the communication, persuasion, and inducement processes that were essential to the cooperative activity he saw as the essence of organization.

The divergence from the classical approaches should be obvious. Rather than stating prescriptive principles, Barnard purports to describe the empirical reality of organizations. He treats the role of the executive as central, but he barely mentions formal authority and formal organizational structure. In effect, he implies that those factors are not particularly important to understanding how organizations really operate. Mainly, however, Barnard had gone beyond observations about empirical realities of the workplace and social forces there to apply such ideas to a more comprehensive analysis of the organization as an operating system, to be analyzed as such rather than formally and artificially prescribed. His approach was apparently exhilarating to many researchers, including one of the preeminent social scientists of the century.

Herbert Simon attacked the administrative management school much more directly than Barnard had. In an article entitled "The Proverbs of Administration" in *Public Administration Review*, Simon (1946) criticized the principles of administration as being vague and contradictory. He compared them to proverbs because he saw them as prescriptive platitudes, such as "Look before you leap," that are useless because they are unclear and often balanced by a contradictory proverb: "He who hesitates is lost." The principle of specialization is not clear, for example, because it is never made clear whether one specializes by function, by clientele, or by place. Specialization contradicts the principle of unity of command, which requires that a subordinate report to a superior within his or her specialization. Yet if a school has an accountant, who is obviously a specialist, that accountant must report to an educator. The two principles come into conflict.

Similarly, the principle of span of control conflicts with unity of command. In a large organization, narrow spans of control require many hierarchical levels. There must be many small work units, with a supervisor for each. Then there must be many supervisors above those supervisors to keep the span of control narrow at that level, and so on up. Yet this means that communication up, down, and across will become very cumbersome, and it will be difficult to maintain a clear, direct system of hierarchical authority.

Simon called for more systematic studies of administrative processes to develop concepts and study their relationships and argued that the principles can be useful only as a part of this process. The objective must be to determine when individuals in administrative settings would choose one or the other of the alternatives represented by the principles. As indicated by his critique, such choices are seldom clear. The limits on the ability of organizational members to perform and to be completely rational are major determinants of organizational processes and their effects, and Simon argued that these limits on rationality and ability must be more carefully analyzed. In sum, he argued for a more empirical and analytical approach to organizational analysis.

Hammond (1990) argues that Simon's critique of Gulick and others in the administrative management school overlooked major strengths of that approach. As mentioned above, they did seek to analyze challenges that managers constantly face for which later researchers have not really found answers and that have a continuing influence on organizational structure in government. Still, most organization theorists agree that Simon's rejection of the principles had the stronger influence on subsequent work in that field (Hammond, 1990).

Simon pursued these ideas further in *Administrative Behavior* (Simon, 1948). As the title indicates, he was interested in analyzing actual behavior rather than stating formal prescriptions or principles. He drew on Barnard's idea of an equilibrium of inducements and contributions and extended it into a more elaborate discussion of an organization's need to provide sufficient inducements to members and external constituencies and supporters for it to survive.

Like Barnard, Simon was concerned with the complex process of inducement and persuasion and with abstract incentives such as prestige, power, and altruistic service in addition to material incentives. He saw the uncertainties and contradictions posed by the principles purporting to guide administrative decisions. Either as cause or as consequence, his attention to these issues appears to have been related to a continuing interest in a fundamental question: Amid such uncertainty and complexity, how are administrative choices and decisions made? The principles of administration were based on the assumption that administrators could and would be rational in their choices of the most efficient mode of organization. Much of economic theory assumed the existence of "economic man"—an assumption that firms and individuals would be strictly rational in maximizing profits and personal gain. Simon observed that in administrative settings, there are always uncertainties. "Administrative man" is subject to cognitive limits on rationality. Strictly rational decisions and choices are elusive, because information and time for decisions are limited. Even where there is abundant information, human cognition is limited—human mental capacity is too limited to process all the information. Whereas the other formulations assumed maximizing behavior in decision making, Simon coined a new concept: Rather than maximize, administrative man will "satisfice." Satisficing involves choosing the best of a limited set of alternatives so as to optimize the decision within constraints on information and time. Thus, an administrator does not make the maximally rational decision, because that is essentially impossible. The administrator makes the best possible decision within constraints of time, resources, and cognitive capacity.

This conception of the decision process was a more significant departure than it may seem at first glance. It challenged a fundamental tenet of economic theory. It influenced subsequent research on decision making in business firms, as amplified by *A Behavioral Theory of the Firm,* by Richard Cyert and James March (1963). It was a leading step toward more recent approaches to organizational decision making, as we will see later. Together with Simon's related concerns with actual behavior in organizations and theories of it, the approach was influential in turning organizational analysts in those directions. With James March, Simon later published another influential book, *Organizations* (March and Simon, 1958), in which they further elaborated the inducements-contribution equilibrium theory. They presented an extensive set of propositions about factors influencing the decision by an employee to join and stay with the organization and, once in it, to produce. Simon's conception of decision making in administrative settings, however, appears to be the foremost reason that he was later awarded the Nobel Prize in economics.

Social Psychology, Group Dynamics, and Human Relationships

Another major development in the 1930s was the arrival of Kurt Lewin in the United States as a refugee from Naziism. An immensely energetic intellectual, Lewin was to become one of the most influential social scientists in the history of the field. As a psychological theorist, Lewin developed "field theory" and "topological psychology." His ultimate objective was a mathematicized theory for explaining human actions as a function of both characteristics of the individual and the conditions impinging on that individual at a given time. This may not seem original from a contemporary perspective, but it was distinct at the time from other prominent approaches, such as Freudian psychology, which more heavily emphasized unconscious motives and past experiences.

Lewin's emphasis on the field of forces influencing an individual's actions was particularly suited to his interest in group behaviors and change processes in groups and individuals. He spoke of different psychological regions within a person that corresponded to different activities, such as leadership, and relationships to other regions, such as an executive region (Back, 1972, p. 98). He viewed subgroups within larger groups as regions within the larger field of influences and relations external to the individual and used this formulation to study power, communication, influence, and "cohesion" within groups. This led Lewin to a general conception of change that has been valuable to analysts of groups and organizational change for years.

Lewin argued that groups and individuals maintain a "quasi-stationary equilibrium" in their attitudes and behaviors as a result of balance between forces pressing for change and against change. These forces were components of the field of situational conditions that he emphasized in his approach, and he pointed out that change must involve change in these forces. Groups, for example, involve fields of pressures and influences on an individual within the group. If the person is removed from the group and persuaded to change an attitude but returned to the same field of group pressures, the change is unlikely to be effective. The total field of group pressures must be altered. This involves a three-phase process. First is "unfreezing," or weakening, the forces against change and strengthening the forces for change. Next, the "change" phase moves the group to a new equilibrium point. Then, the "refreezing" phase firmly sets the new equilibrium through such processes as expressions of group consensus.

One of Lewin's better-known experiments in group dynamics illustrates his meaning. During World War II, Lewin sought to aid the war effort by engaging in research on methods of encouraging consumption of under-utilized foods as a way of conserving resources. He conducted an "experiment" on convincing housewives that they should use more beef hearts in preparing meals. He assembled the housewives in groups and presented them with information favoring the change. They then discussed the matter, aired and resolved their concerns about the change ("unfreezing"), and came to a consensus that they should use more beef hearts. In groups in which the housewives made a public commitment to do so, more of them adopted the new behavior than in groups where the members made no such public commitment. The group commitment provides an example of "refreezing" through setting group forces at the new equilibrium point.

This project also demonstrates Lewin's interest in "action research," or the analysis, evaluation, and sometimes manipulation of ongoing social processes. He constantly engaged in projects on race relations, leadership, and other practical issues. In one of the earliest experimental studies of leadership in contemporary social science, he and colleagues placed groups of boys under the supervision of men who used laissez-faire, democratic, or authoritarian leadership styles (Lewin, Lippitt, and White, 1939). They concluded that the boys displayed the least aggression when under the democratic leader and preferred the democratic leader to the authoritarian leader. The results were obviously relevant to a major social issue during that period, when fascism was a powerful political force in Europe.

The intellectual leader of a group of social scientists interested in research on group processes, Lewin was instrumental in the establishment of the Research Center for Group Dynamics at MIT and the first National Training Laboratory, which was for years to be a leading center for training in group processes. These activities had an interesting set of diverse, sometimes opposing influences on later work. Although Lewin's own experiments often amounted to demonstration projects aimed at making a point instead of tightly designed experiments, his efforts were among the first applications of reasonably rigorous experimental methods to the analysis of human behavior (using control groups, for example).

The work of Lewin and his colleagues set in motion the development of experimental social psychology, which led to numerous experiments on group processes and more recently to increasing emphasis on experimental rigor and design. This emphasis, plus an interest in refining the concepts employed in group research, have resulted in an elaborate field in which numerous well-designed experiments are constantly under way on such topics as attitude change and interpersonal perceptions and attributions. The field appears to have deemphasized group research very strongly in favor of these topics.

Some of the important experiments on groups were obviously relevant to organizational behavior. The experiment on leadership contributed to the growing interest in participative leadership styles in organizations. In another classic experiment conducted by members of this group, Lester Coch and John R. P. French (1948) compared work groups in a factory that were faced with a change in work procedures. One group fully participated in the decision to make the change, another group had limited participation, and a third group was simply instructed to make the change. The participative groups made the change more readily and more effectively, with the most participative group doing the best. These sorts of projects were instrumental in making "participative decision making," or PDM, a widely discussed (and sometimes utilized) technique in management theory and practice. Other experiments influenced by the observations from the Hawthorne Experiments and elsewhere included experiments on work groups consisting of college students engaged in tasks in the laboratory, in which the researchers sought to manipulate group pressures experimentally to analyze these processes. Numerous experiments of this sort contributed to the growing literature on industrial psychology and organizational behavior.

Interestingly, Lewin's influence also led to an almost diametrically opposing trend in applied group dynamics. In large part as a reflection on Lewin's interest in applied work, the National Training Laboratory conducted training in group processes for governmental and industrial organizations. After Lewin's death, the group dynamics movement split into two movements. In addition to the researchers who emphasized rigorous experimental research on group concepts, a large group continued to emphasize industrial applications and training in group processes. They tended to reject experimental procedures in favor of experiential, intuitive learning in group sessions. Their work contributed importantly to the development of the field of organization development. It also led to the widespread use of T-groups, sensitivity sessions, and encounter-group techniques during the 1960s and 1970s (Back, 1972, p. 99).

The Human Relation Emphasis

The Hawthorne Experiments and related work and the research on group dynamics were producing insights about the importance of social and psychological factors in the workplace and the potential value of participative management, enhancing employee self-esteem, and other efforts to improve human relations in organizations. A number of writers who began to emphasize such factors came to be characterized as representing a human relations movement, even though the actual boundaries of this so-called movement are not very clear.

Very influential on the thinking of some of these authors was a theory of human needs put forward by the psychologist Abraham Maslow. Maslow argued that there were certain major categories of human needs, which were arranged in a "hierarchy of prepotency." The lowest category would dominate a person's motives until it was sufficiently fulfilled, and then the next-highest category would dominate, and so on. The categories, in order of prepotency, were the physiological needs, the safety needs, the love needs, the esteem needs, and the self-actualization needs. The self-actualization category referred to the need for self-fulfillment, for fulfillment of one's potential, and for becoming all that one is capable of becoming. Thus, as a person fulfills basic psysiological needs, such as the need for food, and moves on up the hierarchy, the person will ultimately become concerned with self-actualization. This notion of a distinction between lower-level needs and a higher order of needs for esteem and for growth and fulfillment was particularly attractive to writers emphasizing human relations in organizations (for more detail on Maslow's formulation, see Chapter Six).

Douglas McGregor, for example, published a book whose title foretells the message: *The Human Side of Enterprise* (1960). McGregor had been instrumental in bringing Kurt Lewin to MIT, and he reflected the influence of both Lewin and Maslow in introducing his conceptions of Theory X and Theory Y. He argued that management practices in American industry were dominated by a view of human behavior that he labeled Theory X. This theory held that employees were basically lazy, passive, resistant to change and responsibility, and indifferent to organizational needs. It is therefore incumbent upon management to take complete responsibility for directing and controlling the organization. Employees must be closely directed, controlled, and motivated by management. McGregor felt that Theory X was implicit in the organizational practices that one could observe in most industrial organizations, in managerial attitudes, and in the classic approaches to management, such as scientific management.

Theory Y was a diametrically different view of employees. Drawing on Maslow's conception of higher-level needs for esteem and self-actualization, McGregor defined Theory Y as the view that employees were fully capable of self-direction and self-motivation. Underutilized though it was, management based on this approach would be more effective because individual self-control is a more effective form of control than close hierarchical direction and supervision. McGregor advocated organizational arrangements allowing more worker participation and self-control through such techniques as decentralization of authority, management by objectives, and job enlargement.

McGregor's advocacy of Theory Y clearly rejected the classical approaches to organization, and that rejection was emphatic in other major works at the time that placed a similar value on releasing human potential in the workplace. Argyris (1957), for example, argued that there were inherent conflicts between the needs of the mature human personality and the needs of organizations. He noted Herbert Simon's argument that organizations are "intendedly rational." Even though they are incapable of perfect rationality, as Simon made clear in developing his concept of satisficing, organizations will strive for it. Especially when this striving takes the form of the classical principles of administration, healthy individuals will experience frustration, failure, and conflict. Healthy individuals desire relative independence, activeness, and use of their abilities. A number of the classical principles, such as those that called for narrow spans of control, clear chain of command and unity of direction, and narrow specialization, were inconsistent with these values. They would foster dependence on superiors and organizational rules, passiveness resulting from reduced individual discretion, and lack of opportunity to use one's abilities resulting from narrow tasks and organizational constraints. Argyris, too, called for further development of such techniques as participative leadership and job enlargement to counter this problem.

As with the classical approaches before them, the proponents of the human relations school in their turn became the targets of scathing criticisms. Critics complained that those writers concentrated too narrowly on one dimension of the organization—the human dimension—and were relatively inattentive to other major dimensions, such as structure, labor union objectives, and environmental pressures. They argued that the human relations types were repeating the mistake of proposing one best way of approaching organizational and managerial analysis, always treating interpersonal and psychological factors as the central, crucial issues. Another complaint was that human relations approaches were often manipulative. For all the nice talk about releasing human potential, participative management, and so on, some critics grumbled about the tendency of such approaches always to serve the ends of management, as if the real objective were to get the workers to acquiesce in the roles that management intended to impose on them in the first place. Even where the motives were pure, some critics asserted, the approach was often naive. Labor unions sometimes objected to participative management projects and similar techniques because they feared that management would later cite the project as a reason that the workers did not really need raises.

Finally, in relation to the development of organization theory, probably the most damaging critique of the approach was that it was simply empirically unfounded, that there was no evidence that improved human relations would necessarily or even usually lead to improved organizational performance (Perrow, 1970b). The upsurge in empirical research that was occurring in the 1950s and 1960s was producing evidence that there was sometimes considerable conflict in very successful organizations and that there was no necessary relationship between individual work satisfaction and individual productivity. Findings such as these made the approach appear less and less viable as a basis for theoretical development.

Like the criticisms of the classical approaches, these criticisms tend to be overblown and a bit unfair and hypocritical. They often overlook the historical perspective of the writers, underestimating the significance of what they were trying to do at the time. They also sometimes distort and overlook the actual positions of some of the contributors, some of whom actually balk at being labeled human relations types and argue that they never intended the simple-minded approaches attributed to them. Nevertheless, it is now widely accepted that the writers often classified into this school did not produce a theoretical base that was sufficiently sound and well substantiated to guide the field.

While they may not dominate theory and research, it would be harmful to overlook the value of the insights that these organizational analysts provided. Examples still abound of management practices that are dysfunctional because of inattention to factors emphasized by this group. When improperly implemented, scientific management techniques have created ludicrous situations in which workers slow down or otherwise disguise their normal behaviors when the management analysts are trying to observe them. Illustrative is the case of a consulting firm that was trying to implement a management improvement system in a large state agency in Florida. The system involved minute analysis of work procedures and activities in a process similar to time-motion methods. Part of the process involved having observers spot-check employees at random intervals to note their activities. If the employee was idle, the observer would duly record that fact. A colleague of mine went to the office of a midlevel administrator in the agency to discuss a research project. Finding the administrator on the phone, she began to back out of his office. He beckoned her back in, explaining that he was not on the phone; he was sitting there trying to think. He was holding the phone to his ear to be sure that the observer would not happen by and record him as being idle. Another administrator was not so careful. After working late into the night on a project and coming in early to complete it, he finally finished and sat back to take a break, without thinking. Too late! The observer happened by and checked his record sheet. Idle! Gotcha! As described in Chapter Eleven, one unit of the U.S. Postal Service built a glass cage in which disabled workers had to sit all day, without being allowed to read. The new postmaster general estimated that the bad morale and distrust spawned by such practices reduced productivity substantially, and he introduced steps to improve communication and participation.

Another example was provided by a management trainee in a large manufacturing firm. He was being rotated through various subunits in the training process and was working with the systems engineers on the design of the assembly-line arrangements. One step in the production process involved having an employee sit and watch two glass water tanks through which refrigerator compressors would be dragged by a wire. If there was a leak in the compressor, an air bubble would be released, and the employee would remove the compressor as defective. The management trainee expressed disgust at the stupid incompetence of the employees, who were constantly failing at this simple task, where all they had to do was sit and watch two tanks of water for eight hours. As a solution, the systems designers changed the procedure so that an employee would sit directly facing a tank and would have to watch only one tank. The management trainee was even more disgusted to find that the employees were so stupid that they could not even handle this simple task!

As these examples illustrate, even several decades after the human relations material began to appear, there are still plenty of instances of dysfunctional management attitudes and procedures that could probably be improved by some reading in the human relations literature. Before turning to the approaches that have superseded this one, then, it is essential to recognize, that, while they may not predominate in theory development and they may not take enough organizational factors into account, managers will overlook these contributions at their peril. The organization where the management trainee worked contacted a university looking for some consultants to help in dealing with a problem of absenteeism and employee vandalizing of products on the assembly line. The vandalism reportedly involved certain perfectly natural bodily functions, description of which would not be shocking to mature individuals except insofar as it might be considered distressing that such acts should be directed toward refrigerators. A concern for academic decorum nevertheless dictates omission of those details. A careful researcher will not jump to conclusions about causal connections between managerial attitudes and such incidents, especially on the basis of hearsay, but one is sorely tempted.

Open-Systems Approaches and Contingency Theory

The criticisms of the human relations approach, increasing attention to general systems theory, and new research findings forced a more elaborate view of organizations. It became increasingly evident that organizations successfully adopt different forms under different circumstances or contingencies. As mentioned earlier, a frequently cited explanation of this trend is that organizational analysts became convinced that both the classical approaches and the human relations approach emphasized one best way to organize and manage. Clearly, the situation is more complex than that. There are a variety of forms of organization that can be effective under certain contingencies of task and technology, size, environment and other factors. The effort to specify these contingencies and the organizational forms matched to them made "contingency theory" the dominant approach in organizational analysis.

At least since the 1950s, researchers associated with the Tavistock Institute in Great Britain were conducting research on "sociotechnical systems," emphasizing the interrelationships between technical factors and social dimensions in the workplace. (Burrell and Morgan, 1980, pp. 146–147). An example of this work is an insightful study of a change in work processes in a coal-mining operation (Trist and Bamforth, 1951), which found that the technical and procedural changes in the work process had significant influences on the social relations within the work group. They treated the organization as a system with interdependent social and technical subsystems, which tended to maintain an equilibrium. In response to disturbances, the system would move to a new point of equilibrium, a new ongoing pattern of interrelated social and technical processes. Additional studies by the Tavistock researchers further developed this view that organizations are systems responding to social, economic, and technological imperatives that have to be satisfied for effective operation of the system—that is, that there are group and individual characteristics, task requirements, and interrelations among them that must be properly accommodated in the design of the organization.

Consistently with their emphasis on organizations as ongoing systems seeking to maintain equilibrium in response to disturbances, Tavistock researchers also began to devote attention to the external environments of organizations. In a widely influential article entitled "The Causal Texture of Organizational Environments," Emery and Trist (1965) noted the increasing flux and uncertainty in political, social, economic, and technological settings in which organizations operate and discussed the influence on the internal operations of organizations of the degree of "turbulence" in their environments. Thus, the emphasis moved toward analysis of organizations as open systems, facing the need to adapt to environmental variations.

In the United States, the most explicit systems approach to organizational analysis appeared in a very prominent text by Daniel Katz and Robert L. Kahn (1966), *The Social Psychology of Organizations*. They undertook to demonstrate how the systems languages of inputs, throughputs, outputs, feedback, and homeostasis could be usefully applied to organizations. In analyzing throughput processes, for example, they sought to differentiate the various major subsystems, maintenance subsystems, adaptive subsystems, and managerial subsystems. Katz and Kahn's effort is regarded as a classic in the organizational literature (Burrell and Morgan, 1980, p. 158), but it is also an example of the general, heuristic nature of the systems approach. Classification of organizational factors and processes, such as inputs, outputs, and designation of subsystems, in and of themselves have no specific theoretical meaning. They say nothing, for instance, about relationships between subsystems or between inputs and outputs. The systems approach has come increasingly to be seen as a framework for organizing information, a "macroparadigm" (Kast and Roenzweig, 1973, p. 16), but not as a precise guide to theory. Theoretically significant, however, is its role in the development of the way that organizations were viewed and analyzed. Researchers increasingly regarded organizations as social entities that display great variation in response to a variety of influences and imperatives.

Besides the efforts to apply systems concepts to organizations, research results were substantiating the view that organizations successfully adopt different forms and patterns in response to contingencies. Researchers in England again played a very influential role. Joan Woodward conducted a study of British industrial firms that would be regarded as pathbreaking. She found that the firms fell into three categories on the basis of the production process or "technology" employed by the organization: The small-batch or unit production system was used by such organizations as shipbuilding and aircraft manufacturing firms; large-batch or mass-production systems were operated by typical mass-manufacturing firms; and continuous production systems were used by petroleum refiners and chemical producers. Most importantly, she concluded that the successful firms within each category showed a similar profile of their management structures, but those profiles differed among the three categories. The successful firms within a category were similar on such dimensions as the number of managerial levels, spans of control, and the ratio of managerial personnel to other personnel, yet they differed on these measures from the successful firms in the other two categories. This indicated that the firms within a category had achieved a successful fit between their structures and the requirements of the particular production process or technology with which they had to deal. The successful firms appeared to be effectively adapting structure to technology.

Another very influential study, reported by Burns and Stalker (1961) in *The Management of Innovation,* further contributed to the view that effective organizational structures are adapted in response to contingencies. They studied a set of firms in the electronics industry in Great Britain. The industry was undergoing rapid change, with new products being developed, markets for the products shifting, and new information and technology available. The firms faced considerable flux and uncertainty in their operating environments. Burns and Stalker felt that they could classify the firms reasonably well into two categories on the basis of their managerial structures and practices: *organic* and *mechanistic* organizations. Their descriptions of the characteristics of these two groups depict mechanistic organizations as bureaucratic organizations designed along the lines of the classical approaches. The name of the category also has obvious implications; these were organizations designed to operate in machinelike fashion. Burns and Stalker argued that the organic type, named to underscore the analogy with living, flexible organisms, was the more successful model in the rapidly changing electronics industry. Such organizations were able to adapt and innovate more effectively under the changing and uncertain conditions as a result of their less rigid structures and procedures and their emphasis on flexibility in communication, supervision, and role definition. The message, however, was not that the mechanistic form is inherently inferior but that it was inferior for the rapidly changing conditions in that industry. The mechanistic form can be more successful under stable environmental and technological conditions, where its emphasis on consistency and specificity would make it more efficient than a more loosely structured organization. Thus, Burns and

Stalker also emphasized the need for a proper adaptation of the organization to contingencies.

While Burns and Stalker tended to blend the concepts of environment and technology, an important research project in the United States heavily emphasized the organization's environment as a determinant of effective structure. Paul Lawrence and Jay Lorsch (1967) studied firms in three separate industries that confronted varying degrees of uncertainty, complexity, and change and concluded that the firms successfully operating in more uncertain, complex, changing environments had more highly differentiated internal structures. They also had more elaborate structures and procedures for integration of the diverse units in the organization. Successful firms facing more environmental stability and certainty showed less differentiation and integration. Lawrence and Lorsch concluded that successful firms must have internal structures as complex as the environments in which they operate.

Other researchers were also rapidly contributing not just to the general contingency view but also to the development of the specific contingencies. Perrow (1973) published a paper that became very widely quoted and cited, in which he developed a concept of organizational technology. He proposed two basic dimensions for the concepts of technology: the predictability of the task (number of exceptions encountered) and the analyzability of the problems encountered. Organizations with nonroutine tasks, high on these dimensions, will have more flexible structures, while organizations with routine tasks will have more formal, centralized structures.

In the same year, James Thompson (1967) published *Organizations in Action*, which was widely regarded as a major integrative statement. Drawing on Herbert Simon's perspective, he depicted organizations as reflecting their managers' and designers' striving for rationality amid pressures against it. He wove together a number of propositions about the ways in which hierarchy, structure, units designed to buffer the environment, and other arrangements are used in the effort to "isolate the technical core"; that is, to create stable conditions for the units doing the basic work of the organization. The ability to do so and the means of doing so are contingent on dimensions of technology and environment. Thompson analyzed technology in terms of the interdependencies among units and individuals required by the work and analyzed organizational environments in terms of homogeneity and stability.

Through the 1960s and 1970s, an upsurge in empirical research on organizations extended and tested these approaches, added new "contingencies" to the set, or at least contributed to the definition and measurement of concepts of structure and other dimensions drawn on by contingency theorists. Peter Blau and colleagues (Blau and Schoenherr, 1971) reported a series of studies showing relationships between organizational size and structure, which added size to the standard set of contingencies. Hage and Aiken (1969) reported a series of studies of social welfare agencies, which provided evidence that routineness of task, joint programs among organizations, and other factors were related to organizational structure and change. Richard Hall and colleagues (Haas, Hall, and Johnson, 1966; Hall, 1968) conducted research on the measurement of bureaucratic characteristics of organizations and variations among organizations on such properties. In England, the Aston researchers (Pugh, Hickson, and Hinings, 1969) conducted their influential effort at empirical measurement of organizations and development of an empirical taxonomy. They interpreted differences in their taxonomic categories as the results of differences in age, size, technology, and external auspices and control. Child (1972) pointed out that in addition to the contingencies of size, environment, and technology usually emphasized by contingency theorists, strategic choices by managers also play an important role in adapting structure. These and numerous other efforts had by the mid 1970s established the contingency approach, the argument that organizational structures and processes are shaped by contingencies of technology, size, environment, and strategic choice, as the central "school" or "movement" in organizational theory. Efforts were being made to translate the contingency observations into prescriptive statements for use in "organizational design" (Galbraith, 1977; Khandawalla, 1977; Starbuck and Nystrom, 1981; Mintzberg, 1989).

Although it is unquestionably the predominant recent approach in organizational theory, the contingency approach also has its problems. It should be obvious from the descriptions of the work on technology and environment that there are substantial differences in the ways that the major researchers define and use the central concepts of the contingency approach. There has been much controversy among researchers about how the concepts are best defined, operationalized, and measured. Moreover, there are frequent conflicts among findings of different studies. Some researchers have found a relationship between technology and structure, for example, and some have not (Hall, 1987). Many of the studies have been fragmented and partial in that they have concentrated on one of the major contingencies to the exclusion of the others, when it is becoming obvious that organizations are influenced by an array of factors, at least including combinations and interactions of the major contingencies (Hall, 1987). In addition, while the research has been very important in moving organization theory toward more realistically elaborate models, and especially toward the recognition of organizational variation, even the related concentration on "organization design" is not yet producing clear and specific guidelines for the management of organizations and the construction of theory.

The developments through the 1960s and 1970s resulted in an elaborate field in which a number of journals are constantly filled with articles reporting empirical studies or conceptual analyses of numerous organizational issues and variables. These journals and numerous books cover dimensions of organizational structure, environment, effectiveness, change, conflict, communication, strategy, technology, interorganizational relations, and related variables.

In addition to the organization design emphasis, by the early 1980s, the field appeared to be moving toward increased emphasis on organizational environments and their relationships or organizational survival and "life cycle." Analysis of organizational life cycles (Kimberly, Miles, and Associates, 1980) was receiving increasing attention, and this emphasis appeared to be generally related to the work on organizational environments, which was receiving even greater attention than earlier. Various scholars sought to develop "natural selection" and "population ecology" models for analysis of how certain organizational forms survive and prosper in certain environmental settings while others do not (Aldrich, 1979; Hannan and Freeman, 1989). There was also increasing attention to external controls on organizations (Pfeffer and Salancik, 1978). These trends appeared to be predominant among organization theorists, while research on internal tasks and structural dimensions seemed to be slackening. This was apparently demonstrated by the frequency of articles appearing (Hall, 1987, p. 200), even though some of the work on structural analysis and task dimensions was actually coming to fruition in books by major authors (Van de Ven and Ferry, 1980; Mintzberg, 1979).

In the closely related work in organizational behavior and organizational psychology, there was a similar trend of elaborate empirical and conceptual development during the 1960s and 1970s. Thousands of articles and books reported work on employee motivation and satisfaction, work involvement, role conflict and ambiguity, organizational identification and commitment, professionalism, leadership behavior and effectiveness, task design, and managerial procedures such as management by objectives and flextime.

In reviewing this richly developed field comprising the interrelated work on organization theory and organizational behavior, an important issue for those interested in public organizations and public management is raised: whether the characteristics of public organizations have been adequately covered in that voluminous literature and whether it has shown sufficient attention to the governmental and political environments of organizations that are obviously so important for understanding public organizations. As discussed in Chapter One, there has been a growing literature on public bureaucracies for some time, but the major typologies propounded by organization theorists have tended not to treat public organizations as a distinct category.

That tendency is also evident in this historical review. The major analyses of organizations either have concentrated on industrial organizations or have sought to develop generic concepts and theories that apply across many types of organizations. Peter Blau (Blau and Schoenherr, 1971), for example, conducted his studies of organizational size in government agencies but drew his conclusions about size as if they applied to all organizations. So have replications of Blau's study (Beyer and Trice, 1979), even though Argyris (1972, p. 10) suggested that Blau may have found the particular relationship that he did find because he was studying organizations governed by civil service systems. Such organizations might respond to differences in size in different ways than do other organizations, such as business firms.

Weber argued that his conception of bureaucracy applied to governmental agencies and private business firms alike (Meyer, 1979). Major figures such as James Thompson (1962) and Herbert Simon (Simon, Smithburg, and Thompson, 1950) have stressed the commonalities among organizations and have suggested that public agencies and private firms are more alike than they are different. Obviously, many of the contributions to organization theory and behavior that have been covered above were aimed at developing a concept or a theory that would apply across many organizations. Nowhere is the implicit inferiority of such distinctions as public and private more evident than in the contingency literature. The categories of task and technology developed by those researchers cross the public and private sectors. The environmental dimensions analyzed emphasize dispersion, uncertainty, and flux. The implication is that the distinctions concerning public and private, market and nonmarket, governmental and nongovernmental, if useful at all, are useful only as specific subdimensions of these more general dimensions.

More recently, there have been developments that tend to close the gap between this generic position and the public bureaucracy literature. As described in Chapter One, during the last two decades, a number of authors and experienced executives cited in this book have made just this sort of complaint about the organization theory literature: It offers an incomplete analysis of public organizations and public management and the influences of their political and institutional environments (Warwick, 1975; Meyer, 1979; Hood and Dunsire, 1981; Pitt and Smith, 1981; Perry and Kraemer, 1983). Complaining also that the public bureaucracy literature has been too anecdotal, too discursively descriptive, and too little concerned with internal structure, behavior, and management in the bureaucracy, they have called for and begun more explicit organizational analyses of the public bureaucracy of the sort described in this book.

References

Aberbach, J. D., Putnam, R. D., and Rockman, B. A. *Bureaucrats and Politicians in Western Democracies.* Cambridge, Mass.: Harvard University Press, 1981.

Abney, G., and Lauth, T. *The Politics of State and City Administration.* Albany: State University of New York Press, 1986.

Adams, J. S. "Inequity in Social Exchange." In L. Berkowitz (ed.), *Advances in Experimental and Social Psychology.* New York: Academic Press, 1965.

Aharoni, Y. *The Evolution and Management of State-Owned Enterprises.* Cambridge, Mass.: Ballinger, 1986.

Alderfer, C. P. *Existence, Relatedness, and Growth: Human Needs in Organizational Settings.* New York: Free press, 1972.

Aldrich, H. E. *Organizations and Environments.* Englewood Cliffs, N. J.: Prentice-Hall, 1979.

Aldrich, H. E., and Pfeffer, J. "Environments of Organizations." In *Annual Review of Sociology,* Vol. 2. Palo Alto, Calif.: Annual Review, Inc., 1979.

Alimard, A., *Management Policy in State Government: The Commonwealth of Virginia.* Richmond: Center for Public Affairs, Virginia Commonwealth University, 1987.

Allen, J. W., and others. *The Private Sector in State Service Delivery: Examples of Innovative Practices.* Washington, D.C.: Urban Institute, 1989.

Allison, G. T. "Public and Private Management: Are They Fundamentally Alike in All Unimportant Respects?" In J. L. Perry and K. L. Kraemer (eds.) *Public Management.* Mountain View, Calif.: Mayfield, 1983.

Ammons, D. N., and Newell, C. *City Executives: Leadership Roles, Work Characteristics, and Time Management.* Albany: State University of New York Press, 1989.

Anderson, W. F., Newland, C., and Stillman, R. *The Effective Local Government Manager.* Washington, D.C.: International City Management Association, 1983.

Angle, H., and Perry, J. L. "An Empirical Assessment of Organizational

Commitment and Organizational Effectiveness." *Administrative Science Quarterly,* 1981, *26,* 1–13.

Anthony, R. N., and Herzlinger, R. *Management Control in Nonprofit Organizations.* Homewood, Ill.: Irwin, 1975.

Argyris, C. "The Individual and Organization: Some Problems of Mutual Adjustment." *Administrative Science Quarterly,* 1957, *2,* 1–24.

Argyris, C. *The Applicability of Organizational Sociology.* London: Cambridge University Press, 1972.

Atkinson, S. E., and Halversen, R. "The Relative Efficiency of Public and Private Firms in a Regulated Environment: The Case of U.S. Electric Utilities." *Journal of Public Economics.* 1986, *29,* 281–294.

Back, K. *Beyond Words.* New York: Russell Sage Foundation, 1972.

Backoff, R. W., and Nutt, P. C. "A Process for Strategic Planning with Specific Application for the Nonprofit Organization." In J. M. Bryson and R. C. Einsweiler (eds.), *Strategic Planning.* Chicago: Planners Press, 1988.

Backoff, R. W., and Rainey, H. G. "The Interdependent Effects of Technological Change, Affirmative Action, Professionalization, and Merit Principles on Contemporary Public Personnel Management." In C. Levine (ed.), *Urban Affairs Annual Reviews.* Vol. 11. Newbury Park, Calif.: Sage, 1977.

Baldwin, J. N. "Public Versus Private: Not That Different, Not That Consequential." *Public Personnel Management,* 1987, *16,* 181–193.

Baldwin, J. N. "A Review of the Literature Comparing Public and Private Employees." Paper presented at the national conference of the American Society for Public Administration, Miami, Fla., 1989.

Baldwin, J. N. "Perceptions of Public Versus Private Sector Personnel and Informal Red Tape: Their Impact on Motivation." *American Review of Public Administration,* 1990, *20,* 7–28.

Ban, C. "The Crisis of Morale and Federal Senior Executives." *Public Productivity Review,* 1987, *11,* 31–49.

Bandura, A. *Social Learning Theory.* Englewood Cliffs, N.J.: Prentice-Hall, 1978.

Banfield, E. C. "Corruption as a Feature of Governmental Organization." *Journal of Law and Economics,* 1975, *18,* 587–605.

Barnard, C. I. *The Functions of the Executive.* Cambridge, Mass.: Harvard University Press, 1938.

Barney, J. B., and Ouchi, W. G. (eds.). *Organizational Economics: Toward a New Paradigm for Understanding and Studying Organizations.* San Francisco: Jossey-Bass, 1986.

Bartol, K. M. "Professionalism as a Predictor of Organizational Commitment, Role Stress, and Turnover: A Multidimensional Approach." *Academy of Management Journal,* 1979, *22,* 815–826.

Barton, A. H. "A Diagnosis of Bureaucratic Maladies." In C. H. Weiss and A. H. Barton (eds.), *Making Bureaucracies Work.* Newbury Park, Calif.: Sage, 1980.

Bass, B. M. *Leadership and Performance Beyond Expectations.* New York: Free Press, 1985.

Baum, E., and James, A. C. "Communication in Public and Private Sector Organizations." Paper presented at the annual meeting of the Academy of Management, Boston, 1984.

Beaumont, E. F. "A Pivotal Point for the Merit Concept." *Public Administration Review,* 1974, *34,* 426–431.

Beck, P. A., Rainey, H. G., Nicholls, K., and Traut, C. "Citizen Views of Taxes and Services: A Tale of Three Cities." *Social Science Quarterly,* 1987, *68,* 223–243.

Beck, P. A., Rainey, H. G., and Traut, C. "Disadvantage, Disaffection, and Race as Divergent Bases for Citizen Fiscal Policy Preferences." *Journal of Politics,* 1990, *52,* 71–93.

Becker, S. W., and Neuhauser, D. *The Efficient Organization.* New York: Elsevier, 1975.

Behling, O., Schriesheim, C., and Tolliver, J. "Present Trends and New Directions in Theories of Work Effort." Journal Supplement Abstract Service of the American Psychological Service, 1973.

Bellante, D., and Link, A. N. "Are Public Sector Workers More Risk Averse Than Private Sector Workers?" *Industrial and Labor Relations Review,* 1981, *34,* 408–412.

Bendor, J., and Moe, T. M. "An Adaptive Model of Bureaucratic Politics." *American Political Science Review,* 1985, *79,* 755–774.

Benn, S. I., and Gaus, G. F. *Public and Private in Social Life.* New York: St. Martin's Press, 1983.

Bennis, W., and Nanus, B. *Leaders: The Strategies for Taking Charge.* New York: Harper & Row, 1985.

Beyer, J. M., and Trice, H. M. "A Reexamination of the Relations Between Size and Various Components of Organizational Complexity." *Administrative Science Quarterly,* 1979, *24,* 48–64.

Birch, D., and Veroff, J. *Motivation: A Study of Action.* Pacific Grove, Calif.: Brooks/Cole, 1966.

Blake, R. R., and Mouton, J. S. "Overcoming Group Warfare." *Harvard Business Review,* 1984, *62,* 98–108.

Blank, R. M. "An Analysis of Workers' Choice Between Employment in the Public and Private Sectors." *Industrial and Labor Relations Review,* 1985, *38,* 211–224.

Blau, P. M. "Decentralization in Bureaucracies." In M. Zald (ed.), *Power in Organizations.* Nashville, Tenn.: Vanderbilt University Press, 1970.

Blau, P. M., and Schoenherr, R. A. *The Structure of Organizations.* New York: Basic Books, 1971.

Blau, P. M., and Scott, W. R. *Formal Organizations.* San Francisco: Chandler, 1962.

Block, P. *The Empowered Manager: Positive Political Skills at Work.* San Francisco: Jossey-Bass, 1987.

Blumenthal, J. M. "Candid Reflections of a Businessman in Washington." In J. L. Perry and K. L. Kraemer (eds.), *Public Management.* Mountain View, Calif.: Mayfield, 1983.

Boschken, H. L. *Strategic Design and Organizational Change: Pacific Rim Seaports in Transition.* University: University of Alabama Press, 1988.

Bower, J. *The Two Faces of Management.* Boston: Houghton Mifflin, 1983.

Bower, J. L., and Christenson, C. J. *Public Management: Texts and Cases.* Homewood, Ill.: Irwin, 1978.

Bowsher, C. A. "OMB Management Leadership." Testimony before the Committee on Governmental Affairs, U.S. Senate, Oct. 31, 1990. U.S. General Accounting Office/T-GGD-91-1.

Boyatzis, R. E. *The Competent Manager.* New York: Wiley, 1982.

Bozeman, B. *All Organizations Are Public: Bridging Public and Private Organizational Theories.* San Francisco: Jossey-Bass, 1987.

Bozeman, B., and Bretschneider, S. "The 'Publicness Puzzle' in Organization Theory: A Test of Alternative Explanations of Differences Between Public and Private Organizations." TIPP Working Paper. Syracuse, N.Y.: Maxwell School, Syracuse University, 1989.

Bozeman, B., and Loveless, S. "Sector Context and Performance: A Comparison of Industrial and Government Research Units." *Administration and Society,* 1987, *19,* 197–235.

Bozeman, B., and Straussman, J. D. *Public Management Strategies: Guidelines for Managerial Effectiveness.* San Francisco: Jossey-Bass, 1990.

Breton, A., and Wintrobe, R. *The Logic of Bureaucratic Conduct.* Cambridge: Cambridge University Press, 1982.

Bretschneider, S. "Management Information Systems in Public and Private Organizations: An Empirical Test." *Public Administration Review,* 1990, *50,* 536–545.

Brock, J. *Managing People in Public Agencies.* Boston: Little Brown, 1984.

Brudney, J. L. *Fostering Volunteer Programs in the Public Sector: Planning, Initiating, and Managing Voluntary Activities.* San Francisco: Jossey-Bass, 1990.

Brudney, J. L., and Hebert, F. T. "State Agencies and Their Environments: Examing the Influence of Important External Actors." *Journal of Politics,* 1987, *49,* 186–206.

Bryson, J. M. *Strategic Planning for Public and Nonprofit Organizations: A Guide to Strengthening and Sustaining Organizational Achievements.* San Francisco: Jossey-Bass, 1988.

Bryson, J. M., and Einsweiller, R. C. (eds.). *Strategic Planning.* Chicago: Planners Press, 1988.

Bryson, J. M., and Einsweiller, R. C. (eds.). *Shared Power.* Lanham, Md.: University Press of America, 1991.

Bryson, J. M., and Roering, W. D. "Applying Strategic Management in the Public Sector." In J. M. Bryson and R. C. Einsweiller (eds.), *Strategic Planning.* Chicago: Planners Press, 1988.

Buchanan, B. "Government Managers, Business Executives, and Organizational Commitment." *Public Administration Review,* 1974, *35,* 339–347.

Buchanan, B. "Red Tape and the Service Ethic: Some Unexpected Differences Between Public and Private Managers." *Administration and Society,* 1975, *6,* 423–438.

Burke, W. W. *Organization Development.* Glenview, Ill.: Scott, Foresman, 1982.

Burkhead, J., and Miner, J. *Public Expenditure.* Chicago: Aldine, 1971.

Burns, J. M. *Leadership.* New York: Harper & Row, 1978.

Burns, T. and Stalker, G. M. *The Management of Innovation.* London: Tavistock, 1961.

Burrell, G., and Morgan, G. *Sociological Paradigms and Organizational Analysis.* London: Heinemann, 1980.

Cameron, K. "Measuring Organizational Effectiveness in Institutions of Higher Education." *Administrative Science Quarterly,* 1978, *23,* 604–632.

Cameron, K., Sutton, R. I., and Whetten, D. A. (eds.). *Readings in Organizational Decline.* Cambridge, Mass.: Ballinger, 1988.

Cameron, K., and Whetten, D. A. (eds.). *Organizational Effectiveness: A Comparison of Multiple Models.* Orlando, Fla.: Academic Press, 1983.

Campbell, J. P. "On the Nature of Organizational Effectiveness." In P. S. Goodman, J. Pennings, and Associates, *New Perspectives on Organizational Effectiveness.* San Francisco: Jossey-Bass, 1977.

Campbell, J. P., Dunnette, M. D., Lawler, E. E., and Weick, K. E. *Managerial Behavior, Performance, and Effectiveness.* New York: McGraw-Hill, 1970.

Campbell, J. P., and Pritchard, R. D. "Motivation Theory in Industrial and Organizational Psychology." In M. D. Dunnette (ed.), *Handbook of Industrial and Organizational Psychology.* Skokie, Ill.: Rand McNally, 1983.

Carroll, G. R., Delacroix, J., and Goodstein, J. "The Political Environments of Organizations: An Ecological View." In B. M. Staw and L. L. Cummings (eds.), *Research in Organizational Behavior.* Vol. 10. Greenwich, Conn: JAI Press, 1988.

Cervantes, A. J. "Memoirs of a Businessman-Mayor." In J. L. Perry and K. L. Kraemer (eds.), *Public Management.* Mountain View, Calif.: Mayfield, 1983.

Chackerian, R., and Abcarian, G. *Bureaucratic Power in Society.* Chicago: Nelson-Hall, 1984.

Chandler, A. D. *Strategy and Structure.* Cambridge, Mass.: MIT Press, 1962.

Chase, G., and Reveal, E. C. *How to Manage in the Public Sector.* Reading, Mass.: Addison-Wesley, 1983.

Cherniss, G. *Professional Burnout in Human Service Organizations.* New York: Praeger, 1980.

Child, J. "Organizational Structure, Environment, and Performance: The Role of Strategic Choice." *Sociology,* 1972, *6,* 1–22.

Chubb, J. E., and Moe, T. M. "Politics, Markets, and the Organization of Schools." *American Political Science Review,* 1988, *82,* 1065–1088.

Chubb, J. E., and Moe, T. M. *Politics, Markets, and America's Schools.* Washington, D.C.: Brookings Institution, 1990.

Clark, P. B., and Wilson, J. Q. "Incentive Systems: A Theory of Organizations." *Administrative Science Quarterly,* 1961, *6,* 129–166.

Coch, L., and French, J.R.P. "Overcoming Resistance to Change." *Human Relations,* 1948, *1,* 512–532.

Cohen, M. D., March, J. G., and Olsen, J. P. "A Garbage Can Model of Organizational Choice." *Administrative Science Quarterly,* 1972, *17,* 1–25.

Cohen, S. *The Effective Public Manager.* San Francisco: Jossey-Bass, 1988.

Connolly, T. "Some Conceptual and Methodological Issues in Expectancy Models of Work Performance Motivation." *Academy of Management Review,* 1976, *1,* 37–47.

Contino, R., and Lorusso, R. M. "The Theory Z Turnaround of a Public Agency." *Public Administration Review,* 1982, *42,* 66–72.

Conway, M., and Fiegart, F. B. "Motivation, Incentive Systems, and the Political Party Organization." *American Political Science Review,* 1968, *62,* 1159–1173.

Cook, J. D., Hepworth, S. J., Wall, T. D., and Warr, P. B. *The Experience of Work.* London: Academic Press, 1981.

Coursey, D., and Bozeman, B. "Decision-Making in Public and Private Organizations: A Test of Alternative Concepts of 'Publicness.'" *Public Administration Review,* 1990, *50,* 525–535.

Coursey, D., and Rainey, H. G. "Perceptions of Personnel System Constraints in Public, Private, and Hybrid Organizations." *Review of Public Personnel Administration,* 1990, *10,* 54–71.

Crane, D. P., and Jones, W. A. *The Public Manager's Guide.* Washington, D.C.: Bureau of National Affairs, 1982.

Crow, M., and Bozeman, B. "R&D Laboratory Classification and Public Policy: The Effects of Environmental Context on Laboratory Behavior. *Research Policy,* 1987, *16,* 229–258.

Cyert, R. M. (ed.). *The Management of Nonprofit Organizations with Emphasis on Universities.* Lexington, Mass.: Heath, 1975.

Cyert, R. M., and March, J. G. *A Behavioral Theory of the Firm.* Englewood Cliffs, N.J.: Prentice-Hall, 1963.

Daft, R. L. *Organization Theory and Design.* St. Paul, Minn.: West, 1989.

Dahl, R. A., and Lindblom, C. E. *Politics, Economics, and Welfare.* New York: Harper & Row, 1953.

Davis, S. M., and Lawrence, P. R. *Matrix.* Reading, Mass.: Addison-Wesley, 1977.

Davis, T.R.V. "OD in the Public Sector: Intervening in Ambiguous Performance Environments." In J. L. Perry and K. L. Kraemer (eds.), *Public Management.* Mountain View, Calif.: Mayfield, 1983.

Decker, J. E., and Paulson, S. K. "Performance Improvement in a Public Utility." *Public Productivity Review,* 1988, *11,* 52–66.

Demerath, N., Marwell, G., and Aiken, M. *Dynamics of Idealism.* San Francisco: Jossey-Bass, 1971.

Denhardt, R. B. *Theories of Public Organization.* Pacific Grove, Calif.: Brooks/Cole, 1984.

Dess, G. G., and Beard, D. W. "Dimensions of Organizational Task Environment." *Administrative Science Quarterly,* 1984, *29,* 52–73.

Dessler, G. *Organization Theory.* Englewood Cliffs, N.J.: Prentice-Hall, 1987.

Dewey, J. *The Public and Its Problems.* Chicago: Swallow Press, 1927.

DiIulio, J. J. "Recovering the Public Management Variable: Lessons from Schools, Prisons, and Armies." *Public Administration Review,* 1989, *49,* 127–133.

DiMaggio, P. J., and Powell, W. R. "The Iron Cage Revisited: Institutional Isomorphism and Collective Rationality in Organizational Fields." *American Sociological Review,* 1983, *48,* 147–160.

Dobbin, F. R., and others. "The Expansion of Due Process in Organizations." In L. G. Zucker (ed.), *Institutional Patterns and Organizations.* Cambridge, Mass.: Ballinger, 1988.

Doig, J. W., and Hargrove, E. C. (eds.). *Leadership and Innovation.* Baltimore, Md.: Johns Hopkins University Press, 1987.

Dominick, J. "Business Coverage in Network Newscasts." *Journalism Quarterly,* 1981, *58,* 184.

Donahue, J. D. *The Privatization Decision.* New York: Basic Books, 1990.

Downs, A. *Inside Bureaucracy.* Boston: Little, Brown, 1967.

Downs, C. W. *Communication Audits.* Glenview, Ill.: Scott, Foresman, 1988.

Downs, G. W., and Larkey, P. *The Search for Government Efficiency: From Hubris to Helplessness.* New York: Random House, 1986.

Downs, G. W., and Mohr, L. B. "Conceptual Issues in the Study of Innovation." *Administrative Science Quarterly,* 1976, *21,* 700–714.

Drake, A. W. "Quantitative Models in Public Administration: Some Educational Needs." In A. Drake, L. Keeney, and P. Morse (eds.), *Analysis of Public Systems.* Cambridge, Mass.: MIT Press, 1972.

Drucker, P. F. "Managing the Public Service Institution." *Public Interest,* 1973, *33* (Fall), 43–60.

Drucker, P. F. "Measuring Business Performance." *Wall Street Journal,* Aug. 3, 1976, p. 16.

Dunsire, A., Hartley, K., Parker, D., and Dimitrou, B. "Organizational Status and Performance: A Conceptual Framework for Testing Public Choice Theories." *Public Administration,* 1988, *66,* 363–388.

Dye, T. R. *Understanding Public Policy.* Englewood Cliffs, N.J.: Prentice-Hall, 1981.

Eadie, D. C. "Building the Capacity for Strategic Management." In J. L. Perry (ed.), *Handbook of Public Administration.* San Francisco: Jossey-Bass, 1989.

Elling, R. C. "The Relationships Among Bureau Chiefs, Legislative Committees, and Interest Groups: A Multistate Study." Paper presented at the annual meeting of the American Political Science Association, Washington, D. C., 1983.

Elling, R. C. "Civil Service, Collective Bargaining, and Personnel-Related Impediments to Effective State Management: A Comparative Assessment." *Review of Public Personnel Administration,* 1986, *6,* 73–93.

Emmert, M. A., and Crow, M. M. "Public-Private Cooperation and Hybrid Organizations." *Journal of Management,* 1987, *13,* 55–67.

Emmert, M. A., and Crow, M. M. "Public, Private, and Hybrid Organizations: An Empirical Examination of the Role of Publicness." *Administration and Society,* 1988, *20,* 216–244.

Emery, F. E., and Trist, E. L. "The Causal Texture of Organizational Environments." *Human Relations,* 1965, *18,* 21–32.

Ehrenhalt, A. "Privatization Without Ideology." *Governing,* 1990, *3,* 63–64.

Etzioni, A. "Mixed Scanning: A 'Third' Approach to Decision Making." *Public Administration Review,* 1967, *27,* 385–392.

Etzioni, A. "Mixed Scanning Revisited." *Public Administration Review,* 1986, *46,* 8–14.

Etzioni, A. *A Comparative Analysis of Complex Organizations.* New York: Free Press, 1975.

Etzioni, A. *The Moral Dimension.* New York: Free Press, 1988.

Evans, M. G. "Organizational Behavior: The Central Role of Motivation." *Yearly Review of Management of the Journal of Management,* 1986, *12,* 203–223.

Fesler, J. "Public Administration and the Social Sciences: From 1946 to 1960." In F. C. Mosher (ed.), *Public Administration: Past, Present, and Future.* University: University of Alabama Press, 1975.

Fiedler, F. E. *A Theory of Leadership Effectivness.* New York: McGraw-Hill, 1967.

Fiedler, F. E., and Garcia, J. E. *New Approaches to Leadership: Cognitive Resources and Organizational Performance.* New York: Wiley, 1987.

Filley, A. C., House, R. J., and Kerr, S. *Managerial Process and Organizational Behavior.* Glenview, Ill.: Scott, Foresman, 1976.

Fiorina, M. P. "Flagellating the Federal Bureaucracy." *Society,* 1983, *20,* 66–74.

Fishbein, M., and Ajzen, I. *Belief, Attitude, Intention, and Behavior: An Introduction to Theory and Research.* Reading, Mass.: Addison-Wesley, 1975.

Florkowski, G. W., and Lifton, D. E. "Assessing Public Sector Productivity Incentives: A Review." *Public Productivity Review,* 1987, *43,* 53–70.

Fottler, M. D. "Management: Is It Really Generic?" *Academy of Management Review,* 1981, *6,* 1–12.

Frederickson, H. G., and Hart, D. K. "The Public Service and the Patriotism of Benevolence." *Public Administration Review,* 1985, *45,* 547–553.

French, J.R.P., and Raven, B. " The Bases of Social Power." In D. Cartwright and A. Zander (eds.), *Group Dynamics.* New York: Harper & Row, 1968.

French, W. L., and Bell, C. H. *Organization Development.* Englewood Cliffs, N.J.: Prentice-Hall, 1978.

Fried, R. C. *Performance in American Bureaucracy.* Boston: Little Brown, 1976.

Fry., B. R. *Mastering Public Administration.* Chatham, N.J.: Chatham House, 1989.

Gabris, G. T. (ed.). "Why Merit Pay Plans Are Not Working: A Search for Alternative Pay Plans in the Public Sector — A Symposium." *Review of Public Personnel Administration* 1987, *7,* 9–90.

Galbraith, J. *Organizational Design.* Reading, Mass.: Addison-Wesley, 1977.

Garson, G. D., and Overman, E. S. *Public Management Research Directory,* Vols. 1 and 2. Washington, D.C.: National Association of Schools of Public Affairs and Administration, 1981, 1982.

Gawthorp, L. C. *Bureaucratic Behavior in the Executive Branch.* New York: Free Press, 1969.

Georgiou, P. "The Goal Paradigm and Notes Towards a Counter Paradigm," *Administrative Science Quarterly* 1973, *18* (Sept.), 291–310.

Gerth, J. "A Blend of Tragedy and Farce." *New York Times,* July 3, 1990, p. C1.

Gerth, H., and Mills, C. W. *From Max Weber: Essays in Sociology.* New York: Oxford University Press, 1946.

Goggin, M. L., Bowman, A. O., Lester, J. P., and O'Toole, L. J. *Implementation Theory and Practice.* Glenview, Ill.: Scott, Foresman, 1990.

Gold, K. A. "Managing for Success: A Comparison of the Public and Private Sectors." *Public Administration Review,* 1982, *42,* 568–575.

Golembiewski, R. T. "Civil Service and Managing Work." *American Political Science Review,* 1962, *56,* 964–969.

Golembiewski, R. T. "Organization Development in Public Agencies: Perspectives on Theory and Practice." *Public Administration Review,* 1969, *29,* 367–368.

Golembiewski, R. T. "Organizing Public Work, Round Three: Toward a New Balance Between Political Agendas and Management Perspectives." In R. T. Golembiewski and A. Wildavsky (eds.), *The Costs of Federalism.* New Brunswick, N.J.: Transaction, 1984.

Golembiewski, R. T. *Humanizing Public Organizations.* Mount Airy, Md.: Lomond, 1985.

Golembiewski, R. T. "Contours in Social Change: Elemental Graphics and a Surrogate Variable for Gamma Change." *Academy of Management Review,* 1986, *11,* 550–566.

Golembiewski, R. T. "Public-sector Management Today: Advanced Differentiation and Early Institutionalization." *Yearly Review of Management of the Journal of Management,* 1987a, *13,* 323–338.

Golembiewski, R. T. "Public-Sector Organization: Why Theory and Practice Should Emphasize Purpose, and How to Do So." In R. C. Chandler (ed.), *A Centennial History of the American Administrative State.* New York: Free Press, 1987b.

Golembiewski, R. T. "Differences in Burnout, by Sector: Public vs. Business Estimates Using Phases." *International Journal of Public Administration,* 1990, *13,* 545–560.

Golembiewski, R. T., Proehl, C. T., and Sink, D. Success of OD Applications in the Public Sector: Toting Up the Score for a Decade, More or Less. *Public Administration Review,* 1981, *41,* 679–682.

Goodman, P. S., Pennings, J. M., and Associates. *New Perspectives on Organizational Effectiveness.* San Francisco: Jossey-Bass, 1977.

Goodsell, C. T. *The Case for Bureaucracy.* Chatham, N.J.: Chatham House, 1985.

Gordon, J. R. *Organizational Behavior.* Newton, Mass.: Allyn & Bacon, 1990.

Gortner, H. F., Mahler, J., and Nicholson, J. B. *Organization Theory: A Public Perspective.* Homewood, Ill.: Dorsey Press, 1987.

Greiner, J. M., and others. *Productivity and Motivation: A Review of State and Local Government Initiatives.* Washington, D.C.: Urban Institute Press, 1981.

Greiner, L. E. "Patterns of Organizational Change." *Harvard Business Review,* 1967, *45,* 119–128.

Griffin, R. W. *Management.* Boston: Houghton Mifflin, 1987.

Griffin, R. W. "Work Redesign Effects on Employee Attitudes and Behaviors: A Long-Term Field Experiment." In F. Hoy (ed.), *Academy of Management Proceedings.* Washington, D.C.: Academy of Management, 1989.

Gross, B. M. "What Are Your Organization's Objectives?" In W. R. Nord (ed.), *Concepts and Controversy in Organizational Behavior.* Pacific Palisades, Calif.: Goodyear, 1976.

Gruneberg, M. M. *Understanding Job Satisfaction.* London: Macmillan, 1979.

Guion, R. M., and Landy, F. J. "The Meaning of Work and Motivation to Work." *Organizational Behavior and Human Performance,* 1972, *7,* 308–339.

Gulick, L. "Notes on the Theory of Organization." In L. Gulick and L. Urwick (eds.), *Papers on the Science of Administration.* New York: Institute of Public Administration, 1937, 3–13.

Guralnick, D. B. (ed). *Webster's New World Dictionary of the American Language.* New York: Simon & Schuster, 1980.

Guyot, J. F. "Government Bureaucrats Are Different." *Public Administration Review,* 1960, *20,* 195–202.

Haas, J. E., Hall, R. H., and Johnson, N. J. "Toward an Empirically Derived Taxonomy of Organizations." In R. V. Bowers (ed.), *Studies of Behavior in Organizations.* Athens: University of Georgia Press, 1966.

Hackman, J. R., and Oldham, G. R. *Work Redesign.* Reading, Mass.: Addison-Wesley, 1980.

Hackman, J. R., and Porter, L. W. "Expectancy Theory Predictions of Work Effectiveness." *Organizational Behavior and Human Performance,* 1968, *3,* 417–426.

Hage, J., and Aiken, M. "Routine Technology, Social Structure and Organizational Goals." *Administrative Science Quarterly,* 1969, *14,* 366–376.

Hall, R. H. "Professionalization and Bureaucratization." *American Sociological Review,* 1968, *33,* 92–104.

Hall, R. H. *Organizations: Structure and Process.* Englewood Cliffs, N.J.: Prentice-Hall, 1987.

Hall, R. H., and Quinn, R. E. *Organization Theory and Public Policy.* Newbury Park, Calif.: Sage, 1983.

Hammond, T. H. "In Defence of Luther Gulick's 'Notes on the Theory of Organizations.' " *Public Administration,* 1990, *68,* 143–173.

Hannan, M. T., and Freeman, J. *Organizational Ecology.* Cambridge, Mass.: Harvard University Press, 1989.

Harris, J. P. *Congressional Control of Administration.* Washington, D.C.: Brookings Institution, 1964.

Hartman, R., and Weber, A. *The Rewards of Public Service.* Washington, D.C.: Brookings Institution, 1980.

Hayward, N. *Employee Attitudes and Productivity Differences Between the Public and Private Sectors.* Washington, D.C.: Productivity Information Center, National Technical Information Center, U.S. Department of Commerce, 1978.

Heclo, H. "Issue Networks and the Executive Establishment." In A. King (ed.), *The New American Political System.* Washington, D.C.: American Enterprise Institute, 1978.

Heneman, H. G., and Schwab, D. P. "Evaluation of Research on Expectancy Theory Predictions of Employee Performance." *Psychological Bulletin,* 1972, *78,* 1–9.

Hersey, P., and Blanchard, K. H. *Management of Organizational Behavior.* Englewood Cliffs, N.J.: Prentice-Hall, 1982.

Hersey, R. D. "Government Moves to Revise Its Salary Structure." *New York Times,* May 11, 1989, p. 1.

Herzberg, F. "One More Time: How Do You Motivate Employees?" *Harvard Business Review,* 1968, *46,* 36–44.

Herzberg, F., Mausner, B., Peterson, R. O., and Capwell, D. F. *Job Attitudes: Review of Research and Opinion.* Pittsburgh, Pa.: Psychological Service of Pittsburgh, 1957.

Hickson, D. J., and others. "A 'Strategic Contingencies' Theory of Interorganizational Power." *Administrative Science Quarterly,* 1971, *16,* 216–229.

Hickson, D. J., and others. *Top Decisions: Strategic Decision Making in Organizations.* San Francisco: Jossey-Bass, 1986.

Hirschman, A. O. *Shifting Involvements.* Princeton, N.J.: Princeton University Press, 1982.

Hjern, B., and Porter, D. O. "Implementation Structures: A New Unit of Administrative Analysis." *Organization Studies,* 1981, *2,* 211–227.

Hofstetter, C. R. "Organizational Activists: The Bases of Participation in Amateur and Professional Groups." *American Politics Quarterly,* 1973, *1,* 244–276.

Holdaway, E., Newberry, J. F., Hickson, D. J., and Heron, R. P. "Dimensions of Organizations in Complex Societies: The Educational Sector." *Administrative Science Quarterly,* 1975, *20,* 37–58.

Holzer, M. "Productivity In, Garbage Out: Sanitation Gains in New York." *Public Productivity Review,* 1988, *11,* 37–50.

Hood, C. *The Tools of Government.* London: Macmillan, 1983.

Hood, C., and Dunsire, A. *Bureaumetrics: The Quantitative Comparison of British Central Government Agencies.* University: University of Alabama Press, 1981.

House, R. J. "A Path-Goal Theory of Leader Effectiveness." *Administrative Science Quarterly,* 1971, *16,* 321–338.

House, R. J., and Dessler, G. "The Path-Goal Theory of Leadership: Some Post Hoc and A Priori tests." In J. G. Hunt and L. L. Larson (eds.), *Contingency Approaches to Leadership*. Carbondale: Southern Illinois University Press, 1974.

House, R. J., and Mitchell, T. R. "Path-Goal Theory of Leadership." *Journal of Contemporary Business*, 1974, *3*, 81–97.

House, R. J., and Rizzo, J. R. "Role Conflict and Ambiguity as Critical Variables in a Model of Organizational Behavior." *Organizational Behavior and Human Performance*, 1972, *7*, 467–505.

House, R. J., and Singh, J. V. "Organizational Behavior: Some New Directions for I/O Psychology." *Annual Review of Psychology*, 1987, *38*, 669–718.

Houston, D. J., and Delevan, S. M. "Public Administration Research: An Assessment of Journal Publications." *Public Administration Review*, 1990, *50*, 674–681.

Hummel, R. *The Bureaucratic Experience*. New York: St. Martin's, 1982.

Huntington, S. P. *American Politics: The Promise of Disharmony*. Cambridge, Mass.: Belknap Press, 1981.

Ingraham, P. W. "Transition and Policy Change in Washington." *Public Productivity Review*, 1988, *12*, 61–72.

Ingraham, P. W., and Ban, C. (eds.). *Legislating Bureaucratic Change: The Civil Service Reform Act of 1978*. Albany: State University of New York Press, 1984.

Ingraham, P. W., and Rosenbloom, D. H. "The New Public Personnel and the New Public Service. *Public Administration Review*, 1989, *49*, 116–124.

Janis, I. L. "Groupthink." *Psychology Today*, Nov. 1971, p. 43.

Jencks, C. "The Hidden Prosperity of the 1970s." *Public Interest*, 1984, *77*, 37–61.

Johnson, D. W., and Johnson, F. P. *Joining Together: Group Theory and Group Skills*. Englewood Cliffs, N.J.: Prentice-Hall, 1975.

Judis, J. B. "Mission Impossible." *New York Times Magazine*, Sept. 25, 1989, p. 30.

Kahn, R. F., and others. *Organizational Stress: Studies in Role Conflict and Ambiguity*. New York: Wiley, 1964.

Kanter, R. M. "Power Failure in Management Circuits." In J. M. Shafritz and J. S. Ott (eds.), *Classics of Organization Theory*. Homewood, Ill.: Dorsey Press, 1987.

Kast, F. E., and Rosenzweig, J. E. (eds.) *Contingency Views of Organization and Management*. Chicago: Science Research Associates, 1973.

Katz, D., Gutek, B. A., Kahn, R. L., and Barton, E. *Bureaucratic Encounters: A Pilot Study in the Evaluation of Government Services*. Ann Arbor: Survey Research Center, Institute for Social Research, University of Michigan, 1975.

Katz, D., and Kahn, R. L. *The Social Psychology of Organizations*. New York: Wiley, 1966.

Katzell, R. A., and Yankelovich, D. *Work, Productivity, and Job Satisfaction*. New York: Psychological Corporation, 1975.

Kaufman, H. "Administrative Decentralization and Political Power." *Public Administration Review,* 1969, *29,* 3.

Kaufman, H. *Are Government Organizations Immortal?* Washington, D.C.: Brookings Institution, 1976.

Kaufman, H. *The Administrative Behavior of Federal Bureau Chiefs.* Washington, D.C.: Brookings Institution, 1979.

Keeley, M. "Impartiality and Participant-Interest Theories of Organizational Effectiveness." *Administrative Science Quarterly,* 1984, *29,* 1–12.

Kelman, S. "The Grace Commission: How Much Waste in Government?" *Public Interest,* 1985, *78,* 62–82.

Kelman, S. *Making Public Policy.* New York: Basic Books, 1987.

Kelman, S. "Defense Bureaucracy's Corrupting Influence." *Wall Street Journal,* July 7, 1988, p. 22.

Kelman, S. "The Making of Government Good Guys." *New York Times,* July 26, 1989, Business Section, p. 1.

Kenny, G. K., Butler, R. J., Cray, D., and others. "Strategic Decision Making: Influence Patterns in Public and Private Sector Organizations." *Human Relations,* 1987, *40,* 613–631.

Kerr, S. "On the Folly of Rewarding A, While Hoping for B." In J. S. Ott (ed.), *Classic Readings in Organizational Behavior.* Pacific Grove, Calif.: Brooks/Cole, 1989, pp. 114–126.

Kettl, D. F. *Government by Proxy.* Washington, D.C.: CQ Press, 1988.

Kettl, D. F. "The Image of the Public Service in the Media." In The Volcker Commission, *Leadership for America.* Lexington, Mass.: Heath, 1989, pp. 95–112.

Kettl, D. F. "The Perils — and Prospects — of Public Administration." *Public Administration Review,* 1990, *50,* 411–419.

Khandawalla, P. *Organization Design.* San Diego, Calif: Harcourt Brace Jovanovich, 1977.

Kiel, L. D. "Nonequilibrium Theory and Its Implications for Public Administration." *Public Administration Review,* 1989, *49,* 544–551.

Kilpatrick, F. P., Cummings, M. C., and Jennings, M. K. *The Image of the Federal Service.* Washington, D.C.: Brookings Institution, 1964.

Kimberly, J. R. "Organizational Size and the Structuralist Perspective: A Review, Critique, and Proposal." *Administrative Science Quarterly,* 1976, *21,* 577–597.

Kimberly, J. R., Miles, R. H., and Associates. *The Organizational Life Cycle. Issues in the Creation, Transformation, and Decline of Organizations.* San Francisco: Jossey-Bass, 1980.

Kingdon, J. W. *Agendas, Alternatives, and Public Policies.* Boston: Little, Brown, 1984.

Klein, H. J. "An Integrated Control Theory Model of Work Motivation." *Academy of Management Review,* 1989, *14,* 150–172.

Kopelman, R. E., and Thompson, P. H. "Boundary Conditions for Expectancy Theory Predictions of Work Motivation and Job Performance." *Academy of Management Journal,* 1976, *19,* 237–258.

Kotter, J. P., and Lawrence, P. R. *Mayors in Action.* New York: Wiley-Interscience, 1974.

Kovach, K. A., and Patrick, S. L. "Comparisons of Public and Private Subjects on Reported Economic Measures and on Facet Satisfaction Items for Each of Three Organizational Levels." Paper presented at the annual meeting of the Academy of Management, Washington, D.C., 1989.

Kraemer, K. L., and Perry, J. L. "Institutional Requirements for Research in Public Administration." *Public Administration Review,* 1989, *49,* 9–16.

Kreitner, R., and Luthans, F. "A Social Learning Approach to Behavioral Management." In J. R. Gordon (ed.), *Organizational Behavior.* (2nd ed.) Newton, Mass.: Allyn and Bacon, 1987.

Kurke, L. E., and Aldrich, H. E. "Mintzberg Was Right! A Replication and Extension of the Nature of Managerial Work." *Management Science,* 1983, *29,* 975–984.

Lachman, R. "Public and Private Sector Differences: CEOs' Perceptions of Their Role Environments." *Academy of Management Journal,* 1985, *28,* 671–679.

Ladd, E. C. "What the Voters Really Want." In J. L. Perry & K. L. Kraemer (eds.), *Public Management.* Mountain View, Calif.: Mayfield, 1983.

Landy, F. J., and Guion, R. M. "Development of Scales for the Measurement of Work Motivation." *Organizational Behavior and Human Performance,* 1970, *5,* 93–103.

Larson, M. *The Rise of Professionalism.* Berkeley: University of California Press, 1977.

Lasko, W. "Executive Accountability: Will SES Make a Difference?" *The Bureaucrat,* 1980, *9,* 6–7.

Lau, A. W., Pavett, C. M., and Newman, A. R. "The Nature of Managerial Work: A Comparison of Public and Private Sector Jobs." *Academy of Management Proceedings,* 1980, 339–343.

Lawler, E. E. *Pay and Organizational Effectiveness.* New York: McGraw-Hill, 1971.

Lawler, E. E. *Motivation in Work Organizations.* Pacific Grove, Calif.: Brooks/Cole, 1973.

Lawrence, P. R., and Lorsch, J. W. *Organization and Environment.* Cambridge, Mass.: Harvard University Press, 1967.

Leavitt, H. J. "Some Effects of Certain Communication Patterns on Group Performance." *Journal of Abnormal and Social Psychology,* 1951, *46.*

Lerner, A. W., and Wanat, J. "Fuzziness and Bureaucracy." *Public Administration Review,* 1983, *43,* 500–509.

Lester, J. P., Bowman, A. O., Giggin, M. L., and O'Toole, L. J. "Public Policy Implementation: Evolution of the Field and Agenda for Future Research." *Policy Studies Review,* 1987, *7,* 200–216.

Levine, C. H. (ed.). *Managing Fiscal Stress.* Chatham, N.J.: Chatham House, 1980a.

Levine, C. H. "Organizational Decline and Cutback Management." In C. H. Levine (ed.), *Managing Fiscal Stress.* Chatham, N.J.: Chatham House, 1980b.

Levy, S. J. "The Public Image of Government Agencies." *Public Administration Review,* 1963, *23* (Mar.), 25–29.

Lewin, K., Lippitt, R., and White, R. K. "Patterns of Aggressive Behavior in Experimentally Created 'Social Climates.' " *Journal of Social Psychology,* 1939, *10,* 271–299.

Lewis, E. B. *Public Entrepreneurship.* Bloomington: Indiana University Press, 1980.

Lewis, E. B. "Admiral Hyman Rickover: Technological Entrepreneurship in the U.S. Navy." In J. W. Doig and E. C. Hargove (eds.), *Leadership and Innovation.* Baltimore, Md.: Johns Hopkins University Press, 1987.

Lewis, G. B. "In Search of the Machiavellian Milquetoasts: Comparing Attitudes of Bureaucrats and Ordinary People." *Public Administration Review,* 1990, *50,* 220–227.

Lichter, R. S. "Media Power: The Influence of Media on Politics and Business." *Florida Policy Review,* 1988, *4,* 35–41.

Lichter, R. S., Rothman, S., and Lichter, L. *The Media Elite.* Bethesda, Md.: Adler and Adler, 1986.

Light, P. C. "When Worlds Collide: The Political-Career Nexus." In G. C. Mackenzie (ed.), *The In-and-Outers.* Baltimore, Md.: Johns Hopkins University Press, 1987, pp. 77–99.

Lindblom, C. E. "The Science of Muddling Through." *Public Administration Review,* 1959, *19,* 79–88.

Lindblom, C. E. *Politics and Markets.* New York: Basic Books, 1977.

Linsky, M. *Impact: How the Press Affects Federal Policymaking.* New York: Norton, 1986.

Lipset, S. M., and Schneider, W. *The Confidence Gap: Business, Labor, and Government in the Public Mind.* Baltimore, Md.: Johns Hopkins University Press, 1987.

Lipsky, M. *Street-Level Bureaucracy.* New York: Russell Sage Foundation, 1980.

Locke, E. A. "Toward a Theory of Task Motivation and Incentives." *Organizational Behavior and Human Performance,* 1968, *3,* 157–159.

Locke, E. A. "What Is Job Satisfaction?" *Organizational Behavior and Human Performance,* 1969, *4,* 309–336.

Locke, E. A. "The Nature and Causes of Job Satisfaction." In M. D. Dunnette (ed.), *Handbook of Industrial and Organizational Psychology.* Skokie, Ill.: Rand McNally, 1976.

Lodahl, T. M., and Kejner, M. "The Definition and Measurement of Job Involvement." *Journal of Applied Psychology,* 1965, *49,* 24–33.

Long, N. E. "Power and Administration." *Public Administration Review,* 1949, *9,* 257–264.

Lowi, T. *The End of Liberalism.* New York: Norton, 1979.

Lynch, B. P. "An Empirical Assessment of Perrow's Technology Construct." *Administrative Science Quarterly,* 1974, *19,* 338–356.

Lynn, L. E. *Managing the Public's Business.* New York: Basic Books, 1981.

Lynn, L. E. *Managing Public Policy.* Boston: Little, Brown, 1987.

Lynn, N. B., and Wildavsky, A. (eds.). *Public Administration: State of the Discipline.* Chatham, N.J.: Chatham House, 1990.

MacAvoy, P. W., and McIssac, G. S. "The Performance and Management of United States Federal Government Enterprises." In P. W. MacAvoy, W. T. Stanbury, G. Yarrow, and R. J. Zeckhauser (eds.), *Privatization and State-Owned Enterprises.* Boston: Kluwer Academic Publishers, 1989.

McCauley, C. D., Lombardo, M. M., and Usher, C. H. "Diagnosing Management Development Needs: An Instrument Based on How Managers Develop." *Journal of Management,* 1989, *15,* 389–404.

McCurdy, H. E., and Cleary, R. "Why Can't We Resolve the Research Issue in Public Administration?" *Public Administration Review,* 1984, *44,* 49–55.

MacDonald, F. *Novus Ordo Seclorum: The Intellectual Origins of the Constitution.* Lawrence: University of Kansas Press, 1985.

McFadden, D. "The Revealed Preferences of a Government Bureaucracy: Empirical Evidence." *Bell Journal of Economics,* 1976, *7,* 55–72.

McGregor, E. B. "Administration's Many Instruments: Mining, Refining, and Applying Charles Lindblom's *Politics and Markets."Administration and Society,* 1981, *13,* 347–375.

McGregor, D. *The Human Side of Enterprise.* New York: McGraw-Hill, 1960.

McKelvey, B. *Organizational Systematics.* Berkeley: University of California Press, 1982.

Macy, J. W. *Public Service: The Human Side of Government.* New York: Harper & Row, 1971.

Maier, N.R.F. "Assets and Liabilities in Group Problem Solving: The Need for an Integrative Function." *Psychological Review,* 1967, *74,* 239–249.

Mainzer, L. C. *Political Bureaucracy.* Glenview, Ill: Scott, Foresman, 1973.

Maitland, L. "Focus of H.U.D. Inquiry: An Obscure and Influential Woman." *New York Times,* May 31, 1989, p. 11.

Malek, F. V. "The Development of Public Executives: Neglect and Reform." *Public Administration Review,* 1974, *34,* 230–233.

March, J. G. "The Business Firm as a Political Coalition." *Journal of Politics,* 1962, *24,* 662–678.

March, J. G., and Olsen, J. P. (eds.). *Ambiguity and Choice in Organizations.* Bergen, Norway: Universitepsfarbaget, 1976.

March, J. G., and Olsen, J. P. "Garbage Can Models of Decision Making in Organizations." In J. G. March, and R. Weissinger-Baylon (eds.), *Ambiguity and Command.* White Plains, N.Y.: Pitman, 1986, pp. 11–35.

March, J. G., and Olsen, J. P. *Rediscovering Institutions: The Organizational Basis of Politics.* New York: Free Press, 1989.

March, J. G., and Simon, H. A. *Organizations.* New York: Wiley, 1958.

Marmor, T. R. "Entrepreneurship in Public Management: Wilbur Cohen and Robert Ball." In J. W. Doig and E. C. Hargrove (eds.), *Leadership and Innovation.* Baltimore, Md.: Johns Hopkins University Press, 1987, pp. 246–281.

Marmor, T. R., and Fellman, P. "Policy Entrepreneurship in Government: An American Study." *Journal of Public Policy,* 1986, *6,* 225–253.

Marsh, R. M., and Mannari, H. "Technological Implications Theory: A Japanese Test." *Organization Studies,* 1980, *1,* 161–183.

Martin, S. *Managing Without Managers: Alternative Work Arrangements in Public Organizations.* Newbury Park, Calif.: Sage, 1983.

Mascarenhas, B. "Domains of State-Owned, Privately Held, and Publicly Traded Firms in International Competition." *Administrative Science Quarterly,* 1989, *34,* 582–597.

Maslow, A. H. *Motivations and Personality.* New York: Harper & Row, 1954.

Maynard-Moody, S., Stull, D. D., and Mitchell, J. "Reorganization as Status Drama: Building, Maintaining, and Displacing Dominant Subcultures." *Public Administration Review,* 1986, *46,* 301–310.

Mazmanian, D. A., and Sabatier, P. A. (eds.). *Effective Policy Implementation.* Lexington, Mass.: Heath, 1981.

Mechanic, D. "Sources of Power of Lower Participants in Complex Organizations." *Administrative Science Quarterly,* 1962, *7,* 349–363.

Meier, K. J. *Politics and the Bureaucracy.* Pacific Grove, Calif.: Brooks/Cole, 1987.

Meyer, J. W., and Rowan, B. "Institutionalized Organizations: Formal Structure as Myth and Ceremony." In J. W. Meyer and W. R. Scott (eds.), *Organizational Environments: Ritual and Rationality.* Newbury Park, Calif.: Sage, 1983.

Meyer, M. W. *Change in Public Bureaucracies.* London: Cambridge University Press, 1979.

Meyer, M. W. " 'Bureaucratic' vs. 'Profit' Organization." In B. L. Staw and L. L. Cummings (eds.), *Research in Organizational Behavior.* Greenwich, Conn.: JAI Press, 1982.

Michelson, S. "The Working Bureaucrat in the Nonworking Bureaucracy." In C. H. Weiss and A. H. Barton (eds.), *Making Bureaucracies Work.* Newbury Park, Calif.: Sage, 1980.

Miles, R. E., and Snow, C. C. *Organizational Strategy, Structure, and Process.* New York: McGraw-Hill, 1978.

Miles, R. H. "A Comparison of the Relative Impacts of Role Perceptions of Ambiguity and Conflict by Role." *Academy of Management Journal,* 1976, *19* (Mar.), 25–35.

Miles, R. H. *Macro Organization Behavior.* Glenview, Ill.: Scott, Foresman, 1980.

Miles, R. H. *Managing the Corporate Social Environment.* Englewood Cliffs, N.J.: Prentice-Hall, 1987.

Miles, R. H., and Petty, M. M. "Relationships Between Role Clarity, Need for Clarity, and Job Tension and Satisfaction for Supervisory Roles." *Academy of Management Journal,* 1975, *18,* 877–883.

Miliband, R. *The State in Capitalist Society.* New York: Basic Books, 1969.

Miller, G. J., and Moe, T. M. "The Positive Theory of Hierarchies." In H. F. Weisberg (ed.), *Political Science: The Science of Politics.* New York: Agathon, 1986.

Miller, J. C. "A Presidential Veto for Pork Spending." *Wall Street Journal,* Jan. 30, 1990, p. A18.

Milward, H. B., and Rainey, H. G. "Don't Blame the Bureaucracy." *Journal of Public Policy,* 1983, *3,* 149–168.

Milward, H. B., and Wamsley, G. "Interorganizational Policy Systems and Research on Public Organizations." *Administration and Society,* 1982, *13,* 457–478.

Mintzberg, H. *The Nature of Managerial Work.* New York: Harper & Row, 1972.

Mintzberg, H. *The Structuring of Organizations.* Englewood Cliffs, N.J.: Prentice-Hall, 1979.

Mintzberg, H. *Power in and Around Organizations.* Englewood Cliffs, N.J.: Prentice-Hall, 1983.

Mintzberg, H. *Mintzberg on Management.* New York: Free Press, 1989.

Mintzberg, H., Raisinghani, D., and Theoret, A. "The Structure of Unstructured Decisions Processes." *Administrative Science Quarterly,* 1976, *21,* 266–273.

Mitchell, T. R. "Expectancy Models of Job Satisfaction, Occupational Preference, and Effort: A Theoretical, Methodological, and Empirical Appraisal." *Psychological Bulletin,* 1974, *81,* 1053–1077.

Mitnick, B. M. *The Political Economy of Regulation.* New York: Columbia University Press, 1980.

Molnar, J. J., and Rogers, D. L. "Organizational Effectiveness: An Empirical Comparison of the Goal and System Resource Approaches." *Sociological Quarterly,* 1976, *17,* 401–413.

Mooney, J. D. "The Scalar Principle." In J. D. Mooney and A. C. Reiley (eds.), *The Principles of Organization.* New York: Harper & Row, 1930.

Morgan, G. *Riding the Waves of Change: Developing Managerial Competencies for a Turbulent World.* San Francisco: Jossey-Bass, 1988.

Morris, T. D., Corbett, W. H., and Usilander, B. L. "Productivity Measures in the Federal Government." *Public Administration Review,* 1972, *32,* 753–763.

Morrisey, G. L. *Management by Objectives and Results in the Public Sector.* Reading, Mass.: Addison-Wesley, 1976.

Morse, P. M., and Bacon, L. W. (eds.). *Operations Research for Public Systems.* Cambridge, Mass.: MIT Press, 1967.

Mosher, F. *Democracy and the Public Service.* New York: Oxford University Press, 1982. (Originally published 1968.)

Mosher, F. C. (ed.). *American Public Administration: Past, Present, Future.* University: University of Alabama Press, 1975.

Mott, P. E. *The Characteristics of Effective Organizations.* New York: Harper & Row, 1972.

Mowday, R. T., Porter, L. W., and Steers, R. M. *Employee-Organization Linkages.* Orlando, Fla.: Academic Press, 1982.

Muchinsky, P. "A Comparison of Within- and Across-Subjects Analyses of the Expectancy-Valence Model for Predicting Effort." *Academy of Management Journal,* 1977, *20,* 154–158.

Murray, C. *Losing Ground.* New York: Basic Books, 1984.

Murray, H. A. *Explorations in Personality.* New York: Oxford University Press, 1938.

Murray, M. A. "Comparing Public and Private Management: An Exploratory Essay." *Public Administration Review, 1975, 35,* 364–371.

Musolf, L., and Seidman, H. "The Blurred Boundaries of Public Administration." *Public Administration Review,* 1980, *40,* 124–130.

National Academy of Public Administration. *Revitalizing Federal Management.* Washington, D.C.: National Academy of Public Administration, 1986.

National Academy of Public Administration. *Privatization: The Challenge to Public Management.* Washington, D.C.: National Academy of Public Administration, 1989.

National Center for Productivity and Quality of Working Life. *Employee Attitudes and Productivity Differences Between the Public and Private Sectors.* Washington, D.C.: National Center for Productivity and Quality of Working Life, 1978.

National Commission on Productivity and Work Quality. *Productivity: Employee Incentives to Improve State and Local Government Productivity.* Washington, D.C.: U.S. Government Printing Office, 1975.

National Commission on the Public Service. *Leadership for America: Rebuilding the Public Service.* Washington, D.C.: National Commission on the Public Service, 1989.

Nigro, L. G. (ed.). *Decision Making in the Public Sector.* New York: Marcel Dekker, 1984.

Niskanen, W. A. *Bureaucracy and Representative Government.* Chicago: Aldine, 1971.

Nord, W. R. "A Political-Economic Perspective on Organizational Effectiveness." In K. Cameron and D. A. Whetten (eds.), *Organizational Effectiveness: A Comparison of Multiple Models.* Orlando, Fla.: Academic Press, 1983.

Nutt, P. C. "Types of Organizational Decision Processes." *Administrative Science Quarterly,* 1984, *29,* 414–450.

Nutt, P. C., and Backoff, R. W. "A Strategic Management Process for Public and Third-Sector Organizations." *Journal of the American Planning Association,* 1987, *53,* 44–54.

Olshfski, D. F. "Critical-Incident Analysis of the Individual and Organizational Environment of Public-Sector Executives." In J. Rabin, G. Miller, and W. B. Hildreth (eds.), *Handbook of Strategic Management.* New York: Marcel Dekker, 1989.

Olshfski, D. "Politics and Leadership: Political Executives at Work." *Public Productivity and Management Review,* 1990, *13,* 225–244.

Organ, D. W., and Greene, C. N. "Role Ambiguity, Locus of Control, and Work Satisfaction." *Journal of Applied Psychology,* 1974, *59,* 101–102.

Osborne, D. *Laboratories of Democracy.* Boston: Harvard Business School Press, 1990.

Ott, J. S. *The Organizational Culture Perspective.* Pacific Grove, Calif.: Brooks/ Cole, 1989.

Ouchi, W. *Theory Z: How American Business Can Meet the Japanese Challenge.* Reading, Mass.: Addison-Wesley, 1981.

Paine, F. T., Carroll, S. J., and Leete, B. A. "Need Satisfactions of Managerial Level Personnel in a Government Agency." *Journal of Applied Psychology,* 1966, *50,* 247–249.

Park, C., Lovrich, N. P., and Soden, D. L. "Testing Herzberg's Motivation Theory in a Comparative Study of U.S. and Korean Public Employees." *Review of Public Personnel Administration,* 1988, *8,* 40–60.

Parker, D. "Is the Private Sector More Efficient?" *Public Administration Bulletin,* 1985, 2–23.

Parkinson, C. N. *Parkinson's Law.* Boston: Houghton Mifflin, 1957.

Patchen, M. *Some Questionnaire Measures of Employee Motivation and Morale.* Ann Arbor: Survey Research Center, Institute for Social Research, University of Michigan, 1965.

Perrow, C. "Departmental Power and Perspective in Industrial Firms." In M. N. Zald (ed.), *Power in Organizations.* Nashville, Tenn.: Vanderbilt University Press, 1970a.

Perrow, C. *Organizational Analysis.* Belmont, Calif.: Wadsworth, 1970b.

Perrow, C. "A Framework for Comparative Analysis of Organizations." In F. E. Kast and J. E. Rosenzweig (eds.), *Contingency Views of Organization and Management.* Chicago: Science Research Associates, 1973.

Perry, J. L. "Merit Pay in the Public Sector: The Case for a Failure of Theory." *Review of Public Personnel Administration,* 1986, *7,* 57–69.

Perry, J. L. (ed.). *Handbook of Public Administration.* San Francisco: Jossey-Bass, 1989.

Perry, J. L., and Babitsky, T. T. "Comparative Performance in Urban Bus Transit: Assessing Privatization Strategies." *Public Administration Review,* 1986, *46,* 57–66.

Perry, J. L., and Kraemer, K. L. (eds.). *Public Management.* Mountain View, Calif.: Mayfield, 1983.

Perry, J. L., and Miller, T. K. "The Senior Executive Service: Has It Worked?" Paper presented at the annual meeting of the American Political Science Association, San Francisco, Aug. 1990.

Perry, J. L., Petrakis, B. A., and Miller, T. K. "Federal Merit Pay, Round II: An Analysis of the Performance Management and Recognition System." *Public Administration Review,* 1989, *49,* 29–37.

Perry, J. L., and Porter, L. W. "Factors Affecting the Context for Motivation in Public Organizations." *Academy of Management Review,* 1982, *7,* 89–98.

Perry, J. L., and Rainey, H. G. "The Public-Private Distinction in Organization Theory: A Critique and Research Strategy." *Academy of Management Review,* 1988, *13,* 182–201.

Perry, J. L., and Wise, L. R. "The Motivational Bases of Public Service." *Public Administration Review,* 1990, *50,* 367–373.

Peters, B. G. "The Problem of Bureaucratic Government." *Journal of Politics,* 1981, *43,* 56–81.

Peters, B. G. *The Politics of Bureaucracy.* New York: Longman, 1984.

Peters, B. G., and Hogwood, B. W. "The Death of Immortality: Births, Deaths, and Metamorphoses in the U.S. Federal Bureaucracy, 1933–1982." *American Review of Public Administration,* 1988, *18,* 119–133.

Peters, T. J. "Restoring American Competitiveness: Looking for New Models of Organizations." *Academy of Management Executive,* 1988, *2,* 104–110.

Peters, T. J., and Waterman, R. H. *In Search of Excellence: Lessons from America's Best-Run Companies.* New York: Harper & Row, 1982.

Petty, M. M., McGee, G. W., and Cavender, J. W. "A Meta-Analysis of the Relationships Between Individual Job Satisfaction and Individual Performance." *Academy of Management Review,* 1984, *9,* 712–721.

Pfeffer, J. *Power in Organizations.* Boston: Pitman, 1981.

Pfeffer, J. *Organizations and Organization Theory.* Boston: Pitman, 1982.

Pfeffer, J., and Salancik, G. R. *The External Control of Organizations.* New York: Harper & Row, 1978.

Pinder, C. C. *Work Motivation.* Glenview, Ill.: Scott, Foresman, 1984.

Pitt, D. C., and Smith, B. C. *Government Departments: An Organizational Perspective.* London: Routledge & Kegan Paul, 1981.

Poister, T. H. "Crosscutting Themes in Public Sector Agency Revitalization." *Public Productivity Review,* 1988a, *11,* 29–35.

Poister, T. H. (ed.). "Success Stories in Revitalizing Public Agencies." *Public Productivity Review,* 1988b, *11,* 27–103.

Poister, T. H., and Larson, T. D. "The Revitalization of PennDOT." *Public Productivity Review,* 1988, *11,* 85–103.

Pondy, L. R. "Organizational Conflict: Concepts and Models." *Administrative Science Quarterly,* 1967, *12,* 296–320.

Porter, E. A., Sargent, A. G., and Stupak, R. J. "Managing for Excellence in the Federal Government." *New Management,* 1986, *4,* 24–32.

Porter, L. W. "Job Attitudes in Management: Perceived Deficiencies in Need Fulfillment as a Function of Job Level." *Journal of Applied Psychology,* 1962, *46,* 375–384.

Porter, L. W., and Lawler, E. E. *Managerial Attitudes and Performance.* Homewood, Ill.: Irwin, 1968.

Porter, L. W., and Von Maanen, J. "Task Accomplishment and the Management of Time." In J. L. Perry and K. L. Kraemer (eds.), *Public Management.* Mountain View, Calif.: Mayfield, 1983.

Porter, M. E. *Competitive Advantage.* New York: Free Press, 1985.

Powell, T. E., and Ogilvie, J. R. "The Divergence of Public and Private Administration: An Empirical Assessment of an Outmoded Model." Unpublished paper, Department of Management, University of Hartford, 1990.

President's Council on Management Improvement. *Applying the Best in Government! Improving the Management of Human Resources in the Federal Government Through a Public-Private Partnership.* Washington, D.C.: Office of the Assistant Secretary for Personnel Administration, U.S. Department of Health and Human Services, 1987.

Pressman, J. L., and Wildavsky, A. B. *Implementation*. Berkeley: University of California Press, 1973.

Price, J. L. *Handbook of Organizational Measurement*. Lexington, Mass.: Heath, 1972.

Pugh, D. S., Hickson, D. J., and Hinings, C. R. "An Empirical Taxonomy of Work Organizations." *Administrative Science Quarterly*, 1969, *14*, 115–126.

Quinn, J. B. *Strategies for Change: Logical Incrementalism*. Homewood, Ill.: Irwin, 1980.

Quinn, R. E. *Beyond Rational Management: Mastering the Paradoxes and Competing Demands of High Performance*. San Francisco: Jossey-Bass, 1988.

Quinn, R. E., and Cameron, K. "Organizational Life Cycles and Shifting Criteria of Effectiveness: Some Preliminary Evidence." *Management Science*, 1983, *29*, 33–51.

Quinn, R. E., and Rohrbaugh, J. "A Spatial Model of Effectiveness Criteria: Towards a Competing Values Approach to Organizational Analysis." *Management Science*, 1983, *29* (3), 363–377.

Raines, H. "Bureaucrats: Scapegoats Again for Reagan and Staff." *Louisville Courier Journal*, Oct. 23, 1981, p. 1.

Rainey, G. W. "Implementation and Managerial Creativity: A Study of the Development of Client-Centered Units in Human Service Programs." In D. J. Palumbo and D. J. Calista (eds.), *Implementation and the Policy Process*. New York: Greenwood Press, 1990.

Rainey, G. W., and Rainey, H. G. "Breaching the Hierarchical Imperative: The Modularization of the Social Security Claims Process." In D. J. Calista (ed.), *Bureaucratic and Governmental Reform*. JAI Research Annual in Public Policy Analysis and Management. Greenwich, Conn.: JAI Press, 1984.

Rainey, H. G. "Perceptions of Incentives in Business and Government: Implications for Civil Service Reform." *Public Administration Review*, 1979, *39*, 440–448.

Rainey, H. G. "Reward Preferences Among Public and Private Managers: In Search of the Service Ethic." *American Review of Public Administration*, 1982, *16*, 288–302.

Rainey, H. G. "Public Agencies and Private Firms: Incentive Structures, Goals, and Individual Roles." *Administration and Society*, 1983, *15*, 207–242.

Rainey, H. G. "Public Management: Recent Research on the Political Context and Managerial Roles, Structures, and Behaviors." *Yearly Review of Management of the Journal of Management*, 1989, *15*, 229–250.

Rainey, H. G. "Public Management: Recent Developments and Current Prospects." In N. Lynn and A. Wildavsky (eds.), *Public Administration: State of the Discipline*. Chatham, N.J.: Chatham House, 1990.

Rainey, H. G., Backoff, R. W., and Levine, C. L. "Comparing Public and Private Organizations." *Public Administration Review*, 1976, *36*, 233–246.

Rainey, H. G., and Milward, H. B. "Public Organizations: Policy Networks and Environments." In R. H. Hall and R. E. Quinn (eds.), *Organizational Theory and Public Policy*. Newbury Park, Calif.: Sage, 1983.

Rainey, H. G., Traut, C., and Blunt, B. "Reward Expectancies and Other Work-Related Attitudes in Public and Private Organizations: A Review and Extension." *Review of Public Personnel Administration*, 1986, *6*, 50–73.

Rainey, H. G., and Wechsler, B. "Executive Transition in Government." *Public Productivity Review*, 1988, *12*, 43–45.

Rawls, J. R., Ullrich, R. A., and Nelson, O. T. "A Comparison of Managers Entering or Reentering the Profit and Nonprofit Sectors." *Academy of Management Journal*, 1975, *18*, 616–622.

Rehfuss, J. *The Job of the Public Manager*. Homewood, Ill.: Dorsey Press, 1989.

Reston, J. "Back to Basics." *New York Times*, Feb. 6, 1977, p. 15.

Rhinehart, J. B., and others. "Comparative Study of Need Satisfaction in Governmental and Business Hierarchies." *Journal of Applied Psychology*, 1969, *53*, 230–235.

Ring, P. S. "Strategic Issues: What Are They and from Where Do They Come?" In J. M. Bryson and R. C. Einsweiler (eds.), *Strategic Planning*. Chicago: Planners Press, 1988.

Ring, P. S., and Perry, J. L. "Strategic Management in Public and Private Organizations: Implications of Distinctive Contexts and Constraints." *Academy of Management Review*, 1985, *10*, 276–286.

Ripley, R. B., and Franklin, G. A. *Policy-Making in the Federal Executive Branch*. New York: Macmillan, 1975.

Ripley, R. B., and Franklin, G. A. *Bureaucracy and Policy Implementation*. Homewood, Ill.: Dorsey Press, 1982.

Ripley, R. B., and Franklin, G. A. *Congress, the Bureaucracy, and Public Policy*. Homewood, Ill.: Dorsey Press, 1984.

Rizzo, J. R., House, R. J., and Lirtzman, S. E. "Role Conflict and Ambiguity in Complex Organizations." *Administrative Science Quarterly*, 1970, *15*, 150–163.

Roberts, N. C. "Public Entrepreneurship." In P. J. King and N. C. Roberts (eds.). *Policy Entrepreneurship*. San Francisco: Jossey-Bass, forthcoming.

Roberts, N. C., and King, P. J. "Policy Entrepreneurs: Catalysts for Innovative Public Policy." In F. Hoy (ed.), *Proceedings of the Annual Meeting of the Academy of Management*. 1988.

Roberts, N. C., and King, P. J. "The Process of Public Policy Innovation." In A. Van de Ven, H. Angle, and M. S. Poole (eds.), *Research on Management of Innovation*. Cambridge, Mass.: Ballinger, 1989.

Roessner, J. D. "Incentives to Innovate in Public and Private Organizations." In J. L. Perry and K. L. Kraemer (eds.), *Public Management*. Mountain View, Calif.: Mayfield, 1983.

Roethlisberger, F. J., and Dickson, W. J. *Management and the Worker*. Cambridge, Mass.: Harvard University Press, 1939.

Rogers, D. L., and Molnar, J. "Organizational Antecedents of Role Conflict and Ambiguity in Top-Level Administrators." *Administrative Science Quarterly*, 1976, *21*, 598–610.

Rogers, E. M., and Argawala-Rogers, R. *Communication in Organizations.* New York: Free Press, 1976.

Rogers, E. M., and Kim, J. "Diffusion of Innovations in Public Organizations." In R. L. Merrit (ed.), *Innovation in the Public Sector.* Newbury Park, Calif.: Sage, 1985.

Rohrbaugh, J. "Operationalizing the Competing Values Approach: Measuring Performance in the Employment Service." *Public Productivity Review,* 1981, *5,* 141–159.

Rokeach, M. *The Nature of Human Values.* New York: Free press, 1973.

Romzek, B. S. "Employee Investment and Commitment: The Ties That Bind." *Public Administration Review,* 1990, *50,* 274–382.

Romzek, B. S., and Dubnick, M. J. "Accountability in the Public Sector: Lessons from the *Challenger* Tragedy." *Public Administration Review,* 1987, *47,* 227–239.

Romzek, B., and Hendricks, J. "Organizational Involvement and Representative Bureaucracy: Can We Have It Both Ways?" *American Political Science Review,* 1982, *76,* 75–82.

Rosen, B. *Holding Government Bureaucracies Accountable.* New York: Praeger, 1989.

Rosenbaum, D. E. "Estimate on Deficit Is Raised Sharply." *New York Times,* July 7, 1990a, p. A10.

Rosenbaum, D. E. "A Financial Disaster with Many Culprits." *New York Times,* June 6, 1990b, p. 1.

Rosenberg, M. *Occupations and Values.* New York: Free Press, 1957.

Rosenbloom, D. H. *Public Administration.* New York: Random House, 1989.

Rourke, F. E. *Bureaucracy, Politics, and Public Policy.* Boston: Little, Brown, 1984.

Rubin, I. S. *Shrinking the Federal Government: The Effect of Cutbacks on Five Federal Agencies.* New York: Longman, 1985.

Rubin, M. S. "Sagas, Ventures, Quests, and Parlays: A Typology of Strategies in the Public Sector." In J. M. Bryson and R. C. Einsweiler (eds.) *Strategic Planning.* Chicago: Planners Press, 1988.

Ruffat, J. "Strategic Management of Public and Nonmarket Corporations." *Long-Range Planning,* 1983, *16,* 74–84.

Rumsfeld, D. "A Politician-Turned-Executive Surveys Both Worlds." In J. L. Perry and K. L. Kraemer (eds.), *Public Management.* Mountain View, Calif.: Mayfield, 1983

Ruttenberg, S. H., and Gutchess, J. *Manpower Challenge of the 1970s: Institutions and Social Change.* Baltimore, Md.: Johns Hopkins University Press, 1970.

Salamon, L. M. (ed.). *Beyond Privatization: The Tools of Government Action.* Washington, D.C.: Urban Institute, 1989.

Saleh, S. D., and Hosek, J. "Job Involvement: Concepts and Measurements." *Academy of Management Journal,* 1976, *19,* 213–224.

Sandeep, P. "Why Government Can't Always Get the Best." *Government Executive,* Mar. 1989, p. 64.

Sanders, R. P. "The 'Best and Brightest': Can the Public Service Compete?"

In the Volcker Commission, *Leadership for America*. Lexington, Mass.: Heath, 1989.

Savas, E. S. *Privatization: The Key to Better Government*. Chatham, N.J.: Chatham House, 1987.

Savas, E. S., and Ginsburg, S. G. "The Civil Service: A Meritless System?" *Public Interest*, 1973, *32*, 72–84.

Schachter, S. "Deviation, Rejection, and Communication." *Journal of Abnormal and Social Psychology*, 1951, *46*, 190–207.

Schachter, S. *The Psychology of Affiliation*. Stanford, Calif.: Stanford University Press, 1959.

Schay, B. W. "Effects of Performance-Contingent Pay on Employee Attitudes." *Public Personnel Management*, 1988, *17*, 237–250.

Schein, E. H. *Organizational Culture and Leadership: A Dynamic View*. San Francisco: Jossey-Bass, 1985.

Schott, R. L. "The Professions in Government: Engineering as a Case in Point." *Public Administration Review*, 1978, *38*, 126–132.

Schuler, R. S. "Role Perceptions, Satisfaction, and Performance Moderated by Organizational Level and Participation in Decision Making." *Academy of Management Journal*, 1977, *20*, 159–165.

Schuster, J. R. "Management Compensation Policy and the Public Interest." *Public Personnel Management*, 1974, *3*, 510–523.

Schuster, J. R., Colletti, J. A., and Knowles, L. "The Relationship Between Perceptions Concerning Magnitude of Pay and the Perceived Utility of Pay: Public and Private Organizations Compared." *Organizational Behavior and Human Performance*, 1973, *9*, 110–119.

Schwartz, J. E. *America's Hidden Success: A Reassessment of Twenty Years of Public Policy*. New York: Norton, 1983.

Schwenk, C. R. "Conflict in Organizational Decision Making: An Exploratory Study of Its Effects in For-Profit and Not-For-Profit Organizations." *Management Science*, 1990, *36*, 436–448.

Scott, W. R. "The Adolescence of Institutional Theory." *Administrative Science Quarterly*, 1987, *32*, 493–511.

Scott, W. R., and Meyer, J. W. "The Organization of Societal Sectors." In J. W. Meyer and W. R. Scott (eds.), *Organizational Environments: Ritual and Rationality*. Newbury Park, Calif.: Sage, 1983.

Seidman, H. "Public Enterprises in the United States." *Annals of Public and Cooperative Economy*, 1983, *54*, 3–18.

Seidman, H., and Gilmour, R. *Politics, Position, and Power*. Boston: Little, Brown, 1986.

Selznick, P. *Leadership and Administration*. New York: Harper & Row, 1957.

Selznick, P. *TVA and the Grass Roots*. New York: Harper & Row, 1966.

Shapiro, E. "New Products Clog Groceries." *New York Times*, May 29, 1990, p. B1.

Shapiro, Z. "Expectancy Determinants of Intrinsically Motivated Behavior." *Journal of Personality and Social Psychology*, 1983, *34*, 1235–1244.

Sharkansky, I. "The Overloaded State." *Public Administration Review*, 1989, *49*, 201–203.

Sherif, M., and Sherif, C. *Groups in Harmony and Tension.* New York: Harper & Row, 1953.

Sherwood, F. P., and Page, W. J. "MBO and Public Management." In J. L. Perry and K. L. Kraemer (eds.), *Public Management.* Mountain View, Calif.: Mayfield, 1983.

Sherwood, F. P., and Rainey, H. G. "Management Policy in the State Government of Florida." In P. Downing (ed.), *Florida State University Policy Sciences Annual,* Tallahassee: Policy Sciences Program, Florida State University, 1983.

Sherwood, F. P., and Wechsler, B. "The 'Hadacol' of the Eighties: Paying Senior Managers for Performance." *Review of Public Personnel Administration,* 1986, *7,* 27–41.

Shore, L. M., Thornton, G. C., and Newton, L. A. "Job Satisfaction and Organizational Commitment as Predictors of Behavior Intentions and Employee Behavior." In F. Hoy (ed.), *Academy of Management Proceedings.* Academy of Management, 1989.

Siegel, G. B. "Who Is the Public Employee?" In W. B. Eddy (ed.), *Handbook of Organization Management.* New York: Marcel Dekker, 1983.

Siegel, G. B. "The Jury Is Still Out on Merit Pay in Government." *Review of Public Personnel Administration,* 1987, *7,* 3–15.

Sikula, A. F. "The Values and Value Systems of Governmental Executives." *Public Personnel Management,* 1973a, *2,* 16–22.

Sikula, A. F. "The Values and Value Systems of Industrial Personnel Managers." *Public Personnel Management,* 1973b, *2,* 305–309.

Simon, H. A. "The Proverbs of Administration." *Public Administration Review,* 1946, *6,* 53–67.

Simon, H. A. *Administrative Behavior.* New York: Free Press, 1948.

Simon, H. A. "On the Concept of Organizational Goal." In F. E. Kast and J. E. Rosenzweig (eds.), *Contingency Views of Organization and Management.* Chicago: Science Research Associates, 1973.

Simon, H. A., Smithburg, D. W., and Thompson, V. A. *Public Administration.* New York: Knopf, 1950.

Simon, M. E. "Matrix Management at the U.S. Consumer Product Safety Commission." *Public Administration Review,* 1983, *43,* 357–361.

Sims, H. P., Szilagyi, A. D., and McKemey, D. R. "Antecedents of Work-Related Expectancies." *Academy of Management Journal,* 1976, *19,* 547–559.

Skinner, B. F. *Science and Human Behavior.* New York: Free Press, 1953.

Smith, F. J. "Index of Organizational Reactions." *JSAS Catalogue of Selected Documents in Psychology,* 1976, *6,* 54.

Smith, M. P., and Nock, S. L. "Social Class and the Quality of Life in Public and Private Organizations." *Journal of Social Issues,* 1980, *36,* 59–75.

Smith, P. B. *Groups Within Organizations.* New York: Harper & Row, 1973.

Smith, P. C., Kendall, L. M., and Hulin, C. L. *The Measurement of Satisfaction in Work and Retirement.* Skokie, Ill.: Rand McNally, 1969.

Solomon, E. E. "Private and Public Sector Managers: An Empirical Investigation of Job Characteristics and Organizational Climate." *Journal of Applied Psychology,* 1986, *71,* 247–259.

Spann, R. M. "Public Versus Private Provision of Governmental Services." In T. E. Borcherding (ed.), *Budgets and Bureaucrats: The Sources of Government Growth*. Durham, N.C.: Duke University Press, 1977.

Sperry, R. L. "To Prevent Scandal: Oversight *and* Management." *Government Executive*, July 1990, pp. 59–60.

Stanley, D. T. *The Higher Civil Service*. Washington, D.C.: Brookings Institution, 1964.

Starbuck, W. H. "Organizations and Their Environments." In M. D. Dunnette (ed.), *Handbook of Industrial and Organizational Psychology*. New York: Wiley, 1983.

Starbuck, W. H., and Nystrom, P. C. "Designing and Understanding Organizations." In P. C. Nystrom and W. H. Starbuck (eds.), *Handbook of Organizational Design*. New York: Oxford University Press, 1981.

Starke, F. A., and Behling, O. "A Test of Two Postulates Underlying Expectancy Theory." *Academy of Management Journal*, 1975, *18*, 703–714.

Staw, B. M. *Intrinsic and Extrinsic Motivation*. Morristown, N.J.: General Learning Press, 1976.

Staw, B. M. "Organizational Behavior: A Review and Reformulation of the Field's Outcome Variables." *Annual Review of Psychology*, 1984, *35*, 627–666.

Steers, R. M. "Problems in the Measurement of Organizational Effectiveness." *Administrative Science Quarterly*, 1975, *20*, 546–558.

Steers, R. M. *Organizational Effectiveness: A Behavioral View*. Pacific Palisades, Calif.: Goodyear, 1977.

Steiner, I. D. *Group Process and Productivity*. Orlando, Fla.: Academic Press, 1972.

Steiss, A. W. *Management Control in Government*. Lexington, Mass.: Heath, 1982.

Stephens, J. E. "Turnaround at the Alabama Rehabilitation Agency." *Public Productivity Review*, 1988, *11*, 67–84.

Stevens, J. M., Wartick, S. L., and Bagby, J. *Business-Government Relations and Interdependence: A Managerial and Analytical Perspective*. New York: Praeger, 1988.

Stewart, R. B. "The Reformation of American Administrative Law." *Harvard Law Review*, 1975, *88*, (June), 1667–1711.

Stockfish, J. A. *The Political Economy of Bureaucracy*. Morristown, N.J.: General Learning Press, 1972.

Stone, A. B., and Stone, D. C. "Appendix: Case Histories of Early Professional Educational Programs." In F. C. Mosher (ed.), *American Public Administration: Past, Present, Future*. University: University of Alabama Press, 1975.

Stone, D. C. "Administrative Management: Reflections on Origins and Accomplishments." *Public Administration Review*, 1990, *50*, 3–20.

Swiss, J. E. *Public Management Systems*. Englewood Cliffs, N.J.: Prentice Hall, 1991.

Szilagyi, A. D., Sims, H. P., and Keller, R. T. "Role Dynamics, Locus of Control, and Employee Attitudes and Behavior." *Academy of Management Journal*, 1976, *19*, 259–276.

Taylor, F. W. *The Principles of Scientific Management.* New York: Harper & Row, 1919.

Tehrani, M., Montanari, J. R., and Carson, K. R. "Technology as Determinant of Organization Structure: A Meta-Analytic Review." In L. R. Jauch and J. L. Wall (eds.), *Proceedings of the Annual Meeting of the Academy of Management* 1990.

Thibaut, J. W., and Kelley, H. H. *The Social Psychology of Groups.* New York: Wiley, 1959.

Thomas, K. W. "Conflict and Conflict Management." In M. D. Dunnette (ed.), *Handbook of Industrial and Organizational Psychology.* New York: Wiley, 1983.

Thompson, F. J. *Personnel Policy in the City.* Berkeley: University of California Press, 1975.

Thompson, F. J. "Managing Within Civil Service Systems." In J. L. Perry (ed.), *Handbook of Public Administration.* San Francisco: Jossey-Bass, 1989.

Thompson, J. D. "Common and Uncommon Elements in Administration." *Social Welfare Forum,* 1962, 181–201.

Thompson, J. D. *Organizations in Action.* New York: McGraw-Hill, 1967.

Tichy, N. M., *Managing Strategic Change.* New York: Wiley, 1983.

Tichy, N. M., and Ulrich, D. "The Leadership Challenge—A Call for the Transformational Leader." *Sloan Management Review,* 1984, *26,* 59–68.

Tierney, J. T. *The U.S. Postal Service.* Dover, Mass.: Auburn House, 1988.

Tolbert, P. S. "Resource Dependence and Institutional Environments: Sources of Administrative Structure in Institutions of Higher Education." *Administrative Science Quarterly,* 1985, *30,* 1–13.

Tolbert, P. S., and Zucker, L. G. "Institutional Sources of Change in the Formal Structure of Organizations: The Diffusion of Civil Service Reform, 1880–1935." *Administrative Science Quarterly,* 1983, *28,* 22–39.

Tolchin, M. "Sixteen States Failing to Pay Required Medicare Costs." *New York Times,* Mar. 9, 1989, p. 45.

Traut, C., and Rainey, H. G. "The Information Gathering Practices of City Officials." Paper presented at the annual meeting of the American Political Science Association, Atlanta, Ga., 1989.

Trist, E. L., and Bamforth, K. W. "Some Social and Psychological Consequences of the Longwall Method of Coal Getting." *Human Relations,* 1951, *4,* 3–38.

Tullock, G. *The Politics of Bureaucracy.* Washington, D.C.: Public Affairs Press, 1965.

Tullock, G. *Private Wants, Public Means.* New York: Basic Books, 1970.

U.S. Department of Health and Human Services, Social Security Administration, Office of Strategic Planning. *2000: A Strategic Plan.* SSA Publication no. 01-001. Washington, D.C.: U.S. Department of Health and Human Services, 1988.

U.S. Department of the Treasury, Internal Revenue Service. *Internal Revenue Service Strategic Plan.* IRS Document 6941. Washington, D.C.: U.S. Department of the Treasury, 1984.

U.S. General Accounting Office. *Social Security: Actions and Plans to Reduce*

Agency Staff. GAO/HRD-86-76BR. Washington, D.C.: U.S. General Accounting Office, 1986.

U.S. General Accounting Office. *Federal Pay: Comparisons with the Private Sector by Job and Locality.* GAO/GGD-90-81FS. Washington, D.C.: U. S. General Accounting Office, 1990.

U.S. Merit Systems Protection Board. *Working for the Federal Government: Job Satisfaction and Federal Employees.* Washington, D.C.: U.S. Merit Systems Protection Board, 1987.

U.S. Office of Personnel Management. *Federal Employee Attitudes.* Washington, D.C.: U.S. Office of Personnel Management, 1979, 1980, 1983.

Valle, F. P. *Motivation: Theories and Issues.* Pacific Grove, Calif.: Brooks/Cole, 1975.

Van de Ven, A. H. "Review of H. E. Aldrich, *Organizations and Environments.*" *Administrative Science Quarterly,* 1979, *24,* 320–326.

Van de Ven, A. H. "Early Planning, Implementation, and Performance of New Organizations." In J. R. Kimberly, R. H. Miles, and Associates, *The Organizational Life Cycle: Issues in the Creation, Transformation, and Decline of Organizations.* San Francisco: Jossey-Bass, 1980.

Van de Ven, A. H., and Delbecq, A. L. "A Task-Contingent Model of Work Unit Structure." *Administrative Science Quarterly,* 1974, *19,* 183–197.

Van de Ven, A. H., Delbecq, A. L., and Koenig, R. "Determinants of Coordination Modes Within Organizations." *American Sociological Review,* 1976, *41,* 322–338.

Van de Ven, A. H., and Ferry, D. L. *Measuring and Assessing Organizations.* New York: Wiley-Interscience, 1980.

Vaughn, R. G. *The Spoiled System.* New York: Charterhouse, 1975.

Viteritti, J. P. *Across the River: Politics and Education in the City.* New York: Holmes and Meier, 1983.

Viteritti, J. P. "Public Organization Environments: Constituents, Clients, and Urban Governance." *Administration and Society,* 1990, *21,* 425–451.

Volcker Commission. *Leadership for America: Rebuilding the Public Service.* Lexington, Mass.: Heath, 1989.

Von Mises, L. *Bureaucracy.* New Haven, Conn.: Yale University Press, 1944.

Vroom, V. H. *Work and Motivation.* New York: Wiley, 1964.

Vroom, V. H., and Jago, A. J. "Decision-Making as a Social Process: Normative and Descriptive Models of Leader Behavior." *Decision Sciences, 1974, 5,* 743–769.

Vroom, V. H., and Yetton, P. W. *Leadership and Decision-Making.* Pittsburgh, Pa.: University of Pittsburgh Press, 1973.

Wahba, H., and House, R. J. "Expectancy Theory in Work and Motivation: Some Logical and Methodological Issues." *Human Relations,* 1974, *28,* 121–147.

Waldman, S., Cohn, B., and Thomas, R. "The HUD Ripoff." *Newsweek,* Aug. 7, 1989, pp. 16–22.

Waldo, D. *The Administrative State.* New York: Holmes and Meier, 1984. (Originally published 1947.)

Wall Street Journal. "GE Takes $450 Million Pretax Charge on Losses for Defective Compressor." May 7, 1990, p. 1.

Walsh, A. H. *The Public's Business: The Politics and Practices of Government Corporations.* Cambridge, Mass.: MIT Press, 1978.

Wamsley, G. L., and Zald, M. N. *The Political Economy of Public Organizations.* Lexington, Mass.: Heath, 1973.

Wamsley, G. L., and others. *Refounding Public Administration.* Newbury Park, Calif.: Sage, 1990.

Wanous, J. P., and Lawler, E. E. "Measurement and Meaning of Job Satisfaction." *Journal of Applied Psychology,* 1972, *56,* 95–105.

Warwick, D. P. *A Theory of Public Bureaucracy.* Cambridge, Mass.: Harvard University Press, 1975.

Waste, R. J. *Power and Pluralism in American Cities.* New York: Greenwood, 1987.

Webber, R. A. "Staying Organized." *The Wharton Magazine,* 1979, *3,* 16–23.

Wechsler, B., and Backoff, R. W. "Policy Making and Administration in State Agencies: Strategic Management Approaches." *Public Administration Review,* 1986, *46,* 321–327.

Wechsler, B., and Backoff, R. W. "The Dynamics of Strategy in Public Organizations." In J. Bryson and R. C. Einsweiller (eds.), Chicago: American Planning Association, 1988.

Weick, K. E. *The Social Psychology of Organizing.* Reading, Mass.: Addison-Wesley, 1979.

Weidenbaum, M. L. *The Modern Public Sector: New Ways of Doing the Government's Business.* New York: Basic Books, 1969.

Weinberg, M. W. *Managing the State.* Cambridge, Mass.: MIT Press, 1977.

Weinberg, M. W. "Public Management and Private Management: A Diminishing Gap?" *Journal of Policy Analysis and Management,* 1983, *3,* 107–125.

Weiss, D. J., Dawis, R. V., England, G. W., and Lofquist, L. H. *Manual for the Minnesota Satisfaction Questionnaire.* Minneapolis: Industrial Relations Center, University of Minnesota, 1967.

Weiss, H. L. "Why Business and Government Exchange Executives." In J. L. Perry and K. L. Kraemer (eds.), *Public Management.* Mountain View, Calif.: Mayfield, 1983.

Whetten, D. A. "Interorganizational Relations." In J. Lorsch (ed.), *Handbook of Organizational Behavior.* Englewood Cliffs, N.J.: Prentice-Hall, 1987.

Whetten, D. A. "Sources, Responses, and Effects of Organizational Decline." In K. Cameron, R. I. Sutton, and D. A. Whetten (eds.), *Readings in Organizational Decline.* Cambridge, Mass.: Ballinger, 1988.

White, J. D. "On the Growth of Knowledge in Public Administration." *Public Administration Review,* 1986, *46,* 15–25.

Wholey, J. S. *Evaluation: Promise and Performance.* Washington, D.C.: Urban Institute, 1979.

Whorton, J. W., and Worthley, J. A. "A Perspective on the Challenge of Public Management: Environmental Paradox and Organizational Culture." *Academy of Management Review,* 1981, *6,* 357–361.

Wildavsky, A. *The New Politics of the Budgetary Process.* Glenview, Ill.: Scott, Foresman, 1988.

Williamson, O. E. *Markets and Hierarchies.* New York: Free Press, 1975.

Williamson, O. E. "The Economics of Organizations: The Transaction Cost Approach." *American Journal of Sociology,* 1981, *87,* 548–577.

Wilmers, R. G., and Reilly, W. F. "Decay in New York's Civil Service." *New Republic,* 1973, *169,* 18–22.

Wilson, J. Q. *The Amateur Democrat: Club Politics in Three Cities.* Chicago: University of Chicago Press, 1966.

Wilson, J. Q. "Innovation in Organization: Notes Toward a Theory." In L. A. Rowe and W. B. Boise (eds.), *Organizational and Managerial Innovation: A Reader.* Pacific Palisades, Calif.: Goodyear, 1973a.

Wilson, J. Q. *Political Organizations.* New York: Basic Books, 1973b.

Wilson, J. Q. "The Politics of Regulation." In J. Q. Wilson (ed.), *The Politics of Regulation.* New York: Basic Books, 1980.

Wilson, J. Q. *Bureaucracy.* New York: Basic Books, 1989.

Wise, C. R. "Public Service Configurations and Public Organizations: Public Organization Design in the Post-Privatization Era." *Public Administration Review,* 1990, *50,* 141–155.

Witt, E. "Paying What They're Worth." *Governing,* 1989, *3,* 28–33.

Wolf, C. *Markets or Governments: Choosing Between Imperfect Alternatives.* Cambridge, Mass.: MIT Press, 1988.

Woll, P. *American Bureaucracy.* New York: Norton, 1977.

Woodward, J. *Industrial Organization: Theory and Practice.* London: Oxford University Press, 1965.

Yarwood, D. L., and Enis, B. M. "Advertising and Publicity Programs in the Executive Branch of the National Government: Hustling or Helping the People?" In D. L. Yarwood (ed.), *Public Administration: Politics and the People.* New York: Longman, 1987.

Yates, D., Jr. *The Politics of Management: Exploring the Inner Workings of Public and Private Organizations.* San Francisco: Jossey-Bass, 1985.

Yuchtman, E., and Seashore, S. E. "A System Resource Approach to Organizational Effectiveness." *American Sociological Review,* 1967, *32,* 891–903.

Zald, M. N. "On the Social Control of Industries." *Social Forces,* 1978, *57,* 79–101.

Zaltman, G., Duncan, R., and Holbek, J. *Innovations and Organizations.* New York: Wiley, 1973.

Zander, A. *Groups at Work: Unresolved Issues in the Study of Organizations.* San Francisco: Jossey-Bass, 1977.

Name Index

A

Abcarian, G., 7
Aberbach, J. D., 64, 175, 180
Abney, G., 57, 59, 64, 116, 180
Adams, J. S., 135–136
Aharoni, Y., 30
Aiken, M., 101, 102, 155, 288
Alderfer, C. P., 124, 125
Aldrich, H. E., 32, 41, 167, 173, 174, 290
Alimard, A., 213
Allison, G. T., 5, 7, 54, 74, 94, 114, 152, 165, 166, 173, 174, 176
Ammons, D. N., 173, 174, 179
Anderson, W. F., 181
Angle, H., 149
Argawala-Rogers, R., 193
Argyris, C., 101, 102, 283, 290
Atkinson, S. E., 32, 220

B

Babitsky, T. T., 220
Back, K., 279, 281
Backoff, R. W., 5, 32, 34, 89, 91, 92
Bacon, L. W., 80
Bagby, J., 22
Baldwin, J. N., 16, 32, 140, 141, 152, 153
Ball, R., 183–184, 247
Bamforth, K. W., 286
Ban, C., 42
Bandura, A., 164
Barnard, C. I., 75, 126, 128, 212, 276–277, 278
Barney, J. B., 18
Bartol, K. M., 151
Barton, A. H., 5, 99, 121

Barton, E., 3, 53
Bass, B. M., 169
Baum, E., 203
Beard, D. W., 41
Beck, P. A., 53, 250
Behling, O., 137
Bell, C. H., 235, 236
Bellante, D., 142
Bendor, J., 82
Benn, S. I., 24
Bennis, W., 168, 172
Beyer, J. M., 102, 106, 290
Blake, R. R., 159, 199, 213
Blanchard, K. H., 163
Blau, P. M., 25, 101, 102, 288, 290
Block, P., 73, 78
Blumenthal, J. M., 31, 54, 114, 173
Blunt, B., 141
Boschken, H. L., 92, 93
Bower, J., 7
Bower, J. L., 7
Bowman, A. O., 68, 117
Boyatzis, R. E., 152, 154, 167, 175, 203
Bozeman, B., 5, 16, 26, 28, 29, 30, 31, 112, 114, 115, 140, 142, 151, 261
Breton, A., 5
Bretschneider, S., 32, 114, 140, 202
Brock, J., 7
Brudney, J. L., 57, 64, 180, 257
Bryson, J. M., 39, 44, 88, 89, 92, 201, 245
Buchanan, B., 31, 112, 121, 152, 153, 154, 175, 201
Burke, W. W., 236, 237
Burns, J. M., 167, 169
Burns, T., 39, 100, 287
Burrell, G., 269, 274, 275, 276, 286
Bush, G., 3, 64

Subject Index

A

Achievement, need for, 135

Administrative Behavior (Simon), 278

Administrative management school, 271–274; reactions to, 274–279

Agencies, 25–26, 27; with excellence, 256; and public organizations, 62–64. *See also* Public agencies

Agendas, and public policy process, 67–68

Alabama Divisions of Rehabilitation and Crippled Children Service, 242; mission statement of, 91

Attentive publics, 51

Authority, public and economic, 26, 28–30

B

Behavior modification, 139; and leadership, 163–164

Behavioral Theory of the Firm, A (Cyert and March), 279

Budgets, 60–61

Bureaucracy: types of, 109; Weber's construct of, 270–271

Bureaucrat bashing, 2

C

Centralization, 101

Change: large-scale, 240–249; planned, 232; and public managers, 264; reasons to resist, 232–233; resistance to, 232; types of, 233–234

Charlotte, N.C., city government of, 255

Civil Services Reform Act of 1978, 8, 254

Clients, 56

Co-optation, 39

communication, 192–193; assessments and audits of, 193; managing, 198–200; problems in, 194–195; and public organizations, 200–204; roles in, 193

Competence, 48–49

Complexity, 102; and public managers, 262–263

Conflict, 195–196; bases of, 196–197; managing resolution of, 198–200; outcomes, suppression, and escalation of, 198; and public organizations, 200–204; stages and modes of, 197–198; types of, 196

Constituents, 56

Contingency theory, 18, 287–291; and decision making, 83–84; of leadership, 159–160; and organizational environments, 40–41, 43. *See also* Strategic contingencies

Corporations, with excellence, 251–254

Courts, and public organizations, 61–62

D

Decisions: contingency perspectives on, 83–84; garbage can model of, 86–87; incremental processes of, 84–85; and logical incrementalism, 85–86; and mixed scanning, 85; in organizations, 79; process model of, 86; rational models for, 80; rational techniques for, 80–81; and rationality, 81–83

Differentiation, 40; horizontal and vertical, 102

E

Eastman Kodak, 253

Efficiency, of organizations, 220–222

Electoral politics, 64

333